Integrating Innovation

This book is available as a free fully-searchable ebook from
www.adelaide.edu.au/press

Integrating Innovation:

South Australian Entrepreneurship Systems and Strategies

Edited by

Göran Roos and Allan O'Connor

Entrepreneurship, Commercialisation and Innovation Centre
The University of Adelaide

THE UNIVERSITY
of ADELAIDE

UNIVERSITY OF
ADELAIDE PRESS

Published in Adelaide by

University of Adelaide Press
The University of Adelaide
Level 14, 115 Grenfell Street
South Australia 5005
press@adelaide.edu.au
www.adelaide.edu.au/press

The University of Adelaide Press publishes externally refereed scholarly books by staff of the University of Adelaide. It aims to maximise access to the University's best research by publishing works through the internet as free downloads and for sale as high quality printed volumes.

For the full Cataloguing-in-Publication data please contact the National Library of Australia: cip@nla.gov.au

ISBN (paperback) 978-1-922064-90-5
ISBN (ebook: pdf) 978-1-922064-91-2
ISBN (ebook: epub) 978-1-922064-92-9
ISBN (ebook: mobi) 978-1-922064-93-6

Editor: Rebecca Burton
Editorial support: Julia Keller
Book design: Zoë Stokes
Cover design: Emma Spoehr
Cover image: Sergey Nivens, source — 123rf.com

Contents

Chapter Abstracts

The aim of this chapter is to set the context for the content to follow. It discusses the origin of the idea for this work and the South Australian contextual setting that has inspired the concept that innovation is integrated through firm and socio-economic levels. It proffers the ideas that entrepreneurship is a key contributor to an ecosystem that integrates innovation and that the tools of intellectual capital management are important for understanding how that ecosystem functions to integrate innovation. It then provides an overview of the chapters and outlines the structure of the book before concluding with the challenge that this endeavour undertakes.

This chapter examines the theoretical and policy discourse that has informed South Australia's innovation policy since the 1980s. The recommendations and policy strategies to support innovation have changed little during this time, and yet South Australia's productivity improvement through innovation still lags behind other states and economic regions of similar size. This chapter considers where impediments may lie in South Australia's innovation system and argues that there is a need to move beyond the current policy path dependency that relies upon behaviours and attitudes that have traditionally served to maintain stability and control. The state needs to invest in gaining a different and more holistic understanding of the contribution and value contributed by diverse knowledge taxonomies, from both the HASS and STEM disciplines, and the multiple monetary and non-monetary transactions that inspire and support innovation across the economy.

3 — A patent perspective of South Australian innovation: An indicator within the regional innovation system story

Kym Teh, The University of Adelaide
Göran Roos, The University of Adelaide

This article explores innovation performance in the context of patent data from South Australia (SA). The analysis highlights underlying assumptions and limitations of such an approach, although certain conclusions concerning that state's innovation trajectory are suggested. Integral to this exploration are the economic, regulatory and constitutional features that affect and define the nation of Australia, of which SA is one of six states. The SA patent activity analysis launches a discussion of the state's regional innovation system (RIS). Uniquely, this research exploration brings together the two elements of examining an innovation system unit that is smaller than a nation and linking that with the state's innovation performance.

4 — Innovation system symbiosis: The impact of virtual entrepreneurial teams on integrated innovation and regional innovation systems

Gavin Artz, University of South Australia

The experience of technology entrepreneurship in Adelaide, South Australia, hints at a symbiosis between the evolution of a regional innovation system, the changes that such a system causes in managerial and cultural forms at the company level, and how these new collaborative forms then feed back into the regional innovation system as well as link to national and international innovation networks. Through an examination of the MEGA entrepreneurship education program and the working relationships between organisations and companies that have grown around it, specifically the digital media company rezon8, *virtual entrepreneurial teams enabled by cross-institutional and cross-organisational collaborations are explored.*

PART 2: FIRM-LEVEL PERSPECTIVES

5 — Do clusters matter to the entrepreneurial process? Deriving a conceptual model from the case study of Yalumba

Huanmei Li, The University of Adelaide
Allan O'Connor, The University of Adelaide

Although the importance of industrial clusters in inspiring regional entrepreneurship has been increasingly recognised, little is known about the dynamic mechanism through which the cluster involvement of a firm influences its entrepreneurial process. This chapter initiates an attempt to conceptually model the interactions between multidimensions of industrial cluster involvements, a firm's entrepreneurial process and its entrepreneurial performance. Using Yalumba as a case study, our analysis suggests the feasibility and practicality of the proposed model. We subsequently discuss the implication of the chapter for future industry cluster and entrepreneurial process research and practice.

6 — Operationalising innovation: Hotwiring the creative organisation

Fiona Kerr, The University of Adelaide

In order to thrive in the twenty-first century, organisations need not only to be able to recognise complexity and sustainability as key components of business, but also to be able to foster and harness them. Those who operate successfully in such an environment go beyond organisational learning and strategy planning to building adaptive, innovative capabilities which result in sustained competitive advantage. This chapter explores how such adaptation and innovation are coupled with a capacity for strategic innovation and the ability to 'hotwire' across industry boundaries, and how such abilities ultimately decouple organisations from the confining need to know what is over the horizon in order to be able to deal with it.

industries development in South Australia (SA). We contrast an intellectual capital (IC) perspective employing IC analysis tools (Roos, Pike, & Fernström, 2005) with a complex systems analysis model (McKelvey, 2004). The government's interventions addressed major gaps in the sector; and the IC analysis was able to create deeper insights into the resources and capabilities exposing the knowledge resource interdependencies between three major stakeholder sectors.

10 — A diagnostic tool for assessing innovation readiness

Paul Shum, University of Western Sydney

Using data-mining methods to classify the sampled companies, an 'innovation-ready' category is identified. Their scores in innovation capabilities and environment are consistently higher in all dimensions than that of the 'Non-innovation ready' category. This study overcomes problems of previous innovation studies by developing systematically an innovation readiness framework that is based on intellectual capital and captures a more complete set of innovation capabilities with associated enterprise-wide interlocking mechanisms and required cultural change. This benchmark innovation profile will help practitioners from SMEs with stringent resource constraints to more accurately and consistently target important areas for improving their organisation's innovation capabilities.

11 — Developing a framework for the management of Critical Success Factors in organisational innovation projects: A case of Enterprise Resource Planning systems

Jiwat Ram, The University of Adelaide
David Corkindale, University of South Australia

The complexities of the organisational innovation process of ERP systems pose serious challenges for the uptake of such innovations in SMEs. Researchers have therefore identified a large number of critical success factors (CSFs) to help achieve success at various stages of this innovation process. However, little is known about how the identified CSFs are to be managed. We present a framework for the management of nine commonly identified CSFs. The proposed framework will help SMEs in putting together an action plan to successfully manage the ERP innovation process. The framework can also serve as a basis for the development of a theory of the management of CSFs.

CONCLUSION

12 — Innovation and entrepreneurship: Building the systems and strategies for South Australia

Allan O'Connor, The University of Adelaide
Göran Roos, The University of Adelaide

Through review of the submitted chapters, a number of key issues emerge that illustrate the difficulty of integrating innovation. Of primary importance is recognition that innovation in South Australia (SA) is interdependent with systems that influence the firm and individuals, as well as national and international systems of innovation. Intellectual capital is shown to be a useful lens, particularly given that system integration is heavily dependent on the human, relational and structural elements which facilitate innovation. Four strategies for SA are suggested for the development of an assistive ecosystem for integrating innovation, and a future research agenda is mapped out which, if pursued, will strengthen our understanding and engagement with the systems of innovation.

Notes on Contributors

Jane Andrew is an educator and researcher working at the University of South Australia in the School of Art, Architecture, and Design, where she is the Director of matchstudio, an interdisciplinary research and professional practice studio that supports students' transition from university to work. Jane's early career as a designer-maker, together with her role as Executive Director of Craftsouth (now Guildhouse), inspired her teaching and research career, which focuses on the contribution of 'creative capital' to economic development. Collaborative, trans-disciplinary practice, value networks and systems thinking are other areas of her research focus. In 2004 she was awarded an APAI scholarship and commenced a PhD as part of an ARC Linkage Project at the Centre for Labour Research/Australian Institute for Social Research and the Department of the Premier and Cabinet's Strategic Projects Division.

Gavin Artz is an economic development professional exploring large-scale innovation. He works for the South Australian Government developing and implementing the strategies and policies needed to build an effective regional innovation system. He holds an MBA from the University of South Australia and a BA in Politics from La Trobe University, and is currently a PhD candidate at the University of South Australia researching innovation. Gavin has been the CEO of the Australian Network for Art and Technology and was a founding Director of the Australian Design Alliance. He has been a participant on the FutureEverything Award International Advisory Group (UK), Innovation and Business Skills Australia Expert Working Group, P2P International IP and Commercialisation Forum Steering Committee (UK) and Chair of ISEA2013.

Peter Balan joined the University of South Australia following a career in market research, marketing and company management in France, Germany, Switzerland, the UK and Australia. He was the Foundation Head of the University's School of Marketing and the Foundation Director of his university's Centre for the Development of Entrepreneurs. His research is in innovation capability, entrepreneurial orientation and business model innovation, as well as in entrepreneurship education.

Eva Balan-Vnuk combines qualitative and quantitative methods, namely concept mapping and Qualitative Comparative Analysis (QCA), in her research to investigate aspects of innovation and entrepreneurship, including business models. Prior to academia, Eva spent nine years working for Microsoft in Europe, Middle East, Africa and Asia, in a variety of sales, marketing, strategy and management roles. After having completed her PhD to better understand the business model strategies of sustainable social enterprises, she now works for Microsoft in Australia, working with customers to help them identify ways to become more innovative. Eva is a Visiting Research Fellow at the University of Adelaide.

David Corkindale completed a science degree, worked for a pharmaceutical company and gained a Masters in Business and Operational Research (OR) and then worked in OR for a major engineering company in the UK for some years. Becoming interested in marketing, he ended up working in research for the largest advertising agency in London. He moved to be on the marketing faculties of a major Business School in the UK and then in Canada, gaining a PhD along the way, before coming to Australia. He is now Professor of Marketing at the University of South Australia, where he was instrumental in establishing the School of Marketing. He has specialised in the role of marketing in the commercialising of new technology, has done a range of assignments in this and is now undertaking research on choice behaviour online. He has published five books and many papers in academic journals.

Graciela Corral de Zubielqui is the Associate Head (Research) and a lecturer in the postgraduate Project Management and Innovation area in the Entrepreneurship, Commercialisation and Innovation Centre at the University of Adelaide. She completed her PhD in the area of innovation, globalisation and SMEs performance. She also holds a Bachelor of Economics (Honours) and a Master in Economics and Business Administration. She worked in projects which linked government departments, industry and university. Her research interests include innovation, knowledge transfer, collaboration activities between government, industry and university, SMEs performance and impact on regional economic development.

Vernon Ireland is Director of Project Management for the University of Adelaide. Previously he has been Corporate Development Director of Fletcher Challenge Construction, responsible for people and business systems improvement in the USA, New Zealand, Australia, Pacific and Asian businesses, in the $2 billion pa company; in academe he was the foundation Dean of Design, Architecture and Building at the University of Technology, Sydney. He has conducted staff development programs with the Shanghai Construction Commission, Defence Materiel Organisation and Thales Australia. He supervises seven PhD students, one on linear projects and six on complex systems and projects. He has been awarded the Engineers Australia Medal (2008), the Rotary International Gold Medal for contributions to vocational education (2006) and the Magnolia Silver Medal from the Shanghai Government (2000) for contributions to Chinese overseas relations.

Fiona Kerr is a specialist in systems and neural complexity at the University of Adelaide, having spent nearly thirty years in the business world working in the areas of organisational creativity and transformation before entering academia. This sometimes meant embedding in an organisation or a bureaucracy for up to three years to assist in innovative systemic change. Fiona still consults to businesses and governments in a number of countries, working with systems complexity on a number of levels, from increasing adaptivity in small organisations to a whole-of-government perspective on their role in enabling and growing innovative capacity, and value chain network analysis. She became interested in the cognitive aspects of leaders who shape innovative systems, and the increase in complexity of staff in adaptive organisations, and is now researching cognitive differences in creative leaders. She is a regular speaker on the practices and neuroscience of creating and leading adaptive organisations.

Huanmei Li (Mushui) did her PhD at the University of Adelaide. Her thesis is on the innovation and marketing performance of Australian wineries. Specifically her research was about how management practices of wine companies can best leverage region-specific tangible and intangible resources to successfully pursue opportunities and to achieve innovation and market performance. During her time as a PhD student, she was also involved in several projects on the innovation behaviours of SMEs and the wine industry. Currently she works as a project assistant at Vanderlee and Associates and she is Chinese wine market advisor at the Barossa Grape and Wine

Association. She is also the Executive President at the Wine Australia Promotion Association (WAPA).

Allan O'Connor is the postgraduate Academic Director for Innovation and Entrepreneurship at the Entrepreneurship, Commercialisation and Innovation Centre at the University of Adelaide. Allan combines his extensive experience in confronting the growth issues of small and medium enterprises and business start-up to inform his teaching and research. Allan's main teaching interests are in the assessment of business opportunities, entrepreneurial strategy and developing research skills. Since 2012 he has co-authored the leading Asia Pacific text, *Entrepreneurship Theory, Process and Practice*, with Professors Howard Frederick and Donald Kuratko. His research examines the intersection between entrepreneurship, innovation and socio-economic development, which has led to the development of the Australian Cluster Observatory and an in-depth study of entrepreneurial ecosystems. In application, his research is designed to inform policy makers, regional development agencies and the practicing entrepreneur with respect to creating and managing the resources necessary to foster and develop innovation and entrepreneurship in response to the strategic challenges of economic change.

Jiwat Ram has published in top tier journals in project management and information systems areas, including the *International Journal of Project Management*, and the *International Journal of Production Economics*. His work is highly received with his papers ranked in the Top 25.

Göran Roos is chairing the Value Add and Industrial Growth Sub-Committee of the Economic Development Board in Adelaide. He is a member of the Council for Flinders University; Stretton Fellow appointed by the City of Playford at the University of Adelaide; Adjunct Professor at ECIC, University of Adelaide; Adjunct Professor at University of Technology Sydney Business School; and Adjunct Associate Professor in the College of Business, Nanyang Business School, Nanyang Technological University, Singapore. Göran was appointed *Manufacturing for the Future* Thinker in Residence by the South Australian Premier for the year 2011. He was selected for the Committee for Economic Development of Australia (CEDA) Top 10 Speeches in 2013 and is a fellow of the Australian Academy of Technological Sciences and Engineering (ATSE).

Pi-Shen Seet is Associate Professor in Management at Flinders Business School. Previously he was Senior Lecturer at University of Adelaide's Business School and taught MBA/MCommerce courses on Entrepreneurship, Organisation Behaviour and Leadership, and he was awarded the Scott Henderson Award for Excellence in Learning & Teaching. A Philosophy, Politics & Economics graduate from Oxford University, he completed his PhD at Judge Business School, University of Cambridge, where he taught on undergraduate and postgraduate courses. He is visiting scholar at the Nanyan Technopreneurship Centre, Singapore, and is part of the Family Business Education and Research Group based at the University of Adelaide.

Paul Shum is currently a research fellow participating in an ARC-funded project on supply chain management. Over the last two years, Paul was an Assistant Professor, teaching finance and economics at the Hong Kong Shue Yan University. He is also the Director of Finance of a startup software company incubated at the Hong Kong Science and Technology Park, adjacent to the Chinese University of Hong Kong. Prior to his appointments in Hong Kong, Paul worked at universities in Australia, teaching and researching accounting and management, particularly in innovation and commercialisation. Before joining the academic field, Paul had more than fifteen years of industry experience in accounting, marketing and management. He worked at large resources companies BHP and Santos in marketing and planning. He has been a fellow CPA for ten years. He holds an MBA from the University of Adelaide, a PhD, a B Econ (Hon), a Grad Dip in Advanced Manufacturing Technology, and a Grad Dip in Accountancy.

Kym Teh is a PhD candidate of the Entrepreneurship, Commercialisation and Innovation Centre of the University of Adelaide, and the school manager of that university's School of Population Health. His research is in the area of higher education (universities), entrepreneurship, and exploring the adaptive responses of universities to transformational change. Kym is also an Adjunct Lecturer at the School of Information Technology and Mathematics at the University of South Australia, and has been an Adjunct Lecturer at Flinders Law School, Flinders University. Kym graduated from the University of Adelaide with qualifications in law, and postgraduate qualifications in computer science, and science and technology commercialisation. Amongst his professional roles, he has been an Executive General Manager, Strategy & Innovation, and Economic Development, of EDS Australia (which is now Hewlett Packard), Senior Strategy Advisor to the Science, Technology and Innovation Directorate of the Government of South Australia, and a technology law partner.

Foreword

'Innovation happens through regional, social and economic system dynamics [and] relies on a systems view of entrepreneurship' (Chapter 1, this book). It is this systems perspective on entrepreneurship and innovation, and in particular a focus on the ways in which entrepreneurship strategies and systems work in support of integrating innovation, which best define *Integrating Innovation: South Australian Entrepreneurship Systems and Strategies*.

The contribution made by this collective of researchers distinguishes itself on multiple levels.

Firstly, it does so through the delineation of national, regional and firm-level innovation systems. It may be intuitively understood that stimulating innovation at the firm level leads to productivity growth, and that entrepreneurial skills at a firm level are important contributors to the innovation performance of a nation. It is another matter to clearly articulate the characteristics of, and key actors within, national, regional and firm-level innovation systems and to represent how they interact to bring about improved regional socio-economic performance. *Integrating Innovation: South Australian Entrepreneurship Systems and Strategies* provides an important frame of reference for an audience seeking to apply the concepts discussed to their professional and personal context as they read by maintaining an holistic perspective of the innovation systems whilst explaining the difference between and interdependencies across the national, regional and firm tiers.

Secondly, the authors address the role of innovation and entrepreneurship in building the absorptive capacity within economies. This is particularly relevant for small economies like that of South Australia seeking to shift to better diversified and more globally relevant activities. The competitiveness gains to be made through better collaboration, learning and management capability at a firm level will translate to improved competitiveness of the region.

Finally, there are moments in the reading of this collection where one imagines the authors' intended audience: 'Dear Policymaker' might have introduced the discussion of South Australia's innovation performance. Suggested areas of focus include:

- strengthening of inter-systems relationships across the national, regional and firm levels through facilitated knowledge exchange, effective communications and strong policy/program alignment

- development of new tools and methodologies to foster and manage collaboration and competition, including instruments that promote entrepreneurship and are likely to have significant impact on the innovation performance of regional economies

- prioritisation of strategies that allow firms to share transaction costs and hedge risks associated with innovation

- focus on innovation infrastructure (technological capabilities, physical environments or the places that attract the all-important creative human capital and knowledge, skills and training) which enables the innovation effort.

The complexity of the task of mapping, interpreting and diagnosing the state's innovation needs is not to be underestimated, but *Integrating Innovation: South Australian Entrepreneurship Systems and Strategies* constructively brings into focus the role of government policy which facilitates, enables and catalyses the connections, outreach and knowledge bases that are at the heart of a state regional innovation system.

I commend this work to the reader, both as an instructive and regionally relevant discussion on the relationship between innovation and entrepreneurship for systems impact, and as an invitation to be part of the future of innovation performance in South Australia.

Megan Antcliff
Director, Strategic Projects and Innovation
Director, Tonsley Redevelopment, Department of State Development, South Australia

Introduction

The idea of integrating innovation:

1

Entrepreneurship and a systems perspective

Göran Roos, The University of Adelaide
Allan O'Connor, The University of Adelaide

Introduction: The ambition of this book

In 2011, the South Australian [SA] Government enlisted the services of Professor Göran Roos as Adelaide Thinker in Residence to examine the innovation challenges faced by the manufacturing sector. Professor Roos's brief was to work with a group of ten small- to medium-sized manufacturing firms and two government departments to guide the participants through a process that would actively engage them in business model innovation. At the time, a group of researchers were also engaged to work with the firms and government agencies to help document specific aspects and challenges confronted by the firm's leaders and managers and the government agencies that seek to facilitate regional transformation and transition.

Professor Roos's residency inspired this book and, with the support of the University of Adelaide Press, we issued a call for South Australian research that would not only demonstrate the drivers and processes of innovation but also illustrate the interdependencies of innovation across multiple levels, ranging from the individuals with innovation ideas and ambitions through to government support agencies that create the supporting context and infrastructure for innovation.

Although the manufacturing sector provided the setting for Professor Roos's work, for contributions to this book we loosened this constraint. We purposefully invited open submissions for research that dealt with innovation and correspondingly entrepreneurship from any perspective as long as it was original research based in South Australia which offered insight on the idea of integrating innovation through entrepreneurship strategies and systems. We welcomed articles that addressed relevant and related subjects pertinent to the South Australian innovation system. As a result we attracted articles dealing with both innovation and entrepreneurship that varied from not-for-profit firms with social missions to the research and development division of a pharmaceutical company; from public infrastructures such as education and intellectual property patenting systems to private infrastructures of Enterprise Resource Planning systems.

The book itself is designed as a seed for an innovative idea and its editors held three ambitions for the work. The first was to draw together initially South Australian research and researchers (later we wish to expand this collective) who are actively engaged in creating and contributing to new knowledge about innovation by adopting a systems view of entrepreneurship. The second was to facilitate a growth in understanding about the linkages between innovation and entrepreneurship and how these two distinct ideas are necessarily intertwined, how they interact and with what effect. The third ambition was to examine and establish a language that has relevance to the concept of integrated innovation and entrepreneurship. We felt that the field of intellectual capital offered a systems view that provided such a language; and consequently we review each article in the concluding chapter to draw together the salient points from each of the contributing authors and construct the links between innovation and entrepreneurship when considered through the lens of an intellectual capital system.

This introductory chapter is designed to provide the context for the subsequent chapters. It first outlines the South Australian economic context, which leads to the second discussion of the manufacturing sector and how the definition of manufacturing has changed. This introduces the idea of a much broader range of sectors that are responsible for innovation, and provides the platform for a much more open approach to thinking about innovation within the state's context.

Next we consider the question of how important it is to consider innovation as an integrated system concept. This section discusses the different levels, antecedents and the broad range of influences on innovation. It particularly draws attention to the government role in innovation and how policy environments are changing to respond to the complexity of issues of such things as stimulating innovation.

We then discuss entrepreneurship with respect to the extent to which it is a study of a system that extends beyond a conceptual study of individual entrepreneurs. This system has a specific purpose and that is to introduce innovation. Hence we establish here the link between entrepreneurship and innovation. The discussion then moves toward the elements that are predominant in a social system that generates innovation and the deficiencies of academic studies in this critical area of concern. Lastly, we outline the language and tools of intellectual capital [IC] to provide a point of reference on the challenges of integrating innovation before the chapter draws to its conclusion.

The characteristics of the SA economy

South Australia is a small economy and, significantly, the smaller the size of the economy, the less relevant neo-classical economic theory is (Roos, 2012). A small economy does not have the opportunity that a large economy has to spontaneously generate optimal responses to change. Left to its own devices, compared to a large economy, a small economy as a whole has a higher risk of decline. To express it in neo-classical economic terminology, the smaller the economy, the more market failure becomes a feature of the economy as a whole.

The increasing openness of a small economy does not change its propensity for market failure, since its ability to digest and make use of knowledge is affected by its 'absorptive capacity' (Roos, 2012). The absorptive capacity of an economy is based on a firm's ability to recognise the value of new information, assimilate it and apply it to commercial ends. If the absorptive capacity does not increase while the information inflow increases, the economy will still not perform any better.

As a result of the resources boom, Australia — and South Australia — faced the risk of the so-called Dutch Disease: a term applied when the wealth generated by a country's booming resources sector drives up the exchange rate and inflates the domestic economy, making the country (and its manufacturing sector) less internationally competitive and compromising its long-term economic prosperity (Government of South Australia, 2012b). The South Australian economy is vulnerable to a high-cost environment, driven by the high exchange rate and terms of trade.

Many firms, as well as many government support systems, are yet to identify how to compete in this new environment. Failing to come to terms with this new dynamic will mean that the existing potential for agility and innovation, especially in small to medium enterprises [SMEs], is unlikely to be realised.

This necessitates a call to action to improve the competitiveness of the South Australian economy, especially through strengthening the innovation system to boost the absorptive capacity, collaboration and learning by firms, the level of firm management capability, and a shift to more balanced, diverse and high-value activities with global reach.

SA manufacturing: An innovation lead indicator

The South Australian manufacturing sector has been subjected to significant changes through globalisation, the repositioning of international markets, increased demands for customer responsiveness, and customisation and growth in global supply chains (Spoehr, 1999). Today, the challenge is ongoing with increasing complexity in global supply chains and new emerging demand for green technologies and products (Future Manufacturing Industry Innovation Council, 2011). According to the South Australian Plan (Government of South Australia, 2012b), in 1991 manufacturing accounted for 1 in 6 jobs and in 2011 this number had declined to 1 in 10.

As a result of the sectoral changes, together with the intensification of foreign competition, the comparative disadvantages in some manufacturing activities and the high value of the Australian dollar, the imperative for South Australian firms to engage with business model innovation and experiment with diversity is becoming increasingly urgent. While Australia generally faces an ongoing structural adjustment to the new global competitive environment, South Australia in particular risks losing proportionally 6700 jobs during the period up to 2016/17 (Government of South Australia, 2012b).

However, perhaps contrary to popular belief, South Australian manufacturing is not in terminal and in inevitable decline, nor is manufacturing an old industry whose death should be accepted to make way for growth industries like resources and services. In essence, the South Australian Manufacturing Green Paper (Government of South Australia, 2012a) argues several points including the following:

- Manufacturing still employs around 1 million Australians and has done so, more or less, since the 1960s.

- In SA, 10 per cent of the workforce is in manufacturing (79 000 jobs).

- Manufacturing still accounts for 8.7 per cent of GDP and most of Australia's high-value exports.

- In SA in 2011, manufacturing contributed $8.9 billion or 10 per cent of the Gross State Product and, importantly, there is evidence that manufacturing has a substantial multiplier effect on the rest of the economy by being a carrier of technological change and by driving jobs, investments and sales in other sectors.

While statistics suggest that the manufacturing sector's share of the Australian economy and rate of employment is declining, it is a relative downturn, characteristic of most developed countries. In absolute terms, manufacturing remains a substantial and important generator of economic activity and jobs, especially since most manufacturing firms are also directly involved in the services part of the economy. Manufacturing includes myriad activities in addition to production, such as design, logistics, customer solutions, support services and research. Its economic contribution is often underestimated as these other discrete manufacturing activities are not counted as 'manufacturing' in national statistics. And yet, firms involved in (sometimes oblique) sub-sectors of manufacturing are a major part of the South Australian economy, characterised by the small to medium enterprise sector.

Contemporary evidence suggests that innovation is not simply the fruit of research and commercialisation. Rather, the reality of innovation more commonly in evidence is a fluid, interactive, cumulative process involving a wide array of learning and problem-solving activities, with multiple actors drawing on a variety of resources, forming and reforming combinations of knowledge (Lam, 2004). Value-adding innovation also requires entrepreneurial management that couples new knowledge with commercial potential to a customer and, importantly, a market promoting adoption and diffusion (Zubielqui, Lindsay, & O'Connor, 2014).

Is an integrating innovation perspective important?

The UK Government paper, *Innovation and Research Strategy for Growth* (Department for Business, Innovation and Skills, 2011) is a cogent and comprehensive presentation of evidence from academic scholarship and empirical studies by the OECD, NESTA, the EU and others. It shows a wider set of links between research knowledge and innovation, as well as elements of innovation that go way beyond research.

The Australian experience of innovation operating in many different modes at the enterprise level, including in SMEs, is documented in a series of studies over fifteen years by the Australian Business Foundation. Chief among these are the seminal study, *The High Road or The Low Road?* (Marceau, Manley, & Sicklen, 1997), linking innovation to productivity and growth; the collection of expert papers on the hidden human dimensions of innovation, *Inside the Innovation Matrix* (Australian Business Foundation (ED), 2008); and the recent analysis and case studies of business model innovation by Scott-Kemmis (2012). This body of work substantiates the variety of value creation and value-capturing activities undertaken by innovative enterprises and their workforces that meet market needs in exceptional ways, generate revenue, and transform business methods and capabilities to serve customers worldwide. These are not restricted to large firms or to high-tech sectors, but are pervasive across the economy.

At the heart of these innovative activities is the constant search and analysis by enterprises for market opportunities and how they integrate these with their own design, management, finances, engineering and organisational capabilities to gain and retain a distinctive competitive edge. Further, innovation in firms equally depends on a wider innovation environment, a system that has the infrastructure, finance, information and institutions that support firms taking the risks and reaping the rewards of business change, whether radical or incremental.

Too often innovation is a term whose meaning is obscured by vagueness and overuse. Of even greater concern, outdated and inaccurate understandings of innovation are widely held by business and government decision makers and by the general public. Further, there is little appreciation of how productivity growth can be improved by the innovative behaviour of enterprises and their workforces. This results in misguided views about innovation capabilities and how they contribute to a firm's competitive advantage, particularly when faced with concurrent shifts in the global economic competitive environment.

Being innovative is more than coming up with new ideas or inventions, and it does not simply equate with commercialising scientific discoveries or technology breakthroughs. At its simplest, innovation is doing something new that is both useful and valued, and it requires an entrepreneurial management for its exploitation. The OECD (2011) report on skills for innovation and research suggests that a broad range of skills, including 'soft skills' such as entrepreneurial skills and capabilities, will become an increasingly important contribution to innovation in a nation. Similarly, Shane (2008) emphasises that would-be entrepreneurs need to be armed with skills that make them more successful, rather than just being encouraged to start a business. A key feature of such skills is the ability to implement transformative change in response to needs or problems that really matter to a customer, which creates a market and benefits a community.

From a policy perspective, an understanding of how to best stimulate and support the transformation of small- to medium-sized firms and assist the transition of others is not readily apparent. Part of the problem is embedded in the complexity of the relationships between the motivations and drivers of individual business owners or Chief Executive Officers, the issues and challenges faced by the management teams of firms confronting the need for change, and the dynamics that firms encounter within their regional environment. However, few studies have ever examined the interrelationships from within the dynamics of the firm to understand how broad policy approaches would or could impact behavioural change at such intimate levels of the firm and the individual.

Modern innovation policy will no longer be simplistic in its demarcation between portfolios. Marton and Phillips (2005, p. 81) attest that the characteristics of modern policy-making, leading into the future, will be 'forward looking, outward looking, integrated and participatory, inclusive of the views, values, objectives and practices of all concerned parties and based on lessons systematically learned from ongoing experience'. Policy-making organisations are faced with a greater need to provide new solutions driven by an array of stakeholders (Hess & Adams, 2002; Yapp, 2005).

Entrepreneurship: A system that integrates innovation

The earliest studies of entrepreneurship were conducted by economists who recognised the contribution of the entrepreneur in altering market economic systems (Hébert & Link, 1982). More recently, the idea of the entrepreneur as also contributing to social system changes has resulted in the emergence of social entrepreneurship as an area of research (Christie & Honig, 2006; Thompson, Alvy, & Lees, 2000; Peredo & Chrisman, 2006; Peredo & McLean, 2006; Nicholls, 2010). One of this chapter's authors, O'Connor (2013), more particularly makes distinctions between types of entrepreneurship that may occur within the knowledge, social and corporate sectors of a national economy and argues that these tend to converge on the issue of expansion and growth of an economy.

Audretsch (2004, p. 188) traces the development of entrepreneurship with respect to its contribution to national economic systems and concludes that entrepreneurship serves 'as a mechanism facilitating the spill over of knowledge', and that in order for public policy 'to promote innovation and economic growth' there is a need for instruments that promote entrepreneurship. However, Audretsch continues by highlighting the need for future research 'to explicitly identify what exactly those instruments are and how public policy can best be deployed to promote innovative entrepreneurship'.

The process of entrepreneurship is centrally concerned with the recognition, discovery and/or creation of opportunity (Alvarez & Barney, 2005; Schendel & Hitt, 2007; Shane & Venkataraman, 2000). Substantivists view opportunity as a symbolic interaction between entrepreneurs and their environment (Dimov, 2011). Adner and Kapoor (2010) also claim that value recognition and appropriation happens through ecosystem interactions and interdependencies often mapped as an industry value chain, or perhaps better described as a value web from a systems perspective. In adopting a systems approach, it is important to recognise that the study of entrepreneurship does not start and stop with the actions of an entrepreneur or their firm but extends to the interactions and interdependencies of the entrepreneur, as the principle actor, and their firm, as a mediator, with the social, market and macro-economic environments.

The concept of panarchy (Gunderson & Holling, 2002) suggests that change within systems happens along various layers within the system and at different rates. Each system layer contained within the whole acts simultaneously to conserve and stabilise on the one hand and to generate and test innovations on the other (Holling, 2001). If one is to consider each layer of value creation in a value web, then it follows that different firm or actor interactions at each layer not only create but also reconfigure and/or destroy value. In order for the ecosystem to change and adapt, an innovation must succeed within each layer, and the entrepreneur must envision and align not only one system layer but each successive and/or dependent system layer.

By way of example, technology systems must interact with social systems, and therefore advances in technology face two challenges; first, gaining a foothold in one or more of the successive technology value systems, and second, making sure that the inner and outer (or upstream and downstream) social value systems align with the technological advance (described as an ecology strategy by Iansiti and Levien, 2004). To confront both of these challenges, technologists must address not only the intersections between the economic and technology systems but also the social system intersections that carry and distribute information.

The introduction of innovation into an ecosystem represents a reorganisation phase (see Gunderson & Holling, 2002; Holling, 2001), which is the least examined and the least understood phase (Holling, 2001). McKelvey (2004) argued that reductionist methods fail entrepreneurship research, as the nature of entrepreneurship as a phenomenon resembles a complexity science whereby causality is considered through multiple lenses: the objective action and reaction among predictable and universal behaviours; the specific objectives of participating actors that shape specific behaviour; localised material conditions that alter the substance of, or inputs into, innovation and entrepreneurial venturing; and lastly, the influence of top-down and bottom-up hierarchical and institutional structures that impose means and ways of creating actor interactions.

The conclusion is that we can view the economy as an open system in dynamic disequilibrium. As a consequence, structural changes manifested in the contraction and death of old enterprises and the birth and growth of new ones are compelling evidence of an efficient economy at work. Holling (2001) outlines how human systems differ from systems of nature due to three factors — foresight/intentionality, communication and technology — and it is the entrepreneur who is a central actor in creating dynamic changes through these particular attributes of human systems.

The elements of an integrated innovation system

The complex interaction of market forces involving changing consumption preferences, changing production processes, changing production costs, changing market offerings, changing levels of value creation, changing levels of value appropriation and changing trade patterns results in a dynamic industrial structure in terms of scope, profitability and location. These complex interactions have been the focus of many researchers and have resulted in many theoretical developments to help us in our understanding over a very long time. Some of the key insights, heavily simplified, are in chronological order:

- Industry locates to where rent opportunities are largest (von Thünen, 1826 [1966]).

- Patterns of trade are a consequence of shifting comparative advantages among regions (Heckscher, 1919).

- Economic activity is a constantly shifting spatial interaction between people and property (Lösch, 1939).

- Technological innovations are the driving force in a continually evolving capitalist system. Firms successfully deploying new technologies will replace those that do not, resulting in the birth and death of firms — a process known as 'creative destruction'. Technological innovation often creates temporary monopolies, allowing abnormal profits that are then removed by rivals and imitators. These temporary monopolies are necessary to provide the incentive necessary for firms to develop new products and processes (Schumpeter, 1911; 1939; 1942).

So far we can conclude that the most important elements of a regional innovation system are:

- knowledge, new to the firm, the industry or the world (a human attribute)

- competent people (a human attribute)

- an environment conducive to innovation (a structural attribute).

To these elements at least three further criteria that create the dynamic flow of innovation activity by entrepreneurs and their firms must be integrated into the system for successful innovation:

- The innovation must be desired by the market.

- A high level of value creation must be achieved through the innovation.

- A high proportion of the value created must be captured by the innovating firm.

We will discuss each of these in turn at its related systems level.

Knowledge

Knowledge new to the world is most frequently achieved through basic research carried out at universities and research institutes. Due to the existing pressures of the financial markets, it is difficult for listed corporations to invest in basic research, which by its very nature is long-term, risky and ever more expensive. In one survey of Chief Financial Officers in US firms, 80 per cent responded that they would cut R&D, if necessary to meet their firm's next-quarter's profit projections (Graham, Harvey, & Rajgopal, 2005).

For example, only one of every ten thousand chemicals investigated by pharmaceutical firms is approved for patient use (National Research Council, 2010). It is estimated to cost on average $802 million and take an average of twelve years to transition one new chemical from the exploratory phase to use by United States patients (Hewitt & Lowy, 2001). This is a large barrier to commercial investors. Under these boundary conditions, when publically listed firms are investing less in basic research and more in applied research and development, it is increasingly left to privately held firms, foundations, non-government organisations and government to fund basic research. This is consistent with the notion that governments should assume responsibility for supporting activities that produce benefits to society as a whole but not necessarily commensurately to the individual performer or underwriter. This means that research universities and research institutes will have to assume the primary responsibility for performing basic research, with the funding coming from federal government and foundations.

Knowledge new to the industry is most frequently developed through applied research at universities and research and technology organisations. In this area the contributions of the universities are frequently overestimated and the contributions of the research and technology organisations underestimated. The following statement illustrates this: 'To be blunt, if anything, there is a tendency in the literature to perhaps overplay the role of universities and underplay the role of the private sector in generating innovative technology clusters' (Betts & Lee, 2004).

Knowledge new to the firm is inherently executed as R&D-type activities within the firm or as collaborative activities between the firm and outside agencies (other firms, universities, research and technology organisations, etc.). Again the role of universities tends to be overestimated, as illustrated by the fact that in Government

Voucher programs aimed at enabling firms to involve themselves to higher degree in collaborative R&D with universities and research and technology organisations the overwhelming majority of vouchers are cashed in with research and technology organisations, not universities (ICS Ltd, 2010). New knowledge on the firm level covers a broad area including traditional scientific and engineering knowledge development but also areas like design and business models that are not normally classified as R&D.

Competent people

The key source of value creation in any nation resides in its people. The economist Jonathan Hughes (1973), argues that the economic wellbeing of any society is dependent on economic value creation, which in turn is strongly dependent on innovation, and since innovations are realised by a minority of the society's citizens, it has a very high dependence on these individuals for its continued economic wellbeing (Schramm, 2010). Given the ever-increasing speed of knowledge development, the demands on all categories of employees are higher than ever and will continue to increase, and this poses a challenge for the ability of firms to find a sufficient number of qualified employees in the available pool of potential employees. This situation is reaching critical status in the areas of engineering and science, where many OECD countries are unable to provide a future supply of these types of graduates sufficient in quality and quantity to enable the domestic industry to put to use available new knowledge and to grow at the speed for which the market provides the potential. In one instance, a firm seeking to hire employees was able to find only 47 who were qualified out of an applicant pool of 3600 (Rich, 2010); and almost one-third of US manufacturing companies responding to a recent survey say they are suffering from some level of skills shortages (*People and profitability: A time for change*, 2009).

The impact on quantity can be overcome by importing skilled talent if the attraction of the country is great enough but once a nation's ability to innovate, and hence to attract the type of individuals who are desirable from an economic perspective, have declined sufficiently the decline becomes self-reinforcing as quality students no longer seek to attend that nation's universities and high-calibre graduates seek work in more attractive nations. The impact of the quality at all levels of education cannot be underestimated. In a study by McKinsey and Company (2009) the researchers conclude that if United States youth could match the performance of students in Finland, America's economy would be between 9 and 16 per cent larger. That equates to between 1.3 and 2.3 *trillion* dollars each year.

An environment conducive to innovation

What are the environmental requirements conducive to innovation? In a seminal study, Cushing (2001) objectively and systematically compared the effects of three common theories explaining economic growth — the social capital theory, the human capital theory and the creative capital theory. He found no evidence that social capital leads to regional economic growth; in fact, the effects were negative. He found that the human capital theory of economic growth is not as straightforward to interpret as the proponents may argue, in spite of it providing a good statistical account for regional growth. He further found that the creative capital theory produced equally strong if not stronger results than the human capital theory; and the Bohemian and Innovative Indices had especially high predictive power for regional economic growth (Florida, 2004). Like all theories, criticism can be directed at both the study's content and its scope (see, for example, Storper & Scott, 2009) but it is likely to contain some truth that can be simplified down to a shift in behaviour from individuals going to where the jobs are to jobs going to where the individuals are. This increases the importance of having locations that are attractive to individuals who will innovate and generate economic growth.

Once we have transformed the new knowledge to new offerings it is essential to bring these new offerings to market with the highest possible speed. Time is of the utmost importance in this process and any delay can have catastrophic consequences for economic value creation. The ever-increasing speed can be illustrated by the fact that it took almost two years for 1 million iPods to be sold, 74 days for 1 million iPhones (Apple Sells One Millionth iPhone, 2007), and 28 days for 1 million iPads (Apple Sells One Million iPads, 2010). Any environment that increases the friction, and hence slows down the process of getting an offering to market, undermines the whole innovation-driven economic value creation process.

One of the environmental issues is cost of labour. Experience from Sweden and Finland shows that if the cost of labour can be kept below 15 per cent of total cost there is normally no value to be had from outsourcing to countries with lower labour costs. This is due to the negative effects incurred by increasing the distance between development and production, management and production, lead customers and production, and so on.

Another environmental issue to consider is legal risk. In the US, firms spend more than twice as much on litigation as on research (National Science Board, 2010). The class-act law-suit 'business' equals around 3 per cent of the GDP in the US. It is obvious that this type of situation will discourage firms from taking risks, and the launch of a new offering inherently entails risk; hence this has a not insignificant negative impact on the propensity to innovate.

A further environmental issue is Tax Policy. Obviously both corporate and private tax, and direct and indirect tax, will impact the attractiveness of a region as well as the attractiveness of exerting additional effort in pursuit of additional wealth for both individuals and companies. It is worth noting that the actual effectiveness of policies like R&D tax credits is very low — what looks like a statistically reported increase in R&D spending (which explains why all econometric and research papers using reported R&D statistics end up arguing for its positive effects) is frequently just a reclassification of other expenses into R&D expenses and not an increase in the actual R&D executed (which becomes obvious when in-depth interviews are executed in firms).

Regulation can be both a barrier and a driver of innovation. It becomes a barrier when it imposes friction in the process from offering development to market without providing a larger long-term benefit to the firm. It becomes a driver for innovation when it forces the firm to develop new offerings that enable the firm to reach new global markets faster than competitors. Having a policy philosophy that uses regulation as a driver of innovation builds on the thesis that health, safety, and environmental goals can be co-optimised with economic growth through technological innovation.

The approach that needs to be taken in creating an atmosphere conducive to innovation is outlined in an article by Ashford, Ayres, and Stone (1985):

> [A] regulator must assess the innovative capacity of the target industrial sector. The target sector may be the regulated industry, the pollution control industry, or a related industry capable of producing substitute technology. The analysis should focus principally on the process of technological change within the possible responding sectors. The regulator should analyze a sector's 'innovative dynamic' rather than its existing, static technological capability. An assessment

of this innovative dynamic requires a historical examination of the pattern of innovation in the regulated industry, an evaluation of the technological capabilities of related sectors having incentives to develop compliance or substitute technology, and a comparison between the regulated sector and analogous sectors with documented technological responses to regulation. The assessment should include an analysis of the industry's existing technological capabilities as well as a reasoned prediction of its innovative potential under the challenge of regulation. This kind of assessment will assist the design of regulations promoting innovation beneficial both to public health and the environment, and to economic growth within the responding industrial sector. (p. 422)

The relationship between regulation and innovation is complex. When drastic innovation redefines the very framework for implementing and operating technologies it often means entering unregulated territory or breaking existing rules. Drastic innovations that generate paradigm shifts in value creation (for example, ICT, Biotechnology, Nanotechnology) call for a more holistic consideration of the link between innovation and mobilisation of value on the one hand, and regulation on the other.

Access to capital is a further perpetual environmental issue. In regions where access to venture capital is scarce, firms have developed alternative sources of funding like lead customer risk funding, business angel funding, university alumni fund funding or peer-to-peer lending. Peer-to-peer lending [P2P] is one of the clearest examples of modern financial innovation, as entrepreneurs have harnessed the internet and its associated economies of scale to exert competitive pressure on more traditional lending practices. As described by Brill (2010), P2P lending relies on online platforms that connect borrowers with lenders. These platforms are operated by firms that enable the initial connection between lenders and borrowers and that service the loans after they have been originated. The draw of P2P lending for both borrowers and lenders is that the companies serving as intermediaries charge just a small fee for their services — around 1 per cent.

Other environmental issues relate to:

- intellectual property protection
- freedom of distortions like crime and corruption
- free market access, which will result in emotionally charged events:

- o IBM's PC business is now owned by a Chinese company (Augustine, 2007, p. 17)
- o Bell Laboratories is now owned by a French company (Zarroli, 2006)
- o Volvo Car is now owned by a Chinese company after having been acquired from a US company (Reed, 2010)
- access to necessary infrastructure like roads (see, for example, Canning & Bennathan, 2004; 2000), rail, ports and airports but also energy, water, sanitation and ICT-infrastructure (for an interesting review see, for example, Skogseid, 2007).

Geographic proximity to key markets is also an important but decreasing environmental issue for innovation. The decreasing importance is due to increased global mobility combined with a higher digital content of the offering for which the transportation cost is very small compared to the corresponding cost of its physical equivalent. For example, the cost of sending a metal part for a car from Australia to the US is substantially higher than sending the corresponding digital file that can be uploaded to the machine tools for direct manufacture of the same part. The proximity issues are now more related to the benefit that can be derived from locating factories near potential customers; engineering facilities near factories; and research laboratories near engineering facilities (National Research Council, 2010).

To wrap up the range of issues that contribute to creating an environment conducive to innovation, Hindle, Yencken, and O'Connor (2011) suggest the various policy initiatives related to the different challenges faced by a firm. Figure 1.1 highlights a sample range of government policy focus areas, such as entrepreneurial capacity, finance and industry, innovation and market as areas that deserve attention if a government is to influence the creation and growth of high potential businesses.

The innovation must be desired by the market

This can either be achieved through an in-depth understanding of the value drivers in the mind of the customer (using sophisticated techniques like Conjoint Value Hierarchy [CVH]; see Roos, Pike, & Fernström, 2006, pp. 227-82) or using an intuitive approach with the assumption that customers cannot value what they do not know. These choices are not to be seen as mutually exclusive but rather as endpoints of a scale where it is also possible to move from one to the other in a cyclic way.

Policies influencing entrepreneurial capacity (e.g. education and training, immigration)
Policies influencing finance and industry (e.g. macroeconomic including: monetary, market regulation)
Policies influencing innovation (e.g. microeconomic: research and development, firm support and incentives)
Policies influencing the market (e.g. microeconomic: regional development, consumer incentives)

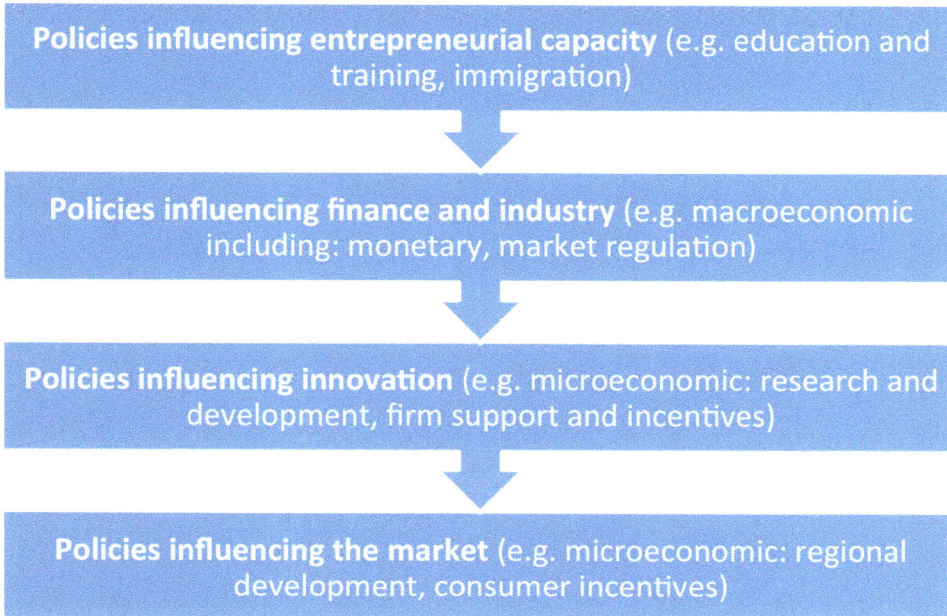

Figure 1.1: Policy initiatives related to the different challenges faced by a firm.
Source: Courtesy of the authors.

High value creation must be achieved through the innovation

High value creation is achieved by innovating offerings that are in high demand by customers and then rapidly bringing them to market with operational excellence in order to initially extract innovation-based monopoly rents followed by rents from superior competitive advantage grounded in operational excellence.

A high proportion of the value created must be captured by the innovating firm

The business model (for a detailed discussion see Osterwalder, 2004; further developed in Roos & Pike, 2009; and outlined in detail in Roos, von Krogh, Roos, & Fernström, 2010) of the firm will determine its ability to appropriate value in its existing business environment. Hence business model innovation becomes the key to increasing the appropriation of value. The power of the business model can be seen in the business model innovation. For example, Apple's iPhone went from a global market share of nothing to a global market share of 2.5 per cent in 18 months, whilst at the same time moving from a share of the profit pool in the industry of 0 per cent to a profit pool share of 45 per cent, forcing all other players to reduce their profit pool share and hence their value appropriation (this being most felt by Nokia, with a reduction from around 80 per cent to around 30 per cent).

We next turn to consider how IC systems assist in charting the dynamics of human systems.

The usefulness of IC in understanding innovation and entrepreneurship systems

There is a need to further understand the relationships between intellectual capital resources and the systems and strategies that anticipate environmental and market changes (O'Connor & Yamin, 2011). Furthermore, innovation systems that provide significant regional and community benefit need to be considered from the perspective of cross-institutional frameworks and at national and international levels (Hall, 2005; Spencer, 2003). This necessitates different thinking about organisational form (Harkema & Browaeys, 2002). Hervas-Oliver, Albors Garrigos, and Gil-Pechuan (2011) argue that research addressing the strategies and systems which integrate innovation would be valuable for understanding how different organisations manage their intellectual capital to respond and contribute to innovation systems and develop innovation capability.

In order to create value, entrepreneurs bundle and deploy resources that are not necessarily owned or controlled by the entrepreneur (Stevenson & Jarillo, 1990). Similarly, firms allocate their limited resources between two fundamental processes of creating value and appropriating value. Although both value creation and value appropriation are required for achieving sustained competitive advantage, a firm has significant latitude in deciding the extent to which it emphasises one over the other. Research shows that a stock market reacts favourably when a firm increases its emphasis on value appropriation relative to value creation. This effect, however, is moderated by firm and industry characteristics — in particular, financial performance, the past level of strategic emphasis of the firm and the technological environment in which the firm operates. These results do not negate the importance of value creation capabilities, but rather highlight the importance of isolating mechanisms that enable the firm to appropriate some of the value it has created (Mizik & Jacobson, 2003).

The IC Navigator process developed by Roos and Roos (1997) and further refined by Roos and Pike (2007) offers an example of a powerful diagnostic into how firms actually operate, highlighting the importance of resources and the numerous value-creating pathways that connect them. Some groups of pathways will represent innovation processes, while wholesale changes to the structures will represent changes to the business model. It is possible that the resource-based view of the firm can indicate how different functional (technological and marketing) and integrative (internal and external) capabilities affect product development efficiency (lead time and productivity) and product effectiveness (fit with market needs and quality). However, only the most modern and sophisticated IC methodologies, which account for differences between forms of resources, such as those presented by Roos and Pike (2007), have the capability to explain the detailed interactions and explain real outcomes.

In firm-level analysis, IC refers to blocks or stocks of particular types of assets termed as different types of capitals, i.e. physical, monetary, human, relational and structural capitals. The IC Navigator is largely based upon the aforesaid capitals, although it should be noted that while the IC Navigator incorporates each resource type, it is only the human, relational and structural (referred to as 'organisational') capitals that are of the intellectual form, while physical and monetary capitals are of the traditional form treated more regularly by accounting theories and practices.

Hervas-Oliver et al. (2011, pp. 124-5) escalated the analysis of IC to the regional level by examining twenty-eight indicators used by the European Union across six years, and noted that while

> the traditional break up of national IC based on relational, structural and human, [is] useful and practical, [it] can be questioned due to the fact that similar results are obtained in IC national models without any classification or weight give[n] to any block. Put differently, it seems that further reclassification of the blocks of national IC systems can be developed in order to provide a more comprehensive and economic-friendly tool for policymakers. (pp. 123-5)

It is from this point that we embark upon the journey of discovery by examining the papers presented in this special call for research papers. To date we are aware that innovation consists of applying knowledge new to the firm, the industry or the world to the creation of desirable offerings. These new offerings are then speedily brought to the global market in ways and forms that enable the capture of a large share of the value created through these offerings.

An overview of the proceeding chapters

This book is divided into three sections. The first section clusters chapters that adopt a South Australian regional perspective on innovation. In this section three papers are presented that discuss different aspects of the South Australian approach to innovation. Jane Andrew in her chapter 'Moving beyond policy path dependency: An approach to fostering innovation in South Australia' examines the theoretical and policy discourse that has informed South Australia's innovation policy. The chapter argues the case for a more holistic understanding of the contribution and value contributed by diverse knowledge domains and the multiple forms of transactions that inspire and support innovation across the economy.

The next chapter, 'A patent perspective of South Australian innovation: An indicator within the regional innovation system story', explores South Australia's innovation performance in the context of measuring and analysing patent data. From this analysis the authors, Kym Teh and Göran Roos, bring into focus a discussion of the state's regional innovation system [RIS] and raise pertinent and critical questions about the relevance and performance of such a system.

The third chapter in this section, by Gavin Artz, 'Innovation system symbiosis: The impact of virtual entrepreneurial teams on integrated innovation and regional innovation systems', draws upon the experience of technology entrepreneurship in South Australia. It alludes to a symbiosis between the evolution of a regional innovation system, the changes that such a system causes in managerial and cultural forms at the company level, and how these new collaborative forms then feed back into the regional innovation system as well as linking to national and international innovation networks. The three chapters together provide insight into the regional innovation system dynamics.

The second section provides three chapters that adopt integrative firm-level perspectives, each looking at different ways a firm or firms bring about innovation behaviour. The first chapter in this set, 'Do clusters matter to the entrepreneurial process? Deriving a conceptual model from the case study of Yalumba' by Huanmei Li and Allan O'Connor, attempts to conceptually model the interactions between multiple dimensions of industrial cluster involvements, a firm's entrepreneurial process and a firm's entrepreneurial performance. The chapter draws implications for future industry cluster research and practice and particularly brings the entrepreneurial process into the innovation picture.

The next chapter, by Fiona Kerr, 'Operationalising innovation: Hotwiring the creative organisation', examines the complexity and sustainability of key business and innovation components. Kerr argues that those firms that successfully master complexity build adaptive, innovative capabilities that result in sustained competitive advantage and the ability to transgress industry boundaries.

The third chapter in this section, 'Business model innovation in nonprofit social enterprises', co-authored by Eva Balan-Vnuk and Peter Balan, adopts a different stance by examining nonprofit firms. This chapter proposes two key reasons for business model innovation among nonprofit firms, those reasons being to remain financially viable, and to expand the delivery of important services to the community. The authors further outline six dimensions of innovation capability that enable nonprofit social enterprises to innovate their business models. As a group these chapters provide a contemporary view of how firms integrate innovation into daily performance and practice.

The third section of the book presents four chapters that specifically focus on innovation management practices, particularly in South Australian firms. While the chapters in the second section treat the firms as innovating entities, the chapters in this section look specifically at the ways and means firms are managed in order to bring about innovation. The first chapter in this set, 'Complex systems adjusting stability levels and providing entrepreneurial opportunity', provides a contextual piece that examines the question of how firms discover and exploit entrepreneurial opportunities through the lens of complex systems. The author, Vernon Ireland, argues that in order for firms to benefit from the process of adaptation in changing system emergence, both the firms' organisation and individuals need to quickly sense the change in a complex system and the adaptation process, create meaning from the change in order to identify a direction of that change, and respond quickly to initiate the process using the entrepreneurial techniques and processes of the individual or enterprise. The chapter offers a number of prospective tools and techniques from complex systems management which may be useful and informative to innovative firms.

The next chapter, by Graciela Corral DeZubielqui, Pi-Shen Seet and Allan O'Connor, 'Intellectual capital system perspective: A case study of government intervention in digital media industries', explores how a systems analysis informs strategies of government program intervention using the case of a government-led initiative for the creative industries development in South Australia. The article contrasts an intellectual capital [IC] perspective employing IC analysis tools with a complex systems analysis model. The analysis creates deeper insights into how to manage the resources and capabilities and the knowledge resource interdependencies between the government, university and industry stakeholders.

The following chapter, by Paul Shum, 'A diagnostic tool for assessing innovation readiness', systematically develops an innovation readiness framework based on intellectual capital that captures a complete set of innovation capabilities with associated enterprise-wide interlocking mechanisms and cultural change requirements. This diagnostic tool will help SME practitioners to target more accurately and consistently important areas for improving their organisation's innovation capabilities.

The final chapter in this section, by Jiwat Ram and David Corkindale, 'Developing a framework for the management of Critical Success Factors in organisational innovation projects: A case of Enterprise Resource Planning systems', presents a framework of nine commonly identified Critical Success Factors [CSFs] for the management of the complexities involved in the organisational innovation process of Enterprise Resource Planning [ERP] systems. The authors propose the designed framework to assist SMEs in putting together an action plan to successfully manage the ERP innovation process. They argue that the framework can also serve as a basis for the development of a theory for the management of CSFs. The chapters assembled for the third section provide different viewpoints of how to manage the integration of innovation at different levels, be it at region level or firm level.

The final chapter of the book considers the collection of chapters to illustrate the integrated nature of innovation, and portrays a systems perspective of the interlinkages between the chapters. Innovation is idiosyncratic, and we requested the contributors to this volume to identify the future research agendas that extend from their analysis. The final chapter draws these viewpoints together to chart a course of research development that will increase not only our understanding of how innovation is integrated within South Australia but how the management of the innovation system can be effected and outcomes can be improved.

Conclusion

This chapter has outlined the ambition for this book and presents the underpinning philosophy which we seek to explore through the coming chapters. Innovation is not the responsibility of any single individual, institution, firm or government department but is instead a result of system integration.

South Australia is a small economy that faces a fundamental need to reshape its approach to innovation. The manufacturing sector, as the backbone of the state's economy, has and will continue to change its nature and form. This necessitates a rethink about how innovation happens and how the respective actors within an economy interact and engage with each other. In effect, innovation relies on intersections between people, knowledge, information sharing, ideas, and financial and other resources. Innovation happens through regional, social and economic system dynamics; innovation relies on a systems view of entrepreneurship.

Entrepreneurship can be taken as a study of the entrepreneur and new business creation. However, this conception of entrepreneurship misses the critical link to economic outcomes; the ebb and flow of social and economic fortunes that are underpinned by the actions, reactions and engagement of individuals in a specific social and economic system that brings about innovation and change. In this book we are exploring how the linkages within the system can be conceptualised and made transparent.

Intellectual capital [IC] provides a means to capture the dynamics of innovation systems. Although developed for firm-level analysis and performance monitoring, the principles of IC have broader relevance. The challenge is to repackage and reconceptualise IC for the application to entrepreneurship systems. To this endeavour, this book is dedicated for the benefit of the South Australian entrepreneurial ecosystem.

References

Adner, R, & Kapoor, R. (2010). Value creation in innovation ecosystems: How the structure of technological interdependence affects firm performance in new technology generations. *Strategic Management Journal, 31*, 306-33.

Alvarez, SA, & Barney, JB. (2005). How do entrepreneurs organise firms under conditions of uncertainty? *Journal of Management, 31*(5), 776-93.

Apple Sells One Millionth iPhone. (2007, September 10). Press Release. Retrieved from http://www.apple.com.

Apple Sells One Million iPads. (2010, May 3). Press Release. Retrieved from http://www.cnbc.com/id/36911690.

Ashford, NA, Ayres, C, & Stone, RF. (1985). Using regulation to change the market for innovation. *Harvard Environmental Law Review, 9*, 419-66.

Audretsch, DB. (2004). Sustaining innovation and growth: Public policy support for entrepreneurship. *Industry and Innovation, 11*(3), 167-91.

Augustine, N. (2007). *Is America falling off the flat earth?* Washington, DC: National Academy of Sciences, National Academy of Engineering, Institute of Medicine.

Australian Business Foundation. (2008). *Inside the innovation matrix: Finding the hidden human dimensions.* Sydney: Australian Business Foundation Limited.

Betts, JR, & Lee, CWB. (2004, February 13-14). Universities as drivers of regional and national innovation: An assessment of the linkages from universities to innovation and economic growth. *John Deutsch Institute Conference on Higher Education in Canada*, Queen's University, Canada.

Bounfour, A. (Ed.) (2008). *Organisational Capital: Modelling, measuring and contextualising.* London: Routledge.

Brill, A. (2010, December 3). Peer-to-peer lending: Innovative access to credit and the consequences of dodd-frank. *Legal Backgrounder, 25*(35).

Canning, D, & Bennathan, E. (2007, 22 March). The rate of return to transportation infrastructure. In OECD/ECMT, *Transport infrastructure and economic productivity*, Round Table 132.

Canning, D, & Bennathan, E. (2000). The social rate of return on infrastructure investments. Policy Research Working Paper 2390: World Bank,

Development Research Group, Public Economics and Private Sector Development and Infrastructure, Infrastructure Group.

Christie, MJ, & Honig, B. (2006). Social entrepreneurship: New research findings. *Journal of World Business, 41*, 1-5.

Corral de Zubielqui, G, Lindsay, N, & O'Connor, A. (2014). How product, operations, and marketing sources of ideas influence innovation and firm performance in Australian SMEs. *International Journal of Innovation Management, 18*(2). doi: 10.1142/S1363919614500170.

Cushing, R. (2001, December). *Creative capital, diversity and urban growth.* (Unpublished paper, Austin, Texas).

Department for Business, Innovation and Skills. (2011). *Innovation and research strategy for growth.* UK: The Stationery Office Limited.

Dimov, D. (2011). Grappling with the unbearable elusiveness of entrepreneurial opportunities. *Entrepreneurship: Theory and Practice, 35*(1), 57-81.

Florida, R. (2004). *Cities and the creative class.* London: Routledge.

Future Manufacturing Industry Innovation Council. (2011). *Trends in manufacturing to 2020: A foresighting discussion paper.* Canberra: Future Manufacturing, Department of Innovation, Industry, Science and Research.

Government of South Australia. (2012a). *Manufacturing works: A strategy for driving high-value manufacturing in South Australia.* Retrieved from www.dmitre. sa.gov.au/manufacturing.

Government of South Australia. (2012b). *Manufacturing Green Paper: Setting directions for the transition of manufacturing in South Australia.* Retrieved from www.dmitre.sa.gov.au/manufacturing.

Graham, JR, Harvey, CR, & Rajgopal, S. (2005). The economic implications of corporate financial reporting. *Journal of Accounting and Economics, 40*(1), 3-73.

Gross, HT, & Weinstein, BL. (1986). Technology, structural change, and the industrial policy debate. In Rees, J. (Ed.), *Technology, regions, and policy.* Towota, NJ: Rowman & Littlefield.

Gunderson, L, & Holling, C. (2002). *Panarchy: Understanding transformations in human and natural systems.* Washington, DC: Island Press.

Hall, A. (2005). Capacity development for agricultural biotechnology in developing countries: An innovation systems view of what it is and how to develop it. *Journal of International Development 17*, 611-30.

Harkema, SJM, & Browaeys, MJ. (2002). Managing innovation successfully: A complex process. In *European Academy of Management Annual Conference Proceedings*, EURAM.

Hébert, RF, & Link, AN. (1982). *The entrepreneur — Mainstream views and radical critiques*. New York, USA: Praeger Publishers.

Heckscher, EF. (1919). Utrikeshandelns verkan på inkomstfördelningen. *Ekonomisk Tidskrift, 21*, 1-32.

Hervas-Oliver, JL, Albors Garrigos, J, & Gil-Pechuan, I. (2011). Making sense of innovation by R&D and non-R&D innovators in low technology contexts: A forgotten lesson for policymakers. *Technovation, 31*(9), 427-46.

Hess, M, & Adams, D. (2002). Knowing and skilling in contemporary public administration. *Australian Journal of Public Administration, 61*, 68-79.

Hewitt, P, & Lowy, P. (2001, 30 November). How new drugs move through the development and approval process. Retrieved from www.tufts.edu/med/csdd.

Hindle, K, Yencken, J, & O'Connor, A. (2011). An entrepreneurship policy framework for high-growth firms: Navigating between policies for picking winners and market failure. *International Journal of Entrepreneurial Venturing, Special Edition: Technological Entrepreneurship: Opportunity for High Growth Firms, 3*(4), 324-43.

Holling, CS. (2001). Understanding the complexity of economic, ecological and social systems. *Ecosystems, 4*, 390-405.

Hughes, J. (1973) *The vital few: American economic progress and its protagonists*. New York: Oxford University Press.

Iansiti, M, & Levien, R. (2004, March). Strategy as ecology. *Harvard Business Review*, 82(3), 68-78.

ICS Ltd. (2010, January). *Review of the innovation readiness of SMEs*: A short study undertaken for the Danish Agency for Science, Technology and Innovation. Copenhagen, Denmark.

Lam, A. (2004). Organizational innovation. In Jan Fagerberg, David Mowery and Richard R Nelson (Eds.), *Handbook of innovation*. Oxford University Press.

Lösch, A. (1939). *The economics of location.* Jena: Fischer.

Marceau, J, Manley, K, & Sicklen, D. (1997). *The high road or the low road? Alternatives for Australia's future.* Sydney, NSW: Australian Business Foundation.

Marton, R,& Phillips, SK. (2005). Modernising policy for public value: Learning lessons from the management of bushfires. *Australian Journal of Public Administration, 64,* 75-82.

McKelvey, B. (2004). Toward a complexity science of entrepreneurship. *Journal of Business Venturing, 9,* 313-41.

McKinsey & Company. (2009, April). *The economic impact of the achievement gap in America's schools.*

Mizik, N, & Jacobson, R. (2003). Trading off between value creation and value appropriation: The financial implications of shifts in strategic emphasis. *Journal of Marketing, 67*(1), 63-76.

National Research Council. (2010). *Rising above the gathering storm, revisited: Rapidly approaching category 5.* Washington: National Academies Press.

Nicholls, A. (2010). The legitimacy of social entrepreneurship: Reflexive isomorphism in a pre-paradigmatic field. *Entrepreneurship: Theory and Practice, 34*(4), 611-33.

National Science Board. (2010). Science and engineering indicators: 2010, Appendix tables 4-8 and 4-9. Arlington, VA, USA: National Science Foundation (National Science Board 10-01).

O'Connor, A. (2013). A conceptual framework for entrepreneurship education policy: Meeting government and economic purposes. *Journal of Business Venturing, 28,* 546-63.

O'Connor, A & Yamin, S. (2011). Innovation and entrepreneurship: Managing the paradox of purpose in business model innovation. *International Journal of Learning and Intellectual Capital, 8*(3), 239-55.

OECD. (2011). *Skills for innovation and research.* Retrieved from http://dx.doi.org/10.1787/9789264097490-en.

Ohlin, B. (1933). *Interregional and international trade.* Cambridge: Harvard University Press.

Osterwalder, A. (2004). *The business model ontology: A proposition in a design science approach*. Lausanne, Switzerland, University of Lausanne, École des Hautes Études Commerciales.

Penrose, E. (1995). *The theory of the growth of the firm* (reprinted ed.). New York: Oxford University Press.

People and profitability: A time for change. (2009). USA: Deloitte, Oracle, and the Manufacturing Institute.

Peredo, AM, & Chrisman, JJ. (2006). Toward a theory of community-based enterprise. *Academy of Management Review, 31*, 309-28.

Peredo, AM, & Mclean, M. (2006). Social entrepreneurship: A critical review of the concept. *Journal of World Business, 41*, 56-65.

Pike, S, & Roos, G. (2007). The validity of measurement frameworks: Measurement theory. In A Neely (Ed.), *Business performance measurement: Unifying theory and integrating practice* (pp. 218-36). Cambridge University Press.

Reed, J. (2010, August 2). Geely completes purchase of Volvo for $1.5bn. *Financial Times*. Retrieved from http://www.ft.com/cms/s/0/b25238b6-9e1e-11df-b377-00144feab49a.html#axzz3HxeYCWSo.

Rich, M. (2010, July 1). Factory jobs return, but employers find skills shortage. *The New York Times*. Retrieved from http://www.nytimes.com/2010/07/02/business/economy/02manufacturing.html?pagewanted=all&_r=0.

Roos, G, & Roos, J. (1997). Measuring your company's intellectual performance. *Long Range Planning, 30*(3), 413-26.

Roos, G. (2012). *Manufacturing into the future*. Adelaide Thinker in Residence 2010-11, Adelaide Thinkers in Residence, Government of South Australia, Adelaide, Australia. Retrieved from http://www.thinkers.sa.gov.au/roosreport/files/inc/194455830.pdf.

Roos, G, Pike, S, & Fernström, L. (2006). *Managing intellectual capital in practice*. Waltham, MA: Butterworth-Heinemann, an imprint of Elsevier.

Roos, G, & Pike, S. (2009). An intellectual capital view of business model innovation. In Bounfour, A. (Ed.), *Organisational capital: a modelling, measuring and contextualising* (Vol. 12). Routledge.

Roos, G, von Krogh, G, & Roos, J with Fernström, L. (2010). *Innføring i strategi, 5ᵗʰ edition*. Bergen, Norway: Fagbokforlaget.

Schendel, D, & Hitt, MA. (2007). Introduction to Volume 1. *Strategic Entrepreneurship Journal, 1*, 1-6.

Schramm, C. (2010, April 20). Made in America. In *The National Interest Online*. Retrieved from http://www.jstor.org/discover/10.2307/42896308?uid =3737536&uid=2134&uid=2485224617&uid=2&uid=70&uid=3&uid=24 85224607&uid=60&sid=21104944012237.

Schumpeter, JA. (1911). *Theorie der Wirtschaftlichen Entwicklung*. Jena, Germany: Dunker und Humblot.

Schumpeter, JA. (1939). *A theoretical, historical, and statistical analysis of the capitalist process*. New York: McGraw-Hill.

Schumpeter, JA. (1942). *Socialism, capitalism and democracy*. New York: Harper and Brothers.

Scott-Kemmis, D. (2012). *Responding to change and pursuing growth: Exploring the potential of business model innovation in Australia*. Sydney: Australian Business Foundation.

Shane, SA. (2008). *The illusions of entrepreneurship*. New Haven and London: Yale University.

Shane, S, & Venkataraman, S. (2000). The promise of entrepreneurship as a field of research. *The Academy of Management Review, 25*(1), 217-26.

Skogseid, I. (2007). A study of the dynamics of local adaptation of ICT. (A thesis submitted in partial fulfilment of the requirements for the degree of Doctor Scientarium, University of Oslo, Norway).

Spencer, JW. (2003). Firms' knowledge-sharing strategies in the global innovation system: Empirical evidence from the flat panel display industry. *Strategic Management Journal, 24*(3), 217.

Spoehr, J. (Ed.) (1999). *Beyond the contract state — Ideas for social and economic renewal in South Australia*. Adelaide: Wakefield Press.

Storper, M, & Scott, AJ. (2009). Rethinking human capital, creativity and urban growth. *Journal of Economic Geography 9*(2), 147-67.

Stevenson, HH, & Jarillo, JC. (1990). A paradigm of entrepreneurship: Entrepreneurial management. *Strategic Management Journal, 11*(5), 17-27.

Thompson, J, Alvy, G, & Lees, A. (2000). Social entrepreneurship — A new look at the people and the potential. *Management Decision, 38*, 328-38.

Vernon, R. (1966). International investment and international trade in the product cycle. *Quarterty Journal of Economics, 80*, 190-207.

von Thünen, JJ. (1826). *Der isolierte Staat in Beziehung auf Landwirtschaft und Nationalökonomie.* Hamburg, Perthes. English Translation by CM Wartenberg: The isolated state. Oxford: Pergamon Press (1966).

Yapp, C. (2005, January). Innovation, futures thinking and leadership. *Public Money and Management*, 57-60.

Zarroli, J. (2006, April 3). French Telecom Company Alcatel merging with Lucent. News Press Release.

Part 1

Regional-level perspectives

Moving beyond policy path dependency:

An approach to fostering innovation in South Australia

2

Jane Andrew, University of South Australia

Introduction

> The history we experience is the result of the ideas we pursue.
> (Dwight Waldo, 1952, p. 99)

Stemming from the 1990s, the work of Nelson and Winter (1977), Freeman (1985) and Lundvall (1992) on National Systems of Innovation has been used to argue for a new and more holistic perspective of the roles of policy governance and institutions for innovation. Despite this being acknowledged in South Australia's economic policy discourse at the time, this chapter considers why the state continues to struggle to apply and implement a more holistic approach to stimulating and supporting innovation across the economy. John Dryzek (2001) observes that 'a policy discourse will always feature particular assumptions, judgements, contentions, dispositions, and capabilities' (p. 658) and is often reinforced by the advocacy of strong industry associations and economic ideologies.

Particularly influential in regional innovation policy discourse has been the work of the Organisation for Economic Co-operation and Development [OECD], whose arguments asserting the primary importance of science and technology to regional economic growth have left an enduring legacy of investments heavily weighted towards science, technology and engineering disciplines and industries in an effort to foster innovation and develop South Australia's pool of human capital. Whilst significant immediate opportunities exist for these industries, it is clear that this focus has distracted South Australian policy makers from considering the importance of fields of knowledge within the Humanities, Arts and Social Sciences [HASS] and the valuable role they can play in the state's innovation system and long-term economic development.

Interpreting the concept of innovation

In 2000, at the time of Australia's National Innovation Summit, the OECD led the discourse and research on the role of innovation in economic development. At that time, as now, many governments viewed the OECD's work as a benchmark with which to compare policy experiences, seek answers to common problems, identify good practice (as determined by the theoretical and ideological viewpoints of the dominant member countries) and co-ordinate domestic and international policies. The growing body of research undertaken by the OECD has provided policy makers with reason to increase its support and investment in industries that rely on science and technology as their primary knowledge base and input to production.

The prevailing conceptualisation of innovation

A broad definition of innovation's role in regional economic development offered by the OECD in 2001 states that 'innovations are understood as new creations, which have economic significance by virtue of their adoption within organisations' (p. 12). This statement has contributed to the growing body of discourse focusing on regional economic growth and Endogenous Growth Theory, and has informed a plethora of Australian (national and regional) government economic development reports and policies focusing on stimulating and supporting innovation. Australia's translation of the OECD's concept of innovations of significance was, as it still is, commonly cited within the realms of science, technology and the engineering industries.

This disciplinary/industry bias is demonstrated by Parvitt (1984, as cited in OECD, 2001), who summarises the contexts from which innovation stems and observes that there are sectoral differences in the application and outcomes of the innovation process. Parvitt distils this observation into four sectoral types including:

- *supply-dominated sectors* — such as traditional clothing and furniture, where firms generate few important innovations themselves, but rather import them from other firms

- *scale-intensive sectors* — such as food processing and cement, in which process innovations predominate

- *specialised suppliers* — such as engineering, software and instruments, which are characterised by frequent product innovations, often developed in collaboration with their customers

- *science-based producers* — such as producers of chemicals, biotechnology and electronics, who develop both new products and processes, sometimes in close collaboration with universities and research institutes (OECD, 2001, p. 13).

This widely held typology identifying the places or markets for innovations considered of most economic significance implies that the innovation process conforms to a linear product development and supply model.

Seeking to provide a more nuanced and less production-orientated conceptual framework from which to consider innovation, Sporer's (2008) review of the sociological and economic literature and debates defining innovation reveals that a common distinction is made between discovery, invention and innovation. A 'discovery' contributes a completely new addition to an existing body of knowledge; an 'invention' is the creation of something completely new that did not exist before but is based on existing knowledge; and 'innovation' is based on a combination of discovery and invention. Adding to this discourse, Sporer (2008) outlines three different types of knowledge base and their contribution to innovation. Sporer categorises these types of knowledge as 'synthetic' (engineering-based), 'analytical' (science-based) and 'symbolic' (creative-based).

Policy as a reflection of interpretations of innovation

Policy problems are often complex and comprise many different elements together with many different political arguments and actors participating in more than one discourse at a time (Howlett & Lindquist, 2004); yet, as John Dryzek (2001) observes, 'a policy discourse will always feature particular assumptions, judgements, contentions, dispositions, and capabilities' (p. 658).

Following the lead of many European OECD nations, in February 2000 the Howard government and the Business Council of Australia convened the National Innovation Summit to assess the strengths and weaknesses of Australia's innovation system, and to formulate ways to improve performance in this area. It also sought to provide a framework to address innovation policy issues in a comprehensive and co-ordinated manner.

Two reports were released that significantly influenced policy discourse. A notable addition to this discourse was the acknowledgement of the importance of creativity to Australia's economic prosperity. *Innovation: Unlocking the future* (Innovation Summit Implementation Group, 2000) and *Backing Australia's ability — Real results real jobs* (Commonwealth of Australia, 2001) both articulated a role for creative thinking in the innovation process, while adhering to the technologically focused conceptualisation of the role that creativity plays in the economy. The final report of the Innovation Summit Implementation Group, *Innovation: Unlocking the future* (2000), was delivered after eighteen months of analysis of the strengths and weaknesses of Australia's capacity for innovation. The report makes key recommendations about what actions and investments are necessary to build a solid, sustainable research and development base from which ideas could grow.

The report's recommendations focus on three areas: creating an ideas culture, generating ideas and acting on ideas. Adopting the language of business and enterprise within the policy development and promotion arena, the executive summary of the report states:

> We need to create the right culture to support us in our efforts to become better innovators. For example, improving our vision, attitude and strategic approach to innovation, the entrepreneurial expertise of our managers, and our graduates' skills in creativity, oral business communications and problem solving ... (p. ix)

The following statement entwines the discourse surrounding the knowledge economy, education, management and human resource theory with innovation and entrepreneurship, stating:

> If Australia is to be a nation of successful innovators, we must promote an 'ideas environment'; a culture that nurtures good ideas and supports entrepreneurs ... It also means a commitment to lifelong learning, and establishing creative

working environments to sustain a highly skilled and motivated workforce where excellence in research and innovation can flourish … (p. 2)

Acknowledging creativity's role in the innovation process

The government's innovation objectives describe creativity as important. However, the emphasis is on innovation stemming from creative maths and science within the supply side of the innovation system. This is evidenced by further excerpts from the Innovation Summit report (2000), where it becomes more focused on the Science, Technology, Engineering and Maths [STEM] knowledge typologies, the sectors and industries in which it considers creativity is of most economic benefit, stating:

> Like other countries, Australia is experiencing a shortage in the number of graduates in mathematics, physics, chemistry, and information technology. Yet it is these skills which serve as core building blocks for basic research and development. Such skills shortages will affect the capacity of business to carry out research and development and to conduct knowledge-based activity and will be a significant constraint on investment in vital areas of the New Economy. (p. 6)

The report further states:

> Beyond the commitments already made in areas such as biotechnology, environmental sustainability and health and medical research, we must nurture our research capabilities in the 'enabling' sciences of physics, chemistry and mathematics, and also in the humanities and social sciences. Research in the humanities and social sciences, for example, can enhance the organisational, management, legal and marketing knowledge that is critical to successful innovation. (p. 15)

This linear-supply side-focus on the role of HASS disciplines within the innovation system completely ignores the significant but often unmeasured role that the HASS knowledge taxonomies and, more specifically, the creative professions play in informing all forms of innovations, and interpreting the 'symbolic' and translating this into 'the aesthetic' through design-led approaches to idea generation and creation. Apple Inc. is an example of how the creativity emanating from the STEM and HASS disciplines, when combined, generates innovations that contribute significant economic return and stimulate social change.

Countries such as Sweden, Finland and Germany have embedded in their culture an appreciation for design, and thus have an advantage in arguments for government support for design-led innovation strategies. Designers employ a range of thinking styles ranging from a rational problem solving advocated by Herbert Simon (1969), where positivism is the basis, to Donald Schön's constructivist reflective practice approach, where meaning and value are explored through a conceptual phase. These approaches reflect the spectrum of thinking styles from intuition and artfulness to science and fact applied within the design process. In her chapter 'Time for change: Building a design discipline', Sharon Helmer Poggenpohl (2009) highlights Steven Toulimin's (2001) observation that the dominance of science has diminished the significance of disciplines that deal with less predictable and messy issues of human behaviour and creation. It is perhaps the perceived messiness of the design/design thinking process that has impeded more concerted integration of design into South Australia's innovation landscape. This is despite the long-running advocacy campaigns by design industry associations for innovation policy interventions to invest in programs that support design skills, and the integration of design into mainstream innovation programs. Creative and design-led approaches to foster innovation have struggled to embed themselves in the suite of policy tools used by economic and industry development agencies to support increasing innovative activity across the economy.

Buchanan (1992) argues that the reason for the persistence of the STEM disciplines being the focus of policy responses to fostering innovation is the limited conceptualisation of the forms of knowledge which contribute to innovation more broadly. This, he suggests, has been the result of the increasing specialisation of learning and knowledge through the growth in size and status of academies from the Renaissance to now. The specialisation of fields of study has contributed to the increasing fragmentation of the spheres of knowledge used in examining issues and solving problems faced by society. Buchanan notes that as spheres of knowledge and disciplines have become progressively narrow in scope and more numerous, they have lost 'connection with each other and with the common problems and matters of daily life from which they select aspects for precise methodological analysis' (p. 6).

This observation is reinforced by the UK-based Creative Clusters network, who state on their website (2002):

> Aspects of creativity [artistic/scientific] have diverged so much in our minds that we now see them as distinct, even incompatible, kinds of activity, with different types of learning, behaviour and language. It can be seen in universities, with their separate schools for arts, science and business, in government departments and in the long-standing isolation of business from the arts. (n.p.)

Stoneman (2007) offers a more balanced recognition of the collective contribution the STEM and HASS disciplines make to innovation. Stoneman's diagram makes explicit the connection between the 'soft innovations' contributed by art and creative practices on the one hand, and the 'hard innovations' contributed by science, technology and engineering on the other, both of which collectively contribute to creative products and services that draw on the foundations both of science and technology and of art and creative practices (Howard, 2008, p. 8).

In highlighting the reciprocal and beneficial relationship between the STEM and HASS disciplines, Stoneman (1996) has, however, implied a value bias by differentiating between the hard and solid contribution of science, technology and engineering, and the soft, symbolic and sometimes intangible contribution of creative practices to the ecology of the innovation system.

Ivan Turok (2009) suggests there is a tendency to neglect the wider range of lower status, longer established and 'medium tech' industries with considerable scope for design improvements, process enhancements and market diversification. Arguing for a more nuanced understanding of innovation than that posed by the OECD (2001, p. 12), Jason Potts (2007) argues that the heavy focus on innovation as a business-centric, technical search-and-discovery process largely ignores

> [t]he more complex interactions between producers and consumers, as well as subsequent phases beyond technology innovation, such as adoption and adaptation of a novel product or service to human lifestyles, along with its retention and normalisation by a population of carriers. (p. 7)

Howard (2008) argues that in the emerging global economy, it has become more difficult for businesses to compete on the basis of technology and cost alone. They must compete on 'non-price' factors, such as brand, reputation, product 'look and feel', and their ability to interact with customers. With the emergence of the so-called New Economy in the 1990s highlighting the imperative to innovate, many economic regions in Australia have been considering how they might foster innovation. Business consultants have been busy undertaking numerous industry consultation rounds, policy reviews and report writing. The reports highlight a growing acknowledgement of the role of creativity, design and the design-thinking process, and their potential to contribute to innovations across the economy, and the need to enable the development of these skills within the state's workforce. This, however, requires shifts in the policy discourse from using innovation as an abstract noun to a verb in which people in the workforce become agents and actors in the innovation process across the economy.

In the 2004-05 *State of the Regions* report (National Economics, 2005) there are a number of 'stylised facts' that directly relate to, inform and influence policy perspectives on the role and need for the development of creative capital to foster economic growth and sustainability. Of note is the report's inclusion of the term 'creativity'. The report calls for a focus on developing the regions' human capital by investing in both hard and soft infrastructure that will enable knowledge and creativity to make increased contributions to economic and employment growth.

In a similar vein, in 2005 the Prime Minister's Science Engineering and Innovation Council Working Group [PMSEIC] made recommendations for 'leveraging the intellectual and creative wealth of our nation', and proposed that creativity and design are pivotal in stimulating innovation across a wide variety of industries. The committee cites in particular the broader notion of the creative industries, and highlights OECD countries that have developed strategic initiatives

> [t]o foster innovation through acknowledging and incorporating culture, creativity and design in community and economic growth initiatives, including harvesting the arts, entertainment and creative sectors as key growth sectors of their economies. (p. 7)

PMSEIC's acknowledgement of the potential for the creative industries to make a significant contribution to the economy was informed by two distinct strands of academic and advocacy arguments that grew in intensity from the 1980s. Both arguments advocate a role for creativity and creative individuals in stimulating regional growth and prosperity.

This sentiment coincides with a growing recognition within the business, science and industry sectors of the value of 'creativity' as an element in an organisation's strategic approach to attracting and retaining a knowledgeable and highly skilled workforce, stimulating innovation, and boosting competitiveness to retain and increase market opportunities. To this end Green (2009) asserts that regional economies wanting to realise innovation must invest in capabilities and skills for innovation, in the management of innovation, and in collaboration between a varieties of knowledge sectors. This includes investing not only in the development of knowledge and human capital within the science and technology sectors, but also in the development of creative capital and design capacity.

The process of innovation

Beckman and Barry (2007) have observed that as organisations have been confronted with increasingly complex business challenges, many have sought to understand the more fundamental principles underlying the innovation process, in which design plays an important role.

Within the context of enhancing business performance, the concepts of creativity, innovation and design are commonly defined thus (DTI, UK Treasury, 2005, as cited in Howard, 2008):

- 'Creativity' is the generation of new ideas — either new ways of looking at existing problems, or seeing new opportunities, perhaps by exploiting new technologies or changes in markets.

- 'Innovation' is the successful exploitation of new ideas. It is the processes that carry ideas through to new products, new services, new ways of running the business, or even new ways of doing business.

- 'Design' is what links creativity and innovation. It shapes ideas to become practical and attractive propositions for users or customers. Design may be described as creativity deployed to a specific end. (p. 8)

As acknowledged by Green earlier (2009, p. 92), organisations are increasingly considering the design process and applying it for its ability to draw together knowledge from all fields in developing the most appropriate solution to the issue at hand.

Innovation as a social process

Edquist (1997) suggests that the importance of the social and cultural contexts in which innovations are stimulated and adopted makes the process of innovation much more complex than a simple linear progression adhering to a single knowledge domain or methodological approach. The Review of the National Innovation System (2008, as cited in Green, Agarwal, & Hall, 2009) asserts that

> [m]any government workplace and innovation programs in Australia are directed at technological or scientific innovation while only a few are directed at strengthening innovation management inside organisations, including leadership and culture. (p. 20)

Drawing from academic discourse on knowledge and learning, Charles Owen (2007) developed a conceptual framework that envisaged design as a process of knowledge development, in which both analytic and synthetic knowledge are of equal importance in the translation of theoretical observations and developments into practice in the form of artefacts and institutions (p. 27).

Transforming a social process into an innovation culture

KEA[1] promotes the concept of culture-based creativity and its application to the development of new products and services, stating that

> [c]ulture-based creativity is an essential feature of a post-industrial economy. Culture is the general expression of humanity, the expression of its creativity. Culture is linked to meaning, knowledge, talents, industries, civilisation and values. (KEA European Affairs, 2009, pp. 3-4)

Rather than considering culturally based, economic, scientific or technological innovation as an either/or choice for policy makers, KEA points to the *Oslo Manual's* (2005) guidelines for collecting and interpreting innovation data, where it is recommended that 'policies on innovation need to be developed so as to recognise the cross-sectoral and multi-disciplinary aspect of "creativity" which mixes elements of "culture-based creativity", "economic", as well as "technological" innovation' (as cited in KEA, 2009, p. 8).

Historians, political scientists, anthropologists, economists, sociologists and policy makers have all studied the role of relationships between individuals, organisations and groups in a society's economic development, success and sustainability. Granovetter argues that all economic action is inherently enmeshed in social relations and that all forms of exchange are inherently embedded in social

---

1   KEA is a consultancy based in Brussels specialising in providing advice, support and research in relation to creative industries and sport since 1999.

relationships. Embeddedness, he posits, could take several distinct forms: social ties, cultural practices and political contexts (1973, as cited in Woolcock, 1998, p. 161).

Some twenty or so years after Granovetter observed the importance of social relations to regional innovation and economic development, Lagendijk's (1997) work in this area has been influential in arguing the importance of industry clusters to the wider business environment, and acknowledging the vital role of industry associations, research centres and other 'binding' organisations. It is via these communication hubs that new patterns of collaboration and networking develop and act as catalysts for innovation by sharing tacit knowledge.

It is therefore important for regions wishing to develop and sustain the culture and capacity to innovate that investments are made not only in the formal education sectors where explicit knowledge is shared, but also in initiatives that foster the sharing of tacit knowledge within and across knowledge domains.

Charles Leadbetter (2000) articulates this perspective when he says:

> Culture — not science, technology or even economics — will determine how deeply embedded the New Economy becomes in our daily lives … Economic and scientific modernisation succeeds when it is accompanied by cultural creativity that revolutionises the way we see the world. (p. 228)

Ideas and new technologies in themselves are inert manifestations until they are translated and applied in new combinations, breathing life into new possibilities that inspire the pursuit of business opportunities. As Carlsson (2004) observes, 'only when the actors in the innovation systems and competence blocs interact with each other closely and frequently enough do the new technical possibilities result in economic growth' (pp. 248-9). Carlsson adds:

> Through better connectivity, the design space becomes denser: more ideas are created, new ideas can be tried and implemented (or rejected) more quickly, and the knowledge base can expand through more experimentation. This reflects the supply side (the innovation system) of the market for innovations.
>
> … If the demand side responds appropriately — i.e., if the competence bloc succeeds in selecting and supporting viable new products — economic growth results. (p. 256)

However, as Amidon and Macnamara (2002) have recognised, sustaining the level of communication necessary to foster regional innovation and collaboration within clusters and innovation systems requires leadership and a commitment by stakeholders to the exchange of knowledge on an ongoing basis.

Early attempts to implement an industry cluster and network strategy in South Australia

In the late 1990s, Doug Henton and Kim Walesh from the US consultancy firm Collaborative Economics, and Professor Michael Porter, a world leader in the fields of company strategy and the competitiveness of nations and regions, visited South Australia and influenced policy makers in the state and other Australian regions with their work on industry clusters and networks as part of regional innovation strategies. Following the precepts of these American thinkers, who advocated the clustering of interconnected businesses in order to facilitate activity, interactivity and communication, the South Australian state government established the groundwork for the development north of Adelaide of a *Multifunction Polis* [MFP]. Both the Japanese and the Australian Federal governments promoted and supported the experiment in bringing a critical mass of interrelated organisations and their people together, so widespread was the influence of the idea of clusters as a stimulus to innovation.

The two clusters chosen for the prototype MFP program were defence and multimedia. Plans for their concentration in Adelaide's north reflected the enthusiasm in the early 1990s of those interested in, and working within, industry and cluster programs. In 1994, AusIndustry[2], for example, launched its business networks program, which ran parallel to the MFP's strategy to stimulate industry clusters and networks and other business collaboration programs. Late in 1998, the industry clusters program was transferred to South Australian Business Vision 2010 [SABV2010], during which time defence, multimedia, spatial information and water clusters formed.

Other clusters entered the formative stages of development at this time, including business collaboration programs in international tourism; commercial sport and recreation; environment management products and services; mining and geosciences; arts; business and legal services; the conventions industry; renewable

---

2 AusIndustry was established in 1994. Its primary remit was to deliver business services that build on three key drivers of economic growth — innovation, investment and international competitiveness. These services are now delivered by the Department of Industry through its website, www.business.gov.au.

energy; and healthy ageing. In addition, several major new cluster initiatives in the IT and bioscience industries were emerging outside SABV2010's cluster development program. In a document that was part-review and part-advocacy for continued government funding for the SABV2010 Industry Clusters Program, South Australian economist Professor Richard Blandy cited the European regional innovation systems, observing that the development of sustainable and productive clusters and networks could not be accomplished overnight, but was a 'medium to long-run task, as the time horizon for growth and income targets is typically 5-10 years' (2004).

Blandy's observation supports the findings of other researchers and interested individuals and organisations, many of whom attended the SABV2010 Arts Cluster meetings. All expressed a concern that the funding arrangements for cluster initiatives were commonly too short compared to the time it takes industry clusters to develop and build robust, sustainable and productive relationships between multiple business sectors, generating new market opportunities and innovations. Short-term investment, however, was the norm, which suggests an implicit lack of understanding amongst most policy makers and treasuries of the vital role of 'agency' in the development of knowledge-sharing networks and industry clusters to inform, develop and apply innovations within a diverse array of markets across an economy.

The work of Morgan (1996) and Rosenfield (1997) (as cited in Lagendijk, 1997) also spoke to the contribution and importance of industry clusters to the wider business environment, and acknowledged the important role of industry associations, research centres and other 'binding' organisations. They suggested that it would be via these communication hubs that new patterns of collaboration and networking could develop and act as catalysts for innovation through the sharing of tacit knowledge. This observation was reflected in the call of the 2003 Adelaide Thinker in Residence, Charles Landry, for investment in 'urban animateurs', whose sole role was to 'add value to existing initiatives by identifying opportunities to connect people, organisations, events and conferences and to build Adelaide's potential as a connected and strategic city' (2003, p. 8).

In spite of reasoned support, however, the MFP was abandoned before 2000, and the SABV2010 carriage of the cluster program only lasted for a little over two years. The support for cluster strategies to foster innovation waned irrevocably when the state's economic development agency, the Department for Industry and

Trade [DTI], began redefining its strategic objectives and restructuring to form the Department of Trade and Economic Development [DTED] in 2004.[3]

Overcoming policy path dependency

Cooke and Memedovic (2006) argue that

> [p]olicies pursued by regional governments can enhance the economy, culture and identity of regions, including their institutional capacity to attract, animate and construct competitive advantage. Collective entrepreneurship, by promotion of cooperative practices among actors, may give regions distinctive trajectories in regional economic development. (p. 3)

Henton, Melville, and Walesh (1997), in their book *Grassroots Leaders for a New Economy: How Civic Entrepreneurs are Building Prosperous Communities*, argue that the regions that are most able to succeed in the New Economy practise 'collaborative advantage' and highlight the role of civic entrepreneurs, whom they regard as catalysts for collaboration between community, business and government. That is, the entrepreneurs enjoy tight relationships at the intersection of their business, government, education and community sectors, which provide regional resiliency and a unique ability to set and achieve longer-term development goals.

An intertwining of business management and economic development theory reinforced and informed this growing articulation and approach to economic development. Osborne and Gaebler's (1992) observation, occasional participation and published commentary in the series *Reinventing Government* had a major impact on the way democratic governance was viewed, theorised and implemented through political and administrative systems. Embedded within a neo-classical economic framework, the overriding premise of the political theory of reinvention is that business and enterprise are the key drivers of regional economic success.

Attempts to facilitate a more integrated policy environment

The South Australian Strategic Plan [SASP] was designed to provide an overarching, whole-of-government statement on the state's strategic priorities, and it aspired to address the issue of individual agencies developing their separate sectoral plans in

---

3   After 2004 the department was restructured again in October 2011, forming the agency current at the time of writing, the Department of Manufacturing, Innovation, Trade, Resources and Energy [DMITRE].

isolation from one another. The 2004 SASP states that it provides a framework for agencies to work together to achieve clear overall objectives and ultimately seeks to widen opportunities for all South Australians by focusing on six key strategic objectives.[4] The plan states:

> Our priority is to reinforce South Australia as a place that thrives on creativity and innovation. This capacity to do things differently will be one of the keys to achieving all of our objectives. (Department of the Premier and Cabinet, 2004, p. 3)

'Fostering creativity' was one of the six objectives seeking a more holistic approach to fostering innovation. In 2004 the first iteration of the SASP's 'fostering creativity' objective stated:

> The government recognises its role in providing the right environment for these attributes to flourish in sectors ranging from the arts to manufacturing, and its ability to provide a lead for the rest of the community. Our capacity to do things differently will be one of the keys to achieving all of our objectives. (p. 5)

The government updated the SASP in 2007 and 2011, with the 2011 update including 100 targets across six priority areas. The 2011 SASP prioritises the

> three foundations of a sustainable society: Our Community, Our Prosperity and Our Environment are its organising priorities. The plan also recognises that to nourish a sustainable society 'Our Health, Our Education and Our Ideas' are essential … Targets in the Plan are specific and measurable. They align our top priority visions and goals to specific objectives against which we can measure our success and adjust our strategies accordingly. (Government of South Australia, 2011, p. 14)

What has not changed since the 2004 iteration of the plan is the desire for a more integrated and collaborative approach to policy and the delivery of services to be developed and adopted as a cultural norm across government. This is best summarised by the following statement:

> Neither the objectives nor any individual targets stand alone — they are all part of a larger inter-related framework. Achieving one target should not come at the expense of another. Smart thinking about how we do things can neutralise

---

4   The 2004 SASP strategic objectives were growing prosperity; improving wellbeing; attaining sustainability; fostering creativity; building communities; expanding opportunity (Department of the Premier and Cabinet, 2004, p. 3).

effects on other targets, or even turn them into positives. (Department of the Premier and Cabinet, 2007, p. 11)

It needs to be asked whether there has been significant enough investment in understanding and enabling collaboration across the interrelated framework of policy objectives and targets, or in fostering policy innovation in order to do things differently and move away from policy path dependency.

From smart thinking to design thinking

Just as the application of creativity was adopted as part of the language within business development, by 2010 the term 'design thinking' had become as popular in both the business and policy domains as the term 'creativity' has been over the previous twenty years. The growing awareness of the way the design professions approach considering and resolving problems and the development of new products and processes has increased design thinking's appeal to a number of politicians and policy makers in South Australia.

Although South Australia's design community has been advocating since the 1970s that designers and the creative professions in general make a valuable contribution to the economy, the government has made a distinct lack of investment, and has offered support for the development of the state's design sector at arm's length. The notion of 'design thinking', therefore, only gained significant attention in South Australian policy circles as the result of Laura Lee's Thinkers in Residence, 2009-10. Lee, an advocate of the value of design and design thinking, has always argued for the centrality of integrated design as an agent for a sustainable future and a better human experience, highlighting the importance of collaborative engagement across sectors and disciplines. As she states in her Thinkers in Residence report:

> Integrated design promotes holistic approaches and acknowledges that we need to think, and act, strategically for the long term. We need to inform decision making with research, education and collaborative practices embedded in a flexible and interactive structure that promotes innovative new policies and actions for a prosperous and sustainable future for South Australia. (Lee, 2011, p. 12)

Established in 2010 on the basis of one of the key recommendations of Lee's report, the Integrated Design Commission [IDC] was lauded nationally as Australia's first state-level, cross-government design advisory team. Initially focusing on the urban environment, the IDC contributed significantly to stimulating discussion and projects to enhance Adelaide's quality of life through a multidisciplinary, design-led approach. The Commissioner, Tim Horton, had begun working toward broadening the IDC's scope of industry interaction when state Premier Mike Rann stood down in October 2011. With Mike Rann retiring from state politics, the IDC lost an influential advocate and the commission was disestablished soon thereafter. The SA Government Architect working within the Department of Planning, Transport and Infrastructure subsumed its role. With the release of the state's manufacturing strategy, *Manufacturing works* (DMITRE 2012), articulating the importance of design within the state's innovation system, perhaps the disestablishment of the IDC was premature.

Challenging entrenched perceptions of value

The emphasis on stability and predictability, typical of neo-classical economic models applied through 'bureaucratic proceduralism' within government treasuries, contrasts with the desire to do things differently as urged in the South Australian Strategic Plan, which highlights the difficulty of fostering a culture of creativity and innovation broadly across governments. The contrast and conflict of cultures can be illustrated using Quinn's Competing Values Framework [CVF], (Figure 2.1). CVF emerged in the 1980s from studies of public sector organisational effectiveness in the US. In *Beyond Rational Management*, Quinn (1988) characterised organisations as complex, dynamic and contradictory systems in which managers must fulfil many competing expectations. Conflicting aspirations and entrenched cultural norms are factors that are well-recognised as having the ability to stifle innovation in any aspect of the economy.

Although the South Australian Strategic Plan promoted an underlying vision of collaboration and integration between agencies in an effort to avoid the development of separate sectorial plans in isolation, the act of drawing together government agencies with differing objectives and knowledge taxonomies, along with distinct operational objectives, has proven difficult. Efforts to match the SASP's rhetoric with action have only served to highlight the challenge of developing cohesive policy networks.

Consider, for example, the traditional, internal focus of Treasury and its concern with maintaining stability and control of the state's finances. Contrast these with industry strategies seeking to support the development of clusters and

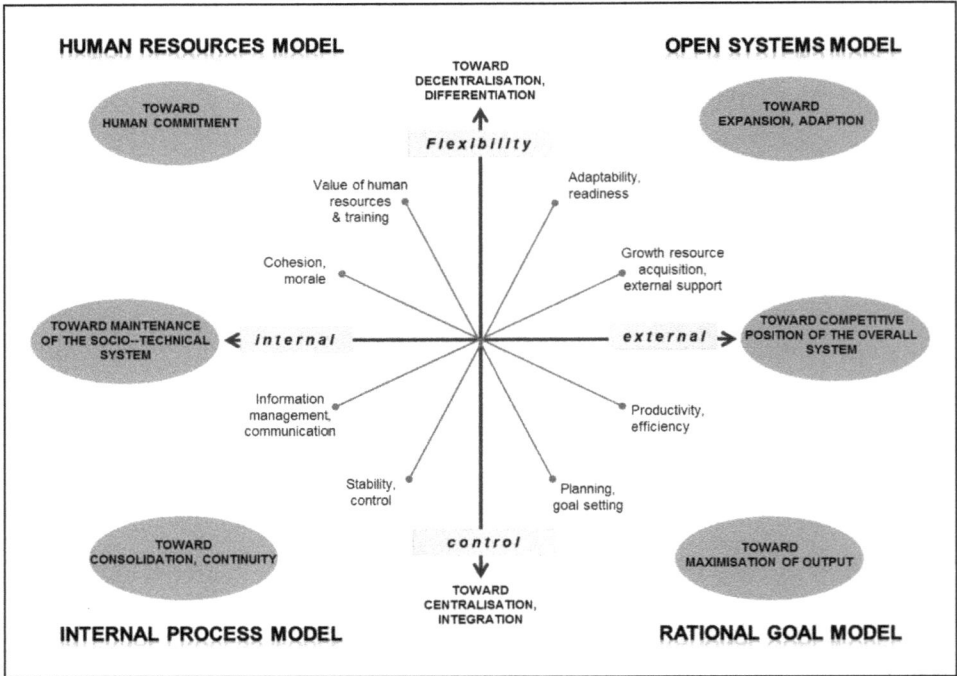

Figure 2.1: Competing Values Framework.
Source: Courtesy of the author, 2012, based on Quinn, 1998, p. 48.

innovative capacity, which are externally focused, with an emphasis on idiosyncratic forms of knowledge, interaction and strategic power. The opposing goals, culture and languages between open-systems models and entrenched neo-liberal economic practices and cultures immediately create impediments to achieving the very thing to which the SASP aspires — fostering innovation within and across government policy domains.

The challenge for a region wishing to change traditional mindsets and integrate such widely disparate cultures is to reconceptualise how a community views itself and the actors within regional innovation. This suggests the need for a reassessment of the concepts and ideas that inform policy and community perceptions of public value and action. One of South Australia's first Thinkers in Residence, Charles Landry (2003), identifies the most inhibiting factor for regions wishing to develop policies that foster the development of creative capacity as 'bureaucratic proceduralism', which he posits 'prevents the identification and exploitation of endogenous creative potential' (2003, p. 46).

New ways of measuring value

Influential in South Australia's policy environment in the 1990s, Collaborative Economics (Henton, Melville, & Walesh, 1997) highlighted the fact that economic innovation requires social innovation, and that assets, networks, culture and the quality of life of the community are cornerstones for regional innovation. However, existing statistical methods do not enable the identification and nuanced measurement of complex and multidimensional innovation systems. Chris Yapp (2005) makes an insightful observation of the inertia common in many public agencies, which prevents them from exploring new ways of envisaging and delivering public value, stating:

> We all want to make our organisations more innovative through radical creativity, and we are all interested in new metaphors. Yet there is also a need for a shift in the organisational logics which sometimes narrow the field of enquiry. (pp. 57-60)

South Australian governments, and the community they serve, therefore, need to acquire a more nuanced appreciation of the ways in which multiple forms of knowledge, creativity and design contribute to an economy. To translate the state's resource of creative capacity into economic advantage, a broader and more sensitive way of measuring the creative contribution is needed, such as Verna Allee's Value Network Analysis [VNA] model (2002).

Applying value network analysis

In the 1990s, business analysis tools, such as value-chain and value-added business analysis, were popular means of identifying and measuring work flows and the input and output of a supply function. Allee (2002) argues that these linear methodologies based on mechanistic industrial production perspectives are not adequate in explaining the complex, interdependent and dynamic relationships between the multiple sets of actors who contribute to organisational or regional economic sustainability and growth.

Allee (2002) draws on living systems theory, knowledge management, complexity theory, system dynamics and intangible asset management theories to offer a methodology for analysing large complex networks. She describes a value network as any set of roles and interactions in which people engage in both tangible and intangible exchanges to achieve economic or social good. Having developed the value network methodology originally to benchmark extremely complex re-engineering projects in 1997, Allee (2002) refined it for capturing transactions and value in the knowledge economy. VNA links specific interactions within the value creating network directly to financial and non-financial scorecards. She proposes that value network analysis methodology

> [i]s grounded in principles of living systems, and represents a decided shift away from mechanistic models. It expands current thinking about intangibles in three important ways.
>
> 1. It goes beyond the asset view of intangibles to also consider intangibles as negotiable and as deliverables.
>
> 2. It proposes a way to model organizations and business relationships as living networks of tangible and intangible value exchanges.
>
> 3. It provides a way to link scorecards and indexes to specific business activities, allowing people to more fully understand the impact of their decisions and actions in both tangible and intangible terms. (p. 2)

Allee (2002, p. 37) argues that a value network generates economic value through complex dynamic exchanges between one or more enterprises, customers, suppliers, strategic partners and the community, and creates three currencies of value, those being:

1. goods, service and revenue [GSR]: exchanges for services or goods, including all transactions involving contracts and invoices, return receipt of orders, requests for proposals, confirmations or payment, and also including knowledge products or services that generate revenue or are expected as part of service (such as reports or package inserts)

2. knowledge: exchanges of strategic information, planning knowledge, process knowledge, technical know-how, collaborative design, policy development and so on, all of which flow around and support the core product and service value chain

3. intangible benefits: exchanges of value and benefits which go beyond the actual service and which are not accounted for in traditional financial

measures, such as a sense of community, customer loyalty, image enhancement, or co-branding opportunities.

Understanding, accepting and using a value network analysis such as that advocated by Allee provides decision makers and other actors with a new path to policy-making as it relates to innovation. Current policy path dependency sees policy makers depending on behaviours and attitudes that have traditionally served to maintain stability and control. The paths to decisions are well-worn, predictable and safe. KPIs can be satisfied. Questions about the value of policies to the public can be reliably answered with stock responses.

Analysing the economy as a network of complex dynamic exchanges will enable individuals, organisations and the system as a whole to understand the value they are contributing and receiving, and the sorts of policies that would facilitate the whole operation.

Conclusion

A growing awareness of the way the creative and design professions approach issues, communicate ideas and develop new products and processes has meant that the term 'design thinking' has become as popular in both the business and policy domains as the term 'creativity' has been over the last twenty years. It is when the differing forms of creativity (artistic, technical and economic) combine, and when innovations in the ways policy problems are conceptualised and addressed, that 'creativity' is best able to address the objectives and targets outlined in the South Australian Strategic Plan. This requires governments, policy makers and industry to shift their thinking about innovation, production of goods, the development of IP, and delivery of services away from a linear production chain model to a systems theory/design thinking approach. In a systems theory model, Bilton (2007) states that 'creativity is dependent upon the relationship between individuals and organisations, not on the competencies within individuals and organisations' (p. 53). Further, he states: '[A] creative economy can only thrive if policy makers, firms and individuals invest in the processes and systems which lie behind it' (p. 171).

Within increasingly contested policy environments stemming from both political and agency-based competition, Markusen (1999, p. 870) draws our attention to 'fuzzy concepts', in which she observes examinations of regional development merely as characterisations of the causes of regional economic growth. A fuzzy concept of particular concern to Markusen is the role of creativity and the creative industries in the economy. Her analysis from an economic geographer's perspective has led her to note that the role of institutions and cultures has become so abstract that they are commonly referred to as 'contingencies' and placed at the boundaries of analysis. Furthermore, she argues:

> The displacement of agents and actions by process nouns entails a shift away from the study of actors, bureaus and social groups, the structures within which they operate, their actions and outcomes, toward a discourse in which processes themselves become the causal agents. (p. 870)

Oughton, Landabasco and Morgan (2002) observe that

> [t]he regional government can play a major role in articulating and dynamising a regional innovation system … [T]he nature of the regional governance system and the wider institutional framework shapes the effectiveness and the efficiency of regional knowledge building/transfer among the different integrating parts of the system, including individual firms, sectoral/value-chain cluster, networks, business service providers, technology centres, university departments, technology transfer centres and development agencies. (p. 102)

Utilising the context-based and less prescriptive conceptual frameworks of Value Network Analysis methodology would provide a means by which South Australia could develop a more nuanced understanding of the ways in which the state's diverse array of creative and design sectors engage and contribute to the economy. This in turn is likely to provide opportunities for sectors that implement the open-process model as part of their operational and innovation models to demonstrate to those who work with a highly structured internal process model the long-term value that is to be gained from investments supporting the development of all forms of knowledge and creativity.

The challenge ahead in South Australia is to build on attempts to operationalise a broader conception of creativity and the value of design, no matter the field of creative practice — one that moves beyond creative quick fixes to an approach that is holistic, multisectoral, multidisciplinary and multidimensional.

Future research recommendations

If South Australia is 'to do things differently', it needs to innovate its innovation polices and instruments to foster innovation. It is worth reflecting on a statement made in 2005 by Stephanie Key, the then South Australian Minister for Employment, Training and Further Education, who said:

> Innovation is not about a few high-profile, high-tech, sectors of the economy; it is about every part of the economy and the need to be smarter in everything we do. Its importance to our economic future development does not mean that we have to turn every business into a mini-University. Rather, it means that we must apply, in new and changing ways, new technologies, new types of work organisation and be constantly open to new skills and ideas. (Department of Further Education Employment Science and Technology, 2005, p. 3)

South Australia's economy cannot rely on the mining and technology sectors to provide long-term economic stability. Nor can the state rely on the car industry to support hundreds of small manufacturing businesses within the car-manufacturing supply chain. Accordingly, a diverse array of knowledge, conceptual and problem-solving expertise, as well as the products and services of South Australian creative individuals and workforces, needs to be considered equally important to achieving all of the state's economic objectives. Applying Allee's (2002) value analysis methodology will generate a more nuanced local knowledge of the state's innovation system across all sectors and therefore inform innovations necessary to develop a more integrated approach to fostering innovation on an economy-wide basis.

References

Allee, V. (2002, November). A value network approach for modelling and measuring intangibles. (White paper, *Transparent Enterprise conference*, Madrid). Retrieved from http://www.vernaallee.com/images/vaa-a-valuenetworkapproach.pdf.

Amidon, D, & Macnamara, D. (2002). 7 C's of knowledge leadership. In CW Holsapple (Ed.), *Handbook on Knowledge Management: Volume 1* (pp. 539-52). Berlin/Heidelberg: Springer-Verlag).

Beckman, SL, & Barry, M. (2007). Innovation as a learning process: Embedding design thinking. *California Management Review, 50*(1), 25-56.

Bilton, C. (2007). *Management and creativity — From creative industries to creative management*. Oxford: Blackwell.

Blandy, D. (2004). *Industry clusters program: A review*. South Australia: Centre for Applied Economics.

Buchanan, R. (1992). Wicked problems in design thinking. *Design Issues, 8*(2), 5-21.

Carlsson, B. (2004). The digital economy: What is new and what is not? *Structural Change and Economic Dynamics, 15*(3), 245-64.

Commonwealth of Australia. (2001). *Backing Australia's ability — An innovation action plan for the future*. Canberra: Commonwealth of Australia.

Cooke, P, & Memedovic, O. (2006). *Regional innovation systems as public goods*. Vienna: United Nations Industrial Development Organization.

Creative Clusters Ltd. (2002). Key concepts: The creative economy. Retrieved from http://www.creativeclusters.com.

Department for Manufacturing, Innovation, Trade, Resources and Energy (DMITRE). (2012). *Manufacturing works*. Adelaide: Government of South Australia.

Department of Further Education Employment Science and Technology (DFEEST). (2005). *Better skills, better work, better state: A strategy for the development of the South Australian workforce to 2010*. Adelaide: Government of South Australia.

Department of the Premier and Cabinet. (2004). *South Australian strategic plan: Creating opportunity*. Adelaide: Government of South Australia.

Department of the Premier and Cabinet. (2007). *South Australian strategic plan 2007*. Adelaide: Government of South Australia.

Dryzek, J. (2001). Legitimacy and economy in deliberative democracy. *Political Theory, 29*(5), 651-69.

Edquist, C. (1997). *Systems of innovation: Technologies, institutions and organisations*. London: Pinter.

Freeman, C. (1985). The economics of innovation: Physical science, measurement and instrumentation, management and education — *IEE proceedings A, 132*(4), 213-21.

Government of South Australia. (2011). *In a great state: South Australia's strategic plan*. Retrieved from http://saplan.org.au/media.

Green, R. (2009). Australia's knowledge-based future — How innovation policy can create long-term growth and jobs. In: UTS Faculty of Business.

Green, R, Agarwal, R, & Hall, J. (2009). Does management matter? Australian management practices research project. *RACMA-09 conference*, Sydney. Retrieved from www.racma.edu.au.

Henton, D, Melville, J, & Walesh, K. (1997). *Grassroots leaders for a new economy: How civic entrepreneurs are building prosperous communities.* San Francisco, CA: Jossey-Bass Publishers.

Howard, J. (2008). *Between a hard rock and a soft space: Design, creative practice and innovation.* (A background paper prepared for the National Innovation Review, Council for the Humanities, Arts & Social Sciences, Canberra).

Howlett, M, & Lindquist, E. (2004). Teaching policy analysis: Policy styles and their implications for training policy analysts. (Unpublished paper, Annual Meeting of the Canadian Political Science Association, University of Manitoba, Canada).

Innovation Summit Implementation Group. (2000). *Innovation: Unlocking the future.* Canberra: Goanna Print.

KEA European Affairs. (2009). *The impact of culture on creativity.* Europe: Directorate-General for Education and Culture.

Lagendijk, A. (1997). *Will new regionalism survive? Tracing dominant concepts in economic geography.* (Discussion paper, CURDS, University of Newcastle upon Tyne).

Landry, C. (2003). *Rethinking Adelaide: 'Capturing imagination'.* Adelaide: Department of Premier and Cabinet, South Australian Government.

Landry, C. (2004). *Imagination and regeneration: Cultural policy and the future of cities.* London: Comedia.

Leadbetter, C. (2000). *Living on thin air: The new economy; with a new blueprint for the 21st century.* London: The Penguin Group.

Lee, L. (2011). *An integrated design strategy for South Australia: Building the future.* Adelaide: Government of South Australia.

Lundvall, BA. (Ed.). (1992). *National systems of innovation: Towards a theory of innovation and interactive learning.* London: Pinter Publishers.

Markusen, A. (1999). Fuzzy concepts, scanty evidence, policy distance: The case for rigour and policy relevance in critical regional studies. *Regional Studies, 33*(9), 869-84.

Maskell, P. (2000). *Social capital, innovation, and competitiveness.* Oxford: Oxford University Press.

Metcalfe, J, Riedlinger, M, Pisarski, A, & Gardner, J. (2006). *Collaborating across the sectors: The relationships between the Humanities, Arts and Social Sciences (HASS) and Science, Technology, Engineering and Medicine (STEM) sectors.* (CHASS Occasional Paper No. 5, Council for the Humanities, Arts and Social Sciences, Canberra).

National Economics. (2005). *State of the regions report 2004-2005.* (Report prepared for the Australian Local Government Association, Melbourne).

Nelson, RR, & Winter, SG. (1977). In search of useful theory of innovation. *Research Policy, 6*(1), 36-76.

Organisation for Economic Co-operation and Development (OECD). (2001). *Cities and regions in the new learning economy.* Paris: OECD.

Osborne, D, & Gaebler, T. (1992). *Reinventing government: How the entrepreneurial spirit is transforming the public sector.* Reading, MA: Addison-Wesley Publishing.

Oughton, C, Landabasco, M, & Morgan, K. (2002). The regional innovation paradox: Innovation policy and industrial policy. *Journal of Technology Transfer, 27*(1), 97-110.

Owen, C. (2007). Design thinking: Notes on its nature and use. *Design Research Quarterly, 2*(1), 16-27.

Poggenpohl, S. (2009). Time for change: Building a design discipline. In SH Poggenpohl & K Satō, *Design integrations: Research and collaboration* (pp. 4-22). Chicago: Intellect, the University of Chicago Press.

Potts, J. (2007). *Innovation: An evolutionary economic view of the creative industries.* The University of Melbourne: UNESCO Observatory, Faculty of Architecture, Building and Planning.

Prime Minister's Science Engineering and Innovation Council Working Group (PMSEIC). (2005). *Imagine Australia: The role of creativity in the innovation economy.* Retrieved from http://www.dest.gov.au.

Quinn, RE. (1988). *Beyond rational management: Mastering the paradoxes and competing demands of high performance.* San Francisco, CA: Jossey-Bass.

Schön, DA. (1987). *Educating the reflective practitioner: Toward a new design for teaching and learning in the professions.* San Francisco, CA: Jossey-Bass.

Sporer, Z. (2008). A present stuck in the past: Innovation and commercialization activities in the OECD and the CEEC. *Revija Za Sociologiju, 39*(1-2), 3.

Stoneman, P. (2007) *An introduction to the definition and measurement of soft innovation.* (Working paper, NESTA, London).

Stoneman, P. (Ed.) (1996). *Handbook of the economics of innovation and technological change.* Oxford: Blackwell.

Toulimin, S. (2001). *Return to reason.* Cambridge, MA: Harvard University Press.

Turok, I. (2009). The distinctive city: Pitfalls in the pursuit of differential advantage. *Environment and Planning A, 41*, 13-30.

Waldo, D. (1952, March). Development of theory of democratic administration. *The American Political Science Review, 46*, 1-103.

Woolcock, M. (1998). Social capital and economic development: Toward a theoretical synthesis and policy framework. *Theory and Society, 27*(2), 151-208.

Yapp, C. (2005, January). Innovation, futures thinking and leadership. *Public Money & Management*, 57-60.

A patent perspective of South Australian innovation:

3

An indicator within the regional innovation system story

Kym Teh, The University of Adelaide
Göran Roos, The University of Adelaide

Introduction

We explore innovation performance in the context of measuring and analysing patent data within the Australian state of South Australia [SA]. However, we discuss and identify the use of patent data to measure innovation performance and the underlying assumptions and any limitations of such an approach in greater detail in this chapter.

Notwithstanding that it has been possible to suggest certain conclusions concerning that state's innovation trajectory from the patent data, integral to this exploration are the economic, regulatory and constitutional features that affect and define the nation of Australia and its states. For the purpose of this research, we launch from a discussion on SA patent activity to discuss the state's regional innovation system [RIS]. The RIS has typically been examined and defined in terms of a nation state. Uniquely, this research exploration brings together the two elements of examining an innovation system unit that is smaller than a nation state — in this case a state in Australia — and linking that with an analysis of that state's innovation performance.

'Innovation'	Character	Source
... is any thought, behaviour or thing that is new because it is qualitatively different from existing forms.	Newness	Barnett (1953, p. 7)
... is any idea, practice, or material artefact perceived to be new by the relevant unit of adoption. The adopting unit can vary from a single individual to a business firm, a city, or a state legislature.	Newness	Zaltman, Duncan, & Holbeck (1984, p. 10)
... [can m]ost generally ... be seen as the synthesis of a market need with the means to achieve and produce a product to meet that need.	Outcome	Moore & Tushman (1982, p. 132)
... is an idea, practice or object that is perceived as new by an individual or other unit of adoption. It matters little, so far as human behaviour is concerned, whether or not an idea is objectively new ... The perceived units of the idea for the individual determine his or her reaction to it. If the idea seems new to the individual, it is an innovation.	Newness	Rogers (1983, p. 11)
... is the process whereby new ideas are put into practice.	Newness/Outcome	Rickards (1985, p. 10)
... = invention + exploitation. The invention process covers all efforts aimed at creating new ideas and getting them to work. The exploitation process includes all stages of commercial development, application, and transfer, including the focusing of ideas or inventions towards specific objectives, evaluating those objectives, downstream transfer of research and/or development results, and the eventual broadbased utilisation, dissemination and diffusion of the technology-based outcomes.	Newness/Outcome	Roberts (1987, p. 3)
... is the adoption of an internally generated or purchased device, system, policy, program, process or service that is new to the adopting organisation	Newness/Outcome	Damanpour (1991, p. 556)

Table 3.1: Definitions of innovation.
Source: Courtesy of the authors, adapted from Doepfer, 2012.

Background

In relation to innovation performance, as assessed through patent data, this chapter specifically discusses the application of a particular approach to selecting the type of 'patent families'. In this case we have chosen the Derwent World Patent Index [DWPI] of families (Thomson Reuters, 2012). The analysis included activity timelines (including 'family' expansion rate); a geographical analysis (source of innovation; destination of innovation); patent grant success rates; entity analysis (sector, portfolio size, number of inventions, entity citations); patents held by individuals; and the same analysis against the dimension of technical categories (such as pharmaceuticals, and agriculture and food), and academic intellectual property.

There is a significant body of research concerning innovation performance, and the particular role of patents as a metric. That research illustrates the strengths, weaknesses and limitations of such an approach. More broadly for example, Hagedoorn and Cloodt (2003) strongly advocate the merits of innovation performance being assessed using multiple indicators, and an example of that approach being applied is Dutta and Benavente's (2011) Global Innovation Index [GII], where patent data is only one of the inputs.

Innovation — Towards a definition

What is innovation? While there may be a range of differing views, Kline and Rosenberg (1986) suggest that innovation is not necessarily something that is well-defined, or even homogeneous, nor can it be identified as entering an economy at a specific point in time.

To further highlight the point that innovation is not necessarily a homogeneous thing or even a homogeneous class of items, Doepfer (2012), by way of example, sets out a range of definitions of innovation, in terms of either its newness or its outcome, as illustrated in Table 3.1.

Notwithstanding that there may be some argument concerning the homogeneity of definitions for innovation, it does appear to be thematic.

Rogers (1998, p. 6), in his work concerning both the definition and measurement of innovation, notes five types of innovation described by the Organisation for Economic Co-operation and Development [OECD]:

- introduction of a new product or qualitative change in an existing product
- process innovation new to an industry
- the opening of a new market
- development of new sources of supply for raw materials or other inputs
- changes in industrial organisation.

Measuring innovation — Patents as an indicator and the notion of value

Outputs and inputs

Rogers (1998), like other researchers and commentators, distinguishes between output and input measures of innovation. Similarly, Dutta and Benavente (2011), in their approach to developing a global innovation index, make that distinction.

The Global Innovation Index project, which the graduate business school INSEAD launched in 2007, highlights the multiple indicator approach, but with the broader objective of attempting to capture the true 'richness of innovation in society', (Dutta & Benavente, 2011, p. 1). The research looks beyond measures of innovation such as the number of PhDs, the number of research articles produced, the research centres created, the patents issued, and research and development expenditure. It also draws an important distinction between input and output measures.

This research is also conducted with reference to countries — whereas the analysis underpinning the research in this chapter is unique in that it addresses the issue of innovation performance by a state (or nation/country sub-unit). In particular, the index comprises two sub-indices: the Innovation Input Sub-Index, and the Innovation Output Sub-Index, with each one being built around five 'pillars' (Dutta & Benavente, 2011, pp. 8-9). The Input Sub-Index includes elements that are considered to enable innovation in relation to the 'national economy': institutions (that is, the political environment, regulatory environment and business environment); human capital and research (that is, education, tertiary education, and research and development); infrastructure (ICT, energy, and general infrastructure); market sophistication (credit, investment, trade, and competition); and business sophistication (knowledge workers, innovation linkages, and knowledge absorption). The Output Sub-Index attempts to collect actual evidence on innovation outputs: scientific outputs (that is, knowledge creation, including patents and other intellectual property [IP]; knowledge impact; and knowledge diffusion); and creative outputs (creative intangibles, and creative goods and services).

In the context of our later discussion, we give specific consideration of the regional innovation system. Perhaps it is useful to note the elements of Dutta and Benevente's Global Innovation Index, which focuses on innovation with respect to nations. To what extent are there linkages between any of those elements at a regional level — that is, at a level that is less than at a national level? This may be particularly instructive when considering the geopolitical-economic dynamics and constraints. For example, from where is government innovation policy most effectively directed?

How many indicators?

Hagedoorn and Cloodt (2003) examine whether it is preferable to use multiple indicators when endeavouring to measure innovative performance, in particular, R&D inputs/expenditure, patent counts and patent citations, and new products (as measured by new product announcements). This is a significant study, examining a large international sample of some 1200 companies, in four high-tech industries. However, for the sectors examined there was sufficient overlap that any one of them could be applied to capture innovation performance.

It is important to note that the context for this research does vary between forms of national measures, whether in the form of an index (or any other metric) assessing the value of a patent, or the innovation performance of a firm. Even so it is useful to consider the range of approaches, which also, as noted above, includes Dutta and Benavente (2011) taking a multiple indicator approach with innovation output and input elements as sub-indices. These approaches are to be contrasted at possibly the other end of the spectrum with single indicator measurements such as the patent success ratio of McAleer and Slottje (2005). As we will discuss later on, in relation to the state of South Australia and an analysis of that state's intellectual property, amongst the matters analysed is a 'success ratio' (Thomson Reuters, 2012). In that instance it is measured as the patent grant to patent application ratio.

An innovation-patent nexus

In terms of empirical approaches, the use of patent data as an index of innovation dominated most early econometric work on innovation (McCann & Ortega-Argiles, 2013). To some extent this is still the most widely used index. However, since the 1990s there has been a concerted effort to use better sources for measuring innovation, driven by two reasons: first, patents reflect very few of the innovations from the services industries (which account for some 70 per cent of value added in advanced economies), and second, patents poorly reflect, say, non-technological innovations. This led to the development of a revised Pavitt-type taxonomy. There were also major developments in the areas of firm-based innovation surveys, focusing on technology business practices, for example (McCann & Ortega-Argiles, 2013).

Much of our discussion so far has at least implied some form of connection between patentability and innovation. Are they in some way equivalent, or is one a test for the other? Put another way, is innovation essential for the granting of a patent, or does patentability indicate that an invention is innovative? If we take the example of the requirements for patentability under the Australian framework, under the most prevalent type of patent, which is the 'standard patent', the so-called level of invention is demonstrating an 'inventive step' over the prior art.

'Inventive step' is defined under the Australian Patents Act and requires a determination of whether an invention would have been obvious to 'a person skilled in the relevant art' (Australian Law Reform Commission, n.p.). This assessment is made in light of the 'common general knowledge', as it existed in Australia before the priority date of the claim. It may also take into consideration prior art information before the priority date that a person skilled in the art could reasonably be expected to have ascertained, understood and regarded as relevant.

In the Australian Law Reform Commission, the Australian High Court considered the inventive step requirement. The Court determined that in assessing whether or not the inventive step requirement has been satisfied, the issue is whether a notional research group in the field 'would have been led directly as a matter of course to pursue one avenue in the expectation that it might well produce the [claimed compound]'. The Court found that the results of a 'routine literature search' that have not entered into the common general knowledge are not relevant to an assessment of inventiveness (Australian Law Reform Commission, n.p.).

In 2001 changes were made to the Australian patent laws affecting the assessment of the inventive step requirement by allowing 'mosaicing' of prior art information during patent examination. Mosaicing allows a patent examiner to assess the inventive step in light of two or more pieces of prior art information in combination, provided that a person skilled in the relevant art could reasonably have been expected to combine such information. Prior to those changes, patent examiners were only permitted to assess the inventive step in light of a single piece of prior art information, alone or combined with common general knowledge in the relevant art in Australia (Australian Law Reform Commission, n.p.).

There are certainly similarities between the inventive step and the concept (or definitions) of innovation. Are they one and the same thing? On the mere construction of 'innovation', it could be reasonably regarded that innovation is a more expansive concept.

Patents and value

There has been a plethora of research conducted concerning the significance of patents in relation to the value of intellectual property, and even concerning the contribution to the value of the enterprise or firm. Perhaps by implication, there is also plenty of research measuring innovation. Indicative of the spread of research addressing these and related matters are the following examples:

- Laitner and Stolyarov (2009) have asserted that there is a connection between the value of a firm, its patents, and the frequency of the citations for those patents. It should be noted that patent clusters and any lag in citations adds complexity to this proposition.

- What is the effect of various research investment inputs on the value of patents? The research examined five sets of factors with respect to possible determinants, and assessed their relative importance: organisation characteristics, inventor characteristics, character of the patent, competitive environment, and the locations (Gambardella, Harhoff, & Verspagen, 2006). Of these determinants (and their associated factors), the inventor's characteristics were the most influential in affecting the value of a patent. Amongst the factors associated with the inventor characteristics are their experience in the organisation, their own 'innovation experience' (as measured by the number of previous patents filed), and inventor effort or motivation (with monetary, career or reputation incentives as proxies for this).

- Is the national patent system in which the patent is filed a factor in affecting its value? The particular research compares patent filings in the United States of America and Germany, concluding that, for comparable inventions, patent filings in Germany have an associated higher value (Bessen & Thoma, 2012).

- This is consistent with the findings from the studies resulting in the Economic Complexity Index. This work identifies the Economic Complexity Index as an indicator of an economy's ability to capture economic value from, for example, innovation activities; and the higher the Index value, the higher this ability. The US Index value is 1.4 and the German index value is 2.0, whereas the Australian Index value is -0.3 (Hausmann et al., 2011).

- There are also a range of 'accounting standards' approaches to determining the value of intellectual property, which includes patents (Singla, 2012). These approaches include assessing the value by the costs incurred, the market valuation (which may be difficult in the case of very new inventions), and the income generated. Singla (2012) suggests that these approaches will, with all other things being equal, produce different results depending on the maturity of the invention or associated product. There are also other methods (the '25% method'), where the licensor receives 25 per cent from the licensee's gross profits arising from the technology (Hagelin, 2004).

- Other instances have applied regression analysis of a firm's market values to derive the value of patent portfolios, using the owner's willingness to pay patent renewal fees, or the owner's estimate of value, as alternative approaches to determining value (Hall, 2009).

- Also, while a patent may be cited as state of the art, it can be cited, too, because it threatens the 'novelty' of new patent applications. This characteristic in itself can affect the value of a patent. A market value approach can be applied to assess the value of a patent with blocking potential. This particular research suggests that patents which receive a higher number of so-called blocking citations may have a higher economic value to firms than other patented inventions (Czarnitzki, Hussinger, & Leten, 2010).

- There has been a significant body of research conducted examining the determinants of value for patents and intellectual property more broadly. Gambardella, Harhoff, and Verspagen (2006) consider a range of factors or determinants that might affect the value of patented inventions. While noting that investment in resources is an important factor, they highlight the importance of inventor characteristics, such as past citations and level of education. Also, the economic value of an invention may rest with the breadth of the inventions produced. This may relate less to equivalent patents or patent families, but is significant for 'complementary technology'.

- This research also indicates that increased resources may be associated with a higher value of the portfolio of inventions (spreading resources across technology-related inventions), and the level of research and development [R&D] is a good predictor of the number of patents. The resources do affect the value of an invention/patent, but perhaps the most significant factor is the inventor characteristics.

In relation to biotechnology in particular, Albino, Petruzzelli, and Rotolo (2009) considered the determinants of patent value. Amongst their determinants they examined scientific knowledge, inter-organisation collaborations, patent scope and technological 'radicalness'. Of these determinants their research suggested that only the organisational breadth of new technology search, the scope of new patents and the radical nature of new technology were significant. Of course, this was by specific reference to biotechnology, which raises the broader question of the extent to which the value of patents (or for that matter the value of intellectual property more broadly) is affected by different ranges of determinants or factors, depending on the sector, industry or technical category.

We raise the above matters as an open question in terms of whether there is a corollary between them and the measure of innovation itself (or even its associated value). Are there further related implications for innovation concerning variations regarding the sector or industry? This is something that we also consider in relation to the regional innovation system.

Analysis of South Australian IP

The Government of South Australia commissioned research entitled 'Analysis of South Australia IP' (Thomson Reuters, 2012). This is perhaps particularly relevant in relation to our later examination of the regional innovation system [RIS] — in particular, uniquely, whether South Australia comprises an RIS. IP is pertinent to any consideration of innovation, notwithstanding our earlier remarks concerning whether there are limitations as to the completeness of IP as a measure of innovation.

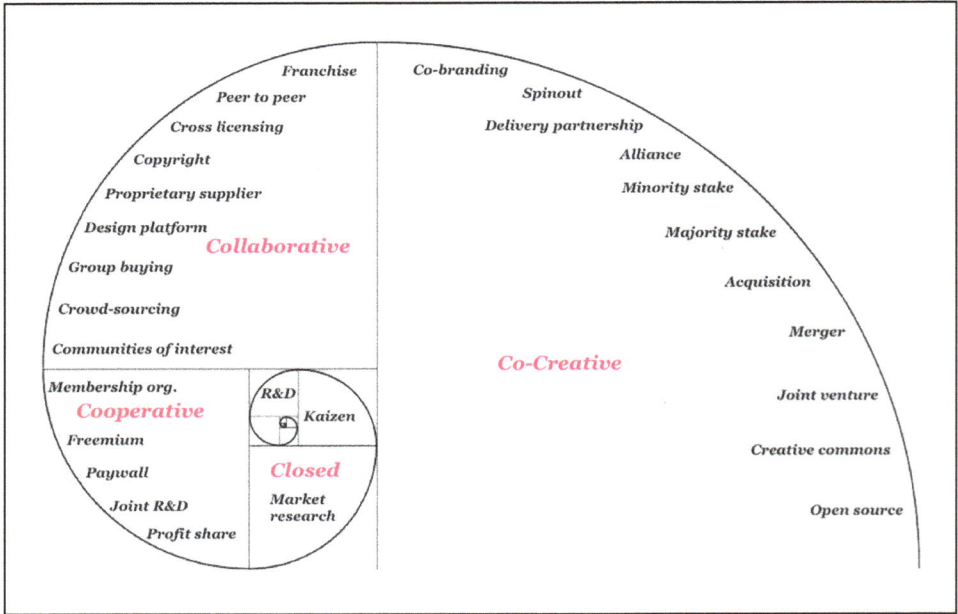

Figure 3.1: Example of ways to form productive partnerships. Some — for example, cross licensing — do depend on IP, whereas others do not.
Source: http://www.100open.com/2013/01/ip-intellectual-paranoia.

The research commissioned by the SA Government was limited to consideration of patent applications and granted patents. Of course, not all innovation is protected by way of patent, both as a matter of strategy or tactics, or due to the specific requirements of patent protection that may preclude certain inventions from that form of IP protection. This question of innovating without using patent protection is becoming increasingly relevant as new forms of collaboration enable and encourage patent- and IP-less innovation (see Figure 3.1 for examples and for the trajectory of development).

It is useful to note that the data collection and analysis used in the research commissioned by the Government of South Australia employed the collection of full patent content on Thomson Innovation, including the Derwent World Patent Index [DWPI]. To focus on the state of South Australia, data was collected from the Australian Patent Register from applicants with an address with a postcode corresponding to that state. Also, in the case of patent documents filed outside

Australia, the search included documents filed by South Australian Patent Attorneys. The DWPI is structured around patent families.

A patent family is, according to Martinez (2010, pp. 10-11), 'a set of patents taken in various countries to protect a single invention (when a first application in a country — the priority — is then extended to other offices)'. In other words, a patent family is 'the same invention disclosed by a common inventor(s) and patented in more than one country' (US Patent and Trademark Office, n.d., n.p.).

There are a range of approaches to patent families, their associated definitions, and types (Martinez, 2010): equivalents (patents that most likely protect the same inventions); extended families (patents protecting the same or related inventions); single priority families (each first filing is treated individually, as the origin of a different family); examiners' technology-based families (patent documents protecting the same technical content); and commercial novelty-based families (patent documents protecting new technical content, which includes data sourced from the DWPI). Each of these patent family types lends itself to particular uses.

The analysis commissioned by the SA Government examined a number of dimensions (Thomson Reuters, 2012), which are in this instance relevant to understanding the extent to which the state of South Australia is in some way a regional innovation system. This IP analysis particularly takes us at least part of the way to understanding IP and perhaps innovation in South Australia — the IP profile of South Australia and some of its entities may provide some pointers to the existence (or otherwise) of innovation systems. The dimensions of this IP analysis include, most importantly for this chapter:

- activity timelines — patent applications/ grants (refer Figure 3.2)

- success — patent grant to patent application ratio (which is also

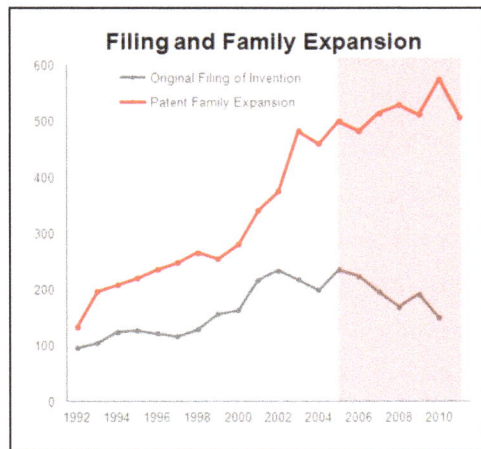

Figure 3.2: Activity timelines.
Source: Thomson Reuters, 2012.

referred to by McAleer and Slottje [2005] as a measure of innovation)

- entity analysis: corporate, academic/government, individual; tiers of number of inventions per entity; filing strategies by Patent Co-operation Treaty [PCT], country; level of citations

- technical analysis — number of inventions per technical category; timeline; growth rates

- strength (Thomson Reuters IP Analytics Strength Index)

- academic IP in South Australia.

% of Landscape by Entity Tier

Tier 3 - 1-3 Inventions 30%

Tier 2 - 4-19 Inventions 15%

Tier 1 - >=22 Inventions 20%

Tier 4 - Individuals 35%

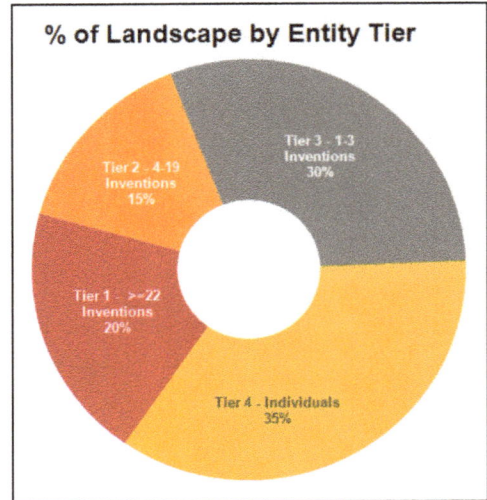

Organisation Portfolio Size Tier Analysis		
Tier	Total Inventions	Number of Entities
Tier 1 - >=22 Inventions	688	18
Tier 2 - 4-19 Inventions	518	76
Tier 3 - 1-3 Inventions	1059	783
Tier 4 - Individuals	1236	1236

Figure 3.3: Inventions per entity.
Source: Thomson Reuters, 2012.

There is a delay of eighteen months between filing a patent application and its publication, which has resulted in not all years of data being complete. However, notwithstanding that, the data and this graph, entitled Filing and [Patent] Family Expansion, are indicative of a gradual decrease since 2005 in the overall number of patent applications pursued by South Australian entities.

The chart and table above (Figure 3.3) show the number of inventions per South Australian entity, including individuals. It is useful to note that a significant and substantial portion of the patents are held by individuals, some 35 per cent of the total.

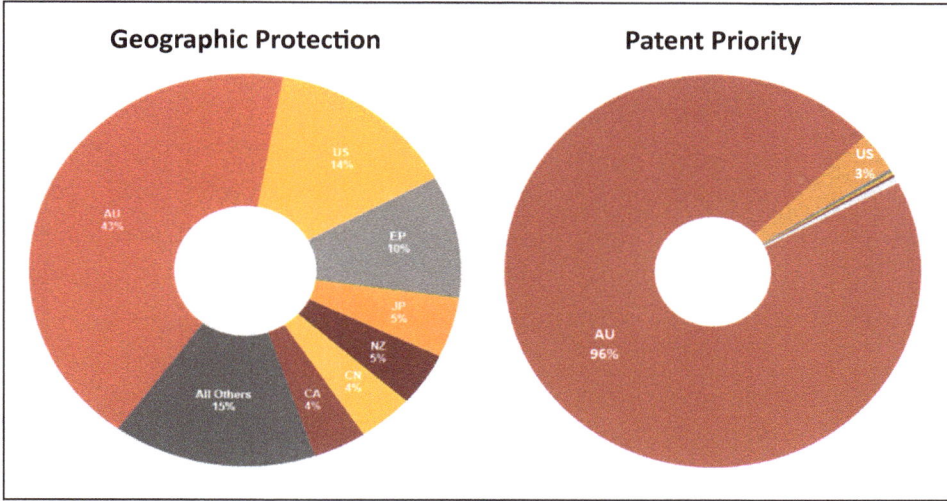

Figure 3.4: Patent source and application distribution.
Source: Thomson Reuters, 2012.

Filing strategies by PCT, country

The charts above (refer Figure 3.4), entitled 'Patent Priority' (as a proxy measure for the geographic source of the invention, and 'Geographic Protection' (indicating the most popular country in which patent protection is sought), show that most South Australian entities pursuing a patent registration claim priority from Australia, exceedingly so with over 96 per cent claiming priority from Australia. Similarly the country where patent protection is most significantly sought is Australia by a substantial margin at 43 per cent, distantly followed by the USA at 14 per cent.

Technical analysis — Technical category

The table below (refer Table 3.2), entitled 'Technology Analysis' (indicating the technical attributes of inventions), shows South Australian inventions (as defined by this research) by technical category. However, this has certain limitations as categories are not mutually exclusive, and multiple categories may be applied to a single invention.

Perhaps, similarly, any analysis of patent data in this way must be moderated in terms of the 'technical categories' that are represented in the region. For example,

Technology Analysis	
Technical Categories	**Inventions**
01 Pharmaceuticals	252
02 Medical Technology and Healthcare	511
03 Agriculture and Food	737
04 Nanotechnology	6
05 Measurement and Instrumentation	411
06 Mining	49
07 Computing and IT	412
08 Electrical Power Production and Distribution, Electri	489
09 Domestic Articles, Personal Care	383
10 Communications	343
11 Semiconductors and Electronic Circuitry	101
12 General Chemistry	216
13 Chemical Engineering	377
14 Lighting/Heating	195
15 Textiles and Paper	78
16 Transport/Automotive	481
17 Civil Engineering	644
18 Optics	141
19 Printing & Photography	88
20 Mechanical Engineering	1468
21 Petroleum	34
22 Nuclear Engineering	15
23 Defense Equipments	22
24 Clean Technology/Environment & Climate Change S	4
25 Amusement/Games/Sports	146
26 Advanced Polymer Processing	102
27 Hybrid, Composite Materials	7
28 Industrial Biotechnology	52
29 Manufacturing Control and Automation	51
32 3D / 4D Printing and Fast Prototyping	7
33 CAD / CAM / CAE	5
34 Wine related	123
35 Water Management	533

Table 3.2: Technology analysis.
Source: Thomson Reuters, 2012.

the pharmaceutical sector tends to be a high user of patent protection when compared with other sectors. The importance of patenting varies by industry (Hall, 2009). So within a region it is arguable that the presence, or otherwise, of a pharmaceutical sector might skew an analysis that focuses on patent data. Other sectors may and do choose to use other forms of protection where intellectual property is integral to a business, using copyright in the case of software or trade secrets protection .

The role of universities in the South Australian innovation environment

As a component of the research mentioned earlier, Thomson Reuters (2012) examined and analysed the patent filing activity of South Australian universities since 1992. This does not include universities that have established a presence in South Australia over recent years such as Carnegie Mellon and University College London, but presumably these universities would have little relevant activity emanating from South Australia, or their patent filings would be made from their home countries. That data and analysis suggests that the role that universities in South Australia play in innovation (as measured by patent activity) is not material. Rather, as suggested by some of the research literature concerning the role of regional universities, the main contribution is that of capabilities development through the skilling of graduates (Varga, 2000; Schartinger, Schibany, & Gassler, 2001; Saxenian, 2000).

Conclusions

Notwithstanding these remarks concerning the use of patents data to assess innovation performance, there are a number of conclusions that we might make about the innovation performance of South Australia. There has been a worldwide surge in patent activity, in part due to the growth in certain industries, such as ICT (Eckert & Langinier, 2013), whereas patent activity has in recent years been declining in South Australia. Does this suggest a decline in innovation in South Australia or a move to other collaborative forms of innovation (see Figure 3.1), or non-patentable innovations like, for example, business models? Innovations may also be protected by forms of intellectual property protection that do not necessarily require registration, such as copyright in the Australian jurisdiction, or trade secret protection as created under contract, or confidential information under the common law. Patent protection is a form of intellectual property protection that requires formal registration. Irrespective of the decline in patent activity in relation to South Australia, that patent activity has specific characteristics: there is a focus on protecting inventions in Australia; a large proportion of patents are held by a large number of individuals; and there are relatively few entities with patents relating to more than twenty-two inventions.

The importance of patenting does vary by industry (Hall, 2009). In addition, in relation to maximising returns from innovation, rarely are patents the most important means. A distinction should be made where there is complexity (where many patents are held by many firms) and discrete instances (where the product is only covered by one or two patents, usually held by a single firm or entity). In the case of complex technologies, 'dispersion' can be a problem. The intention or purpose behind the patent may vary: for a discrete technology, patents may be used to exclude competitors, whereas for a complex technology, a patent may be used as a basis for cross-licensing as well as protection. Different patent strategies may apply in the case of different industries, technologies and patent users — for example, the difference between some manufacturing environments with a focus on materials in contrast to industries that rely on a system. This leads us firstly to the further question of how South Australia, at least in terms of patenting, compares with industries elsewhere, and secondly to a technology-by-technology comparison.

The use of patents as a singular measure of innovation has certain, and not insignificant, limitations. Are innovation and patentability equivalent concepts, or is one necessary for the other, or necessary or sufficient? A multi-indicator approach as alluded to by Hagedoorn and Cloodt (2003) and Dutta and Benevente (2011) has many advantages.

Does South Australia comprise a regional innovation system? The patenting data and analysis does not appear to provide sufficient evidence to support that view. Are we seeing an innovation system, something more like a series of 'clusters', or in some cases merely vertical integration? Even though patent activity may form a necessary part of identifying whether there is an innovation system, it appears that in itself it could never be sufficient as evidence. The definitions or concept of an innovation system seem to have a number of themes in common, one of which is a connectedness of infrastructure, network, and/or interaction. Problematic is the ability to compare 'regions' with one another once we leave the same national boundary — can you compare a state of Australia with a prefecture in Japan, for example? What are the relevant differences in their respective innovation environments or the innovation climate?

A regional innovation system — A suggested approach

We pose the question of whether South Australia comprises a regional innovation system. Also, in relation to the conclusions we have suggested concerning that state's innovation performance, even if there is little or no evidence to indicate the existence of an RIS, should an RIS approach not be considered to enhance innovation performance or capacity? First, to respond to the initial question it is necessary to set out a framework for a regional innovation system, at least at a high level. It is useful to first touch on a concept of the national innovation system. A national innovation system can refer to the creation of innovation within national economies and may be defined as networks 'of institutions [or organisations] in the public and private sector whose activities and interactions initiative, import, modify, and diffuse new technologies' (Freeman, 1987, p. 4). An NIS may also be more broadly regarded as all interrelated institutional actors that create, diffuse and exploit innovations (Doloreux & Parto, 2005, pp. 135, 141), as well as organisations and institutions directly related to searching and exploring technological innovations, such as R&D departments, universities and public institutes (Malerba, 2005, pp. 65-7).

A useful starting point may be to illustrate the components of a national innovation system. In broad terms, an NIS can be broadly defined as all economic, political and other social institutions affecting learning, searching and exploring

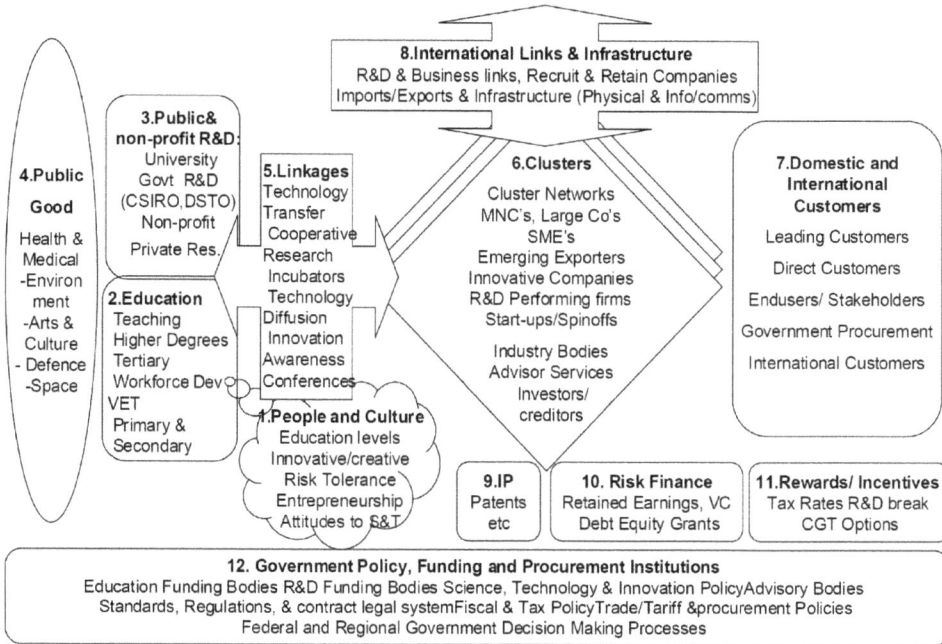

Figure 3.5: Constitution of national innovation systems.
Source: Roos, Fernström, & Gupta, 2005, p. 4.

activities (that is, a nation's universities and research bodies, its financial system, its monetary policies, and internal organisation of private firms) as outlined in Figure 3.5 above.

For a regional innovation system there are some factors that are given due to the national setting, as well as some others that are relevant:

- regional proximity, as a strong influence on corporate and innovation performance, viewed as an analysis of economic, geographic and management factors

- the existence of innovation (of which there are many and varied definitions)

- the relevance of networks in relation to innovation (has geographically and functionally distributed knowledge been unified as a result of collaboration?).

To examine the components of an RIS — that is, the characteristics of a region, the nature of innovation and what constitutes a system — a further review of what may constitute innovation is necessary. While it is not the intention to provide here an in-depth treatise on regional innovation systems, it is important to provide a framework and context for the unique process of exploring the state of South Australia in the context of an RIS. Commonly, innovation systems are examined with respect to national innovation or national innovation systems.

In relation to innovation, in addition to a number of views that we have already canvassed, it is beneficial to broaden our understanding of innovation. As previously noted, it is perhaps risky to treat innovation as something that is precisely defined, or as being something that is necessarily homogeneous.

Below, we discuss each of the elements of a regional innovation system in turn (with innovation having been earlier discussed elsewhere).

'Region' and 'system'

By contrasting the regional innovation system with the national innovation system (as earlier described), we see that the RIS focuses on the regional structures that bind inter-organisational innovation. Typically, exploration of national innovation systems looks to macro economic interests, whereas some commentators suggest that consideration of the RIS might tend to focus on more specific investments to promote innovation. This may become clearer in the case of the example of the state of South Australia (Cooke, 2001). The RIS has been defined in a number of different ways or forms. An RIS

- consists of a production structure (techno-economic structures) and an institutional infrastructure (political-institutional structures) (Asheim & Isaksen, 1997)

- is a complex of innovation actors and institutions in a region, all of which are directly related, with the generation, diffusion and appropriation of technological innovation and an interrelationship between these innovation actors (Chung, 2002)

- consists of interacting knowledge generation and exploitation sub-systems linked to global, national and other regional systems for commercialising new knowledge (Cooke, 2004)

- may be defined as the localised network of actors and institutions in the public and private sectors, whose activities and interactions generate, import, modify and diffuse new technologies within and outside the region (Iammarino, 2005).

Nuances and the regional innovation system

There are two concepts relating to the territorial innovation theory family (Asheim & Coenen, 2005): regional innovation systems [RIS] and clusters (Cooke, Heidenrich, & Braczyk, 2004; Porter, 2000). The innovation system can be viewed in both a narrow and a broad sense. In the narrow construction, the system incorporates the R&D functions of universities, public and private research institutes and corporations. More broadly the system can be viewed as including 'all parts and aspects of the economic structure and the institutional set-up affecting the learning as well as searching and exploring' (Lundvall, 1992, p. 12).

It is important to consider that there are different types of regional innovation systems, resulting in, and affected by, the varying knowledge bases of different industries. The innovation processes are strongly shaped and influenced by their knowledge base. Asheim and Coenen (2005) distinguish between three types of RIS, denoted as:

1. a territorially embedded system, where firms based their innovation activity mainly on localised, inter-firm learning processes stimulated by geographical and relational proximity (for example, where there are networks of SMEs in industrial districts)

2. a regionally networked innovation system, where firms and organisations are also embedded in a specific region, and characterised by localised, interactive learning — there is the intentional strengthening of the region's institutional infrastructure

3. a regionalised national innovation system, where parts of industry and institutional infrastructure are more functionally integrated into national or international innovation systems, and the type of collaboration between organisations tends to be more linear, such as in the case of specific projects.

In a 'learning economy', clusters and the RIS should be regarded as distinct concepts, albeit strongly interrelated ones. The cluster concept is significantly narrower than the RIS and has a strong sectoral connotation, whereas, importantly, the RIS can transcend multiple sectors.

Industry and sector specificity

As noted above, an RIS may transcend multiple sectors. Notwithstanding that proposition, there is a need for different approaches to regional innovation policy (Martin & Trippl, 2013). Regional industries differ strongly in terms of their underlying knowledge bases, and consequently in their policy needs. Regional innovation policies should be designed to address a range of system failures that characterise different institutional settings such as 'organisational thinness', lock-in and fragmentation. In addition, the notion of the differentiated knowledge base is indicative of the industrial variation that may exist within an RIS. Therefore, the approach should typically be customised for different sectors. This observation may be particularly relevant when considering innovation strategy and policy with respect to South Australia.

It can be suggested that under the Sectoral Systems of Innovation (or SSI approach) of Malerba (2002; 2004) different industries may have different competitive, interactive and organisational boundaries that are not necessarily national. Recent research concerning innovation systems supports the view that the region is a key level where innovative capacity is shaped and economic processes co-ordinated and governed. This is perhaps relevant to South Australia, and further reinforces the relevance of an RIS policy approach to that state.

Further developing and supporting the theme of an RIS policy approach, McCann and Ortega-Argiles (2013) note that there is a growing awareness of the links between geography and innovation. There is increasing evidence that certain regions are systematically more disposed towards innovation than others. This has been attributed variously to local industrial structure, agglomeration of externalities, knowledge-related institutions, an environment of entrepreneurship, an innovation- and research-favourable environment, and changing knowledge transaction costs.

Triple Helix

The 'Triple Helix' of University-Industry-Government relations emerged as a metaphor for the operationalisation of the complex dynamics of innovation during the late 1990s (Leydesdorff & Strand, 2013). Under this metaphor, patents can be regarded as events in relation to the interactions in the Triple Helix space. Innovation occurs in a landscape of interactions, collaboration and knowledge exchanges among firms, academic institutions and a range of government agencies. Firms and other agents co-operate and participate in 'networks' at various geographical scales: local, regional, national and international. Contextually a number of factors become significant: the industry structure, role of universities, role of knowledge networks, proximity and localisation, and organisation and culture.

There are interactions in the Triple Helix between economic development, organised knowledge and political control. In this regard it is important to query how one might measure the knowledge base in an economy, and whether that base is more developed at a regional or national level, or vice versa.

The Triple Helix underscores the relevance of government in innovation and regional innovation systems, and, we contend, the importance of the role of public policy development in the RIS field. In general, it can be suggested that regional innovation systems are not sufficient on their own to remain competitive on a globalising economy. Production systems seem to be more important to the innovation system at the regional level. Thus local firms must also have access to national and supra-national innovation systems, as well as to corporate innovation systems from the local firms that have been brought. This line of reasoning is followed to a point where the regional innovation system expands beyond its own boundaries through a process of economic integration (Doloreux & Parto, 2005).

However, in our view the diverse range of opinions and research in this area is strongly suggestive of regional innovation systems being important enablers or catalysts for the development of innovation capacity within a regional setting.

Future research and implications

This research has identified and illuminated many areas for policy analysis and development, and future research. These future directions concern the development of appropriate and effective innovation policy and policy tools that operate at a 'regional level'. In terms of directly related research, what are the elements, factors and influences that comprise the innovation environment or innovation climate which are critical to informing the development of these policies?

Measuring innovation and its value seems to be an ongoing field of research. This research has perhaps suggested other important dimensions that could be added to this fertile field:

- innovation metrics embodied in models that could address a range of economic units: nations/countries, firms and a range of regional concepts
- further research across different innovation environments and climates, identifying the range and different characteristics and attributes — how they influence innovation and to what extent (for example, but not limited to, taxation, intellectual policy, competition, investment, national/regional governance).

In general, there are wide-ranging implications for policy development and the role of governments in enhancing innovation capacity within a regional framework, especially in relation to regions that comprise multisector economies. It appears that it would be fruitful to consider a regional innovation system approach in this regard, but the matter of how to effectively implement a regional innovation system in itself poses a series of vexing challenges that warrant further exploration and research. South Australia might present an appropriately relevant case for such further research.

Acknowledgements

We acknowledge and thank both Dr Nicola Lake and Andrew O'Brien of Thomson Reuters for providing the Analysis of South Australian IP, which was prepared by them on behalf of the Department of Manufacturing, Innovation, Trade, Resources and Energy of the Government of South Australia. In particular we are grateful to Dr Lake for explaining and clarifying their approach to the analysis provided by them. That analysis and the support of Thomson Reuters have been critical in informing and connecting theory with practice in this chapter, within the context of South Australia.

References

Albino, V, Petruzzelli, AM, & Rotolo, D. (2009). Measuring patent value: An empirical analysis of the US biotech industry. Retrieved from http://papers.ssrn.com/sol3/papers.cfm?abstract_id=1400688.

Asheim, BT. (1998). Territoriality and economics: On the substantial contribution of economic geography. In O Jonsson & L-O Olander (Eds.), *Economic Geography in Transition, 74* (pp. 98-109). Lund: The Swedish Geographical Yearbook.

Asheim BT, & Coenen, L. (2005). Knowledge bases and regional innovation systems: Comparing Nordic clusters. *Research Policy, 34*(8), 1173-90.

Asheim, BT, & Gertler, M. (2005). The geography of innovation. In J Fagerberg, DC Mowery, & RR Nelson (Eds.), *The Oxford handbook of innovation* (pp. 291-7). Oxford: Oxford University Press.

Asheim, BT, & Isaksen, A. (1997). Location, agglomeration and innovation: Toward regional innovation systems in Norway? *European Planning Studies, 5*(3), 299-330.

Australian Law Reform Commission. (2004). Domestic legal framework: Types of patents. In ALRC, *Genes and Ingenuity: Gene patenting and human health (ALRC Report 99)*. Retrieved from http://www.alrc.gov.au/publications/5-domestic-legal-framework/types-patents.

Barnett, HG. (1953). *Innovation — The basis of cultural change*. New York: McGraw-Hill.

Bessen, J, & Thoma, G. (2012). Which Patent Systems are better for Inventors? (Preliminary version). Retrieved from http://vhost4.bc.edu/content/dam/files/schools/law/doc/patconpapers/Bessen%20Paper.pdf.

Chung, S. (2002). Building a national innovation system through regional innovation systems. *Technovation, 22*(8), 485-91.

Cooke, P. (2001). Regional Innovation Systems, clusters and the knowledge economy. *ICC 10*(4), 945-74. doi: 10.1093/icc/10.4.945.

Cooke, P. (2004). Regional innovation systems: An evolutionary approach. In P Cooke, M Heidenreich, & H-J Braczyk (Eds.), *Regional innovation systems: The role of governance in a globalized world* (pp. 1-18). London: UCL Press.

Cooke, P, Heidenrich, M, & Braczyk, H-J. (Eds.) (2004). *Regional innovation systems* (2nd ed.). London: Routledge.

Czarnitzki, D, Hussinger, K, & Leten, B. (2010). The market value of blocking patents. Retrieved from http://papers.ssrn.com/sol3/papers.cfm?abstract_id=1803315.

Damanpour, F. (1991). Organizational innovation: A meta-analysis of effects of determinants and moderators. *The Academy of Management Journal, 34*(3), 555-90.

Doepfer, BC. (2012). *Co-Innovation competence: A strategic approach to entrepreneurship in regional innovation structures.* Wiesbaden, Germany: Springer Gabler.

Doloreux, D, & Parto, S. (2005). Regional innovation systems: Current discourse and unresolved issues. *Technology in Society, 27*(2), 133-53.

Dutta, S, & Benavente, D. (2011). Measuring innovation potential and results: The best performing economies. In *The Global Innovation Index, accelerating growth and development* (pp. 3-56). Fontainebleau, France: INSEAD.

Eckert, A, & Langinier, C. (2013). A survey of the economics of patent systems and procedures. *Journal of Economic Surveys, 28*(5), 996-1015. doi: 10.1111/joes.12034, http://onlinelibrary.wiley.com/doi/10.1111/joes.12034/full.

Egan, EJ. (2012). The economics of patent citations: Startup commercialization strategy, value, and success. Retrieved from http://www.edegan.com/wiki/images/0/02/Egan_%282012%29_-_The_Economics_of_Patent_Citations_%28Jan_31st%29.pdf.

Freeman, C. (1987). *Technology policy and economic performance: Lessons from Japan.* London, New York: Pinter.

Gambardella, A, Harhoff, D, & Verspagen, B. (2006). The value of patents. Retrieved from http://www.ffii.se/erik/EPIP2006/Alfonso%20Gambardella_Value%20of%20Patents.pdf.

Hagedoorn, J, & Cloodt, M. (2003). Measuring innovative performance: Is there an advantage in using multiple indicators? *Research Policy, 32*(8), 1365-79.

Hagelin, T. (2004, Spring). Valuation of patent licenses. *Texas Intellectual Property Law Journal, 12*(3), 425-8.

Hall, HH. (2009, 10 June). *The use and value of IP Rights*. (Paper presented at the UK IP Ministerial Forum on the Economic Value of Intellectual Property, London, UK).

Hausmann, R, Hidalgo, C, Bustos, S, Coscia, M, Chung, S, Jimenez, J, Simoes, A, & Yildirim, M. (2011). *The atlas of economic complexity — Mapping paths to prosperity*. Boston: Harvard MIT. Retrieved from: http://chidalgo.com/Atlas/HarvardMIT_AtlasOfEconomicComplexity_Part_I.pdf.

Iammarino, S. (2005). An evolutionary integrated view of regional systems of innovation: Concepts, measures and historical perspectives. *European Planning Studies, 13*(4), 497-519.

Kline, S, & Rosenberg, N. (Eds.) (1986). An overview of innovation. In R Landau & N Rosenbert (Eds.), *The positive sum strategy: Harnessing technology for economic growth* (pp. 275-304). Washington, DC: National Academy Press.

Laitner, J, & Stolyarov, D. (2009, April 3). Derivative ideas and the value of intangible assets. *International Economic Review, 54*(1), 59-95.

Leydesdorff, L, & Strand, O. (2013, September). The Swedish system of innovation: Regional synergies in a knowledge-based economy. *Journal of the American Society for Information Science and Technology, 64*(9), 1890-902.

Lundvall, B-A. (Ed.) (1992). *National systems of innovation: Towards a theory of innovation and interactive learning*. London: Pinter.

McAleer, M, & Slottje, D. (2005). A new measure of innovation: The patent success ratio. *Scienometrics, 63*(3), 421-9.

McCann, P, & Ortega-Argiles, R. (2013). Modern regional innovation policy. *Cambridge Journal of Regions, Economy and Society, 6*(2), 187-261.

Malerba, F. (2002). Sectoral systems of innovation and production. *Research Policy, 31*(2), 247-64.

Malerba, F. (2005). Sectoral Systems of Innovation — A framework for linking innovation to the knowledge base, structure and dynamics of sectors. *Economics of Innovation & New Technology, 14*(1-2), 63-82.

Malerba, F. (Ed.) (2004). *Sectoral Systems of Innovation*. Cambridge: Cambridge University Press.

Martin, R, & Trippl, M. (2013). *System failures, knowledge bases and regional innovation policies.* (Paper no. 2013/13, Lund: Centre for Innovation, Research and Competence in the Learning Economy).

Martinez, C. (2010). *Insight into different types of patent families.* (STI Working paper 2010/2, Madrid: OECD Science).

Moore, WL, & Tushman, ML. (Eds.) (1982). Managing innovation over the product life cycle. In ML Tushman & WL Moore (Eds.), *Readings in the management of innovation* (pp. 131-50). Boston: Ballinger.

Niosi, J. (2011). Building innovation systems: An introduction to the special edition. *Industrial and Corporate Change, 20*(6), 1637-43.

Porter, ME. (2000). Locations, clusters and company strategy. In GL Clark, MP Feldman, & MS Gertler (Eds.), *The Oxford handbook of economic geography* (pp. 253-74). Oxford: Oxford University Press.

Rickards, T. (1985). *Stimulating innovation: A system approach.* London: Pinter.

Roberts, EB. (Ed.) (1987). Introduction: Managing technological innovation. In EB Roberts (Ed.), *Generating technological innovation* (pp. 3-21). New York: Oxford University Press.

Rogers, EM. (1983). *Diffusion of innovations.* New York: Free Press.

Rogers, M. (1998, May). *The definition and measurement of innovation.* (Working Paper No. 10/98, Melbourne: Melbourne Institute of Applied Economic and Social Research).

Roos, G, Fernström, L, & Gupta, O. (2005, November). *National innovation systems: Finland, Sweden & Australia compared, Learnings for Australia.* (Report prepared for the Australian Business Foundation, Sydney).

Saxenian, A. (2000). *Regional advantage: Culture and competition in Silicon Valley and Route 128.* Cambridge, MA: First Harvard University Press.

Schartinger, D, Schibany, A, & Gassler, H. (2001). Interactive relations between universities and firms: Empirical evidence for Austria. *Journal of Technology Transfer, 26*(3), 255-68.

Singla, A. (2012). Valuation of intellectual property. Retrieved from http://bus6900. alliant.wikispaces.net/file/view/article233.pdf.

Thomson Reuters. (2012, August). *Analysis of South Australian IP.* (Report prepared for Department for Manufacturing, Innovation, Trade, Resources and Energy, Government of South Australia).

US Patent and Trademark Office. Glossary. Retrieved from http://www.uspto.gov/main/glossary.

Varga, A. (2000). Local academic knowledge transfers and the concentration of economic activity. *Journal of Regional Science, 40*(2), 289-309.

Varga, A, Jarosi, P, & Sebestyen, T. (2011). Modelling the growth effects of regional knowledge production: The GMR-Europe model and its applications for EU Framework Program policy impact simulations. Retrieved from http://www.ekf.vsb.cz/projekty/cs/okruhy/weby/esf-0116/databaze-prispevku/clanky_ERSA_2011/ERSA2011_paper_01426.pdf.

Zaltman, G, Duncan, R, & Holbeck, J. (1984). *Innovations and organizations.* Malabar: Krieger.

Innovation system symbiosis:

4

The impact of virtual entrepreneurial teams on integrated innovation and regional innovation systems

Gavin Artz, University of South Australia

Introduction

When considering research and public policy on the topic of innovation, there is a tendency to focus on medium and large business, with limited consideration given to small and micro business (Thomas, Miller, & Murphy, 2011, p. 6). In part, this is a hangover from the era of twentieth-century mass production and the massive scale required to be competitive at an industrial level. The capacity for the amateur inventor or 'gentleman scientist' to have a significant technological, scientific or commercial impact seemed to have been lost over this period. However, cracks began to show in this paradigm late in the twentieth century.

Moore's Law arose from, and helped to drive, the micro processor innovations of the late twentieth century by explaining that computer power doubles every eighteen months and is mirrored by declining cost for that computing power (Mack, 2011). The inevitable outcome has been the lowering of barriers to digital access and the expansion of the pool of people who can participate in innovation on an industrial scale. Notably, this has opened up opportunities for technological innovation and the businesses based on these innovations to start from more humble beginnings —

Hewlett Packard and Google from a shed and, more recently, Facebook from a dorm room. This evolution has increased over the first decade of the twenty-first century to a point where 'the need for corporate innovation has never been greater [but where] incumbents are outmaneuvered by new insurgents' (Engel, 2011, p. 42). This sets the stage for some of the most disruptive innovations to come from amateurs, enthusiasts and tinkerers.

Business models like crowdsourcing and crowdfunding highlight how, in the digital realm, both the software and, progressively, the hardware are being developed by people who would traditionally be considered consumers. A business like Kickstarter demonstrates this changing paradigm. Through the provision of the right tools, Kickstarter proves that a community can generate ideas, make choices of resource allocation and bring a product to market — with the added benefit of being certain that a market exists (Gobble, 2012). This approach is possible because affordable and extensive access to communication channels, cheap computing power and shared knowledge have combined to enable a culture of collaboration (Hippel, 2005; Muhdi & Boutellier, 2011).

This technological and cultural change has implications for how we comprehend innovation integration and what a regional innovation system may encompass. The networked nature of open innovation, the capacity for small and micro business to be a sustainable competitor to medium and large business, and the growth of innovation outside of institutions and traditional industrial processes can provide a different lens through which to view innovation in South Australia [SA]. The experience of technology entrepreneurship in Adelaide (the capital city of SA) hints at a symbiosis between the evolution of a regional innovation system, the changes that such a system causes in managerial and cultural forms at the company level, and how these new, collaborative cultures and managerial approaches then feed back into the regional innovation system, linking it to national and international innovation networks. This chapter examines integrated innovation within a regional innovation system, using the case of the MEGA entrepreneurship education program (described in more detail below) and the working relationships between organisations and micro and small businesses that have grown around MEGA — specifically the digital media company *rezon8*. This examination looks at the formation of virtual entrepreneurial teams within social networks that are enabled by cross-institutional, as well as cross-organisational, collaborations. It also looks at how this can inform a view of a regional innovation system that promotes, and is in turn influenced by, integrated innovation at the company level.

The examination begins with a critical exploration of integrated innovation with reference to the models of innovation emerging from digital industries, and how this approach can be understood as a significant shift in the way that innovation is treated across all industries. The chapter then applies the implications of this to the concepts of regional innovation, and explores the case of MEGA to illustrate how, through this lens, a regional innovation system in SA may be examined with a greater relevance to local culture and aspirations.

Integrating innovation and open innovation

Traditional, closed innovation systems associated with large business are linear and siloed, tending toward a stage-gate approach to take a product from idea to market (Buffington, Amini, & Keskinturk, 2012). This view echoes the earlier research of Bernstein and Singh (2006), who argued that the traditional staged models found in the literature on innovation require a deeper consideration of the complexity of relationships across stages if success factors are to be truly evaluated. They highlighted that a standard, value-chain approach to innovation within organisations was not optimal and that the stages should not be seen as separate, siloed activities. Florén and Frishammar (2012) support this view, arguing that informal organisation, cross-functional reviews and more flexible screening processes, as well as greater internal and external collaboration, are needed if financially beneficial ideas are to be brought to market. This speaks to the complex social and knowledge-sharing factors that underlie innovation integration, even when considering closed innovation.

This complexity of integrated processes and social factors is mirrored in the more networked approach found in open innovation dialogues. Chesbrough's (2006) formative work on the conception of open innovation suggests that, particularly for digital- and technology-oriented business, a different conception of integrated innovation needs to be considered. Chesbrough argues that innovation must be more collaborative across businesses and that the innovators must also co-create with consumers. This is integration of innovation beyond the organisation — integration that starts to become inclusive of stakeholder networks to build diverse relationships that create value (Gould, 2012). In this type of environment, where businesses see themselves as a part of an ecosystem or network, open innovation's focus on collaboration becomes a framework that allows for successful innovation, while making the boundaries between the business and competitors more porous (Han, Oh, Im, Oh, Pinsonneault, & Chang, 2012).

While open innovation encompasses integrated innovation beyond the organisation, there is a further consideration to include in a discussion of contemporary integrated innovation. Toffler's (1980) phenomenon of the 'pro-sumer', a contraction of both the producer and consumer into the one entity, was an early harbinger of open innovation, but also suggests more than just customisation or shallow co-creation with the customer. In many ways the idea of the pro-sumer is a constrained version of Hippel's (2013) 'innovation communities'. Both concepts seek to define innovation collaborations that are inclusive of non-institutional and non-organisational based innovators. Hippel uses the terms 'open user innovation' (2013) or 'democratising innovation' (2005) to contextualise these widely distributed communities, which rely on open-source technologies, knowledge sharing and collaboration, into a broader innovation system.

When moving beyond the notion that only business or institutions innovate to one where they exist in a collaborative ecosystem of innovation communities, the questions about innovation integration become more complex and hint at more fundamental social/cultural aspects of innovation.

Integrating innovation beyond the organisation

Innovation is regularly presented as the route for developed economies to maintain a competitive advantage. Many countries have attempted to rise to this challenge by developing a creative economy through policies that link social and cultural activities with business and economic activities, thereby identifying the crucial role that creativity plays (UNCTAD, 2010, p. 27). Innovation can be seen as key to this challenge, because definitions of innovation share a common process of the application of creativity. This focus on intellectual capital is at the heart of any innovation system, but it also highlights a central dichotomy in integrating innovation at an organisational or regional level. There exists a dichotomy between developing new ideas and bringing those new ideas to market (Baer, 2012). This dichotomy is more complex than it may first seem, because it includes a dichotomy between the people and environments that encourage new ideas and the people and structures that are needed to bring a product to market (Baer, 2012). Like the concept of democratised innovation, the dichotomy between creativity and its application raises questions about the institutions and communities where innovation can come from.

West (2002) does not view tensions between these two aspects of innovation as having a significant impact on the capacity to bring ideas to market. However, as participatory expectations brought about by technological change increasingly have an impact on both society and business, these tensions will become more apparent (Busarovs, 2011; Poetz & Schreier, 2012). At the start of the twenty-first century, the OECD predicted that economic success will not be reliant on the uniformity of mass production, but on a need to 'break with the rigid and hierarchical methods of the past and embrace solutions based on greater personal accountability, internal motivation and uniqueness' (Michalski, Miller, & Stevens, 2000, p. 91). In making this prediction the OECD was highlighting how the conditions that encourage creativity will have a significant impact on successful economic activity. When we consider the most common applications of creativity in innovation, we see that creativity is typically imagined as being applied to resolve known problems, based on the current usage of a product by customers (Verganti, 2011). This has the side-effect (p. 386) of often limiting innovation to 'incremental' improvements which focus on resolving known problems for the most profitable customers (Christensen & Raynor, 2004).

Angel (2006) points out that this focus on incremental innovation has led to a phenomenon more akin to productivity improvement rather than innovation, thus diminishing the transformative capacity of innovation in economies. Verganti (2009) explores this transformative capacity through cases of groundbreaking innovation, and has subsequently found that they rely on 'radical innovation of meaning' (2011). This innovation is not based on resolving known problems for customers (incremental innovations) but on radically finding unknown problems of meaning. The groundbreaking nature of disruptive innovation would suggest that it requires an acceptance of a different quality of creativity in innovation processes. In recasting the components of an innovation system, it is perhaps beneficial to look beyond the types of creativity allowed in business to find a more culturally rooted concept of creativity.

Aligning creativity with a deeper cultural and human meaning within a capitalist dialogue of 'creative industries' challenges what type of creativity is appropriate to a richer innovation ecosystem. Deleuze (1990 [1995]) developed the contemporary philosophical grounding for this challenge by characterising creativity as being developed by the creator exploring and continually embellishing their work: a creator who 'creates their own impossibilities and thereby creates possibilities' (p. 133). In this description, Deleuze's creator seeks Verganti's radical innovation of meaning and it is the capacity of this type of creator to find new, unthought-of problems so as to create a new socio-cultural regime that sets disruptive innovation apart from incremental innovation (Verganti, 2011). Kozbelt, Begetto, and Runco argue that it is this very type of problem-finding that is crucial to the creative process, particularly in relation to finding previously unspecified problems (2010, p. 34). Yet innovation in a business context often confuses creativity with fashion, or with reproduction based on variation (Jeanes, 2006, p. 130). Business seeks novelty as outcome and this focus creates new variation, but it does not create new concepts that change the way we think. In Verganti's terminology, traditional views of creativity within innovation may produce product improvement but not new meaning, and it is this new meaning that leads to disruptive innovations. Perhaps it is the integration of broader social and cultural activity into an innovation system that allows for truly groundbreaking innovation to occur. This highlights that there is not necessarily a need to generate more creativity, but a need to find ways of better integrating creativity into innovation processes (Mueller, Melwani, & Goncalo, 2012).

This returns us to the dichotomy between the preferred environments for both creativity and the application of creativity. Entrepreneurial teams are inherently transdisciplinary in conception, and this framework provides an insight into ways of maintaining intrinsic motivation crucial for creativity, while benefiting from the extrinsic motivations that can be helpful in the application of creativity (Marion, Dunlap, & Friar, 2012). This capacity for maintaining intrinsic motivation for creative researchers can conceivably be enhanced by considering how virtual entrepreneurial teams work. Existing literature has characterised these virtual teams in relationship to their use of information and communication technology (Kimble, 2011; Sadri & Condia, 2012). However, as information and communication technology has become embedded in social and business communication, perhaps what is more appropriate, when considering how to manage the integration of social and cultural creativity into business and regional innovation systems, is the specific cultural shift of a 'cross-functional team that is pulled together for a specific purpose' (Johnson, Heimann, & O'Neill, 2001) or of teams 'distributed across geographical distance, time and organizational boundaries' (Au & Marks, 2012). In this way these virtual teams have much more the flavour of social networks where 'transactions are based on relationships, rather than on economic rationality' (Meyskens, Carsrud, & Cardozo, 2010, p. 434). In considering this way of working, we can imagine an innovation system that is capable of integrating a broad range of human activity, transforming it for both commercial and social benefit. This capacity to integrate a broad range of activity also opens opportunities for micro and small business to become more important in innovation systems, as the network requires non-redundant, heterogeneous connections to form the optimal mechanism for transforming social and cultural meaning into economic benefit (Kijkuit & Ende, 2007).

Innovation: Micro and small business

The OECD recognises that micro business and small to medium enterprises [SMEs] make up the majority of businesses and have been the 'major engine of growth in employment and output' (OECD, 2004, p. 17). The OECD defines micro business as having 2 to 9 employees and small business as having 10 to 49 employees. This international experience is mirrored in Australia, albeit at a slightly smaller scale, linking the local experience in SA to international norms. In Australia, the Australian Bureau of Statistics [ABS] defines a micro business as employing less than 5 staff (this includes non-employing businesses), and a small business as employing between 5 and 20 employees. In the private sector, 96 per cent of businesses fit these criteria (ABS, 2008). With regard to innovation in Australia, the ABS in 2010 reported that in the micro business category, only 35.7 per cent had any innovation activity, with small businesses having 54.7 per cent of business involved. This statistic is contrasted with 74.3 per cent of large businesses involved in any innovation activity, in a context where only 44 per cent of Australian businesses are involved in innovation activity (ABS, 2011).

The crucial economic role of micro and small business would seem to fall short when it comes to innovation, and deserves some further exploration. When considering technological innovation in micro and small business, collaborative environments are of particular benefit (Nieto & Santamaría, 2010). For small businesses to be successful innovators in the market, these collaborative environments need to exist at every stage of innovation development and require access to broader regional innovation networks, such as institutional research (Fukugawa, 2006; Varis & Littunen, 2012). The traditional focus of innovation on larger businesses and institutions would seem to be justified by the ABS figures cited above, but the low involvement in innovation by micro and small business may indicate that the specific collaborative and networked ecologies that benefit these businesses in an innovation context are being overlooked.

This becomes more apparent when reviewing the difficulties of developing and maintaining an innovation culture in large businesses and institutions. Marion, Dunlop, and Friar (2012) argue that large firms are being encouraged to become adaptable like small entrepreneurial businesses if they are to maintain the skills needed for innovation within a larger company. Their research concluded that

> [w]hile small firm practices often run counter to traditional product development practices of large firms, it is this difference that opens the doorway for novel opportunities. Small, new ventures are hungry, look for resources and need to successfully commercialize a new innovation or die trying. (p. 334)

As demonstrated by technology industries, there is often a need to acquire smaller technology companies that can focus on innovation if the levels of innovation required for competitiveness are to be maintained (Ferrary, 2003; Kleer & Wagner, 2013). This difficulty in innovating is also true of the academies dedicated to the creation of new knowledge. In Australia, researchers feel that there is a lack of resources available for research and development [R&D] and commercialisation, and that lack is leading to very uneven success rates (Harman, 2010). There are some powerful exceptions to this. For example, the experiments that Ford has developed which allow staff to 'tinker' (as Ford describes it) have raised patents by 30 per cent for the company (Flaherty, 2012). There is also the example of the global technology companies' long-awaited financial settlement with the CSIRO for the use of their wi-fi technology, which grew from cosmological research (Krishna, 2012). These exceptions, though, seem to be attempts to develop micro and small business outlooks in larger businesses and institutions based on harnessing the drive, vision and creativity of individuals. Once again these examples only serve to highlight the potential for innovations that come from the democratisation of innovation and a network of micro and small business working within a more traditional innovation system.

Regional innovation systems as value networks

Small business innovation is enhanced by peer-to-peer learning networks, with inexperienced actors benefiting from developing 'shared cognitive structures' (Bessant,

Alexander, Tskekouras, Rush, & Lamming, 2012, p. 1092). Small businesses are able to be competitive innovators by collaborating with each other in inter-organisational learning networks that develop co-innovations (Westerlund & Rajala, 2010). While regional innovation systems often reference the sharing of knowledge across a network, there remains a strong theme of mediation via institutions. This is often characterised as downward spillover from institutional research centres to the private sector, with the private sector's role being to maintain a readiness to absorb and bring to market this intellectual capital. A regional innovation system is a more complex network of actors, and an expectation that regional spillover effects will occur by perusing this top-down view does not make for a dynamic regional innovation system (Grigore, 2011).

If we step outside of these state and institutional perspectives to more open innovation or entrepreneurial perspectives, regional innovation systems may be seen as what Allee, Cooke, Harmaakorpi, Sotarauta, and Wallin (2010) call 'value networks'. These value networks are 'sets of roles and interactions creating specific business, economic or social outcomes through complex dynamic exchanges of tangible and intangible value' (p. 35). This is not so much a top-down flow of research and intellectual capital, but a complex network of government, business, academia, amateur and community actors that are equally involved in transacting tangible and intangible value across the network. This seems more aligned with Westerlund and Rajala's (2010) observations than with theory around regional or national innovation systems and is more sympathetic to concepts of open and democratic innovation. By making room for intangible value, the concept of value networks seems much closer to the spirit of regional innovation systems — that is, a complex cross-disciplinary network open to a community of innovators, including institutions, where public policy can be shaped by the network as much as it in turn shapes the network. This speaks of a more symbiotic relationship between the nodes of the network in any innovation system.

Case studies

The proceeding discussion sets the scene for an examination of a particular organisation, MEGA, as a key component of a regional innovation system that works with micro and small business. This capacity to work with micro and small business sits within a network of institutions and not-for-profits and opens up access to social, cultural and commercial potential that would normally not be integrated into an innovation process.

Methodology and method

Remenyi, Williams, Money, and Swartz (2009) argue that because business research deals with the human-created phenomenon of the organisation — which in turn is made up of individuals and their relationships to each other, to organisational systems and to other individuals external to the organisation — non-positivist approaches are better suited to exploring this more subjective landscape. In examining this more subjective landscape, Yin (2009) argues that the case study approach is useful when engaging in an in-depth examination of contemporary events, where the boundaries between the case and context are not clearly defined. Yin goes on to argue that the most important application of the case study methodology is to 'explain the presumed causal links in real-life interventions that are too complex' (p. 19) for other methods. The detail that a narrative can provide helps to build an explanation that can communicate to a broad audience the phenomenon that is being examined. Due to these considerations, this chapter takes a descriptive case study approach.

The two case studies in this chapter demonstrate the interconnectivity of the innovation system and the companies that it supports. The focus on MEGA and participant company *rezon8* allows an investigation into technology-based innovation in SA that is dependent on both micro business activity as well as what may be considered amateur technology invention and development, which has corollaries to concepts of open and democratised innovation. The method of research combined unstructured interviews with the key founders of both MEGA and *rezon8*, personal observation and reference to secondary data from reports published on a limited basis by MEGA, as well as information as presented on the websites of both MEGA and *rezon8*. Website information only describes, in their own words, how the businesses represented their activity to a broader public.

It should be noted that I have been a member of the MEGA working group since 2007 and have volunteered as a lecturer, mentor and practice pitch panel member. I have also been an advisory board member for *rezon8*. These experiences have allowed observation, but they also mean that I have been a factor in influencing the development of these organisations.

MEGA and a South Australian innovation system

Overview

MEGA commenced in 2005 in Adelaide (SA) and billed itself as a master-class entrepreneurship program. The focus of the master-class activity has always been digital industries, but it was initially intended to service the mobile phone industry through supporting businesses that developed embedded content for mobile phones. From 2009 the external environments saw a convergence of portable platforms for computing and led to a broader digital technology focus in the MEGA program.

Context

Creative business in SA

The constituents of MEGA are classified as part of the creative industries in SA. The Australian Research Council [ARC] research project 'Creative Economy: Investigating South Australia's Creative Industries' took place from 2003-06 and gives an insight into the industry that MEGA sought to service over this period. Documents that accompanied the presentation of preliminary findings of the ARC research (Innes, Anyanwu, Burgan, & Sorell, 2007), highlighted the fact that the percentage of the creative workforce in SA for 2006 sat at 4 per cent, which is 1 per cent below the national average. SA only accounted for 5 per cent of creative business activity in Australia as a whole. With few exceptions, these creative businesses can be classed as small businesses with an average of fourteen staff and with average sales of $550 000. As opposed to other states in Australia, SA creative businesses relied heavily on volunteerism and high levels of reinvestment back into the creative business to make it sustainable. This correlates with the reasons given for why a creative business was located in SA. Personal, family and quality-of-life factors were the most significant reasons for having a business in SA. With this underling rationale, it is not surprising to find that 58 per cent of employment within the industry is identified as self-employed.

This paints a picture of creative business in SA as characterised by small businesses that are driven by self-employed creative practitioners seeking modest incomes to support a career that they find intrinsically satisfying.

Early mobile industry

When MEGA initially started up, the smart phone revolution brought about by Apple's innovations, with its App Store, and Google, with its more open approach to operating systems, had yet to occur. Low-powered hardware and the multitude of configurations required across phone models and brands were a significant barrier to entry. This meant that there were few defined paths to market and — in the case of the game 'Coolest Girl in School', developed by SA business Champagne for the Ladies — led to only a few sales as the result of international media coverage. Those companies that carved a niche in this emerging industry had to continually adapt to the developing technology and business models evolving in the mobile, digital industry. This combination of niche technology skills and rapid change resulted in a mismatch between the skills possessed by students who were graduating from tertiary institutions and the needs of the industry.

Technology education in SA during the first decade of the twenty-first century

Case study participants reported that industries associated with digital media during the first decade of this century saw skills education become a significant issue in producing industry-ready graduates. The pace of change in the industry made it difficult for education providers to keep up. The time taken to develop and implement curriculum, and the time it took for a student to achieve a qualification, could mean that the skills taught were four years out of date by the time the student graduated. These difficulties in providing appropriate skills in an institutional education setting were exacerbated by a change in how businesses operated. Technology-oriented business were the first to feel the impact of broadband, social media and aggregated information on how information was shared within an industry and how relevant industry skills were developed. These industries have a propensity for sharing information amongst a community of practice. This results in a peer-to-peer sharing of experiences, tutorials and networks as a way of keeping the community abreast of trends and changes. This is not an education based on peer-reviewed texts or textbooks, but a community of practice creating the industry while learning about how it works — a situation that we are still living through today.

MEGA: Cross-disciplinary inclusiveness and collaboration

MEGA grew from early digital economy exploration by the Department of Further Education, Employment, Science and Technology [DFEEST]. DFEEST was, at the time of writing, a department within the SA Government, and MEGA developed out of a proposal for a 'Virtual Digital Media Centre' in the context of a government push toward a greater role for science and technology in the SA economy. The proposal relied on a multifaceted partnership between industry, government and tertiary education institutions. Ultimately this proposal was not successful, but it did indicate that there was willingness to collaborate across organisations and institutions to develop the industry.

Although MEGA came out of DFEEST, it was driven by individuals. In the wake of the failure of the proposal, Peta Pash, a Program Manager within the department, with industry partners

Che Metcalfe from Kukan Studio, Shane Bevin from Monkeystack, Paul Daley, who had been involved in the establishment of Mnet, and Professor Andy Koronios made a decision that the project should be pursued. It was this mutual recognition of skill-gaps by the industry and vocational education and training sector that led to the formation of MEGA.

Peta Pash ensured that MEGA was founded on partnerships and inclusiveness through taking on a supportive role — allowing industry to take the lead. This capacity to develop a platform for industry collaboration set the tone for MEGA, as explained in MEGA's 2010/2011 report:

> MEGA commenced in South Australia in 2005 as a way to build better collaboration between industry, education and government to build the size and capacity of the mobile content and application industry to take advantage of global markets. (Pash, 2011, p. 5)

In this sense MEGA is a key aspect of a collaborative regional innovation system focused on digital media.

This collaboration is crucial to how MEGA's education program is delivered. Key to this is integration with industry, allowing for peer-to-peer training within a framework that is accredited with TAFE, as well as the University of South Australia, the University of Adelaide and Flinders University. This collaboration is embedded over three levels:

1. *Working Group*: The working group is made up of industry representatives who volunteer their time to collaborate and support the planning, implementation and evaluation of the program. This group is made up of representatives from business, government and not-for-profits.

2. *Tutors*: Tutors are industry experts, including academic researchers, who volunteer their time to develop and

present workshops. In this way both theoretical and real-life experiences get presented to those undertaking MEGA. This peer education overcomes the problems raised earlier with regard to ensuring that contemporary industry knowledge is shared.

3. *Mentor*: Often one and the same person as the tutors, the mentors have six meetings (usually weekly) with participants to reinforce the workshop sessions and impart their real-world experience and knowledge. One of the most important roles of the mentors is to take curriculum information and embed it in the outlook of the participants, orienting them to the requirements of industry. A side-effect of the mentor process is that participants quickly move from students to peers in the industry they aspire to participate in.

Process

As the MEGA report states:

> MEGA takes place across a four month period taking participants through the process of market research, idea generation/ exploration/evaluation, feasibility testing against markets, return on investment, technology, developing a business plan and the pitch process. The program culminates in a pitch to a panel of national industry leaders at a high profile Pitch Event in front of a large audience of potential investors and stakeholders. (Pash, 2011, p. 7)

Workshops take place weekly, with mentors being introduced through this process. There are technology- and marketing-specific mentors available in the workshops and opportunities to have feedback from the broad array of mentors at designated times in the workshop series.

MEGA has a history of attracting participants with a broad range of backgrounds, from engineering, design, arts, health, digital media and film. On the whole, participants have little entrepreneurial experience, but there are exceptions to this. Feedback by participants highlights that broadening experience beyond their specific area of expertise to an understanding of general business processes is a significant benefit of MEGA.

While initially MEGA was intended for participants who wished to start their own fast growth businesses, it has been expanded to include product development, social innovations and entrapreneurship activity. *rezon8*'s experience, below, is an example of the experience of a company involved in the MEGA program.

rezon8

rezon8 — now sadly no longer in existence — was, at the time of writing this chapter, a digital media company based in Adelaide that was incorporated during participation in MEGA 2010. *rezon8* billed itself as specialising in the 'development and implementation of interactive and immersive digital solutions supported by cloud-based data analysis services for the advertising, urban planning, and art and entertainment industries' (*rezon8*, 2012). Before *rezon8* started as a company, the founders were a creative team made up of artist Jimmy McGilchrist and IT professional Darryn Van Someren. Together they created an interactive artwork entitled *Swarm*, displayed on the large public screen situated at Federation Square in Melbourne, Australia.

Swarm used cameras to place the public in the screen. This reality was then augmented by animated butterflies that were attracted to the participant's image and that interacted with the participant's movements. This interaction mainly consisted of a naturalistic behavior of the butterflies to avoid movement by the participant. To make the artwork possible, the founders had to develop proprietary software and configure existing hardware in a unique way to achieve the interaction.

The founders participated in MEGA to develop the skills needed to capitalise on the success of their artistic endeavors. As with many participants in MEGA who come from a creative background, the initial focus was on developing creative business opportunities. In *rezon8*'s case the initial focus was seeking opportunities in advertising and marketing to develop interactive creative content. Through the education program and exposure to technical, marketing and business mentors, there was an understanding that the unique intellectual property [IP] created not only had a creative (artistic) component but also a technology component. The Australian Network for Art and Technology [ANAT] had been a long-time sponsor of MEGA and provided me as a mentor for the *rezon8* team. Through the combination of the MEGA education program and the mentorship with partner ANAT, both the creative and commercial components were honed as viable intellectual property in the marketplace beyond the art world.

Another supporter in the MEGA network was local company Monkeystack. The founders of *rezon8* had been participating in a mentorship program hosted by Monkeystack. Monkeystack's Shane Bevin is a volunteer on the MEGA working group and made *rezon8* aware of the opportunity. Post MEGA, *rezon8* was able to relocate to the Moneystack offices. This symbiotic collaboration was important to the growth of the company, as Monkeystack operated within an existing network of media and advertising companies and, as a digital design and animation studio, also possessed skills and experience that complemented *rezon8*'s and filled gaps in the emerging business. Monkeystack were able to collaborate with *rezon8* to develop unique marketing content that led to projects such as *Curious Creatures*, which has found a market internationally as a part of open-air festivals. In 2012, *Curious Creatures* was also shortlisted for the Interactive Award (art category) at SXSW (the annual South by South West music, film and interactive conference and festival held in Austin, Texas), benefiting from collaboration with the art R&D program at Splendid and the Interarts Office at the Australia Council for the Arts.

The success of the artistic work allowed the continued development of interactive artwork to become an R&D component of the business. This market for R&D allows the creation of cutting-edge interactions for customers that welcome risk; this in turn allowed *rezon8* to push hardware and software and to drive product innovation. In the case of *Curious Creatures*, these creative consultancies were opportunities to explore what is possible with the technology under development by *rezon8* and to get instant feedback from a large audience of festival attendees.

While the creative development occurred in digital media and advertising, *rezon8* developed a hardware and software product called Interacta. Described by *rezon8*:

> Interacta uses real-time augmented reality software and hardware that can be easily combined with existing digital screen networks or installed separately as a complete unit … [Y]ou'll also be able to track the results thanks to our intelligent data collection software. It allows you to track who is actually watching your advertising and even how they are responding to it. Using facial recognition software, Interacta can even help determine reactions to your advertising message and what influences it might be having on your sales. (rezon8, 2012, n.p.)

This system is much more ambitious than supplying niche, customised advertising experiences. To make this possible *rezon8* developed an entrepreneurial team through equity offerings and a virtual entrepreneurial team through collaboration. Building this team enabled *rezon8* to fill skill-gaps as well as seek out mentors and advisory board members that could fill experience and knowledge-gaps.

MEGA continued to support and connect *rezon8* through an alumni of participants and mentors. Collaboration by MEGA alumni allows knowledge-sharing to continue across the network, enabling alumni companies and mentors to collaborate. In this way the MEGA alumni have been able to draw together as a virtual entrepreneurial team.

Conclusions

An examination of the path taken by the company *rezon8* through MEGA and the associations developed with mentors and other participating teams makes it apparent that cross-institutional frameworks, as well as cross-organisational networks, are important factors affecting how an individual company will view its intellectual capital and what approaches to innovation are available to it. The transdisciplinary environment created by MEGA allowed *rezon8* to call on expertise from a number of diverse fields. These collaborations have contextualised art creation as a profitable approach to R&D and have recognised the valuable intellectual capital in this practice and how it can be translated into other markets. This innovation has only been possible, though, because of the collaborative environment formed through the linking of like-minded organisations, companies and mentors by MEGA. This, in turn, flows into the collaborative culture that feeds virtual entrepreneurial capacity and enriches the regional innovation system. Not only does MEGA link academic, government and industry partners, but MEGA also connects these macro players to community participation, not-for-profits and emerging micro businesses to create a more inclusive regional innovation system.

The capacity of MEGA to act as a network hub allows an exchange of tangible and intangible value across the network. This gives the regional innovation system centered on MEGA the flavour of a value network. By seeing these regional innovation systems as a value network, it may be possible to open up innovation opportunities for micro and small business. Unlike situations that may be encountered in large organisations, the entrepreneurial start-up integrates innovation into its core reason for being. Traditional stage-gate and siloed approaches to managing innovation in large businesses is not evident in the micro and small business innovation that

MEGA supports, as demonstrated by rezon8. These businesses work in a space that feels more like disruptive and democratised innovation, where a creative community collaborates to quickly and cheaply bring ideas to market based on a deeper cultural and/or social meaning.

The case of MEGA demonstrates how transdisciplinary entrepreneurial team development, facilitated by state-government-sponsored training, has helped create an environment comprising micro and small companies. These companies are geographically close and similar in collaborative outlook, but are also linked into national and global networks. This has enabled these separate companies to collaborate and draw on skills and networks beyond those found within their own businesses, scale expertise and capacity to fulfill customer needs on a project-by-project basis, while still pursuing strategic goals. This virtual team approach has the capacity to strengthen regional, national and international networks that then affect the nature of the regional innovation system.

Future research recommendations

This case study has been purposefully narrative to describe the intent and aspirations of the participants. In this sense it has attempted to contextualise self-assessed roles of individuals and institutions within the broader environment and theoretical concepts. There are limitations to this narrative of relationships between micro and small business innovators and regional innovation systems. This description does not explore the important role of investors. To some extent this is due to the lack of connection to these aspects of the innovation system and the relative immaturity of technology start-up culture in SA. Having described the innovation system, a number of opportunities for further research arise.

Longitudinal research focusing on success factors for technology start-ups that have grown outside of academic research support and medium and large business, in relation to critical support from actors in the regional innovation system, would be valuable.

An exploration more firmly based in social network theory has potential to provide a more precise analysis of the regional innovation system in SA. A quantitative approach should be taken to assess this perception of the roles played against the reality of the interconnection. A social network analysis of the ecosystem may be useful in impartially codifying the relationships and roles across the network.

As the value of micro and small businesses is mostly tied up in intellectual capital, further research into investment in the innovation system would be valuable. This chapter has only partially touched on this key element, which could play a crucial role in the sustainability of the innovation system this chapter describes. The size and flexibility of these businesses, combined with ready access to international markets, could conceivably mean that international investment may cause businesses to move offshore, undermining the strength of the network that made these businesses possible in the first instance.

References

ABS. (2008). Counts of Australian Business Operators 2006-2007. Canberra, Australia: Australian Bureau of Statistics.

ABS. (2011). 8167.0 — Selected Characteristics of Australian Business, 2009-10 Retrieved 14 June 2012, from http://www.abs.gov.au/ausstats/abs@.nsf/Products/8167.0~2009-10~Main+Features~Business+Innovation?

Allee, V, Cooke, P, Harmaakorpi, V, Sotarauta, M, & Wallin, J. (2010). The Matrix — Post cluster innovation policy. In A Eriksson (Ed.), *VINNOVA Report VR 2010:10*. Sweden.

Angel, R. (2006). Putting an innovation culture into practice. *Ivey Business Journal, 70*(3), 1-5.

Au, Y, & Marks, A. (2012). 'Virtual teams are literally and metaphorically invisible': Forging identity in culturally diverse virtual teams. *Employee Relations, 34*(3), 271-87. doi: 10.1108/01425451211217707.

Baer, M. (2012). Putting creativity to work: The implementation of creative ideas in organisations. *Academy of Management Journal, 55*(5), 1102-19. doi: 10.5465/amj.2009.0470.

Bernstein, B, & Singh, PJ. (2006). An integrated innovation process model based on practices of Australian biotechnology firms. *Technovation, 26*, 561-72.

Bessant, J., Alexander, A., Tsekouras, G., Rush, H., & Lamming, R. (2012). Developing innovation capability through learning networks. *Journal of Economic Geography, 12*(5), 1087-112.

Buffington, J, Amini, M, & Keskinturk, T. (2012). Development of a product design and supply-chain fulfillment system for discontinuous innovation. *International Journal of Production Research, 50*(14), 3776-85. doi: 10.1080/00207543.2011.588269.

Busarovs, A. (2011). Crowdsourcing as user-driven innovation: New business philosophy's model. *Journal of Business Management, 4*, 53-60.

Chesbrough, HW. (2006). *Open innovation: The new imperative for creating and profiting from technology.* Boston: Harvard Business School Press.

Christensen, CM, & Raynor, ME. (2004). *The innovator's solution: Creating sustaining successful growth.* Boston: Harvard Business School Publishing.

Deleuze, G. (1995). *Negotiations 1972-1990.* (M Joughin, Trans.). New York: Columbia University Press. (Original work published in 1990).

Engel, JS. (2011). Accelerating corporate innovation: Lessons from the venture capital model. *Research Technology Management, 54*(3), 36-43. doi: 10.5437/08953608x5403007.

Ferrary, M. (2003). Managing the disruptive technologies life cycle by externalising the research: Social network and corporate venturing in the Silicon Valley. *International Journal of Technology Management, 25*(1, 2), 165.

Flaherty, J. (2012). Ford + TechShop: Getting employees to tinker. Retrieved from http://www.wired.com/design/2012/05/ford-techshop.

Florén, H, & Frishammar, J. (2012). From preliminary ideas to corroborated product definitions: Managing the front end of new product development. *California Management Review, 54*(4), 20-43. doi: 10.1525/cmr.2012.54.4.20.

Fukugawa, N. (2006). Determining factors in innovation of small firm networks: A case of cross industry groups in Japan. *Small Business Economics, 27*(2,3), 181-93. doi: 10.1007/s11187-006-0010-2.

Gobble, MAM. (2012). Everyone is a venture capitalist: The new age of crowdfunding. *Research Technology Management, 55*(4), 4-7.

Gould, RW. (2012). Open innovation and stakeholder engagement. *Journal of Technology Management & Innovation, 7*(3), 1-11.

Grigore, C. (2011). Regional innovation from a theoretical perspective. *Inovare Regionala-Notuni Teoretice, 13*(1), 251-4.

Han, K, Oh, W, Im, KS, Oh, H, Pinsonneault, A, & Chang, RM. (2012). Value cocreation and wealth spillover in open innovation alliances. *MIS Quarterly, 36*(1), 291-316.

Harman, G. (2010). Australian university research commercialisation: Perceptions of technology transfer specialists and science and technology academics. *Journal of Higher Education Policy & Management, 32*(1), 69-83. doi: 10.1080/13600800903440568.

Hippel, EV. (2005). *Democratizing innovation.* Cambridge, MA: MIT Press.

Hippel, EV. (2013). Open user innovation. In M Soegaard, & RF Dam (Eds.), *The encyclopedia of human-computer interaction* (2nd ed.). Aarhus, Denmark: The Interaction Design Foundation. Retrieved from http://www.interaction-design.org/encyclopedia/open_user_innovation.html.

Innes, M, Anyanwu, C, Burgan, B, & Sorell, M. (2007). *Creative economy: Investigating South Australia's creative industries.* (Unpublished paper from a forum presentation of preliminary findings, The University of Adelaide, South Australia).

Jeanes, EL. (2006). 'Resisting creativity, creating the new': A Deleuzian perspective on creativity. *Creativity & Innovation Management, 15*(2), 127-34. doi: 10.1111/j.1467-8691.2006.00379.x.

Johnson, P, Heimann, V, & O'Neill, K. (2001). The 'wonderland' of virtual teams. *Journal of Workplace Learning, 13*(1), 24-30.

Kijkuit, B, & van den Ende, J. (2007, September). The organizational life of an idea: Integrating social network, creativity and decision-making perspectives. *Journal of Management Studies, 44*(6), 864-82.

Kimble, C. (2011). Building effective virtual teams: How to overcome the problems of trust and identity in virtual teams. *Global Business & Organizational Excellence, 30*(2), 6-15. doi: 10.1002/joe.20364.

Kleer, R, & Wagner, M. (2013). Acquisition through innovation tournaments in high-tech industries: A comparative perspective. *Economics of Innovation & New Technology, 22*(1), 73-97. doi: 10.1080/10438599.2012.703487.

Kozbelt, A, Begetto, RA, & Runco, MA. (2010). Theories of creativity. In JC Kaufman & RJ Sternerg (Eds.), *The Cambridge handbook of creativity* (pp. 20-47). New York: Cambridge University Press.

Krishna, BM. (2012). Payoff from Wi-Fi patent swells to $829 million but, time is running out for CSIRO to cash in. Retrieved from http://anthillonline.com/payoff-from-wi-fi-patent-swells-to-829-million-but-time-is-running-out-for-csiro-to-cash-in.

Mack, CA. (2011). Fifty years of Moore's law. *IEEE Transactions on Semiconductor Manufacturing, 24*(2), 202-7. doi: 10.1109/tsm.2010.2096437.

Marion, T, Dunlap, D, & Friar, J. (2012). Instilling the entrepreneurial spirit in your R&D team: What large firms can learn from successful start-ups. *IEEE Transactions on Engineering Management, 59*(2), 323-37. doi: 10.1109/tem.2011.2147792.

Meyskens, M, Carsrud, AL, & Cardozo, RN. (2010). The symbiosis of entities in the social engagement network: The role of social ventures. *Entrepreneurship & Regional Development, 22*(5), 425-55. doi: 10.1080/08985620903168299.

Michalski, W, Miller, R, & Stevens, B. (2000). Towards the creative society: 21st century social dynamics. *Foresight, 2*(1), 85-94.

Mueller, JS., Melwani, S, & Goncalo, JA. (2012). The bias against creativity: Why people desire but reject creative ideas. *Psychological Science (Sage Publications Inc.), 23*(1), 13-17. doi: 10.1177/0956797611421018.

Muhdi, L, & Boutellier, R. (2011). Motivational factors affecting participation and contribution of members in two different Swiss innovation communities. *International Journal of Innovation Management, 15*(3), 543-62.

Nieto, MJ, & Santamaría, L. (2010). Technological collaboration: Bridging the innovation gap between small and large firms. *Journal of Small Business Management, 48*(1), 44-69. doi: 10.1111/j.1540-627X.2009.00286.x.

Organisation for Economic Co-operation and Development (OECD). (2004). *Effective policies for small business: A guide for the policy review process and strategic plans for micro, small and medium enterprise development.* Vienna: OECD.

Pash, P. (2011). *MEGA SA Final Report 2010/2011.* Adelaide: DFEEST.

Poetz, MK, & Schreier, M. (2012). The value of crowdsourcing: Can users really compete with professionals in generating new product ideas? *Journal of Product Innovation Management, 29*(2), 245-56. doi: 10.1111/j.1540-5885.2011.00893.x.

Remenyi, D, Williams, B, Money, A, & Swartz, E. (2009). *Doing research in business and management: An introduction to process and method*. London: SAGE Publications Ltd.

rezon8. (2012). *rezon8*. Retrieved from http://www.rezon8.com.au/. (Website and organisation at time of publication no longer in existence).

Sadri, G, & Condia, J. (2012). Managing the virtual world. *Industrial Management, 54*(1), 21-5.

Thomas, B, Miller, C, & Murphy, L. (2011). *Innovation and small business: Volume 1*. London: Ventus Publishing.

Toffler, A. (1980). *The Third Wave*. New York: William Morrow.

United Nations Conference on Trade and Development (UNCTAD). (2010). *Creative economy report 2010*. Retrieved from http://unctadxiii.org/en/SessionDocument/ditctab20103_en.pdf.

Varis, M, & Littunen, H. (2012). SMEs and their peripheral innovation environment: Reflections from a Finnish case. *European Planning Studies, 20*(4), 547-82. doi: 10.1080/09654313.2012.665034.

Verganti, R. (2009). *Design-driven innovation: Changing the rules for competition by radically innovating what things mean*. Boston: Harvard Business School Publishing Corp.

Verganti, R. (2011). Radical design and technology epiphanies: A new focus for research on design management. *Journal of Product Innovation Management, 28*(3), 384-8. doi: 10.1111/j.1540-5885.2011.00807.x.

West, MA. (2002). Sparkling fountains or stagnant ponds: An integrative model of creativity and innovation implementation in work groups. *Applied Psychology: An International Review, 51*(3), 355-87.

Westerlund, M, & Rajala, R. (2010). Learning and innovation in inter-organizational network collaboration. *Journal of Business & Industrial Marketing, 25*(6), 435-42. doi: 10.1108/08858621011066026.

Yin, RK. (2009). *Case study research: Design and method* (4th ed.). Thousand Oaks, CA: SAGE Inc.

Part 2

Firm-level perspectives

Do clusters matter to the entrepreneurial process?

Deriving a conceptual model from the case study of Yalumba

5

Huanmei Li, The University of Adelaide
Allan O'Connor, The University of Adelaide

Introduction

Industrial clusters are geographic concentrations of interconnected companies and institutions in a particular field (Porter, 1990). In recent decades, researchers have paid much attention to the important role played by industrial clusters in inspiring regional entrepreneurship, economic competitiveness and productivity. In the field of entrepreneurship research, sources of opportunity and the entrepreneurial behaviours to exploit these opportunities are considered as two main research areas (Shane & Venkataraman, 2000). Judging from the success of some industrial clusters in various parts of the world and existing research outcomes, industrial clusters and entrepreneurship are closely related phenomena (Rutherford & Holmes, 2007; Wennberg & Lindqvist, 2010). However, most of the research on the impacts of industrial clusters on entrepreneurship focuses on innovation, firm creation or firm growth effects of clusters at the regional level. Limited research has been found in the literature to explore the interaction between industrial clusters and entrepreneurial processes systematically at the firm level.

This chapter attempts to address the above research limitation by deriving a conceptual model articulating the integrated components of industrial clusters, entrepreneurial behaviours in established firms and types of entrepreneurial opportunities. In doing so, we illustrate two fundamental entrepreneurship research questions. What are the sources of entrepreneurial opportunities in clusters? And what are the entrepreneurial behaviours that established firms use to exploit the entrepreneurial opportunities? To respond to these questions we conduct a review of the literature and test it against a case study.

There are six sections in this chapter. In the following section we analyse eight components of industrial clusters. In the section after that we discuss the entrepreneurial process: entrepreneurial opportunities and entrepreneurial management behaviours of established firms. In the next section we present a conceptual model of the entrepreneurial process within industrial clusters and provide propositions about their dynamic interactions. On this basis, in the next section, we conduct an analysis on the case study of Yalumba in the Barossa wine region of South Australia which shows that the entrepreneurial process is active and evident in clusters and that the research in this area is worthwhile. We discuss research limitations and future research directions in the final two sections of the chapter.

Identifying eight components of industrial clusters at the firm level

Industrial clusters are viewed as regional innovative systems, market organisations (Maskell & Lorenzen, 2004), social market constructions (Bagnasco, 1999), contexts of territorial production (Ratti, Bramanti, & Gordon, 1997) and socio-economic environments that support vibrant innovative and transactional activities. The research on industrial clusters has yielded a long list of factors that contribute to the competitiveness of firms within clusters (Aleksandar, Koh, & Leslie, 2007) and to regional economic growth (Cooke, 2001). These key factors include geographic agglomeration (Porter, 1996), economies of scale and scope (Gordon & McCann, 2000), knowledge spillover (Iammarino & McCann, 2006), shared resources (Molina-Morales & Martínez-Fernández, 2008), networking between clustered firms (Karlsson, Johansson, & Stough, 2005), and interaction between firms and supporting organisations (Romero-Martínez & Montoro-Sánchez, 2008). Besides this, industrial clusters involve a sense of belonging, co-operation culture, transportation and transaction cost savings (McCann, Arita, & Gordon, 2002). These factors also include affluent social and venture capital (Cooke, Clifton, & Oleaga, 2005), skilled/semi-skilled labour pools, abundant opportunities, advanced technologies, innovative environment, localised and specialised suppliers and buyers (Porter, 1998), increased legitimacy (Klyver, Hindle, & Meyer, 2008), regional identity, decreased 'newness' and the proliferation of entrepreneurial examples (Romero-Martínez & Montoro-Sánchez, 2008).

Though there is much literature describing various factors, especially on a theoretical level contributing to cluster advantages, the existing literature shows inconsistent research results. This is due to the following reasons: firstly, there is no consistent view about what we mean when we talk about industrial clusters and hence conflicting results from cluster research can occur depending upon the perspective taken — for instance, a pure agglomeration or a complex system perspective. Secondly, the empirical research examines the advantages that clusters bring mostly from a pure agglomeration perspective (Folta, Cooper, & Baik, 2006). The arguments supporting cluster development from this research perspective are often criticised for imitation and homogeneous behaviours (Rocha, 2002) and for mimetic isomorphism (Pouder & St John, 1996) as it occurs in clusters, particularly from a life cycle viewpoint of clusters. Thirdly and most importantly, the analysis of clusters at the firm level lacks an integrating theoretical framework exploring the principal components of clusters to set up a general analysis framework. Given the above research limitations and needs, we attempt, from a review of the literature, to develop an integrating framework of industrial clusters. This framework could help cluster researchers identify and recognise the principal factors as well as the relationships among them to advance the quality of further conceptual and empirical research.

For decades, the advantages brought by geographic proximity — such as agglomeration economies (Marshall, 1890), transportation cost savings (Weber, 1909), external scale economies (Krugman, 1991) and local markets (Porter, 1990) — have been the centre of industrial cluster research. However, the knowledge spillover effects, learning effects, collective efficiency and embeddedness cannot be explained just by applying geographic proximity. Granovetter (1985) has pointed out that economic action is embedded in structures of social relations. In a case such as clusters, social relations become so prominent that it is impossible to ignore them. The classic approach to research on industrial clusters, especially in empirical research, is a focus on the regional or national level, without giving consideration to the micro dynamism of cluster firms. Therefore, this chapter points out the social relations of firms within clusters. Sternberg and Litzenberger (2004) identify three key factors of clusters: spatial concentration of firms, co-operation between firms and co-operation between firms and institutions. Other scholars also point out that clustered firms' external networks are crucial in overcoming cluster-specific generated weaknesses such as lock-in effects and path dependence. Therefore, based on the studies of the above scholars and other existing literature, this chapter identifies four key factors of clusters and their associated key effects.

The first key factor of industrial clusters is geographical proximity. Geographical concentration is the key element in defining a cluster and is mostly common among quantitative research on clusters (Baptista & Swann, 1998). Geographic proximity promises the sharing of infrastructure, social institutions, accessing of crucial resources and enjoyment of collective government promotion and programs for the region (McDonald, Tsagdis, & Huang, 2006). Moreover, geographical proximity facilitates the spread of tacit, codified knowledge (Cooke, 2007), offers innovative advantages (Jaffe, Trajtenberg, & Henderson, 1993), saves innovation costs (Cooke, 2007), builds trust relationships, and increases imitation innovations (Romero-Martínez & Montoro-Sánchez, 2008). Geographical proximity is the basic element defining clusters and the basis of other key factors of clusters. In the clusters literature, geographic proximity of firms is simply geographic agglomeration (Sternberg & Litzenberger, 2004), including Marshallian industrial districts and industrial complexes.

The second key factor is inter-firm networks. A prominent feature of geographical clusters is the extensive network of inter-firm linkages supporting knowledge trading and collaborative innovation (McEvily & Zaheer, 1999). Inter-firm networks refer to both formal, market-based transactions and informal, untraded relationships between firms located in the cluster (Storper, 1997). Inter-firm networks provide access to key resources, tacit knowledge and norms, standards or conventions of behaviours and advanced information and technology (Aldrich & Zimmer, 1986) to ensure business success (Dubini & Aldrich, 1991). Furthermore, inter-firm networks reduce environment uncertainty and ambiguity, stimulate initiatives and innovations (Julien, 2007) and contribute to the learning process and entrepreneurial process (Parker, 2010). Based on these characteristics and effects contributed by inter-firm networks, the region where clusters are located becomes a regional innovative network (Camagni, 1991).

The third key factor is institutional networks between clustered firms, research institutions, financial institutions, governments and other supporting agencies (Saxenian, 1996). Research has found that knowledge is not evenly diffused in the cluster but only flows to firms in certain network positions (Giuliani & Bell, 2005); and that firms especially in the position of a structure hole (as a bridging role between clustered firms and other supporting bodies) easily catch opportunities (Burt, 2000). The institutional network concept is also used to refer to social capital (Coleman, 1990) and institutional embeddedness (Van de Ven, 1993). After examination of the metropolitan high-tech cluster in Rome, Pirolo and Presutti (2007) argue that social capital within clusters ensures the acquisition of knowledge. Similarly, Gordon and McCann (2000, p. 720) argue that

> firms within the social network are willing to undertake risky co-operative and joint-ventures without fear of opportunism, willing to reorganise their relationship without fear of reprisals, and are willing to act as a group in support of common mutually beneficial goals.

In this context, all the clustered entities co-ordinate collectively to enhance a cluster's development and then help to build regional identity. Consequently, the cluster becomes an innovative system (Cooke, Gomez Uranga, & Etxebarria, 1997).

The fourth key factor is the external networks of clustered entities. External networks refer to the relationships between clustered bodies and the organisations located outside of the cluster. There are abundant studies that argue that as clusters evolve, the closeness of regional networks will ultimately become an obstacle to cluster development (DiMaggio & Powell, 1983; Menzel & Fornahl, 2007; Pouder & St John, 1996; Tushman & Romanelli, 1985). In contrast, external networks of clusters expose clustered firms to new ideas and visions (Parker, 2010), and stimulate cluster transformation (Tappi, 2005) and entrepreneurial activities (Rocha & Sternberg, 2005). Because of globalisation and the location of multinational corporation branches worldwide, the involvement of industrial clusters in global value chains is the precondition to ensure cluster upgrade and sustainable development. Furthermore, involvement in global value chains creates opportunities for clustered firms (Humphrey & Schmitz, 2002) in the forms of new information, technology

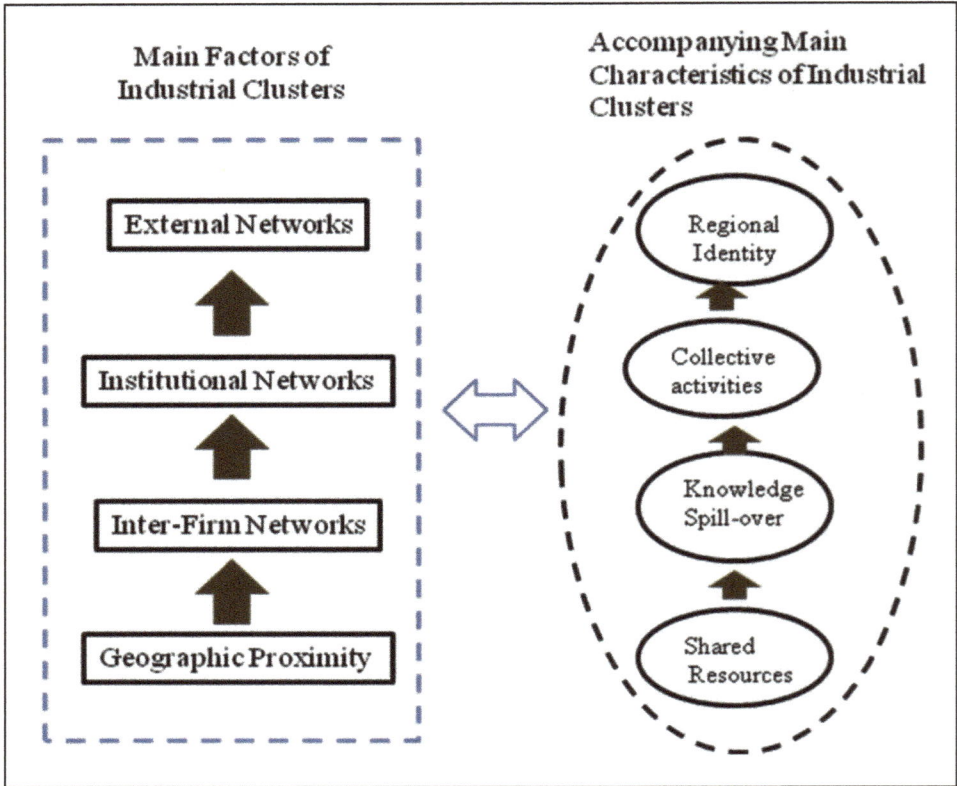

Figure 5.1: The eight components of which clusters are composed.
Source: Courtesy of the authors.

innovation, market expansion and so forth. Thus the networks of clusters are no longer contained within regional or clustered boundaries but are linked to global scope, referred to as an open innovation system (Cooke, 2005).

Prominent effects often accompany the above four key factors of industrial clusters, as shown in Figure 5.1. Firstly, shared public infrastructures and services are often viewed as a basic cluster element. Secondly, the inter-firm networks and institutional networks facilitate codified and tacit knowledge spillover among the clustered firms. Thirdly, the inter-firm and institutional networks promote collective activities and help clustered firms link to organisations outside of clusters. Finally, successful industrial clusters often have a common reputation among the clustered firms such that if one clustered organisation behaves badly or unethically, it will directly or indirectly ruin the reputation of other firms in the same cluster, and vice versa. The collective promotion activities help to build regional identity in domestic or international markets, saving market investment as well as management cost. The above four cluster factors interact with the accompanying characteristics to promote collectively the dynamism of industrial clusters.

An overview of the entrepreneurial process

The entrepreneurial process is the process through which managers employ entrepreneurial methods, practices and decision-making styles to behave entrepreneurially and seize entrepreneurial opportunities. Thus the key point here is how firms can behave entrepreneurially and what types of opportunities are entrepreneurial opportunities. Below, we clarify the dimensions of firm entrepreneurial behaviours and entrepreneurial opportunities.

Entrepreneurial management: A review of the concept and main concerns

Researchers and governments have actively sought entrepreneurship, carried on in the pursuit of business opportunities (Lumpkin & Dess, 1996), as one of the major engines for economic development, innovation, job creation, new start-ups and existing business growth. The research perspectives of entrepreneurship vary between individual, organisation and environment, and are accompanied by definitions of entrepreneurship including new material combinations (Schumpeter, 1934), new entry (Lumpkin & Dess, 1996), creation of organisations (Gartner, 1988) and the process of pursuing opportunities (Shane & Venkataraman, 2000; Stevenson & Jarillo, 1990). In the recent decade, the research focus of entrepreneurship has gradually shifted from psychological characteristics of self-employed individuals to firm-level entrepreneurial management/orientation.

Some useful work has been done to conceptualise and 'practitionalise' firm level entrepreneurship. Based on Miller's (1983) original work on firm-level entrepreneurship, Covin and Slevin (1989) developed a nine-item scale to measure the entrepreneurial posture of firms: innovation, proactiveness and risk-taking. Drawing from strategic management literature, Lumpkin and Dess (1996) proposed a framework of entrepreneurial orientation [EO] for investigating firm-level entrepreneurship: autonomy, innovativeness, risk-taking, proactiveness and competitive aggressiveness. Lumpkin and Dess's research of EO is analogous to Stevenson and Jarillo's (1990) concept of entrepreneurial management [EM], since both reflect the entrepreneurial process of firm.

Stevenson and Jarillo (1990a; 1986) differentiate the opportunity-based entrepreneurial management [EM] from traditional management, which reflects the pursuit of opportunity without regard to the resources currently controlled. The entrepreneurial management practices are reflected in the strategic orientation, resource orientation, management structure, reward philosophy, growth orientation and entrepreneurial culture of a firm (Brown, Davidsson, & Wiklund, 2001; Stevenson & Gumpert, 1985; Stevenson & Jarillo, 1990; Stevenson & Jarrillo-Mossi, 1986). The conceptualisation of opportunity-based EM is consistent with the contemporary opportunity-based definition of entrepreneurship (Eckhardt & Shane, 2003; Shane & Venkataraman, 2000; Venkataraman, 1997) and reflects classical entrepreneurship domains such as Kirzner's (1973) 'opportunity alertness'. After three decades of theoretical and empirical inquiry, EM is widely recognised as an efficient tool to evaluate or measure entrepreneurship in existing organisations and to further our understanding of the entrepreneurial behaviours pursued by existing organisations. Below we discuss six key attributes of EM.

Strategic orientation

Strategy creation is driven by perceived opportunities in the environment, not by the resources required to pursue these opportunities in entrepreneurial management practice. In opportunity-driven strategy, opportunities are the first consideration of managers. Once managers identify opportunities as real, they will marshall the required resources to exploit these opportunities. Almost any opportunity is relevant to the firm (Brown, Davidsson, & Wiklund, 2001) because managers are inclined to create a new business (organisation), instigate renewal or encourage innovation (Sharma & Chrisman, 1999). At the other extreme, the pure trustee's strategy is to utilise the resources controlled by the firm and make use of these resources efficiently. Managers will consider their resources before exploiting any opportunities. In other words, the firm exploits only opportunities requiring the resources under the firm's control.

Resource orientation

Stevenson (as cited in Brown, Davidsson, & Wiklund, 2001) has firstly described dimensions of commitment of resources and control of resources in resource orientation, and Brown, Davidsson, and Wiklund (2001) have then developed this. At one end of the resource commitment continuum, an entrepreneurial firm's resource orientation is to maximise value creation generated by exploiting opportunities while minimising the firm's resources committed. Under the situation of resource orientation, the acquisition and commitment of resources is done in a flexible and multi-step manner (McGrath, 1999), which allows the entrepreneurial firm to adopt new or improved strategies according to the opportunities status without necessarily owning the resources. To maintain this manner of committing resources may be difficult because of pressures created by the accumulation of resources within an organisation (Brown, Davidsson, & Wiklund, 2001), such as capital allocation systems, formal planning systems and certain incentive systems.

At the other end of this continuum are the firms that are considered less entrepreneurial because the commitment of resources is characterised by favouring ownership and control of resources and a thorough analysis in advance before mostly irreversible investments are made. An entrepreneurial firm reduces the resources it uses or owns as much as possible and favours resources (for example, financial capital, intellectual capital, skills and competencies) which are borrowed or rented from others. Such an entrepreneurial resources orientation provides flexibility, which allows SMEs to manage uncertainty by pursuing multiple opportunities (Bradley, Wiklund, & Shepherd, 2011). However, a firm's growth together with the accumulation of resources makes it increasingly difficult to adopt this kind of resource management behaviour.

Management structure

Burns and Stalker (1961) introduced the idea of an organic versus a mechanistic organisational structure. Organic firms are decentralised and informal, emphasising lateral interactions and an equal distribution of knowledge and information throughout the organisation (Lumpkin & Dess, 1996). Meanwhile, mechanistic firms are highly centralised and formal, with a clearly defined hierarchy, authority, responsibility and clearly defined systems to ensure efficiency. An organic organisational structure enables an entrepreneurial firm to manage its rented or borrowed resources flexibly when pursuing opportunities influenced by uncertain environments. Furthermore, to achieve growth from the addition of new products/services or new markets, organic firms are flexible and open to change (Stevenson & Gumpert, 1985).

Reward philosophy

The reward philosophy of an entrepreneurially managed firm reflects interest in creating and harvesting wealth (value) and thus is oriented toward compensations based on how individuals contribute to value creation in pursuing opportunities. The entrepreneurial management structure makes it possible to reward or evaluate employees based on their own individual performance and accountability. Under an entrepreneurial reward philosophy, employees are encouraged to explore potential opportunities, thus developing higher levels of commitment and trust within the firm (Bradley, Wiklund & Shepherd, 2011). In contrast, under a less entrepreneurial reward philosophy, rewards are based on the amount of resources under the individual's control, on hierarchy, and on seniority. Such a reward philosophy will undermine the pursuit of opportunities, since the individuals who control resources tend to limit the usage of these resources to pursue any opportunities under uncertainty.

Growth orientation

Managers in entrepreneurial firms prefer rapid growth to the steady growth that is often the choice of managers in a traditional administrative firm. An entrepreneurial firm is characterised as proactive and competitively aggressive (Covin & Slevin, 1991), utilising all kinds of opportunities and resources to achieve high growth. A traditional administrative firm, in contrast, focuses on resources under its control, tending to avoid rapid growth, which requires more and new resources. The reward philosophy in less entrepreneurial firms decides that it seeks a growth rate which does not jeopardise accumulated resources or create fluctuations in the management track record (Stevenson & Gumpert, 1985). In contrast, high growth often indicates high value creation, thus in entrepreneurially managed firms, managers are inclined to seek high growth rates.

Entrepreneurial culture

Entrepreneurial culture describes the culture of a firm that encourages a broad range of ideas, experimentation, and creativity. An entrepreneurially managed firm regards opportunity as the starting point to conduct business, whereas a traditional administrative firm takes resources under its control as the starting point. Therefore, a firm with an entrepreneurial culture is full of ideas, experimentation and creativity, while there can be a lack of ideas or ideas that just match the owned resources within traditional and more administratively focused firms. An entrepreneurial culture is beneficial to firm growth since growth can be generated from a broad range of opportunities. However, firms that lack an entrepreneurial culture typically generate sales from a more proven and narrow set of opportunities, and this is associated with slower growth rates than entrepreneurial firms (Covin, Green, & Slevin, 2006).

Entrepreneurial opportunity: A review of the concept and main concerns

The concept of opportunities has its roots in Austrian economics and the roles of entrepreneurs have been divided between arbitrageurs (Hayek, 1945; Kirzner, 1973) and innovators (Schumpeter, 1934). One of the fundamental questions of entrepreneurship research, raised by Shane and Venkataraman (2000), is why, when and how opportunities for the creation of goods and services come into existence. This question draws much research attention to the attributes, forms, origins and life cycles of the entrepreneurial opportunity. However, the research on entrepreneurial opportunity is in its infancy and has been characterised by scattered descriptions (Gaglio & Katz, 2001) from a variety of theoretical perspectives. Researchers have viewed an entrepreneurial opportunity as an idea (Davidsson, Hunter, & Klofsten, 2006), an entrepreneurial envisioning or a new means-ends framework (Sarason, Dean, & Dillard, 2006), a project (Casson & Wadeson, 2007) or more commonly as introducing novelty to the market at a profit (Alsos & Kaikkonen, 2004; Companys & McMullen, 2007; DeTienne & Chandler, 2007). The high fragmentation of entrepreneurial opportunity literature has presented a serious obstacle to its theory building.

Casson (1982) defines an entrepreneurial opportunity as a situation in which new goods, services, raw materials and organising methods can be introduced and sold at greater than their cost of production. Following on from Casson's definition,

Venkataraman (1997) defines an entrepreneurial opportunity as a set of ideas, beliefs and actions that enable the creation of future goods and services in the absence of a current market for them. In order to differentiate entrepreneurial opportunities and all other profit opportunities, Shane and Eckhardt (2003) define an entrepreneurial opportunity as a situation in which new goods, services, raw materials, markets and organising methods can be introduced through the formation of new means, ends or means-ends relationships.

However, Plummer, Haynie, and Godesiabois (2007) used the example of Dell Computer's origin to illustrate that even Shane and Eckhardt's (2003) new means-ends framework could confound the idea of an entrepreneurial opportunity, and they appealed for differentiation between objectively new and underexploited opportunities. From the aspect of underexploited opportunities, Singh (2001, p. 11) defined an entrepreneurial opportunity as 'a feasible, profit-seeking potential venture that provides an innovative new product or service to the market, improves on an existing product/service, or imitates a profitable product/service in a less-than-saturated market'. In response to Singh's comments on their definition of an entrepreneurial opportunity, Shane and Venkataraman (2001) rebutted Singh's definition of an entrepreneurial opportunity. According to Shane and Venkataraman (p. 15), firstly, an entrepreneurial opportunity does not have to be exploited by a new venture. It can be exploited by an existing organisation or it can be sold to other organisations or individuals. Secondly, entrepreneurial opportunities do not have to take the form of new products or services. They can also include new organising methods, new raw materials and new geographical markets. Thirdly, an entrepreneurial opportunity should include any market inefficiency due to information asymmetry.

Smith, Matthews, and Schenkel (2009), drawing upon the exchange between Singh and Shane and Venkataraman, define an entrepreneurial opportunity as 'a feasible profit-seeking situation to exploit a market inefficiency that provides an innovative, improved or imitated product, service, raw material, or organising method in a less-than-saturated market' (p. 41). This definition creates more confusion, however, by expanding the entrepreneurial opportunities domain and also blurring the differentiation between entrepreneurial opportunities and all other profit opportunities.

The above statements illustrate the complexity and challenge of establishing a consensus definition of an entrepreneurial opportunity. The basic precondition of an entrepreneurial opportunity is a profitable gap existing in the market (Casson, 1982; Singh, 2000; Smith, Matthews, & Schenkl, 2009), and the exploitation of the profitable gap is often accompanied by innovative application (Casson, 1982; Shane & Eckhardt, 2003; Singh, 2001), whether in products or process. A default position in entrepreneurship research is that entrepreneurial opportunities are not evident, but need entrepreneurial alertness (Gaglio & Katz, 2001; Kirzner, 1973) or entrepreneurial vision (Sadler-Smith, Hampson, Chaston, & Badger (2003). In addition, entrepreneurial opportunities should be feasible by taking legal actions (i.e. actions within the law), using achievable technologies and accessible materials. Besides this, entrepreneurial opportunities cannot be exploited by an existing means-ends framework (Shane & Eckhardt, 2003).

Following the extant works of previous theorists, we define an entrepreneurial opportunity in this research as a feasible profit-seeking situation that influences market balance by providing a new product/service, new raw material, new production methods and new distribution/marketing methods, and by entering new geographical or demographical markets.

The contribution of clustering to entrepreneurial dynamics

A review of the literature reveals that there exist only a few studies analysing the relationship between key components of an industrial cluster and the entrepreneurial behaviours happening in the cluster. However, in the past few years there is a growing tendency toward connecting entrepreneurship and industrial clusters. The majority of the research, on the one hand, oversimplifies entrepreneurship by adopting the number of businesses (Pickles & O'Farrell, 1987), new start-ups (Amit, Muller, & Cockburn, 1995; Giannetti & Simonov, 2004; Pickles & O'Farrell, 1987; Stuart & Sorenson, 2003) or the level of private sector economy (Acs & Armington, 2004) to measure entrepreneurship. On the other hand, most of the existing empirical research on clusters only examines the spatial concentration perspective without considering other crucial factors of clusters. As Romero-Martínez and Montoro-Sánchez (2008) argue, the research on the effects of the cluster key factors are not analysed explicitly or sufficiently.

The main body of existing literature examining cluster benefits on firms usually compares firms within clusters and outside of clusters. It is widely acknowledged that industrial clusters bring opportunities, which require that clustered firms be active, innovative and risk-taking to be able to recognise and exploit these opportunities. In this case, entrepreneurship becomes the essential element for a firm to be able to survive and grow in clusters. The existing research on the relationship between clusters and entrepreneurship mostly centres on the start-up effects of emerging or immature clusters. It is argued theoretically that as clusters mature, innovative inertia arises, where the imitation and homogeneous behaviours of managers (Rocha, 2002), the homogeneous macro culture (Pouder & St John, 1996) and the network closeness (Westlund & Bolton, 2003) will prohibit the development of established firms and the entry of new firms. This argument is inherent in the work of Pouder and St John (1996), who argue that in the convergence phase of industrial clusters, managers within geographic proximate regions are more likely to develop similar models of competition with managers in the same region than with managers outside the clustering region. They further argue that the cognitive homogeneity of managers in clustering regions will cause cognitive bias of competition, innovation inertia and dysfunctional macro culture. However, they do not mention the role of entrepreneurs in the clustering process.

In conclusion, most of the existing arguments regarding the relationship between industrial clusters and entrepreneurship are based on either theoretical assumptions or imprecise empirical analyses. To date, research on the impact that key cluster factors and characteristics have on the entrepreneurial behaviours of established firms, and the entrepreneurial opportunities of clustered regions, is rare. Moreover, research has not arrived at a consensus regarding the interaction between entrepreneurship and industrial clusters. More qualitative research is needed to design the framework for entrepreneurship that occurs in regions and its interactions with regional contexts. Quantitative research should be encouraged using first-hand data to understand the regional entrepreneurship phenomenon. This chapter responds to the research gap by outlining a conceptual model interpreting the relationship between industrial clusters and entrepreneurial process as illustrated in Figure 5.2.

The conceptual model illustrates the general framework of the impacts of key factors and main characteristics of industrial clusters on entrepreneurial behaviours and entrepreneurial opportunities. It also interprets the close relationship between industrial clusters and regional competitiveness, as well as the entrepreneurial process and performance.

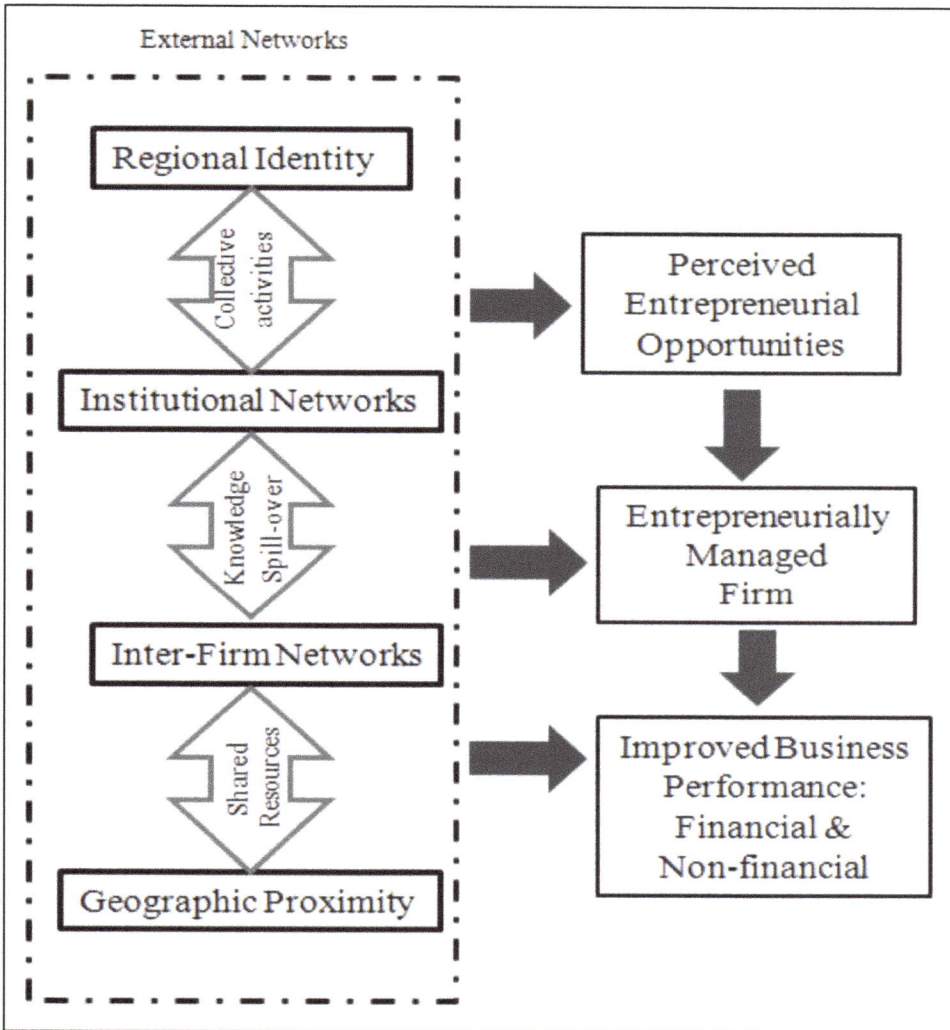

Figure 5.2: The dynamic mechanism between cluster involvement and entrepreneurial process.
Source: Courtesy of the authors.

Industrial clusters are regarded as network-based systems (James, 2005; Keui-Hsien, 2010). James (2005) regards geographical proximity as regional agglomeration, in which the clustered members can access the public infrastructures, services and information. Actors in network-based systems have greater access to each other to learn from and integrate each other's knowledge (Keui-Hsien, 2010), and this, in turn, enhances regional innovation and growth, often referred to as regional innovative networks. At the level of institutional networks, Cooke et al. (1997) link learning to a certain institutional network, and clustered firms can benefit from governmental collective promotions and programs, both of which create learning economies and finally a regional innovative network. The external networks of one cluster decreases the clustered blindness and exposes the cluster to new ideas and visions (Parker, 2010), which is of crucial importance to the cluster's transformation (Tappi, 2005) and upgrade.

Entrepreneurial behaviours and entrepreneurial opportunities are interdependent and interrelated. Entrepreneurial opportunities have been seen as objective, existing independently of entrepreneurial consciousness (Sarasvathy, Dew, Velamuri, & Venkataraman, 2005; Shane & Eckhardt, 2003; Smith, Matthews, & Schenkl, 2009), since they are characterised by generalisability, accuracy and timelessness (McMullen, Plummer, & Acs, 2007). However, there are counter-studies showing that entrepreneurial opportunities are subjective, influenced by an entrepreneur's personal interpretation of a certain situation (Sarason, Dean, & Dillard, 2006). From structuration theory, entrepreneurial opportunities are not an objective existence but are idiosyncratic to the entrepreneur, and entrepreneurs and opportunities are interdependent as a duality (Sarason, Dean, & Dillard, 2006). In this chapter, opportunities are themselves objective but shaped by subjective, idiosyncratic factors. These subjective and idiosyncratic factors condition the creation of new opportunities for the established firms and the firms' ability and willingness to pursue them (Buenstorf, 2007).

Identification of an entrepreneurial opportunity requires entrepreneurial alertness (Kirzner, 1973). Once an entrepreneurial opportunity has been found, the evaluation of whether one particular entrepreneurial opportunity is worth pursuing or not is related closely to a firm's experience and strategies as well as to its abilities. In the exploitation stage of entrepreneurial opportunity, different entrepreneurial opportunities require specific entrepreneurial behaviours to fully exploit them (Eckhardt & Shane, 2003). An entrepreneurial opportunity of new products/ services and new production methods should require entrepreneurial behaviours that emphasise innovativeness; an entrepreneurial opportunity of a new market entry and new distribution/marketing methods should require entrepreneurial behaviours that emphasise risk-taking and proactiveness. Individuals are more likely to identify an entrepreneurial opportunity, but the exploitation of an entrepreneurial opportunity is often through a firm, and thus the supporting context of firms is crucial in the exploitation stage.

Main propositions of the conceptual model

Industrial clusters and entrepreneurship are closely related phenomena; however, research on the entrepreneurial dynamic mechanism of industrial clusters is quite rare. In this section we present three propositions that extend from the conceptual framework. The majority of existing research connecting entrepreneurship and industrial clusters focuses on the start-up effects of industrial clusters or the effect of entrepreneurship to promote the formation of industrial clusters. This research addresses the research gap by constructing a conceptual model that links the different networks existing in an industrial cluster, as well as the accompanied characteristics of different networks, to the entrepreneurial process defined by the interaction between entrepreneurial behaviours and entrepreneurial opportunities.

The argument that entrepreneurship involves networking activity supports the claim that the entrepreneur is embedded in a social network that plays a critical role in the entrepreneurial process (Hoang & Antoncic, 2003). Some entrepreneurs choose to start their firms where their family members, relatives and friends have already had firms — in other words, where they have close ties (Klyver, Hindle, & Meyer, 2008). Network theory suggests that networks benefit entrepreneurs through providing them with access to knowledge, capital, information, advice and other exclusive resources. In addition, networks help entrepreneurs build reputation and social legitimacy (Klyver, Hindle, & Meyer, 2008). Social networks facilitate the access of information (Sorenson, 2003). In sum, these arguments ground Propositions 1a and 1b (below), which suggest a relationship between entrepreneurial opportunities and entrepreneurial management with respect to the depth of industrial cluster involvement by firms.

> Proposition 1a: A firm's depth of involvement in an industrial cluster is closely related to the number of entrepreneurial opportunities that are perceived by the firm.

> Proposition 1b: A firm's depth of involvement in an industrial cluster is closely related to its level of entrepreneurial management behaviours.

Both the geographical concentration of firms as well as the internal and external networks of clusters enable the sharing of resources and infrastructure, strengthen supply to local markets, facilitate information exchange, stimulate co-operation and build regional identity. Wixted (2009) argues that knowledge has a strong tendency to be localised within certain regions. Both codified and tacit knowledge is more easily shared and distributed among localised firms. One basic promise of clusters is to increase opportunities (Rosenfeld, 2003), since clusters are sites of localised positive externalities in labour market pooling, input-output linkages and knowledge spillover (Potter, 2009). Audretsch (1998) argues that innovative ideas based on tacit knowledge cannot be easily transferred across distance, which is why firms always choose to locate in close geographical proximity. Baptista and Swann (1999) believe that information exchange is the prominent feature of geographic concentration and is of foremost importance for technology innovation. Proposition 2 therefore addresses the issues of business performance in relation to industrial clusters.

Proposition 2: A firm's involvement in an industrial cluster and its business performance are closely related.

Opportunity exploitation requires innovation in resources and the combination of resources (Shane, 2012). Entrepreneurial management relates closely to opportunity identification and exploitation (Dimitratos, Voudouris, Plakoyiannaki, & Nakos, 2012; Runyan, Droge, & Swinney, 2008). Entrepreneurially managed firms are more innovative than traditionally managed firms and are more likely to seize entrepreneurial opportunities (Chaston & Scott, 2012). Entrepreneurially managed firms can take first-move advantage and control market entry, dominate distribution channels and set up industry standards (Wiklund, 2006). Entrepreneurially managed firms anticipate and act on future business situations (Venkatraman, 1989). Entrepreneurial behaviours of firms will shape and reshape the entrepreneurial opportunities to fit their pursuit framework, which in turn will affect firm performance. In this process, entrepreneurial behaviours also create certain entrepreneurial opportunities intentionally or inadvertently. Entrepreneurial management encourages an organisation's flexibility and enhances performance (Brown, Davidsson, & Wiklund, 2001; Hughes & Morgan, 2007; Stevenson & Jarillo, 1990). It facilitates knowledge transfer and sharing, helps generate new ideas and is beneficial to organisational culture (Lumpkin, Cogliser, & Schneider, 2009). Propositions 3a and 3b therefore address the issues of business performance in relation to entrepreneurial management.

Proposition 3a: A firm's entrepreneurial management practices and its business performance are closely related.

Proposition 3b: A firm's entrepreneurial management practices and the opportunities that can be perceived by the firm are closely related.

The case study of Yalumba

For many decades, South Australia has been the largest grape grower, wine producer and wine exporter of Australia. The wine industry is integral to the state's economy, society and identity. Wine exports are the third-largest export earner for the state (Chandler, 2010) and the wine industry contributes to employment in many other realms, such as manufacturing, research and tourism. There are seven wine zones and eighteen wine regions in South Australia. Fourteen national industry associations — including regulators, national supplier groups, export councils, federations and research bodies — are located in the South Australian wine cluster (Aylward, 2007). Furthermore, substantial education and training, research, funding and intermediary bodies and various wine industry associations are also located in South Australia. From the industrial cluster perspective, the South Australian wine industry has demonstrated strong cluster characteristics (Roberts & Enright, 2004) and the South Australian wine industry cluster epitomises the innovative model (Aylward, 2007).

Yalumba is Australia's oldest family-owned winery, located in Eden Valley, South Australia. Eden Valley is in the Barossa wine zone, which comprises Barossa Valley and Eden Valley. The foundation history of Yalumba is the story of risk-taking, proactiveness, innovation and alertness to opportunity. Yalumba was founded in 1849 by Samuel Smith, who initially brought thirty acres of vineyard with his first saving. The Yalumba of today is still an extremely progressive organisation, building its innovative reputation on ongoing winemaking and viticultural trials.

In order to improve the competitiveness of the wine industry, in 2009, The Government of South Australia and Adelaide Thinkers in Residence jointly published a report, 'Sustainable value chain analysis: A case study of South Australia wine' (Fearne et al., 2009). The report examined the Oxford Landing/Tesco [OLT] value chain as an example case study. Yalumba owns Oxford Landing Estate, which is based in South Australia. Tesco is the largest supermarket customer for Australian wine in the UK. Below, we test the propositions of our research against the published case to find evidence of whether the four factors (geographic proximity, inter-firm networks, institutional networks and external networks) and the four main characteristics (shared resources, knowledge spillover, collective activities and regional identity) of industrial clusters and the entrepreneurial process are closely related phenomena.

We coded and analysed the text in our report, 'Sustainable value chain analysis: A case study of South Australia wine', using a qualitative analysis software tool, NVivo 9.0. We used this because Computer-Aided Text Analysis [CATA] has higher reliability than human coding, as well as lower cost and greater speed (Neuendorf, 2002), and has been used by other scholars in entrepreneurial orientation analysis (Short, Broberg, Cogliser, & Brigham, 2010). Firstly, we analysed the text for word usage (Morris, 1994) by using the Word Frequency Query to enhance construct validity (Short, Ketchen, Shook, & Ireland, 2010). The result of the Word Frequency Query shows that the article content is closely relevant to the research topic of the chapter. Secondly, we coded the whole article under the interacting factors of the model in the chapter, such as knowledge spillover, institutional networks and entrepreneurial opportunity, to confirm that the key concepts proposed by the conceptual model could be identified within the text. Table 5.1 lists the coded findings. Thirdly, we ran a cluster analysis to check the similarity and relatedness of the concepts used in the chapter and codes, and to verify whether the propositions had validity for further study. The nodes coded show that the factors of the model we propose in this chapter, appearing in one specific region, are interdependent in creating value for consumers.

Table 5.1 demonstrates clearly that Yalumba exhibits industrial cluster involvement characteristics. Yalumba shows strong relationships with internal and external bodies, regional embeddedness and a common reputation with clustered members. The case shows that industrial cluster involvement enables Yalumba to access premium grapes, updated winemaking technology and information, and opportunities related to wine-marketing. Furthermore, industrial cluster involvement appears to continuously encourage the company's management practices to be more outgoing, sustainable and innovative.

The management practices of Yalumba — such as informal relationships, innovative company culture, cutting red tape and easy information exchange — are typical entrepreneurial behaviours (codes 3a to 3q), which may help build the opportunity alertness at Yalumba and facilitate the subsequent opportunity exploration. The entrepreneurial atmosphere of Yalumba creates an environment for the employees to work together to challenge the status quo, and it puts Yalumba in the leading position in innovation in the South Australian wine industrial cluster. The case supports this, as it reveals aspects of positive financial and non-financial performance (codes 2a and 2b).

Figure 5.3 shows that the connections among the concepts of industrial clusters, entrepreneurial behaviours, entrepreneurial opportunities and firm business performance proposed in the model are readily observed when running a word similarity cluster analysis with

Table 5.1 (overleaf): Industrial Cluster and Entrepreneurial Process.
Source: Fearne et al., 2009, page numbers in this table refer to the source document, *Sustainable value chain analysis: A case study of South Australia wine*.

Item ref.	Name	References (%)	Text Sample	Source Various
1	**Industrial cluster**	**99 (59%)**	**Including collective activities, shared resources, geographic proximity, institutional networks, regional identity, external networks, knowledge spill over, inter-firm networks**	
1a			There are also efforts made to educate growers through workshops, seminars and social activities organised.	Page 33
1b	Collective activities	4 (2%)	There are opportunities created for growers to get together and form collaborative relationships (e.g. annual barbeques, educational tours overseas and regular workshops and seminars).	Page 37
1c	Shared resources	2 (1%)	Yalumba, Amcor and Tarac Technologies are all partners in the 14th Adelaide Thinker in Residence program.	Page 18
1d	Geographic proximity	3 (2%)	Grape growers in the Riverland, South Australia. This region produces half of South Australia's grapes and a quarter of Australia's wine, the bulk of which is exported. There are over 1300 registered wine growers in the area.	Page 17
1e			The logistics management must also interface with the Australian Wine and Brandy Corporation (AWBC) to obtain, manage and report on export approval for wine batches.	Page 25
1f	Institutional networks	14 (8%)	This analysis suggests that government R&D funding may be required and justified to investigate how best to reduce the related emissions since there is no commercial driver for firms and chains to do so.	Page 28
1g	Regional identity	6 (4%)	UK consumers who purchase wine from a supermarket regard Australian wines as reliable ('it will never let you down'), good quality and good value. However, Australian wines are rarely on the radar screen when they are looking for something special.	Page 3

1h		The understanding of the customer (Tesco) needs and consumer wants (value) is distinctly limited upstream, particularly amongst input suppliers and growers.	Page 4
1j	25 (15%)	Tesco UK, is the world's fourth largest supermarket and responsible for 25% of all UK wine sales, making it the single largest overseas buyer of Australian wine and the largest customer for Oxford Landing.	Page 17
1k		There are also efforts made to educate growers through workshops, seminars and social activities organised.	Page 33
1m		There are some growers who collaborate but generally, the various groups of growers have more scope for interaction and information sharing.	Page 31
1n	Knowledge spill over 17 (10%)	Yalumba provides a lot of information and advice to their growers through grower liaison officers, winemakers, viticulturists and vineyard managers on maximising their opportunities and efficiencies	Page 33
1p		The relationships between Yalumba and the three divisions of Amcor are generally strong but there is scope to exploit the strong relationships to allow for more innovative designs and improvements to packaging to meet Tesco's needs.	Page 39
1q	Inter-firm networks 28 (17%)	Collotype produces all labels for the Oxford Landing wine. There is a strong two-way information flow between both organisations.	Page 31
1r		The information flow in the OLT value chain was assessed with respect to different functional activities (e.g. quality control, sales, and distribution) and at different levels (e.g. operational or strategic), with the aim of improving efficiency and effectiveness.	Page 34
2	**Business performance** 10 (6%)	**Including financial performance and non-financial performance**	**Various**

			Page
2a	Financial performance	2 (1%)	Yalumba is Australia's oldest family-owned winery and one of the country's largest exporters of wine.	Page 17
2b	Nonfinancial performance	8 (5%)	It was also highlighted that Yalumba has made extra efforts to support the community, local businesses and employ local people from the region.	Page 39
3	**Entrepreneurial behaviours**	**32 (19%)**	**Including strategic orientation, reward philosophy, resource orientation, management structure, growth orientation, entrepreneurial culture**	**Various**
3a	Strategic orientation		They have developed as a team, overcoming operational as well as strategic challenges together.	Page 42
3b		7 (4%)	Strategically develop an innovative value chain through focusing on the willingness to work with suppliers and customers for cooperative improvement.	Page 33
3c	Reward philosophy	1 (1%)	There are many long term employees at all levels, with most senior managers having had experience at operational level.	Page 37
3d	Resource orientation	3 (2%)	Strategically develop an innovative value chain through focusing on the willingness to work with suppliers and customers for co-operative improvement.	Page 42
3e			Yalumba adopts an informal management style, reflecting the personality of senior management and extent of synergies. They have developed as a team, overcoming operational as well as strategic challenges together.	Page 33
3f	Management structure	11 (7%)	It was highlighted that the personnel from Yalumba are flexible and willing to adjust their systems to suit their operations.	Page 39
3g			There were examples of Yalumba staff being commended for being highly approachable, 'natural innovators' and collaborative with a long-term vision and growth strategy.	Page 39

3h	Growth orientation	2(1%)	There were examples of Yalumba staff being commended for being highly approachable, 'natural innovators' and collaborative with a long-term vision and growth strategy.	Page 39
3j	Entrepreneurial culture	8(5%)	They have developed as a team, overcoming operational as well as strategic challenges together.	Page 33
3k			Senior managers are deemed approachable, involved and enthusiastic.	Page 37
3m		28(17%)	In-depth market intelligence (including consumer research) would enable Yalumba to break out of the commodity trap and more effectively reach the distinct market segments, targeting their differential preferences with specific attributes when feasible.	Page 43
3n	Entrepreneurial opportunity		The relationships between Yalumba and the three divisions of Amcor are generally strong but there is scope to exploit the strong relationships to allow for more innovative designs and improvements to packaging to meet Tesco's needs.	Page 39
3p	Product-market	20(12%)	The greatest opportunity for improvement lies in leveraging already strong relationships, to improve the flow of information (strategic and operational) and enable more effective forecasting of supply and demand.	Page 4
3q	Technology	8(5%)	… working closely with Yalumba on the design and production of lighter weight bottles.	Page 17

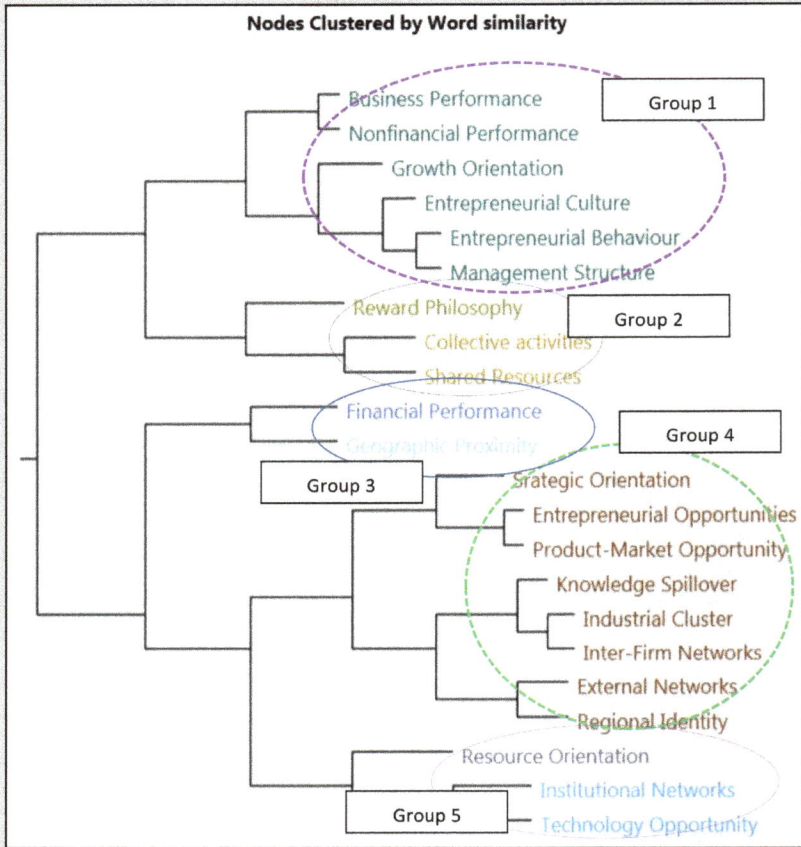

Figure 5.3: Nodes clustered by word similarity.
Source: Courtesy of the authors.

NVivo 9.0. Word similarity cluster analysis means that nodes that have a higher degree of similarity based on the occurrence and frequency of words are shown clustered together, indicating a higher level of relatedness. Sources or nodes that have a lower degree of similarity based on the occurrence and frequency of words are displayed further apart (NVivo9.0, 2012), suggesting low levels of relatedness.

Using this approach we can check the research propositions. In the first instance we can observe in Group 4 of Figure 5.3 that there are many indicators of depth of cluster involvement grouped in close proximity with entrepreneurial opportunities, particularly market-based opportunities. This supports our Proposition 1a, which suggests that a firm's depth of involvement in a cluster is closely related to the number of entrepreneurial opportunities. However, there are also some differences observed with Proposition 1b, which is not so well-supported, due to the distance between the concepts for depth of cluster involvement (Group 4) and those that indicate entrepreneurial management (Group 1). This suggests that the two concepts are more independent, suggesting that involvement in industrial clusters is not necessarily related to entrepreneurial management, and that entrepreneurial management may occur without the presence of an industrial cluster.

We also find that Proposition 2 proves to be unreliable, given that non-financial performance occupies the same grouping as entrepreneurial management and shows less relatedness to the cluster involvement concepts in Group 4. To further confound the propositions, it can be observed that financial performance (Group 3) raised in Proposition 3a, is in close proximity, although not grouped with key entrepreneurial management concepts (in Groups 1 and 2), while Proposition 3b reveals even less relatedness between entrepreneurial management and opportunities.

Discussion

Overall, our analysis reveals that the depth of industrial cluster involvement is closely related to market-based opportunities, and that these two factors may be difficult to distinguish, due to a close correlation. However, the relative failure of Propositions 1b, 2, 3a and 3b suggests that each of the pairs of concepts are likely to be distinguishable factors and therefore may be isolated independently from each other. The extent to which these combined factors leverage the dependent variables of financial and non-financial performance remains unclear, though — as does whether these performances can be improved with the coexistence of factors underpinned by involvement in an industrial cluster.

There are other observations that we may draw from this analysis. For example, geographic proximity is parallel with shared resources and collective activity. This suggests that institutional networks may not provide the necessary condition to generate collective activity as the model suggests but are mostly associated with shared resources and geographic proximity. Another difference worthy of further study is that firm business performance is closely associated with institutional networks.

A study of clusters cannot ignore its commodity/value chain analysis, especially when researching its dynamics (Schmitz, 1995). The case study based on the commodity/value chain of Yalumba illustrates that Yalumba is highly involved in its regional community based on demonstrated clustered development characteristics, while Yalumba's management and marketing practices also express entrepreneurial behaviours and entrepreneurial opportunities. A deeper analysis of the project supports the argument that industrial clusters and entrepreneurship, although independent, are potentially strongly connected phenomena, and research that seeks to further explain the interactive dynamics of the two is necessary.

Conclusion

This chapter identifies gaps regarding research on the relationship between industrial clusters and entrepreneurship. In contrast with prior research, this chapter firstly identifies eight components of industrial clusters, and then describes how the above factors and characteristics contribute to the entrepreneurial process within identified clusters. Rather than focusing on the promoting role of entrepreneurship on the formation of clusters or on the creation role of clusters on start-up enterprises, we focus on the effect of industrial clusters on the established firms located within them. We outline a conceptual model to investigate the interaction between clusters, entrepreneurial behaviours and entrepreneurial opportunities, and this model provides another perspective to address the dynamic mechanism of clusters.

In addition, this chapter provides new perspectives to investigate the complex phenomena of entrepreneurial behaviours and entrepreneurial opportunities. It defines entrepreneurial behaviours as those that are risk-taking, proactive and innovative behaviours aimed at discovering, evaluating, exploiting and creating entrepreneurial opportunities while also constructing a supportive context for entrepreneurial opportunities. This chapter defines an entrepreneurial opportunity as a feasible profit-seeking situation to influence market balance by providing a new product/ service, new raw material, new production methods, new distribution/marketing methods and new geographical markets. This chapter adds valuable arguments to the controversial entrepreneurship research regarding the nature of entrepreneurial opportunity and its relationship with entrepreneurial behaviour. It also suggests ways to measure entrepreneurial behaviours and entrepreneurial opportunities in order to add novel and valuable research outcomes in this area.

Results from descriptive analyses have shown that industrial clusters and entrepreneurial process are closely related phenomena. Given the influences of key factors and main characteristics of industrial clusters on entrepreneurship, we believe it is reasonable to suggest policy strategies to promote entrepreneurship through promoting the development of clusters, especially by stimulating the decisive elements of clusters. It is also reasonable for government strategies to provide more opportunities by stimulating entrepreneurial behaviours in the region.

However, the project also shows a lack of interaction with consumers, which may cause Yalumba to waste some of its investment and opportunity. Our research suggests that Yalumba should not only collaborate and interact with supporting bodies, but should also develop an interactive strategy with consumers both locally and internationally to better understand the markets and stay alert to consumer preferences in order to exploit opportunities.

Future research

It is widely believed that industrial clusters and entrepreneurship are beneficial to individual business performance, regional development and even national competitiveness. In this chapter we have sought to identify the key factors and characteristics of industrial clusters, and to ascertain whether a relationship with the entrepreneurial process could be substantiated. This chapter contributes to a greater understanding of the dynamic interaction between industrial clusters and entrepreneurship. However, more research, both qualitative and quantitative,

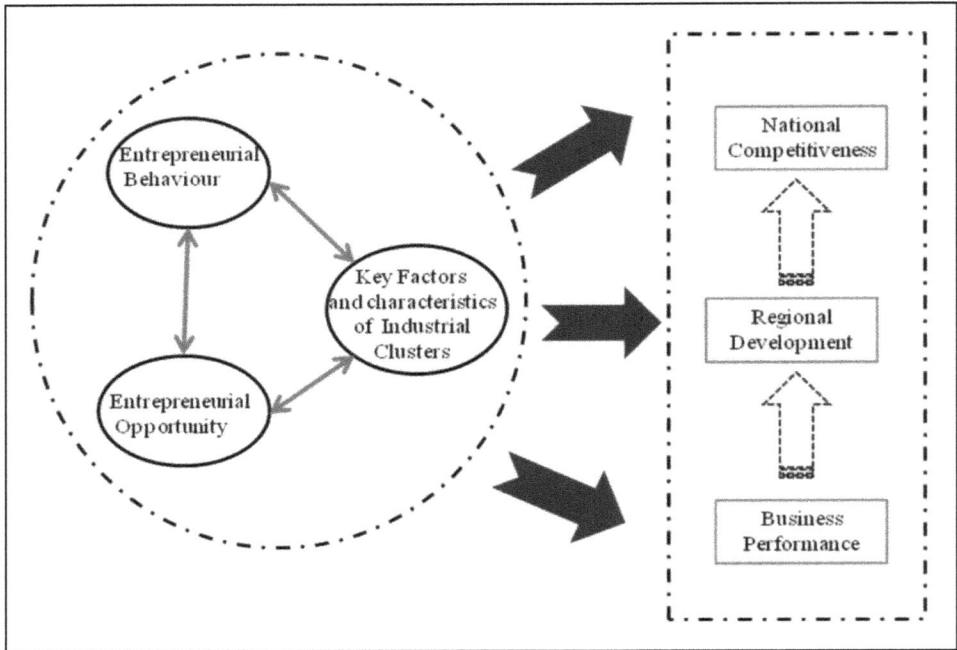

Figure 5.4: Conceptual model for future research.
Source: Courtesy of the authors.

is needed to explore the complex, multidisciplinary and universal phenomena of entrepreneurship and industrial clusters, as well as the interactions between them.

Figure 5.4 shows a future research conceptual model. We propose that future research could focus on how the interactions between industrial clusters, entrepreneurial behaviours and entrepreneurial opportunities influence firm performance, regional development and national competitiveness. Critical future research areas include identifying direct and indirect influential factors of industrial clusters, and identifying the impact pathway of how these key factors and characteristics enhance business performance, regional development and national competitiveness through entrepreneurial behaviours and entrepreneurial opportunities. Further research, both conceptual and empirical, is necessary given the existing and emerging focus and emphasis on policy and practice to develop industrial clusters worldwide.

References

Acs, Z, & Armington, C. (2004). Employment growth and entrepreneurial activity in cities. *Regional Studies: The Journal of the Regional Studies Association, 38*(8), 911-27.

Aldrich, H, & Zimmer, C. (1986). Entrepreneurship through social networks. *The Art and Science of Entrepreneurship, 22*, 3-23.

Aleksandar, K, Koh, SCL, & Leslie, TS. (2007). The cluster approach and SME competitiveness: A review. *Journal of Manufacturing Technology Management, 18*(7), 818-35.

Alsos, GA, & Kaikkonen, V. (2004). Opportunities and prior knowledge: A study of experienced entrepreneurs. *Babson Kauffman Entrepreneurship Research Conference (BKERC)*, Babson College, Wellesley.

Amit, R, Muller, E, & Cockburn, I. (1995). Opportunity costs and entrepreneurial activity. *Journal of Business Venturing, 10*(2), 95-106.

Audretsch, B. (1998). Agglomeration and the location of innovative activity. *Oxford Review of Economic Policy, 14*(2), 18-29.

Aylward, D. (2007). Innovation and inertia: The emerging dislocation of imperatives within the Australian wine industry. *International Journal of Technology and Globalisation, 3*(2), 246-62.

Bagnasco, A. (1999). Teoria del capitale sociale e 'political economy' comparata. *Stato e Mercato, 57*, 351-72.

Baptista, R, & Swann, P. (1998). Do firms in clusters innovate more? *Research Policy, 27*(5), 525-40.

Baptista, R, & Swann, P. (1999). The dynamics of firm growth and entry in industrial cluster: A comparison of the US and UK computer industries. *Journal of Evolutionary Economics, 9*(3), 373-99.

Bradley, SW, Wiklund, J, & Shepherd, DA. (2011). Swinging a double-edged sword: The effect of slack on entrepreneurial management and growth. *Journal of Business Venturing, 26*(5), 537-54.

Brown, TE, Davidsson, P, & Wiklund, J. (2001). An operationalization of Stevenson's conceptualization of entrepreneurship as opportunity-based firm behavior. *Strategic Management Journal, 22*(10), 953-68.

Buenstorf, G. (2007). Creation and pursuit of entrepreneurial opportunities: An evolutionary economics perspective. *Small Business Economics, 28*(4), 323-37.

Burns, T, & Stalker, GM. (1961). *The management of innovation*. London: Tavistock.

Burt, RS. (2000). The network structure of social capital. *Research in Organizational Behavior, 22*, 345-423.

Camagni, R. (1991). Local 'milieu', uncertainty and innovation networks: Towards a new dynamic theory of economic space. In R Camagni (Ed.), *Innovation networks spatial perspectives* (pp. 121-42). London: Belhaven Press.

Casson, M. (1982). *The entrepreneur: An economic theory*. Lanham, MD: Rowman & Littlefield Pub Inc.

Casson, M, & Wadeson, N. (2007). The discovery of opportunities: Extending the economic theory of the entrepreneur. *Small Business Economics, 28*(4), 285-300.

Chandler, N. (2010). Identifying the main economic issues facing the South Australian wine industry. Report prepared for *Economic Issues*, 27. Adelaide: South Australian Centre for Economic Studies.

Chaston, I, & Scott, GJ (2012). Entrepreneurship and open innovation in an emerging economy. *Management Decision, 50*(7), 1161-77.

Coleman, JS. (1990). *Foundations of social theory*. Cambridge: Harvard University Press.

Companys, YE, & McMullen, JS. (2007). Strategic entrepreneurs at work: The nature, discovery, and exploitation of entrepreneurial opportunities. *Small Business Economics, 28*(4), 301-22.

Cooke, P. (2001). Regional innovation systems, clusters, and the knowledge economy. *Industrial and Corporate Change, 10*(4), 945-74.

Cooke, P. (2005). Regional knowledge capabilities and open innovation: Regional innovation systems and clusters in the assymmetric knowledge economy. In S Breschi & F Malerba (Eds.), *Clusters, networks and innovation* (pp. 80-109). Oxford and New York: Oxford University Press.

Cooke, P. (2007). *Regional knowledge economies: Markets, clusters and innovation*. Northampton: Edward Elgar Publishing, Inc.

Cooke, P, Clifton, N, & Oleaga, M. (2005). Social capital, firm embeddedness and regional development. *Regional Studies, 39*(8), 1065-77.

Cooke, P, Gomez Uranga, M, & Etxebarria, G. (1997). Regional innovation systems: Institutional and organisational dimensions. *Research Policy, 26*(4-5), 475-491.

Covin, JG, Green, KM, & Slevin, DP. (2006). Strategic process effects on the entrepreneurial orientation-sales growth rate relationship. *Entrepreneurship: Theory and Practice, 30*(1), 57-81.

Covin, JG, & Slevin, DP. (1989). Strategic management of small firms in hostile and benign environments. *Strategic Management Journal, 10*(1), 75-87.

Covin, JG, & Slevin, DP. (1991). A conceptual model of entrepreneurship as firm behavior. *Entrepreneurship: Theory and Practice, 16*(1), 7-25.

Davidsson, P, Hunter, E, & Klofsten, M. (2006). The discovery process: External influences on refinement of the venture idea. *Feedback, 46*, 13-28.

DeTienne, DR, & Chandler, GN. (2007). The role of gender in opportunity identification. *Entrepreneurship: Theory and Practice, 31*(3), 365-86.

DiMaggio, PJ., & Powell, WW. (1983). The iron cage revisited: Institutional isomorphism and collective rationality in organizational fields. *American Sociological Review, 48*(2), 147-60.

Dimitratos, P, Voudouris, I, Plakoyiannaki, E, & Nakos, G. (2012). International entrepreneurial culture: Toward a comprehensive opportunity-based operationalization of international entrepreneurship. *International Business Review, 21*(4), 708-21.

Dubini, P, & Aldrich, H. (1991). Personal and extended networks are central to the entrepreneurial process. *Journal of Business Venturing, 6*(5), 305-13.

Eckhardt, JT, & Shane, SA. (2003). Opportunities and entrepreneurship. *Journal of Management, 29*(3), 333-49.

Fearne, A, Soosay, C, Stringer, R, Umberger, W, Dent, B, Camilleri, Henderson, D, & Mugford, A. (2009). *Sustainable value chain analysis: A case study of South Australian wine*. Adelaide: Primary Industries and Resources SA.

Folta, TB, Cooper, AC, & Baik, YS. (2006). Geographic cluster size and firm performance. *Journal of Business Venturing, 21*(2), 217-42.

Gaglio, CM, & Katz, JA. (2001). The psychological basis of opportunity identification: Entrepreneurial alertness. *Small Business Economics, 16*(2), 95-111.

Gartner, WB. (1988). Who is an entrepreneur? is the wrong question. *American Journal of Small Business, 12*(4), 11-32.

Giannetti, M, & Simonov, A. (2004). On the determinants of entrepreneurial activity: Social norms, economic environment and individual characteristics. *Swedish Economic Policy Review, 11*(2), 269-313.

Giuliani, E, & Bell, M. (2005). The micro-determinants of meso-level learning and innovation: Evidence from a Chilean wine cluster. *Research Policy, 34*(1), 47-68.

Gordon, I, & McCann, P. (2000). Industrial clusters: Complexes, agglomeration and/or social networks? *Urban Studies, 37*(3), 513-32.

Granovetter, M. (1985). Economic action and social structure: The problem of embeddedness. *Readings in Economic Sociology, 91*(3), 63-8.

Hayek, FA. (1945). The use of knowledge in society. *The American Economic Review, 35*(4), 519-30.

Hoang, H, & Antoncic, B. (2003). Network-based research in entrepreneurship: A critical review. *Journal of Business Venturing, 18*(2), 165-87.

Hughes, M, & Morgan, RE. (2007). Deconstructing the relationship between entrepreneurial orientation and business performance at the embryonic stage of firm growth. *Industrial Marketing Management, 36*(5), 651-61.

Humphrey, J, & Schmitz, H. (2002). How does insertion in global value chains affect upgrading in industrial clusters? *Regional Studies, 36*(9), 1017-27.

Iammarino, S, & McCann, P. (2006). The structure and evolution of industrial clusters: Transactions, technology and knowledge spillovers. *Research Policy, 35*(7), 1018-36.

Jaffe, AB, Trajtenberg, M, & Henderson, R. (1993). Geographic localization of knowledge spillovers as evidenced by patent citations. *The Quarterly Journal of Economics, 108*(3), 577-98.

James, A. (2005). Demystifying the role of culture in innovative regional economies. *Regional Studies, 39*(9), 1197-216.

Julien, PA. (2007). *A theory of local entrepreneurship in the knowledge economy*. Northampton: Edward Elgar Publishing, Inc.

Karlsson, C, Johansson, B, & Stough, R. (2005). *Industrial clusters and inter-firm networks*. Northhampton, MA: Edward Elgar Publishing.

Keui-Hsien, N. (2010). Industrial cluster involvement and organizational adaptation. *Competitiveness Review, 20*(5), 395-406. doi: 10.1108/ 10595421011080779.

Kirzner, IM. (1973). *Competition and entrepreneurship*. Chicago: University of Chicago Press.

Klyver, K, Hindle, K, & Meyer, D. (2008). Influence of social network structure on entrepreneurship participation — A study of 20 national cultures. *International Entrepreneurship and Management Journal, 4*(3), 331-47.

Krugman, PR. (1991). *Geography and trade*. London: MIT Press.

Lumpkin, G, Cogliser, CC, & Schneider, DR. (2009). Understanding and measuring autonomy: An entrepreneurial orientation perspective. *Entrepreneurship: Theory and Practice, 33*(1), 47-69.

Lumpkin, GT, & Dess, GG. (1996). Clarifying the entrepreneurial orientation construct and linking it to performance. *Academy of Management Review, 21*(1), 135-72.

McCann, P, Arita, T, & Gordon, IR. (2002). Industrial clusters, transactions costs and the institutional determinants of MNE location behaviour. *International Business Review, 11*(6), 647-63.

McDonald, F, Tsagdis, D, & Huang, Q. (2006). The development of industrial clusters and public policy. *Entrepreneurship and Regional Development, 18*(6), 525-42.

McEvily, B, & Zaheer, A. (1999). Bridging ties: A source of firm heterogeneity in competitive capabilities. *Strategic Management Journal, 20*, 1133-56.

McGrath, RG. (1999). Falling forward: Real options reasoning and entrepreneurial failure. *Academy of Management Review, 24*(1), 13-30.

McMullen, JS, Plummer, LA, & Acs, ZJ. (2007). What is an entrepreneurial opportunity? *Small Business Economics, 28*(4), 273-83.

Marshall, A. (1890). *Principles of economics* (8th edition). London: Macmillan.

Maskell, P, & Lorenzen, M. (2004). The cluster as market organisation. *Urban Studies, 41*(5), 991-1009.

Menzel, MP, & Fornahl, D. (2007). *Cluster life cycles — Dimensions and rationales of cluster development.* (Workshop paper, Jena Economic Research Papers, 2007-076, n.p.).

Miller, D. (1983). The correlates of entrepreneurship in three types of firms. *Management Science, 29*(7), 770-91.

Molina-Morales, FX, & Martínez-Fernández, MT. (2008). Shared resources in industrial districts: Information, know-how and institutions in the Spanish Tile Industry. *International Regional Science Review, 31*(1), 35-61.

Morris, R. (1994). Computerized content analysis in management research: A demonstration of advantages & limitations. *Journal of Management, 20*(4), 903-31.

Neuendorf, KA. (2002). *The content analysis guidebook.* Thousand Oaks, CA: Sage Publications, Inc.

NVivo9.0. (2012). About cluster analysis. Retrieved from http://help-nv9-en. qsrinternational.com/nv9_help.htm#concepts/about_cluster_analysis.htm.

Parker, R. (2010). Evolution and change in industrial clusters: An analysis of Hsinchu and Sophia Antipolis. *European Urban and Regional Studies, 17*(3), 245-60.

Pickles, AR, & O'Farrell, P. (1987). An analysis of entrepreneurial behaviour from male work histories. *Regional Studies, 21*(5), 425-44.

Pirolo, L, & Presutti, M. (2007). Towards a dynamic knowledge-based approach to the innovation process: An empirical investigation on social capital inside an industrial cluster. *International Journal of Learning and Intellectual Capital, 4*(1-2), 147-73.

Plummer, LA, Haynie, JM, & Godesiabois, J. (2007). An essay on the origins of entrepreneurial opportunity. *Small Business Economics, 28*(4), 363-79.

Porter, M. (1996). Competitive advantage, agglomeration economies, and regional policy. *International Regional Science Review, 19*(1-2), 85-94.

Porter, ME. (1990). *The competitive advantage of nations.* New York: Free Press.

Porter, ME. (1998). Clusters and the new economics of competition. *Harvard Business Review, 76*(6), 77-90.

Potter, J. (2009). Policy Issues in clusters, innovation and entrepreneurship. In J Potter & G Miranda (Eds.), *Clusters, innovation and entrepreneurship* (pp. 21-41). Paris: OECD Publishing.

Pouder, R, & St John, CH. (1996). Hot spots and blind spots: Geographical clusters of firms and innovation. *The Academy of Management Review, 21*(4), 1192-225.

Ratti, R, Bramanti, A, & Gordon, R. (1997). *The dynamics of innovative regions: The Gremi approach*. Aldershot: Ashgate.

Roberts, B, & Enright, M. (2004). Industry clusters in Australia: Recent trends and prospects. *European Planning Studies, 12*(1), 99-121.

Rocha, H, & Sternberg, R. (2005). Entrepreneurship: The role of clusters theoretical perspectives and empirical evidence from Germany. *Small Business Economics, 24*(3), 267-92.

Rocha, HO. (2002). Entrepreneurship and development through clusters: A theoretical model. *British Academy of Management Conference*, London.

Romero-Martínez, AM, & Montoro-Sánchez, Á. (2008). How clusters can encourage entrepreneurship and venture creation: Reasons and advantages. *International Entrepreneurship and Management Journal, 4*(3), 315-29.

Rosenfeld, SA. (2003). Expanding opportunities: Cluster strategies that reach more people and more places. *European Planning Studies, 11*(4), 359-77.

Runyan, R, Droge, C, & Swinney, J. (2008). Entrepreneurial orientation versus small business orientation: What are their relationships to firm performance? *Journal of Small Business Management, 46*(4), 567-88.

Rutherford, TD., & Holmes, J. (2007). Entrepreneurship, knowledge and learning in cluster formation and evolution: The Windsor Ontario tool, die and mould cluster. *International Journal of Entrepreneurship and Innovation Management, 7*(2-5), 320-44.

Sadler-Smith, E, Hampson, Y, Chaston, I, & Badger, B. (2003). Managerial behavior, entrepreneurial style, and small firm performance. *Journal of Small Business Management, 41*(1), 47-67.

Sarason, Y, Dean, T, & Dillard, JF. (2006). Entrepreneurship as the nexus of individual and opportunity: A structuration view. *Journal of Business Venturing, 21*(3), 286-305.

Sarasvathy, SD, Dew, N, Velamuri, SR, & Venkataraman, S. (2005). Three views of entrepreneurial opportunity. In ZJ Acs & DB Audretsch (Eds.), *Handbook of Entrepreneurship Research* (pp. 141-60). New York: Kluwer Academic Publishers.

Saxenian, AL. (1996). *Regional advantage: Culture and competition in Silicon Valley and Route 128*. Cambridge: Harvard University Press.

Schmitz, H. (1995). Collective efficiency: Growth path for small scale industry. *The Journal of Development Studies, 31*(4), 529-66.

Schumpeter, JA. (1934). *The theory of economic development: An inquiry into profits, capital, credit, interest, and the business cycle*. Cambridge, MA: Harvard University Press.

Shane, S. (2012). Reflections on the 2010 AMR Decade Award: Delivering on the promise of entrepreneurship as a field of research. *The Academy of Management Review (AMR), 37*(1), 10-20.

Shane, S, & Eckhardt, J. (2003). The individual-opportunity nexus. In ZJ Acs & DB Audretsch (Eds.), *Handbook of Entrepreneurship Research* (pp. 161-191). New York: Kluwer Academic Publishers.

Shane, S, & Venkataraman, S. (2000). The promise of entrepreneurship as a field of research. *Academy of Management Review, 25*(1), 217-26.

Shane, S, & Venkataraman, S. (2001). Entrepreneurship as a field of research: A response to Zahra and Dess, Singh, and Erikson. *The Academy of Management Review, 26*(1), 13-16.

Sharma, P, & Chrisman, JJ. (1999). Toward a reconciliation of the definitional issues in the field of corporate entrepreneurship. *Entrepreneurship: Theory and Practice, 23*, 11-28.

Short, JC, Broberg, JC, Cogliser, CC, & Brigham, KH. (2010). Construct validation using Computer-Aided Text Analysis (CATA). Organizational Research Methods, 13(2), 320-47.

Short, JC, Ketchen, DJ, Shook, CL, & Ireland, RD. (2010). The concept of 'opportunity' in entrepreneurship research: Past accomplishments and future challenges. *Journal of Management, 36*(1), 40-65.

Simon, H. (1969). *The sciences of the artificial*. Cambridge: MIT Press.

Singh, RP. (2000). *Entrepreneurial opportunity recognition through social networks.* New York: Garland.

Singh, RP. (2001). A comment on developing the field of entrepreneurship through the study of opportunity recognition and exploitation. *Academy of Management Review, 26*(1), 10-12.

Smith, BR, Matthews, CH, & Schenkel, MT. (2009). Differences in entrepreneurial opportunities: The role of tacitness and codification in opportunity identification*. *Journal of Small Business Management, 47*(1), 38-57.

Sorenson, O. (2003). Social networks and industrial geography. *Journal of Evolutionary Economics, 13*(5), 513-27.

Sternberg, R, & Litzenberger, T. (2004). Regional clusters in Germany — Their geography and their relevance for entrepreneurial activities. *European Planning Studies, 12*(6), 767-91.

Stevenson, HH, & Gumpert, DE. (1985). The heart of entrepreneurship. *Harvard Business Review, 85*(2), 85-94.

Stevenson, HH, & Jarillo, JC. (1990). A paradigm of entrepreneurship: Entrepreneurial management. *Strategic Management Journal, 11*, 17-27.

Stevenson, HH, & Jarrillo-Mossi, JC. (1986). Preserving entrepreneurship as companies grow. *Journal of Business Strategy, 7*(1), 10-23.

Storper, M. (1997). *The regional world: Territorial development in a global economy.* New York: The Guilford Press.

Stuart, TE, & Sorenson, O. (2003). Liquidity events and the geographic distribution of entrepreneurial activity. *Administrative Science Quarterly, 48*(2), 175-201.

Tappi, D. (2005). Clusters, adaptation and extroversion: A cognitive and entrepreneurial analysis of the marche music cluster. *European Urban and Regional Studies, 12*(3), 289-307.

Tushman, ML, & Romanelli, E. (1985). Organizational evolution: A metamorphosis model of convergence and reorientation. *Research in Organizational Behavior, 7*, 171-222.

van de Ven, H. (1993). The development of an infrastructure for entrepreneurship. *Journal of Business Venturing, 8*(3), 211-30.

Venkataraman, S. (1997). The distinctive domain of entrepreneurship research. *Advances in Entrepreneurship, Firm Emergence and Growth, 3*(1), 119-38.

Venkatraman, N. (1989). Strategic orientation of business enterprises: The construct, dimensionality, and measurement. *Management Science, 35*(8), 942-62.

Weber, A. (1909). *Über den Standort der Industrien.* Tübingen, Germany: JCB Mohr.

Wennberg, K, & Lindqvist, G. (2010). The effect of clusters on the survival and performance of new firms. *Small Business Economics, 34*(3), 221-41.

Westlund, H, & Bolton, R. (2003). Local social capital and entrepreneurship. *Small Business Economics, 21*(2), 77-113.

Wiklund, J. (2006). The sustainability of the entrepreneurial orientation-performance relationship. In P Davidsson, F Delmar, & J Wiklund (Eds.), *Entrepreneurship and the growth of firms* (pp. 141-155). Northhampton, MA: Edward Elgar Publishing, Inc.

Wixted, B. (2009). *Innovation system frontiers: Cluster networks and global value.* Berlin: Springer Verlag.

Operationalising innovation:

6

Hotwiring the creative organisation

Fiona Kerr, The University of Adelaide

Introduction

In order to thrive in the twenty-first century, organisations need not only to be able to recognise complexity and sustainability as key components of business, but also to be able to foster and harness them. Those who operate successfully in such an environment go beyond organisational learning and strategy planning to building adaptive, innovative capabilities which result in sustained competitive advantage. This chapter explores how such adaptation and innovation are coupled with a capacity for strategic innovation and the ability to 'hotwire' across industry boundaries, and how such abilities ultimately decouple organisations from the confining need to know what is over the horizon in order to be able to deal with it.

Much has been written on how to facilitate and nurture innovation in organisations, but the concepts are often disaggregated and analysed as individual processes, practices or measures. This fails to take into account the complexity of interconnectedness and interdependence which both creativity and innovation entail, whether within the organisation or across markets and industry sectors as *open* innovation gains purchase. The level of interconnectivity renders it challenging to design operational structures and processes, and even organisations which embrace creative problem solving sometimes adopt essentially linear processes in their innovation labs and 'learning gartens'. The problem-solving methods are structured around staged environments and sequential procedures, and this is often not the best format to allow abstract thought.

This does not mean that organisations cannot build structures and processes which facilitate creativity and innovation. Though novel ideas are created in informal spaces and interactions, such opportunities must still be created and facilitated. Further, it must be easy for the outcomes to be captured, and also to be brought to fruition. A level of order is required to support innovative organisations in their steerage and operation. This chapter summarises such order as the intertwined themes of space, time, diversity and interconnectedness.

Each of these themes has multiple, intertwined elements which the innovative organisation builds into their physical and procedural structures and support mechanisms in order to facilitate and nurture innovative practice and creativity. This includes aspects such as the physical layout and flexibility of spaces, and methods of capturing and applying both code-able and non-code-able tacit knowledge. This chapter will also discuss intuitive complex decision-making and the use of reflective networks. Many aspects can be operationalised but operationalisation requires rules, structures, controls, management practices and strategy to be approached in ways which are often counter to common practice.

Innovation is a key driver for economic growth (Pike & Roos, 2007). For the sake of clarity, this chapter makes a simple differentiation between creativity and innovation. Creativity is the conception of novelty, be it a new idea or a new way of perceiving or doing something. Innovation is putting that novelty into practice. The case study this chapter presents, using examples from the same case study throughout, concerns an R&D company in which innovation is critical for survival, and details the shift from potential closure to a highly innovative and successful business. It describes the new, custom-built structure, along with the major features of its operation and how they were designed, implemented and supported by leadership and management practices shaped to assist creativity and innovation. The discussion also offers insight into how these elements interact to hotwire innovative capability in a sustainable manner.

Hotwiring for innovation

What occurs when something is hotwired? Two things which do not normally touch are put in contact and held together until they connect. A spark is generated and this ignites activity. Hotwiring is a good analogy for creating an innovative environment, and such an environment can exist in various forms at different scales, from individual brains to whole-of-industry sectors.

At the individual level, hotwiring gives creative thinkers the time, space and opportunity to build new ideas by connecting disparate information into new neural networks. At the level of people connecting, when they are in a positive environment dealing together with a novel challenge or situation, shared conversation and activity can create new ideas and even affect how those ideas are neurally constructed and shared (Goleman, 2006; Allman, Watson, Tetreault, & Hakeem, 2005), which can result in strongly aligning both goals and purpose going forward (see below).

At the organisational level, minimal blocks to interaction and active support for collaboration will allow these new connections and sparks across different parts of the company. As I have written elsewhere, similar phenomena can occur at higher levels within and across markets, industry sectors and global settings (Kerr, 2012b), and such co-creation is a key feature of open innovation. Organisations that operationalise innovation have flexible and dynamic structures which are minimal and permeable. This allows for the co-ordination and flow of people, ideas and information across diverse parts of the structure. There is an ability for information to flow along 'horizontal human networks' (Meadows, 2008) and for knowledge to be built through relational networks and shared meaning, leading to the co-ordination of shared knowledge, goals and mutual respect (Gittell, Cameron, Lim, & Rivas, 2006), and to the production of new ideas and concepts.

Innovative hotwiring is also about people *physically* coming together where and when they normally would not, as the face-to-face contact which this allows is critical for the firing of particular neurons which lead to the creation of novel thought. It also allows for the most effective capture and dissemination of non-code-able information, such as tacit knowledge. In innovative organisations, the spaces people work in are designed to encourage such contact by increasing the likelihood of physically bumping into each other and talking face to face. There are stairs rather than lifts, as well as cafés, communal eating areas, and other places which encourage informal interaction to increase unpredictable interconnections across all sorts of boundaries (Magadley & Birdi, 2009; Haner, 2005). These interconnections lead to novel ideas.

Such organisations still have structures, boundaries and outcome requirements. The structures include resources, infrastructure and processes built to suit the company and its people. Boundaries and outcome requirements manifest as clear and shared clarification tools, the non-negotiables of a project or process, a shared purpose, and the rules for stopping a project or experiment (Helbing & Lämmer, 2008). There is a wide and appropriate distribution of decision-making across an innovative organisation, so that people can try things and learn from the results. They also have the permission, time and space to stop and reflect, which paradoxically then allows them to move ahead rapidly through increased capacity for novel problem solving and less rework upon implementation. People can reflect alone or in small areas where they incubate ideas and gain insights through divergent thinking. Informal play and 'border-crossing across the organisation' further spark this sort of creative and abstractive thinking process (Haner, 2005).

Setting up an organisation to hotwire ideas, information and people entails an understanding of the major themes and elements of creativity and innovation. The next section of this chapter describes in more detail the themes of time, space, diversity and their interconnectivity across the innovative entity.

The major elements of innovation

Innovation is a serendipitous chess game which favours the versatile, prepared mind. Just like a chess game, innovation involves pieces which move in ways dependent on each other. An unusual move (connection) can inspire a fundamental change in structure and evolution of the situation (game). Many of the pieces have different properties and can do different things. They need to be in the right place at the right time to act, so timing is critical and the game unfolds emergently, with one move depending on another in an opportune pattern. In complexity terms, the game involves interdependence, diversity (heterogeneity), and the layering of moves over time into an emergent strategy.

Moving from analogy to practical terms, this suggests that innovation is rarely 'out of the blue' or spontaneous but instead is cumulative, with ideas building on each other in a layering process which leverages knowledge and capability. Johnson (2010) calls it a 'bricolage' of borrowing old technology and techniques, and combining them into or with new ideas. Often the new layer of innovation comes about from someone with a completely different way of looking at the subject through diverse backgrounds, world views or areas of specialisation, interacting at the right time for those ideas to fall on prepared ground and willing minds.

Space

An appropriate frequency of interaction is critical for successful innovation, and the likelihood of communication and spontaneous face-to-face interaction is crucially dependent on the physical distance between communications partners (Marion, 1999). This means having spatial flow, which enhances the opportunity for people to bump into each other, as the majority of such interaction is unplanned, and is instead a product of chance created by incidental proximity (Backhouse & Drew, 1992). Such proximity occurs if the workplace facilitates informal meetings, whether in cafés or central staircases, where people will pass each other on their daily travels instead of bypassing each other in lifts. Being within-site also allows people to gauge the opportunity to go and chat, and increases the level of general interaction and communication. Face-to-face interaction is also critical for the types of neuronal activity and connectivity which promote the creation of novel ideas, complex problem solving and the release of chemicals which are necessary for the occurrence of the reorganisation of neural nets (neuroplasticity) and even neurogenesis (the growth of new neural nets), as long as there is a high level of trust and shared purpose (Kerr, 2010; Boyatzis, 2006). Such trust and shared purpose requires at least periodic collocation of the members of a virtual team in order to enhance cohesion among its members and allow the innovation that will lead to project success (cf. Boutellier, Gassman, & von Zedtwitz, 2000; Kerr 2012).

Caves and cathedrals

The nature of the physical space is a key variable in both the creative ideation and innovation processes in organisations (Moultrie, Nilsson, Dissel, Haner, & Van der Lugt, 2007). Much work is now being done on the issue of spatial support for creativity and innovation, as there is significant evidence that individual and group activities require, as well as actions needing divergent and convergent thinking, different spaces. Attention should be paid to how the space facilitates or inhibits varying needs for communication, information sharing and collaboration, along with interaction or privacy and quiet reflection (Haner, 2005). Empirical evidence from creative hubs suggests that the size of the space and even the height of the ceilings and windows have a bearing on creative and innovative activity with large, high spaces for preparation and evaluation mixed with small spaces for divergent ideas and imagination so that people cocoon in individually adjustable spaces with various types of technology. This aligns with the phases of divergent and convergent thought which different stages of the creative process entail (Kerr, 2010; Aldous, 2007; Haner, 2005).

Soft factors such as colour, materials and office attractiveness are also an important element of the spatial aspect of creativity. Clauss-Ehlers (2004) found such factors to be the most important single item contributing to perceived wellbeing, and the 'style' of the work environment (including the building and layout) has the ability to inspire, motivate and symbolize innovation and creativity 'simply by being perceived as attractive' (Haner & Bakke, 2004).

The innovative organisation thus pays attention to the proximity of people and spaces to each other. It attends to the style of the spaces, their soft environments and technological tools, and to the provision and layout of a varied physical environment which will facilitate flow and interconnection. Such environments invite the establishment of creative and innovative processes by generating emergent relationships of people through 'hybrid infrastructures for work' (Bakke & Yttri, 2003), which facilitate and enhance innovative practice in a work place.

Time

Timing is important in a number of ways. There has to be a serendipitous alignment of capacity to innovate, assisted by the presence of organisational support for individual and group reflection on both past and new ideas. The timely capture and release of ideas is also needed for such reflection.

New ideas can only proceed when conceptual and technological advances make it possible, be they the layering of concepts and knowledge or the ability to technically build or construct an item. Thus innovation is path- and context-dependent, making it quite different from the notion of best practice.

For many this may be a different concept of innovation — that creative ideas are not sudden sparks of genius but instead build over time, evolving and emerging as new pieces are added from surprising sources. They are slow hunches (Johnson, 2010), and whilst there are 'aha' moments in creativity, such neural sparks are the cognitive amalgamation of a number of pieces of information, knowledge or experience after a period of incubation (which may take minutes, hours, days or years) which form a new neural network in the brain (Saaty & Shih, 2009).

Time for reflection is required for both quick leaps and slowly formed concepts in order to allow the new connections to be made. This calm neural state is the most suitable for creativity, partly due to the release of chemicals that aid the process. It is worth noting that the opposite is also true in terms of stress or pressure triggering the release of chemicals such as cortisol which inhibit or slow the brain from being able to make these connections altogether (Boyatzis, 2006). Whether an innovative idea builds slowly over time or happens in a leap, the organisation needs to enable the innovator to have such time, conversations and exposure to new ideas as is required, along with access to a wide range of judicious information and the permission and opportunity to experiment and act in order to learn.

Time is also required for failure and for multiple attempts to test a concept, as this is a major source of learning. An innovative environment is supportive of informed risk-taking (Heifetz, Grashow, & Linsky, 2009), rather than aiming for closure or a quick-win solution, and operationalising such risk-taking includes agreed rules on when to start and stop. Another way in which time relates to creativity and innovation is the concept of 'pace layering' (Brand, 2000), whereby each level of a healthy society (in this case the organisation) is allowed to operate at its own pace, buffered by slower, larger levels of change but invigorated by faster, smaller cycles of innovation. Many failed attempts at changing a culture or process, or hurrying the creation of something new, are due to the lack of understanding of how such multiple time frames interact, and the lack of ability to either construct successful buffering, or to leave the process alone to readjust its speed and synchronise (Kerr, 2012a; Helbing & Lämmer, 2008).

These temporal concepts align well with innovation's cumulative layering of concept, knowledge and technology.

Heterogeneity/diversity

Uniformity (i.e. if everybody behaves and thinks the same), will lead to a poor adaptation to changing environmental or market conditions. In contrast, a large variety of different approaches (i.e. a heterogeneous population) will imply a large innovation rate. The innovation rate is actually expected to be proportional to the variance of individual solutions. (Helbing & Lämmer, 2008, p. 12)

There are multiple facets to the role that diversity/heretogeneity plays in innovation, and these facets include diversity of people, ideas, spaces, colours, technology, tools and types of thinking. Fostering diversity is critical for organisations adapting to new situations. Operationalised diversity allows for the development of different behavioural roles, multiple perspectives, ideas and approaches. Innovation requires both convergent and divergent thinking at different times during the innovative process, and this is enabled by having a variety of physical spaces, tools, technologies and approaches in order to create the necessary environment (Haner, 2005; Kristensen, 2004; Magadley & Birdi, 2009).

Diversity of mindsets, experience and skills is key to optimising new solutions as these things bring together and recombine individual experience and views of the problem or challenge, leading to fresh options for solutions and ideas. As discussed above, interaction is critical to successful innovation, and therefore, though organisations require rules and structures, these should enhance rather than block connections between diverse people and views.

Diverse tasks, along with a mixture of task and play, are also important for innovative activity as mastery over known tasks increases the confidence to experiment and innovate (De Jong & Den Hartog, 2007). So, too, there should be diverse methods of storing, transferring, integrating and retrieving individual and shared knowledge so that it can be used by a wide range of people. At the whole-of-organisation level, the environment is rarely homogeneous, but instead typically contains multiple states of flux at any one time, with different parts of the organisation existing in varying stages of stability and change. This is in fact the optimum state for a healthy organisation because the parts which are in flux are the parts where the greatest creativity and innovation can occur (Meadows, 2008; Mitleton-Kelly, 2003) as the old practices no longer hold. Innovative organisations task their managers with steering such states rather than settling them down, as such settling in fact acts to suppress adaptation by blocking creativity and minimising emergence.

Figure 6.1 below attempts to put some thematic order to the elements of innovation.

Figure 6.1: The interconnected themes of creativity and innovation.
Source: Courtesy of the author.

The nature of interconnectivity

As this chapter has shown so far, the level of interconnectedness between and within themes shows that disaggregation and siloing within organisations has multiple negative effects. Too often an organisation's performance will be studied in terms of what each section does rather than how it interacts across the structure. Such a review shows what the parts *do* but not how the organisation *works*, and this should be born in mind when operationalising innovation theory.

An idea is a network which can grow and exist at multiple levels, whether at the micro level of a new configuration of neurons within one brain or the shared neural nets of people (multiple brains) working closely together on novel problem solving (Goleman & Boyatzis, 2008). It grows from a clash or meld of new viewpoints as people interact face to face in unpredictable and often self-organised patterns, hence the need for physical spaces which encourage unplanned meetings in a creative workplace. The networked idea takes time and incubation as pieces of the puzzle connect, interact and build into something that can be articulated. Johnson (2010) describes Darwin's theory of evolution as having been 'ready for months before presentation, but delayed because Darwin was "unable of fully thinking it yet"' (p. 118).

Hotwiring the future — Strategic innovation

Although this chapter is not about strategy, it describes the design of workplaces for the emergence of ideas and outcomes. It is therefore relevant to mention the concept of strategic innovation, as opposed to strategic planning, as differentiated below:

> The real world, which models simulate, evolves by surprising. It feeds some slight variation through an incompletely known environment laced with non-linear relations and amplifies results unexpectedly. Planning has traditionally sought to avoid surprises by controlling events and suppressing variations. (Artigiani, 2005, p. 586)

Because strategy building takes place in an unpredictable and uncontrollable system, long-term planning needs to scan that system (be it the company, industry sector or external market) in order to discover emerging conditions and innovative opportunities (Aaltonen, 2007). Long-term plans will always be wrong, so the most innovative and sustainable organisations are those which are skilled in discovering new information (threats, technologies) and generating solutions around them spontaneously, thereby rescuing planners from the unrealistic idea of needing to know the future (Artigiani, 2005).

In terms of the case study this chapter describes, a major issue was anticipating and delivering on strategic plans which held the staff to tightly quantified and timetabled deliverables in a changing and unpredictable market and technological field. When they failed to deliver on what were unrealistic or oversimplified plans they were held accountable. In the redesigned business the executive group adopted scenario building as a major foresight tool. They also promoted intuitive decision-making in planning discussions, as this allowed the introduction of information and knowledge which could not always be justified through linear analysis, yet which introduced valuable insights built up over years of experience (Patton, 2003). They combined this with real-time requirements, and the resultant strategic decisions became more realistic and accurate, and also much more creative.

Thus both creativity and innovation present a rich picture of fast and slow collisions of ideas which build new concepts, crafted by diverse experiences and types of thinking, and facilitated by varied layouts and use of space at different times over the process. The next section looks at operationalising creativity and innovation in the work setting, exploring how to build a culture which leverages such elements to grow an innovative capability within and across the organisation and its people. The section uses the R&D case study throughout in order to illustrate how the major elements were put into practice.

Case study methodology approach and design

The initial context for the empirical research arose from my own direct experience and observations (over many years of management, leadership and advisory positions). I observed consistencies regarding success factors for increasing innovation, which led to initial theory building and the design of the case study. In a long-term empirical study it is difficult to isolate both the endogenous and exogenous forces with respect to innovation. The case design attempted to identify a number of structural, cultural and functional elements which enabled creativity and innovation to be operationalised.

The case study involved an exploratory qualitative field research method which used abduction. This methodology allows for assessment of prior and original theories, and the generation of new knowledge, through 'constant dialogue between theoretical conceptualisation and empirical investigation in a real life context' (Järvensivu & Törnroos, 2010, p. 107). Järvensivu and Törnroos (2010) describe abduction as

> [a]n approach to knowledge production that occupies the middle ground between induction and deduction. Unlike induction, abduction accepts existing theory, which might improve the theoretical strength of case analysis. Abduction also allows for a less theory-driven research process than deduction, thereby enabling data-driven theory generation. (p. 102)

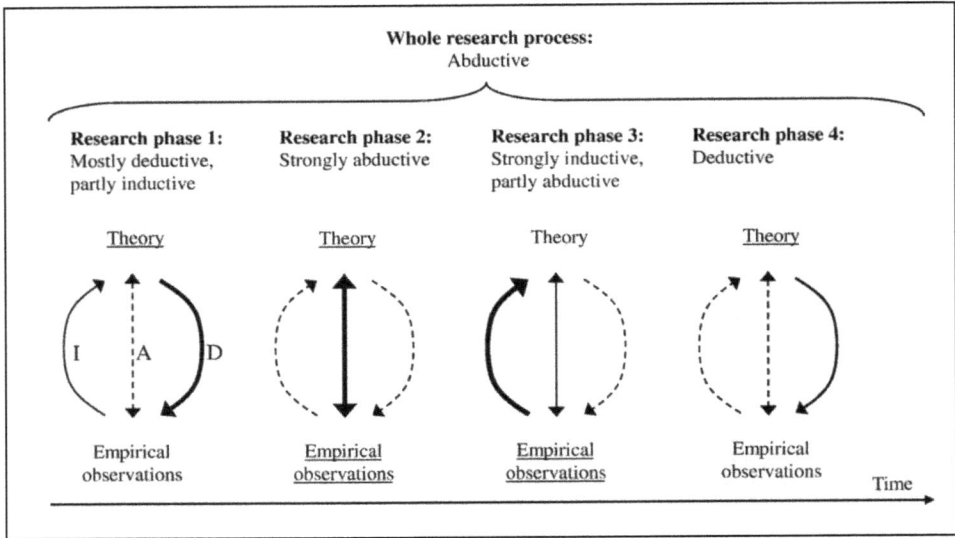

Figure 6.2. Abductive research process as a mix of inductive, abductive and deductive sub-processes.
Source: Järvensivu & Törnroos, 2010, p. 102.

An abductive case study approach suited the case study profile, and the long timeframe and opportunity afforded the research design of systematic combining, an abductive approach to case research. In their so-titled article, Dubois and Gadde (2002) explain that with an abductive approach

> [t]he original framework is successively modified, partly as a result of unanticipated empirical findings, but also of theoretical insights gained during the process. This approach creates fruitful cross-fertilization where new combinations are developed through a mixture of established theoretical models and new concepts derived from the confrontation with reality. (p. 559)

An overarching advantage of this methodology was the learning it offered as an emergent process, by way of the interplay between search and discovery as each new learning was fed back into the prevailing framework, combining systematically over time and experience to guide the new direction (Dubois & Gadde, 2002). The research process can be broken up into phases that contain abductive differences (refer to Figure 6.2). In some phases the researcher's logic *is* 'purely abductive' while in other stages, 'the reasoning may lean more toward deduction or induction. The whole process, however, can be identified as being abductive in general' (Järvensivu & Törnroos, 2010, p. 102).

In Phase 1 there is a preliminary idea of what to study. Phase 2 entails a process of theoretical thinking being influenced by the case study, which in turn influences empirical investigation and further literature research. Phase 3 includes collection and analysis of in-depth empirical data, and Phase 4 is the assessment of validity and analytical generalisability of the results, deduced from generated theory.

The research thus involved developing the evaluative case study using a systematic combining research design (Dubois & Gadde, 2002), and this qualitative exploratory field research method allowed the investigation of a complex set of intricately related variables simultaneously over a period of twelve months. The case study timeframe enabled coverage of all stages from the start of the transformative process through building an innovative structure and infrastructure, and finally bedding in and monitoring success.

Conducting the case study

The aim of the case study was two-fold in terms of required and desired outcomes. The required outcome was to turn a struggling R&D business into a viable entity within twelve months which could successfully hit marketing windows. The desired outcome was to foster a creative capacity that would lead to innovative outcomes such as technological breakthroughs. Both were achieved.

The structure of the case study was a multi-method process. Framing occurred via detailed scene setting from the vice president [VP] of the R&D business, which created shared understanding of the issues, non-negotiables and potential way forward. There were brainstorming sessions with each team around what worked well, what needed to be changed and what would work best going forward. After I had combined and mapped the outcomes, they were presented at an all-staff meeting. There were many information and ideas sessions with groups of all sizes, as well as ongoing work both with and by the VP and executive. Elements explored included a fit-for-purpose structure, infrastructure, management style and configuration, a decision-making process and an environment supportive of creativity and innovation. Weekly management meetings informed this emergent process, as did workshops, direct observations, and examination of archival records, documentation and artefacts. There were monthly updates and discussions, six-monthly all-staff progress talks and workshops using a formal report format, and an interactive discussion site designed by the staff.

A co-created potential structure was put forward to all staff, which was then adapted by three working groups (following, despite the high level of co-creation, a challenging but normal 'storming' session), and subsequently voted in. The new managers ended up being voted in by the challenging process of a secret ballot following the design of a robust process which included discussion and education on the impact and outcomes of these key positions. Key roles were co-designed by myself and staff with relevant knowledge, and a similar process was followed for the concept and design of the star teams (see below), and the organisation's structural levels. The new managers, along with executive and key staff, allocated people across the new structure, and learnt of the difficulty of being responsible for such decisions, as this was one of the activities they were most uncomfortable with. New data bases were designed and built, and new processes and infrastructure put in place. These included remuneration and bonus structures, communication and interactivity methods and tools, project design rules, informal mentoring techniques and values-based performance management (designed by staff at all levels).

There was constant discussion, support, education, and feedback throughout the process at all levels to assist people to share and discuss both progress and issues as the building of an innovative business progressed. Twice during the process this also meant dealing with the emergence of behaviour which was not optimal to success (see below). Over the year, the structure was completely flattened, and the staff subsequently added another layer back in (see sub-heading 'over-flattening' in one of the case study examples below). The increase in maturity of staff at all levels was both obvious and significant, as was the growth of co-creation and innovative capacity. This resulted in the first technological breakthrough in seven years and ensured the viability of the business.

Analysis

Internal hotwiring — Enabling structures

The physical structure of an organisation has many ramifications. It directly affects the culture, as its level of flexibility can impede or facilitate decision-making capability and connectivity. The balance of centralised and distributed decision-making shapes how power is used and activity co-ordinated. Structure impacts the flow and nature of both formal and informal communication and information (Mitleton-Kelly, 2003). Structure also affects the creation of new knowledge by impacting on the capability to take action which is a precursor to learning.

Minimal structure, and uniformity verses flexibility

Creativity and innovation require a minimal structure, which lessens the blocks to connectivity and co-ordination, whereas highly structured or rigid organisational silos halt much of this activity (Helbing & Lämmer, 2008). Minimal structures enable the connection of diverse ideas, people and views through fostering play and experimentation, and maximising serendipitous timing in relation to people's interaction, leading to the layering and leveraging of ideas, new technologies and techniques. There is consistently more opportunity to reflect and allow new ideas to form.

The elements of structural uniformity and flexibility are subtle but fundamental to how an organisation operates. If the structures are too uniform, the processes and methods tend to be standardised and tight, leaving little room for shared learning through exploration of alternatives. Emergence of the most suitable practices for achieving required outcomes is also minimised. Furthermore, it is hard to judge output accurately, as output tends to be quantitative and centralised, whereas most outcomes occur in a dispersed pattern across multiple silos and have substantial qualitative aspects. Thus the highly structured feedback and reward processes are problematic.

Because innovative organisations are knowledge organisations, they are critically dependent on connectivity and the autonomy of informal interaction. Senior decision makers cannot predict or observe these relationships when putting in rules and controls over how people and information will flow and combine. There needs to be a co-ordination capability across functions and up and down levels, together with a balance of centralised and distributed decision-making along with permission to act, as this is the way that people learn and innovate.

The case study in this chapter offers an example of growing a culture supportive of educated risk-taking and multiple experiments, and assisted by organisational structures to support diversity and develop a mindset that questions simple, expedient answers.

Case study example

To begin the rebuilding process, there was collective discussion around what was working well, what was not working and what was not negotiable in terms of resources and output requirements for the business.

This guided the design of a three-phase structure of concept development (inception), analysis and scale-up, with the staff and myself co-constructing three sections with permeable membranes (refer to Figure 6.3) which people could pass through backwards and forwards, depending on the needs of the project or task (they were scientists and engineers, but the analogy is apt). There were handover processes for the work to move to each subsequent phase if no-one was going with it to ensure continuity of knowledge and progress. These included tacit knowledge and ideas. If results in one phase required the process to go back a step, often a team member would go back as well to ensure continuity of knowledge, as this shortened the redesign time. The managers were embedded in each team as well as being part of the executive group, and this allowed them to influence key decisions in terms of practical operational requirements.

Running across the whole structure were small subject-matter expert groups called 'star teams', who could offer advice or train a team member depending on requirements, which also led to a slow 'up-skilling' of all staff over time, thereby broadening their frames of reference, as well as hotwiring informal mentoring activities.

Simple control rules and clear, agreed boundaries

Some structures, such as Gortex's 'lattice organisation' and Buckman's 'influence web', try to mirror flexible structural requirements which allow for an interweaving of processes for new capacities to emerge. This fits with organisational complexity

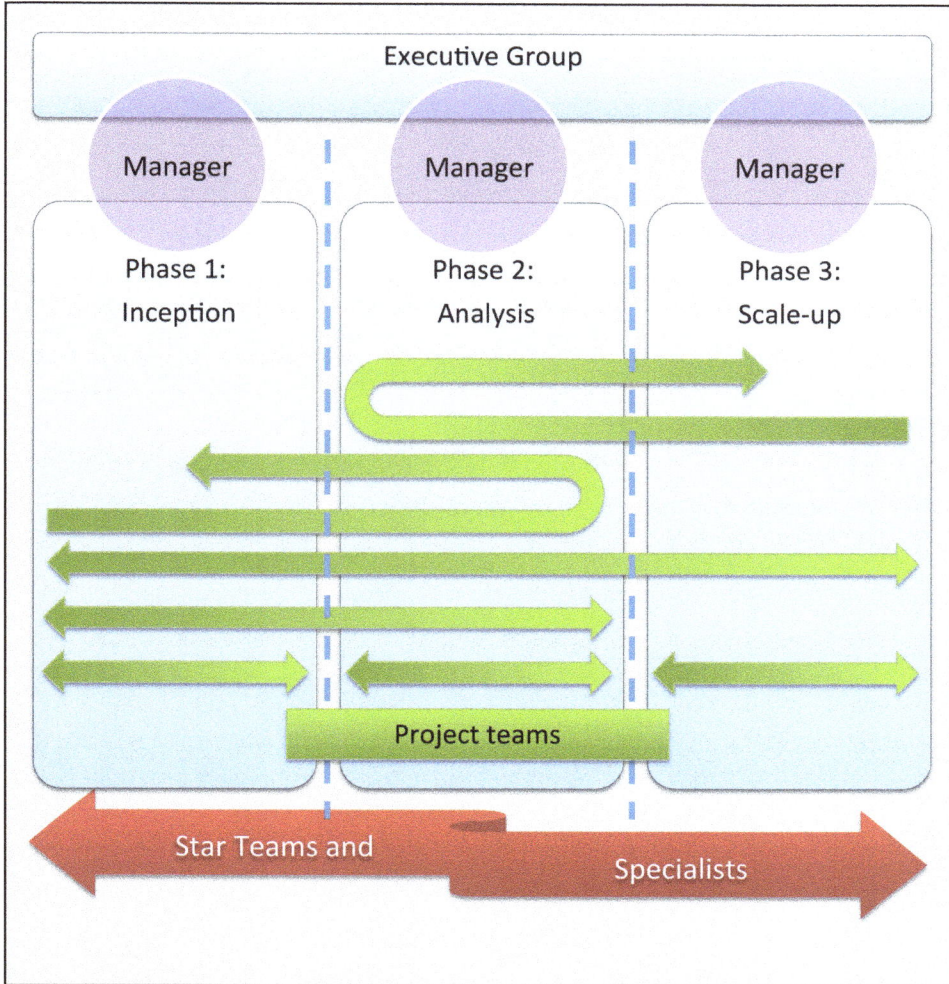

Figure 6.3. New permeable structure.
Source: Courtesy of the author.

theory's self-organisation of people to increase capacity through having fluid and permeable boundaries (Mitleton-Kelly, 2003). Such boundaries are not weak or unclear, but instead are flexible as the nature of work changes, both within and around the organisation. Boundaries are still necessary, including the clarity of shared purpose, but neither boundaries nor roles should block interaction.

Control rules should be simple, with a shared 'why' and an innovative 'how', influenced by minimal regulation loops. These loops should accurately measure what is important, rather than quantifiable, especially as many of the intangible assets around innovation are qualitative. Control rules include such things as employee interaction (organisation charts), resources, outputs (measures, performance appraisals) and real-time control (process rules and types of supervision) (Morrison, 2010).

They should allow for maximum autonomy within the boundaries of understood non-negotiables, shared purpose and appropriate goals. Instead of being based on risk management and compliance, many innovative organisations adopt five categories of control rules which enhance creativity and innovation. They set rules around how to frame the work (key features), its boundaries (which opportunities to explore), its priority rules (ranking), timing (pace of exploration) and exit rules (when to abandon) (Morrison, 2010). These rules provide direction and something to steer against, which is needed in creative, dynamic situations to prevent chaos.

Case study examples

Employee interaction

A common problem when roles are restructured is individuals' retention of tasks which reinforce old ways of working. To minimise this, the group had a celebration tea party to let go of old tasks, old frames and old rules. They wrote each task, rule or process which would no longer be practised on a balloon. They tethered the balloons to tables of champagne and popped them with great ceremony to bring home the point that staff would no longer do these things. The staff designed this ritual as their way of moving forward positively, but it also gave them permission to remind each other if old habits emerged subsequently. The process proved remarkably successful in assisting a change in behaviour and mindset.

Process control

As seen above, the boundaries between phases were structurally clear. There was agreement on what the tasks and deliverables looked like, where they sat, and how people were able to move as required. Handover processes were put in place, and there were accurate and meaningful feedback loops to indicate how successful each stage of the project or process was. If a problem occurred, those with the highest knowledge rather than status discussed and took remedial action.

Output control in terms of interaction

When the group was asked what got in the way of building a great culture, appropriate appraisal was highlighted. With guidance and permission, the staff designed their own system, removing technical capability from the appraisal process, and rebuilding it based on five specific values (i.e. integrity) with descriptors for low, medium and high levels of each, rated by 360-degree feedback in the high-trust atmosphere. This proved extremely powerful in changing behaviour. Technical capability was built into a multilevel open database of self-assessed expertise, which sat permanently on the intranet, and was also used for mentoring and project allocation as skills and expertise were easy to locate. These changes greatly increased collaborative work.

Another aspect of building an innovative culture involved reward. The staff redesigned the pay and bonus methods along with the laboratory timetable processes to allow for personal circumstances — i.e. parents of small children no longer had to do laboratory night shifts but contributed to outcomes and creativity in other ways. The bonus was changed to equal shares, and then abandoned in favour of using the money in other ways which included prizes for (peer reviewed) innovative or creative ideas, attendance at conferences, and in-house programs and celebrations.

It is important that changes, rules and structures are introduced only when there is an understanding of how the system is working, so in the case study the initial review carried out ensured clarity around both the structural interconnections (what went to what) and the dynamic interdependencies of time cycles, queues, bottlenecks and buffers. This informed the design of the new structure, and formed some of the non-negotiables which had to be accommodated.

Status structure — Appropriately distributed decision making/power

A structure will always have power elements. The use of power in relationships often encourages and rewards information control rather than learning. However, in organisations which encourage creativity and innovation, those 'in power' use both formal and informal relationships to openly show an organisational intention to facilitate knowledge sharing and cross-functional collaboration and trust (Lin, 2007). This includes not only inviting disconfirming information from all levels, but visibly acting on it at the top.

Status is also given based on expertise, and such status acts as an effective form of communication in a system as long as people can locate it and use it as required (which is why the database in this case was designed as it was). Thus an innovative, human system is rarely flat or devoid of status or power. It also removes the ability to leverage power in order to get things done. Appropriate use of status can unlock as well as stifle innovation or creativity.

Case study examples

Decision-making capacity and the effect of status

One problem with the original structure was the inability to meet market requirements (generic windows) through a lack of connection between the R&D process and executive decisions on matters of marketing and strategy. The marketing director would travel the world and promise production timings which were not cognisant of technical, compliance and logistical limitations. When the generic windows were subsequently missed, the R&D group were held accountable. In the newly designed structure each phase had a phase manager physically located within the workspace, who also sat on the executive group of senior decision makers (including the marketing director).

To ensure that complex problems and decisions were fully informed, those from project or star teams who had the best knowledge of the situation or technology were included in the decision process to maximise useful information for quality outcomes.

Over-flattening

As part of implementing the new structure and allocating roles, the group voted to have a completely flat structure to show that all staff were of value to outcomes. (The group did this despite advice regarding the potential inequity of equality). Within three months, the senior scientists complained of such inequity, describing the fact that they had to lead, advise and apply many years of experience, yet neither the pay structure nor the decision-making hierarchy reflected this. It was also harder to work out whom to go to in a scientific speciality, as there was no obvious differentiator of the more experienced staff member unless they were personally known.

A structural level was added. This both addressed the equity issue but also put information back into the system by easily allowing people to differentiate levels of capacity, and made various communication processes and logistical collaborations more expedient and fair. This process proved a good surfacing exercise for the group, who had to decide what would be formally valued, and how much it was worth.

It should be noted that this discussion had not been possible for the group at the beginning of this process as they were not able to consider such a complex aspect of what structure brings to the group, but it was now able to occur with a high level of objectivity, highlighting the importance of time for the growth of capacity and maturation.

Over-empowerment

On two particular occasions, sub-optimal emergent behaviour needed to be dealt with. In the first instance the issue of over-empowerment was addressed as a number of staff took the level of decision-making and inclusion too far and the balance had to be restored between decision-making and capability/accountability. At an all-staff meeting I led a discussion on what empowerment was and was not, clarified the levels of capability and responsibility involved, and reinforced the role of managers in an empowered workplace. In the second example, a single individual attempted to hijack the outcome of the secret ballot voting process when he was unsuccessful in gaining a managerial role, and he was subsequently counselled by the VP personally on the work ethics required, and his responsibility to the team.

Physical Spaces

The current work on creative hubs offers insight into what sparks creativity and innovation. It is interesting to investigate what makes Berlin a new Silicon Valley despite other cities investing hugely in trying to create such a cluster of creative activity, but instead growing a technical agglomeration which shares location but not connections or ideas. The features of such creative spaces include the natural heterogeneity of many factors such as buildings (proximity, cost, mix of large and small spaces) and people (from all over the world and quite different fields, from opera to physics). However, though creative centres attract people with such individual diversity, they share an ethical alignment, a sense of curiosity and an attraction to collaborative openness, which in turn increases trust levels (and with that, more nimble capacity for novel ideas). Cheap accommodation and open, light spaces allow people to bump into each other, intermingled with co-working spaces and small cocooning areas, which set up neural dynamic resonance and enhance nimble, creative problem solving (Goleman, Boyatzis, & McKee, 2001; Kerr, 2012a). The high level of self-organised experimentation also allows people to quickly identify what works and what doesn't. For this to be successful, however, the organisation has to be one which openly practices and rewards the sharing and connecting of information and ideas rather than their protection.

It should be noted that this discussion on physical spaces in creative environments involves *unstructured* and *informal* communication, a critical aspect of creativity and innovation. This is lost in organisations that confuse a creative environment and empowerment with having no rules around attending the workplace. Rules should allow flexibility around attendance to enable specific requirements of lifestyle balance or short periods of private reflection if individuals require them. However, this is quite different from working primarily at home or in 'virtual workspaces', as these options minimise the face-to-face and informal interaction required for idea generation.

To summarise

An innovative structure includes connective infrastructures based around human networks to foster relationships and shared meaning (Wheatley, 2006). Processes include valid feedback loops based on accurate real-time information (Helbing & Lämmer, 2008) and common areas and spaces where knowledge sharing is easy, unstructured and encouraged, often with information or idea-sharing devices shaped in ways which invite interaction. Communication infrastructure creates a rich information cascade which can flow where needed at the speed required, supported by practices that push and pull tacit knowledge. Both codifiable and non-codifiable knowledge and information can be captured and passed on in ways people can understand and use. The following section looks at some of these practices in an operational setting.

Internal hotwiring — Enabling practices

Innovation is fostered by information gathered from new connections; from insight gained by journeys into other disciplines or places; from active, collegial networks and fluid, open boundaries. Innovation arises from ongoing circles of exchange, where information is not just accumulated or stored, but created. Knowledge is generated anew from connections that weren't there before. (Wheatley, 2006, p. 113)

A clear sense of purpose and supportive leadership

Innovation occurs most often at the edges between safe practice and the space of the unknown. Whether people *have* to change as the old ways are being removed, or they *want* to innovate, creativity is highest in this space of possibilities (Mitleton-Kelly, 2003). Yet people must feel safe to step into this space, and the leader does this by ensuring that people trust that they will be supported when trying something new. If people do not trust in this support, creativity shuts down. An innovative environment encourages and rewards informed risk-taking, as well as cross-functional and cross-organisational collaboration and trust (Lin, 2007). Their leaders and managers steer rather than control, and invite information which critiques decisions and current methods.

But innovative environments do not task people only with being creative, as people's confidence is maintained by also carrying out tasks successfully. Thus managers should task people with actions to enhance reflective activity. By building performance management systems which drive this, leaders directly influence idea generation and application, as well as 'the creation and implementation of beneficial novelty' (De Jong & Den Hartog, 2007). People become comfortable enough to let go of 'the five C's': consistency, comfort, competence, confidence and control when attempting creative or innovative activity (Seijts, Crossan, & Bilou, 2010).

Case study example

The approach to transforming the R&D business was a radical, emergent process to build a capability to meet market requirements and maximise innovation, while being values-driven and allowing appropriate self-determination regarding the use of people's skills and ideas. The approach produced both excitement and anxiety as a natural consequence of the group being able to make a large number of decisions throughout the process. There was further anxiety due to external pressure from the board for a twelve-month turnaround from loss to profit. The vice president was candid regarding the size of the challenge but established hope, faith and a shared, positive vision for a new entity. He remained supportive throughout the process, including allowing staff to challenge him when necessary, and resourcing activities as required. He supported 'risky' methods of rebuilding the business, such as the voting-in of managers and the design of a new organisational structure, as well as the introduction of new pay and bonus systems, values-based appraisal, level flattening, new seating plans and creative Fridays. Staff devised many of these changes, with a support process which consisted of myself advising or at times co-creating a solution, and the VP actively pushing and supporting the change process until people engaged with it and became comfortable.

Capability to act and make decisions

Such a capability requires clear permissions and agreement on responsibilities as well as accurate feedback mechanisms. An innovative organisation has an infrastructure that supports shared (appropriate) decision-making, is shaped by agreed outcomes and is able to be acted on. In practical terms, there are two main areas in which this enhanced connectivity is important for innovation and creative practice. One is the distribution of authority to make decisions and act to those who can make the best quality decisions. As this is often not the most senior person (at least not alone), both decision-making and the ability to act on those decisions should be appropriately and widely distributed.

Case study example

One of the issues the staff identified was the executive group's lack of understanding in regard to the effect their decisions had on operational work and outcomes (especially marketing). No-one on the executive group was close enough to the actual work, and so, in order to gain insight, part of the new structure included placing the three new section managers physically in their operational groups as well as on the executive group. This enhanced strategic decision quality by creating an understanding of operational requirements.

An even more challenging part of the restructure process was the voting-in of the new managers by secret ballot. The vote was the major criterion (but not the only one) for success, and it was carried out after a rigorous process which ensured people knew what each role had to achieve, and took the vote seriously. Some of the managers were most uncomfortable with this process, and required support throughout it, but were not rescued from it. Confidentiality was maintained (with only one staff member attempting to derail the process as described above). Interestingly, the votes aligned well with success in the other criteria relevant to placement. Another interesting development concerned one of the managers who was voted in. Years before, he had been promoted too early and his inexperience caused issues, which resulted in him returning to his technical role. The VP was worried that this baggage would block the now mature and capable individual from a management role but the staff clearly thought he had matured sufficiently.

The other aspect of a capability to act is the feeling of empowerment and encouragement to play, experiment and fail. All of these activities ensure that creativity and subsequent innovation is maximised. The 'slow hunch' is often informed by multiple misses, and the most outlandish experiment or spectacular failure can produce the best learning. This means that educated risk-taking and multiple experiments (Heifetz, Grashow, & Linsky, 2009) are required by innovative organisations with a culture of high risk, low blame and multiple small strategies to observe progress and recognise points of innovation.

Case study example

Blue sky research (where practical applications are not immediately apparent) had stopped in the R&D business and needed to be brought back to life. The VP allocated Friday afternoons for creative play (in the shape of the skunk works of Lockheed Martin in the 1960s), but little changed. Through conversation, I discovered that the previous boss had tied all innovative activity to direct production and profit outcomes. Therefore, giving people permission to play was now not enough to make them feel safe, as they were used to being measured and their output quantified. This was a revelation in regards to the perception of freedom to experiment, and accordingly, in order to make them more comfortable with such experimentation, the VP put a 'quota' on ideas that had to be of operational use (initially one in ten). This bounded output, and it was arranged for the managers to increase the number of acceptable attempts when a person got close to the maximum (i.e. one in ten became one in twenty, then one in thirty). In addition, reinforcing this perceptive change, activities were recognised and rewarded, such as identification of lessons learned during experiments, and rewarding a high number of new experiments. This also reframed the meaning of a tangible outcome.

We also widened the concept of creative play to incorporate groups from different disciplines, who would meet to play with ideas, discuss concepts and plan cross-functional and cross-disciplinary collaboration. After three months, people were no longer counting failures and had decoupled the need for results from concept creation. Within nine months, the business had developed the first new major technical innovation in three years.

Knowledge creation and dissemination

Knowledge dissemination differs in terms of processes and people. Knowledge capture entails the collection, transfer and integration of personal knowledge, often tacit in nature. To facilitate innovation, such knowledge and experience needs to be captured and retrieved in ways people are comfortable with. Dissemination methods must allow tacit knowledge to be informally explored and exchanged, often in face-to-face situations, mentoring and shadowing activities. Wilson (2002) talks of distinguishing between cognitive (experience of action) and technical (aesthetic experience) knowledge, and there are different ways in which these convert and are passed on. Data that can be coded should sit in databases with functionality that the staff have designed in order to get the data they need in the format and timeframe they need it.

Case study example

Data

Instead of the generic, often clumsy corporate knowledge system, the R&D organisation built systems that captured and defrayed various types of information rapidly and widely. The organisation targeted learning and cross-functional collaboration, and the group designed a multi-level information database to capture and show everyone's skill level, expertise (self-rated) and experience. This was quickly used for mentoring, project group design and knowledge transfer, as people had permission to choose mentors and put together project teams. It remained current as it was updated by individuals rather than a formal administrative HR process, but primarily because it was useful.

Practices that push and pull tacit knowledge

The R&D group had to find a way to reward externalisation of specialist tacit knowledge and experience, as this was not easy to capture and had to be passed on in other ways. A number of measures were implemented including a peer reviewed prize for novel ideas and innovative work; information forums including monthly soapbox talks to present an area of knowledge to all interested R&D staff; public and electronic information packages from anyone going to conferences; and star team presentations and 'skunk work' discussions to ensure that information and learning circulated regularly.

Improving descriptive communication skills (Toastmasters)

As information flow is both pushed and pulled out, the R&D staff identified the lack of capability to communicate ideas as an issue, and chose three ways to improve this. First, they were all trained in Edward de Bono's '6 hats' method for structuring decision-making discussions and meetings so that they were not sidetracked by strong individuals. Secondly, they underwent a 'Toastmasters' program, so that each person could articulate quickly and accurately all aspects of their ideas. All staff grew in capability to push their ideas out, especially formerly reticent (but brilliant) scientists. Thirdly, at executive level there was an annual review of the formation of any gates or blockages to information-cascade down through the organisation — this included talking to people face to face rather than surveys.

Opening up qualitative analysis

Creative environments have decision-making processes that open up inquiry and analysis rather than pushing for closure. This allows the slow hunch to accumulate over time, and it assists in the uncovering or putting forward of disconfirming information to check the veracity of decisions or progress.

The difference between qualitative analysis and data interpretation should be acknowledged — often the latter is driven by simple or limited evaluation criteria and the need to meet short timeframes, which are a fact of life in business. Analysis, as opposed to data interpretation, entails creative thought, and as such people need to have the time, space and opportunity to undertake it through both structured and unstructured methods. Again, here is where heterogeneity of ideas, backgrounds and skills is valuable, with venues and processes that openly encourage the analytical flow. Interestingly, the overall time taken not only to produce but to implement a workable outcome is often shorter using qualitative analysis. This is because, though the initial process may take longer, it includes issues being more accurately identified and both multiple alternatives and contingencies being designed, whereas short-term thinking around activities and data interpretation often results in time lost due to failure or rework.

Case study example

The group identified two previously missing elements which would allow for qualitative analysis. The first was to have informal spaces available with tools for sharing ideas and information, which the group then designed to suit their needs. Some of the tools were deliberately not high-tech, so along with LED screens there were whiteboards, sheets of butcher paper and physical models which could be manipulated.

The group also identified a gap in the capability for analysis and brainstorming of ideas in meetings. Instead the meetings were skewed towards decision-making, and this tended to support the process of closure. After some trial and error, instead of trying to encompass relevant analysis in normal task-driven operational meetings, another type of meeting which was non-task was set up for the group to get together and muse over, discuss and analyse all aspects of a business issue and a deliverable or successful outcome. This meeting format grew in popularity and became an essential part of supporting innovative practice. It also shortened subsequent operational meetings and made them more effective.

Knowledge gatekeepers

Well-constructed systems can have a minimal effect on creativity and innovation if people do not proactively act as transfer-points for knowledge, ideas and information. Rogers (2003) has documented that knowledge flows along interpersonal channels, and that it is opinion leaders who often persuade people to adopt new ideas, acting as focal points in radial networks which are important for innovation. Such opinion leaders act as gateways by providing meaning through increasing understanding around the intent of learning activities, thus giving people context and reinforcing shared goals and alignment. An important point about such knowledge gatekeepers is that they are trusted, which involves personal interaction at some point.

Case study example

The star team members acted as knowledge gatekeepers in various ways. They could sit in on a project team discussion when their speciality was relevant to planning or execution. They could explain the options, possibilities and consequences of technologies and techniques, improving decisions and preventing issues formerly prevalent in project planning. This was the 'short' version of education regarding the star team's technical speciality.

If a greater level of knowledge was required, a star team would be made up of one or two subject-matter experts, as well as a member of each team who would use the process or technology in their project or role. The team members were not expected to become experts, but gained robust knowledge of the impact and requirements of the process/technology. They took that knowledge back into their project teams once they were skilled enough to return.

Lastly, both star team members and other experts from within the projects gave soapbox presentations regularly to the whole staff group in order to raise general knowledge levels. These were very well-

> attended, and were held in a large area adjacent to the canteen, so that people ate, socialised and discussed together following the presentation.

Communication systems that allow the curious to override formal silos

Much of the work on information and communication flow in innovative organisations centres around information moving through human systems along relationships rather than through formal channels (Wheatley, 2006) — the grapevine is an ideal example. A human brain is a good analogy for efficient communication and information flow, where each new piece of information cascades across the whole brain and is taken up and stored where it is relevant. If the brain (or the human) had to stop and decide where each new piece went, we would no longer be able to function. Organisations similarly freeze up when they spend too long trying to direct, edit or restrict information and communication flow. Wheatley describes the use of managers in this way as 'information chastity belts'. Instead, creative organisations tend to have a high level of unstructured communication, which is modelled informally but consistently at all levels.

Case study example

Tools of communication included the soapbox sessions and star teams noted above, as well as unstructured meetings and regular cross-collaborative activity. A useful tool for idea sharing in a research environment (or any creative environment) allowed for an individual with a new idea to enter it into a shared electronic online log which date-stamped the entry and allocated the idea to them. Thus the incentive became to share concepts and innovative ideas, rather than to protect them.

Management communication was openly unstructured at all levels for many types of information. The VP considered that managers and staff could develop judgments regarding who needed to know what, and ensure outcomes. He modelled the expectation that people would not have regular meetings if they could talk as and when required, and where possible this was done face to face instead of emailing, which often saved time and increased both the efficiency and creativity of the outcome. The philosophy was for managers and influencers to 'lean in doorways' and chat rather than lock themselves away in offices trying to decide what was best. A new acceptance of innovative thinking and trying things was consistently reinforced at all levels, largely through encouraging a culture of constant small discussions supported by online information gathering and feedback capability. Topics and nascent ideas were then discussed in larger forums.

Formal information and communication included monthly updates by the VP on progress. Every three months there were traffic-light briefings on both new and existing issues and risks, and the sharing of strategic-level forward plans. These reports and plans remained on the intranet at all times.

Processes for reflection: 'I am here'

As discussed above, reflection is critical for creativity. It allows incubation of ideas and intuitive combinations of information to form because the brain is in the ideal state for new neural connections to occur (Boyatzis, 2008). Reflection allows for surfacing of ideas, and dissonant information can be incorporated by 'pattern breaking' of neural networks, leading to new options and approaches. Reflection is not just something done in a solitary state (though when engaged in such divergent thought people often do so alone). As stated above, it is also important to have periods of concentrating on something other than the task or problem, as this allows neural connections to be made in the background (referred to as incubation), which assists in the formation of new neural networks. This is further enhanced by play and experimentation, especially if it entails crossing organisational or technical borders and if it stimulates ideas and networked ways of seeing things. Novel outcomes are created through allowing the layering needed to form the slow hunches which are built over longer periods, and it is critical to have organisational support for such individual and group reflection on past ideas (Johnson, 2010). This includes areas for such types of activity to occur, often in an informal manner, as such spontaneity is as important as the structured and phased aspects of laboratory work.

As alluded to above, having *too* much time for creative and reflective activity is also not conducive to innovation, as there needs to be a balance between the freedom to creatively reflect and the requirement for effective completion of tasks, which lends the confidence that is gained through pragmatic action (De Jong & Den Hartog, 2007). An interesting tool showing this is Cowan and Darsoe's (2008) graphing of the 'integral structure of wisdom', many aspects of which are very similar to creativity. This contains a horizontal, linear, time-based axis denoting speed and pragmatic competition, with quantified, sequential goal achievement and role definition. The vertical axis depicts depth, stillness and richness, emphasising the intangibles and hidden connections that surround and inform a situation, and denoting increasingly inclusive levels of enquiry through intuition and questioning, leading to what Cowan and Darsoe (2008) term the 'transcendence of dualities'. (This parallels various features of creativity building in the case study in this chapter).

Case study example

In addition to the group reflective activities and processes outlined so far, the R&D staff designed small and large break-out areas. Some were easy to get to and within line of site for communal and cross-border play, while others were tucked away out of sight and human traffic flow for private reflection. There were various combinations of (moveable) seats placed around the grounds and couches placed near the rear patio doors

---

for informal discussion, or a bit of peace and quiet. Some members of staff took a while to be comfortable with relaxing away from their desk, but within three to six months this was no longer a problem.

Summary of key findings from the case study

This section groups the key findings under the headings of space, time, diversity and interconnectedness to illustrate the themes and to ensure a coherent picture.

The theme of space

- The minimal structure appeared to directly increase the level of creative and innovative activity. The ability to move between and across flexible boundaries (hotwiring) was an enabler, as were the minimal (but clear) rules designed by staff around how movement could occur. Thus self-organisation was not impeded.

- The differentiation in physical layout of the workplace allowed for individuals and groups to choose the appropriate venues or spaces as required, greatly enhancing their ability to achieve operational outcomes.

- The organising of physical spaces and flow also proved critical to increasing creative activity and innovation. They included spaces for large group interaction, small group cocooning, individual and group reflection areas which were either private or 'interruptible', and a flow that maximised frequent unplanned encounters by way of corridor placement and team group layouts.

- There were informal areas which were attractive to spend time in, and were equipped with items such as whiteboard walls, which allowed people to share ideas and others to see what was being discussed. Such informal spaces proved to be where the best ideas emanated from. (They also had good coffee!) Staff enjoyed sitting outside to discuss ideas, or walking together, the dynamic resonance of which increases novel ideas and aids memory by stimulating the motor neuron system and producing chemicals which assist in ideation (Kerr, 2013).

The theme of time

- When people's time was allocated across activities which contained both outcome-based tasks along with creative play and reflection time, the resulting innovative outcomes increased (thus empirically backing up De Jong and Den Hartog's work on innovation and task balance).

- Creative play and reflection had to be facilitated formally, and over a period of time, in order for people to perceive it as permissible to engage in such activity, as it had previously been blocked or reframed by tying it to strict outcomes. The implementation of initial quantitative boundaries made staff feel safe, and could then be removed over time as different feedback mechanisms came into play to reward such activity.

- The traction pattern of time in regard to the progress of successful change followed an exponential rather than linear time-path. In practical terms there was a prolonged time of acceptance of the need for change and assimilation of new outcomes, but once such commitment was made by people, progress was then rapid.

- The VP also had to understand the non-linear nature of time in change. He became uncomfortable near the end of the structural redesign phase (around five months), when a 'storming' process appeared ready to halt progress. The exponential nature of traction was stressed to him and he was convinced not to react to the volatile nature of this part of the process, but to allow staff an agreed period of a week to work through the process. Within that week, the working groups produced three edited structures and one was unanimously voted in. Activity then increased markedly and adoption of the process took off.

The theme of diversity

- A key part of the successful change to innovative practice was the high level of staff inclusion in the re-engineering process. Staff were encouraged and enabled to debate and define clear outcome requirements and non-negotiables, which then acted as shared boundaries with which staff designed their structure. This meant they were fully invested in the outcome.

- The processes which allowed for both formal and informal discussion and cross-pollination of ideas and activities across diverse parts of the organisation facilitated a sharp increase in all forms of creative experimentation and innovative activity.

- The redesign of data and knowledge capture to suit the heterogeneous requirements of both formal and informal interaction and knowledge was another strong enabler in terms of allowing innovative experiments and projects to occur, as well as tacit knowledge to be distributed widely.

- The wider distribution of permission to make decisions and to act allowed a more diverse mix of people to take action, collaborate and learn, markedly increasing the amount of novel ideas and outcomes over a few months. The appropriate distribution of decision-making fostered bounded autonomy (within clear goals and purpose), and led to the staff's clarification of what success looked like across diverse outcomes, and where responsibility sat.

- 'Knowledge gatekeeper' was not a formal role. In previous change processes there had been 'change champions', but these roles had not worked, due to their imposed status (as is predominantly the case). Instead, the knowledge gatekeepers included a diverse group of people with different skills and roles, but with the critical personal capability to convince others to try new things or understand why changes were happening. Thus staff saw gatekeepers as credible, effective and valuable, and made use of them.

The theme of interconnectivity

- With regard to operational rules, the capacity for creative thinking and innovative behaviour was still latent within the R&D group but had been blocked by simplistic, linear rules from senior corporate decision makers linking innovative activity to producing direct profit. Such tight rules had a multiplicity of effects, many of which were hard to illustrate as simple cause and effect because of the complex nature of their interaction.

Over time, however, changes made to activities including risk, timeframe setting, play and collaboration saw creativity and innovation climb, and the result was a new technical breakthrough within nine months.

- Regarding information flow and reach, we adopted a 'brain cascade' analogy. As explained above, this means information and data is not sequestered and controlled as it enters the system but instead flows widely, and is held in easily accessed formats to be taken up by interested parties as required. This means that effort is spent less on shaping rules, procedures and blockages, and more on agreeing on the process of central capture and storage in order to minimise blocks and maximise access. Curiosity across silos was both enhanced and rewarded by ensuring full transparency of people's skills and experience through the shared database. An expectation was created that this database should be used for such activities as increasing the growth of both formal and tacit skills, locating mentors and putting together project teams. People ensured that their information was both current and comprehensive, as it had direct, practical outcomes.

Collaboration as an organisational meta-capability

- The higher level of collaboration meant that taking responsibility became easier, and so taking responsibility subsequently increased. Such collaboration also appeared to raise the level of social maturation in the group, and both of these things supported innovative activity.
- The importance of collaboration as a meta-capability was borne out within a year with the successful technical breakthrough and the highly functioning organisation. Its value was also proven when at a later stage the overseas arm of this global joint venture subsequently restructured and took over the now successful R&D business. They sent a new GM over to Australia, whereupon the strongly autocratic individual undid many of the changes outlined in this chapter and replaced it with what he saw as a clean, efficient hierarchical structure, which was driven by tight, linear rules and non-collaborative procedures. This resulted in nearly half of the staff (including nearly 70 per cent of the managers) leaving. When I asked these individuals, upon following up with the organisation one year later,

why they left, a major theme was that they 'could not go backwards', but have taken their lessons with them into various organisations. It is also worth noting that the venture failed within two years.

In addition to the themes above, a consistent thread was leadership and trust

- A clear enabler of the emergent process towards innovative capacity was a leader who demonstrated complex thinking, including a high tolerance for ambiguity and risk-taking, along with a clear sense of purpose and shared values.

- The leader engendered trust in the people undergoing the change, both initially and throughout the process. He was able to paint a picture of potential success, and maintained the characteristics of listening, honesty, passion and candid, pragmatic optimism.

- Staff also felt trust in me as an experienced facilitator skilled in building innovative businesses, and in the co-creative process which facilitated the building of ideas and outcomes rather than imposing them.

- Trust between myself and the VP was also critical, especially during two phases of the process: the slow initial period which entails the lessening of resistance and assimilation of a new way of being, and in the storming phase. Both of these times tempted the VP to tighten control, but his faith in the process and his ability to deal with ambiguity allowed him to let the system settle.

Conclusion

The empirical evidence aligns with much of the literature around managing organisations as complex adaptive human systems, particularly around maximising the potential for creativity and innovation. This is said to occur most effectively when the organisation (system) is in a 'disequilibrium state', as there is a maximisation of knowledge generation, innovative ideas and novelty through learning (Mitleton-Kelly, 2003; Gupta & Anish, 2011).

A high level of commitment was gained from employing a guided self-organisation process which included all staff, bounded by non-negotiables and a clear, shared purpose. The rules put in place to maintain direction were minimal and wherever possible did not impede interconnectivity between people, ideas, movement, communication or knowledge. Such simple rules enabled creativity (Brown & Eisenhardt, 1998) and, along with distributed decision-making capacity, reflected Handy's (1992) concept of 'subsidiarity'[1] in allowing people to be effective.

The distribution of authority to decide and act also appeared to increase creativity and innovation, as it allowed the exercise of judgement, a process which is critical in order for learning to take place, yet which usually resides with power and authority (Handy calls this 'robbing people of their opportunity to learn'). The ability to exercise judgement also is thought to increase problem-solving capability and maximise the potential for raising cognitive complexity (Kira & van Eijnatten, 2008) and creative capacity due to increasing cognitive scripts. This appeared to occur.

Case study results suggested that, regarding innovation management, the VP and managers directly influenced both idea generation and application by exhibiting behaviours which combined daily management behaviour with deliberate actions that stimulated innovation (Bueno, Anton, & Salmador, 2008). Other forms of management behaviour conducive to creativity included consultation; autonomy tempered with support for initiatives; 'tending' and mentoring appropriately; and building a safe yet high-risk environment. Deliberate actions included the framing of what was meant by innovation; creating possibilities for idea generation; practising open and transparent communication of ideas ('cascade'); and facilitating avenues for knowledge sharing, diffusion and creation.

During the process it was fundamental that the focus was maintained on building an enabling structure and accompanying practices which supported outcome achievement along with maximising innovative activity and creative experimentation. A shared understanding of these concepts framed activities, and the pragmatic optimism of high expectations helped to maintain momentum both during the change journey and in the new way of working.

The maturation of the group appeared to be aided by being supported through the change process but not rescued from it (Heifetz, Grashow, & Linsky, 2009). This was true even when people did not wish to take on responsibility for some of the more difficult aspects, such as the placement of individuals in the new structure, or being voted in as a manager. A trusted facilitator aided the process, strongly aided by being

---

1   'Subsidiarity' is an organising principle which states that a matter ought to be handled by the smallest, lowest, or least centralised authority capable of addressing that matter effectively.

embedded within the organisation. This resulted in a high level of knowledge around organisational dynamics and outcome requirements, and the ability to embed and localise co-creation and shape relevant change techniques to suit the level of readiness of the group whilst maintaining constant pressure for them to move forward. The result was a guided process of shaping, building and running an innovative business. (Interestingly, this process has been successfully repeated in other types and sizes of organisation. For more examples, see Kerr, 2012a.)

Implications for future research

Limitations of the present research's abductive method centre on the lack of possible quantification and control in regard to the potential mediation effect of other variables, some of which are unknowable in a complex field setting. This, however, should not stop robustly constructed abductive field studies from being carried out, as qualitative data is often all that is available in the early stages of research into new areas such as the construction of operational capacity for creativity and innovation.

There are many potential areas of future research suggested by this case study in regard to operationalising innovation and hotwiring for creativity.

With regard to the themes this chapter presents, research could investigate whether one factor is more important than another in specific circumstances. For instance, is it more important to have adequate time built in across the process of becoming creative and innovative than it is to ensure spatial features which increase creative capacity, or do space and time interact in some form of facilitative pattern as the process unfolds? Does the pattern change depending on the circumstances?

Alternatively, is the key a high level of diversity around such things as organisational make-up, skill type, problem solving, play or decision-making?

With their high level of interconnection, does variance in any of the themes (of time, space, diversity) influence organisational design, and how? Or is it the other way around: does a high level of variance in business sector or operational outcome requirements influence the themes' interconnections — i.e. does operationalising innovation in a 'Google' environment affect connectivity compared to a manufacturing assembly line, and how?

Does the relative importance of any of the themes to each other change over time in an increasingly innovative organisation?

With regard to leadership style, though it appears to have a strong impact on the operationalisation of innovation, how creative and innovative can an organisation become *despite* its leadership? If this is possible, to what extent is it possible, and what are the drivers and enablers?

How important is the role of skilled facilitation, and what is the effect of this emanating from within or outside the original organisation? Is it only important at the start of the process? Are adequate support and allocation of authority the most important factors for the facilitator? Relatedly, how does the effectiveness or damage of ill-equipped or standardised external facilitation compare to in-house facilitation alone in terms of operationalising innovation?

Such future research will contribute valuable insight into the important area of growing creative capacity and the ability to innovate — both vital capabilities in an increasingly complex and unknowable future.

References

Aaltonen, M. (2007). *The third lens: Multi-ontology sense-making and strategic decision-making* (1st ed.). Aldershot: Ashgate Publishing Limited.

Aldous,CR. (2007). Creativity, problem solving and innovative science: Insights from history, cognitive psychology and neuroscience. *International Education Journal, 8*(2), 176-86.

Allman, JM, Watson, KK, Tetreault, NA, & Hakeem, AY. (2005). Intuition and autism: A possible role for von Economo neurons. *Trends in Cognitive Sciences, 9*(8), 367-73.

Artigiani, R. (2005). Leadership and uncertainty: Complexity and the lessons of history. *Futures, 37*(7), 585-603.

Ashmos, D, Duchon, D, McDaniel, R, & Huonker, J. (2002). What a mess! Participation as a simple managerial rule to 'complexify' organizations. *Management Studies, 39*(2), 189-206.

Backhouse, A, & Drew, P. (1992). The design implications of social interaction in a workplace setting. *Environment and Planning B: Planning and Design, 19*, 573-84.

Bakke, JW, & Yttri, B. (2003, June 17-19). Hybrid infrastructures for knowledge work. *Proceedings of the Fourth International Space Syntax Symposium.* London: UCL.

Boutellier, R, Gassman, O, & von Zedtwitz, M. (2000). *Managing global innovation: Uncovering the secrets of future competitiveness* (2nd revised ed.). New York: Springer.

Boyatzis, RE. (2006). Intentional change theory from a complexity perspective. *Journal of Management Development, 25*(7), 607-23.

Boyatzis, RE. (2008). Leadership development from a complexity perspective. *Consulting Psychology Journal: Practice and Research, 60*(4), 298-313.

Brand, S. (2000). *The clock of the long now: Time and responsibility.* New York: Basic Books.

Brown, S, & Eisenhardt, K. (1998). *Competing on the edge* (1st ed.). Boston: Harvard Business School Press.

Bueno, E, Anton, JM, & Salmador, MP. (2008). Knowledge creation as a dynamic capability: Implications for innovation management and organisational design. *International Journal of Technology Management, 41*(1-2), 155-68.

Clauss-Ehlers, CS. (2008). Sociocultural factors, resilience, and coping: Support for a culturally sensitive measure of resilience. *Journal of Applied Developmental Psychology, 29*(3), 197-212. doi: 10/1016/j.appdev.2008.02.004.

Cowan, D, & Darsoe, L. (2008). Wisdom: A backdrop for organizational studies. In D Barry & H Hansen (Eds.), *The SAGE handbook of new approaches in management and organization* (1st ed., pp. 332-43). London: SAGE Publications.

De Jong, J, & Den Hartog, D. (2007). How leaders influence employees' innovative behaviour. *European Journal of Innovation Management, 10*(1), 41-64.

Dubois, A, & Gadde, LE. (2002). Systematic combining: An abductive approach to case research. *Journal of Business Research, 55*(7), 553-60.

Gittell, J, Cameron, K, Lim, S, & Rivas, V. (2006). Relationships, layoffs, and organizational resilience. *Applied Behavioural Science, 42*(3), 300-29.

Goleman, D. (2006). *Social intelligence: The new science of human relationships* (1st ed.). New York: Bantam Books.

Goleman, D, & Boyatzis, R. (2008, September). Social intelligence and the biology of leadership. *Harvard Business Review, 86*(9), 74-81.

Goleman, D, Boyatzis, R, & McKee, A. (2001, December). Primal leadership: The hidden driver of great performance. *Harvard Business Review, 79*(11), 42-51.

Gupta, A, & Anish, S. (2011). *Insights from complexity theory: Understanding organizations better.* Retrieved from http://tejas.iimb.ac.in/articles/12.php.

Handy, C. (1992, November-December). Balancing power: A new federalist paper. *Harvard Business Review, 70*(6) 59-71.

Haner, U. (2005). Spaces for creativity and innovation in two established organizations. *Creativity and Innovation Management, 14*(3), 288-98.

Haner, U, & Bakke, J. (2004, June 20-24). On how work environments influence innovation — A case study from a large ICT Company. *CD-ROM Proceedings of the XV Annual Conference of the International Society for Professional Innovation Management (ISPIM)*, Oslo.

Heifetz, RA, Grashow, A, & Linsky, M. (2009). *The practice of adaptive leadership: Tools and tactics for changing your organization and the world.* Boston: Harvard Business School Publishing.

Helbing, D, & Lämmer, S. (2008). Managing complexity: An introduction. In D Helbing (Ed.), *Managing complexity: Insights, concepts, applications* (1st ed., pp. 1-16). Berlin: Springer-Verlag.

Järvensivu, T, & Törnroos, JÅ. (2010). Case study research with moderate constructionism: Conceptualization and practical illustration. *Industrial Marketing Management, 39*(1), 100-8.

Johnson, S. (2010). *Where good ideas come from: The natural history of innovation.* New York: Riverhead Books.

Kerr, F. (2010, December 8-10). 'It Is what we are here for — A once in a lifetime chance': A tale of inspirational leadership. *Proceedings of the 24th Annual Australian and New Zealand Academy of Management Conference (ANZAM): Managing for Unknowable Futures.* Adelaide: Australia.

Kerr, F. (2012a). Creating and leading adaptive organisations: The nature and practice of emergent logic. (PhD thesis, University of Adelaide, South Australia).

Kerr, F. (2012b, February). Hot-wiring the innovative organisation. *Necessary Conversations: Innovative Leaders Conference*. (Keynote address, Singapore Raffles Town Club, Singapore).

Kerr, F. (2013, November 27-29). Neuroleadership: How trust facilitates creativity. *Creative Innovation Conference*. (Conference paper, Melbourne, Australia).

Kira, M, & van Eijnatten, F. (2008). Socially sustainable work organizations: A chaordic systems approach. *Systems Research and Behavioral Science, 25*(6), 743-56.

Kristensen, T. (2004). The physical context of creativity. *Creativity and Innovation Management, 13*(2), 89-96.

Lin, H. (2007). Knowledge sharing and firm innovation capability: An empirical study. *International Journal of Manpower, 28*(3), 315-32.

Magadley, W, & Birdi, K. (2009). Innovation labs: An examination into the use of physical spaces to enhance organizational creativity. *Creativity and Innovation Management, 18*(4), 315-25.

Marion, R. (1999). *The edge of organization: Chaos and complexity theories of formal social systems* (1st ed.). Thousand Oaks: SAGE.

Meadows, DH. (Ed.) (2008). *Thinking in systems: A primer*. White River Junction, VT: Chelsea Green Publishing Company.

Mitleton-Kelly, E. (2003). *Complex systems and evolutionary perspectives on organisations: The application of complexity theory to organisations*. Kidlington: Elsevier Science.

Moody, J, & Nogrady, B. (2006). *The sixth wave: How to succeed in a resource-limited world*. Sydney: Random House.

Morrison, T. (2010). The strategic leadership of complex practice: Opportunities and challenges. *Child Abuse Review 19*(5), 312-29.

Moultrie, J, Nilsson, M, Dissel, M, Haner, U, & Van der Lugt, R. (2007). Innovation spaces: Towards a framework for understanding the role of the physical environment in innovation. *Creativity and Innovation Management, 16*, 53-65.

Patton, JR. (2003). Intuition in decisions. *Management Decisions, 41*(10), 989-96.

Pike, S, & Roos, G. (2007, October 15-16). The future of intellectual capital.

Fourth International Conference on Intellectual Capital, Knowledge Management and Organisational Learning, Bellville, South Africa.

Rogers, EM. (2003). *Diffusion of innovations* (5th ed.). New York: Simon & Schuster.

Saaty, TL, & Shih, HS. (2009). Structures in decision making: On the subjective geometry of hierarchies and networks. *European Journal of Operational Research, 199*(3), 867-72.

Seijts, G, Crossan, M, & Bilou, N. (2010). Coping with complexity. *Ivey Business Journal, 74*(3), n.p. Retrieved from http://www.iveybusinessjournal.com/topics/leadership/coping-with-complexity.

Surman, M. (2012). Using the open principles of the web to create creative tech communities. (Audio podcast retrieved from http://www.abc.net.au/radionational/programs/spark/spark-170/3804704).

Wheatley, MJ. (2006). *Leadership and the new science: Learning about organization from an orderly universe* (3rd ed.). San Fransisco: Berrett-Koehler Publishers, Inc.

Wilson, T. (2002). The nonsense of 'knowledge management'. *Information Research, 8*(1), 144.

Business model innovation in nonprofit social enterprises

7

Eva Balan-Vnuk, The University of Adelaide
Peter Balan, University of South Australia

Introduction

Nonprofit social enterprises innovate their business models; however, little is known regarding why they do this, nor what capabilities they need to innovate their revenue-generating activities. In this qualitative exploratory research, we examined five nonprofit social enterprises in South Australia, and found that these organisations consciously innovate their business models for two key reasons: to remain financially viable, and to expand the delivery of important services to the community. In addition, we identified six capabilities that enable nonprofit social enterprises to support their business model innovation.

The nonprofit sector makes a significant contribution to the Australian economy, and performs functions that government and the private sector are either unwilling or unable to provide (Australian Government, 2010; Salamon, 1993). Recognised as an outcome of social entrepreneurship (Mair & Marti, 2006), social enterprises are part of the nonprofit sector, and adopt business models (Austin, Stevenson, & Wei-Skillern, 2006; di Domenico, Haugh, & Tracey, 2010; Zahra, Gedajlovic, Neubaum, & Shulman, 2009).

Innovation in social entrepreneurship is enacted with the aim of fulfilling a primary social mission to create social value (Weerawardena & Mort, 2006), and also to remain competitive (Weerawardena & Mort, 2012). In response to the growing emergence of social enterprises globally, and the positive social impact these organisations deliver, there are increasing calls for empirical research to investigate the 'business models' of social enterprises (Certo & Miller, 2008; Yunus, Moingeon, & Lehmann-Ortega, 2010; Zahra et al., 2009).

Although the relevance of business models for nonprofit social enterprises has been established (Bagnoli & Megali, 2011; Weerawardena & Mort, 2012), and a business model framework for social business has been proposed (Yunus et al., 2010), the mechanisms employed by such enterprises to innovate their business models have not been clarified. This gap in the literature makes it difficult to ascertain which skills or capabilities nonprofit social enterprises must acquire in order to develop and innovate their business models, and to provide guidance to nascent nonprofit social enterprises to increase their chance of organisational survival.

This exploratory qualitative investigation of five nonprofit social enterprises in South Australia seeks firstly to discover why they innovate their business models, and secondly to identify the specific innovation capabilities that enable them to innovate their business models. We identify two key reasons for business model innovation in this chapter, namely that the adoption of business models helps these social enterprises to achieve financial sustainability, and to generate funds to expand the provision of important services. We also identify six capabilities required to support business model innovation in social enterprises: a clear understanding of the organisation's social mission, access to specialised knowledge, access to external expertise, ability to respond to needs of clients and/or beneficiaries, access to alliances and partnerships, and ability to experiment with pilot programs.

This chapter is structured as follows. First, we outline the theoretical background underpinning nonprofit social enterprises, business models, and business model innovation. Next, we present the research questions, explain the data collection process and analysis method, and provide a description of participant organisations. We then present findings from the empirical fieldwork along with verbatim extracts, and we summarise these in the discussion section. The chapter concludes with recommendations for future research and with final remarks.

Theoretical background

Nonprofit organisations and nonprofit social enterprises

Nonprofit organisations (NPOs) exist to address public needs through the delivery of services or programs that would otherwise be unavailable to those in need (Morris, Webb, & Franklin, 2011). NPOs are defined by two key characteristics: promotion of a social value, and prohibition of profit distribution to shareholders (Considine, 2003). These organisations are predominately created as an outcome of social entrepreneurship activities (Weerawardena & Mort, 2006), and arise when an individual or a group focuses on creating social value to alleviate or remedy social problems (Peredo & McLean, 2006). Caroline Chisholm's activities, which earned her the title of the 'emigrant's friend' (Bogle, 1993), are an early example of social entrepreneurship in Australia. There are over 600 000 nonprofit organisations in Australia, employing over 890 000 people, and accounting for 4.1 per cent of GDP. It is considered that 59 000 of these NPOs are financially significant, and it is estimated that approximately half of the sector's income is self-generated, excluding contracted government services (Australian Government, 2010). These organisations include co-operatives, associations, clubs, charities, trusts, volunteer and grassroots organisations, as well as social enterprises (Lyons, 2001). Although the emphasis on revenue generation is not as prominent as in the for-profit sector, NPOs are still required to be financially viable so that they may continue to operate (Young, Jung, & Aranson, 2010).

Due to reduced access to appropriate and reliable sources of funding, NPOs are becoming increasingly entrepreneurial (Weerawardena, McDonald, & Mort, 2010). Entrepreneurial behaviour requires being innovative, proactive and prepared to take risks (Miller, 1983). This behaviour in nonprofit social enterprises is driven by three key reasons (Dees, 1998):

1. the requirement to be financially viable and grow new revenue streams

2. the need to respond to growing numbers of beneficiaries who require support

3. the desire to address new opportunities for social value creation.

As a result, social entrepreneurship 'encompasses the activities and processes undertaken to discover, define, and exploit opportunities in order to enhance social wealth by creating new ventures or managing existing organisations in an innovative manner', and these activities and processes include 'adopting business models' in order to sustain creative solutions to social problems that are commonly large-scale and difficult to address (Zahra et al., 2009, p. 519).

This research focuses on nonprofit social enterprises as organisations that undertake activities to firstly create social value and secondly generate revenue through the provision of goods and services. The key difference between social enterprises and traditional NPOs is that social enterprises actively engage in trading activities (Lyon & Sepulveda, 2009). These trading activities are a core component of these organisations as they reduce dependence on external funding sources such as government grants, donations and bequests, which may be unreliable and may not continue into the future (Shaw & Carter, 2007). As social enterprises typically provide unique services and products to a specific group of beneficiaries, there would be a significant negative effect should the social enterprise be unable to continue its operations (Weerawardena & Mort, 2012).

Business model and business model innovation

The term 'business model' gained prominence with the internet boom, with one of the first references made in the context of electronic commerce (Timmers, 1998). Despite growing consensus that the term 'business model' describes how an organisation creates and captures value (Teece, 2010) and develops sustainable competitive advantage (Morris, Schindehutte, & Allen, 2005), a clear unifying definition is lacking (George & Bock, 2011). The business model construct has been examined in the e-commerce, innovation and strategy domains (Zott, Amit, & Massa, 2011), and the lack of a consistent definition is partly due to the multivalent nature of the construct (Baden-Fuller, Demil, Lecocq, & MacMillan, 2010). For example, George and Bock (2011) define the business model as 'the design of organizational structures to enact a commercial opportunity' (p. 99), while according to Stewart and Zhao (2000), the business model 'is a statement of how a firm will make money and sustain its profit stream over time' (p. 290). In addition, although various approaches have been made to operationalise the business model (Fritscher & Pigneur, 2010), this area of academic inquiry remains fragmented. In this study we replace the term 'firm' with 'organisation'; however the meaning does not change when applied to social enterprises.

The social enterprise and social entrepreneurship literatures both implicitly and explicitly link the business model construct to the organisation's ability to be financially sustainable, which depends on the organisation's revenue-generating activities (Darby & Jenkins, 2006; Liu & Ko, 2012; Wilson & Post, 2013; Zahra et al., 2009). Although it is generally accepted that social enterprises have business models in place (Bagnoli & Megali, 2011; Short, Moss, & Lumpkin, 2009), the factors that influence social enterprise business model innovation remain unclear and require further investigation (Certo & Miller, 2008; Yunus et al., 2010). Ongoing financial sustainability that allows these organisations to serve beneficiaries now and in the future is critical (Weerawardena & Mort, 2012), so understanding how nonprofit social enterprise business models can be innovated is valuable.

The literature makes it clear that it is not enough for an organisation to have a business model; it is argued that the business model cannot remain static or unchanged, but needs to be the subject of innovation. This is because it is proposed that business model innovation is 'the only way to escape cut-throat competition and sustain competitive advantage' (Matthyssens, Vandenbempt, & Berghman, 2006, p. 752). Further, business model innovation is considered to be among 'the most sustainable forms of innovation' (Sosna, Trevinyo-Rodríguez, & Velamuri, 2010, p. 384), and is seen as offering business an 'alternative or complement to product or process innovation' (Amit & Zott, 2012, p. 41). Matzler, Bailom, von den Eichen, & Kohler (2013) confirmed the importance of business model innovation by citing IBM's 2009 CEO survey, observing that nearly 100 per cent of CEOs were actively seeking to change their business through business model innovation — an increase from 37 per cent in the IBM 2006 CEO survey (Pohle & Chapman, 2006).

In other studies, businesses that have been considered to be successful in the business model innovation process have been identified as having 'an orientation towards experimenting … a balanced use of resources' and a 'coherence between leadership, culture and employee commitment' (Achtenhagen, Melin, & Naldi, 2013, p. 427). Successful business model innovation has been found to bring together 'positioning', 'product and service logic', 'value creation logic', 'marketing and sales logic', and 'profit formula' in a fashion that delivers a sustainable and differentiated position in the market (Matzler et al., 2013, p. 33). It is argued that failure to adopt all of these individual aspects in the process of business model innovation will see the organisation either fail to create and/or capture increased value (Teece, 2010).

Although gaining sustainable competitive advantage may be less prominent for social enterprises, it is critical for these enterprises to ensure ongoing financial sustainability to serve beneficiaries in the future (Oftedal, 2013; Weerawardena & Mort, 2012). This suggests that, in a changing business environment, social enterprises should innovate their business model to ensure they can meet their goals. Business model innovation is here operationalised as 'the ongoing management process of developing and introducing improvements and replacements' (Mitchell & Coles, 2004, p. 41). This management process comes in the form of new 'product and service offerings to customers and end users that were not previously available' through 'the combination of "who", "what", "when", "where", "why", "how", and "how much" an organisation uses to provide its goods and services' (Mitchell & Coles, 2004, p. 17).

While there has been growing attention given to business model innovation, its theoretical paradigm is unclear (Schneider & Spieth, 2013). This has led to the development of a number of different theoretical perspectives regarding business model innovation, namely the resource-based view of the firm, the dynamic capabilities view of the firm, or the strategic entrepreneurship view (Schneider & Spieth, 2013). In practice, these different perspectives have led to a variety of proposed methods for business model innovation, such as:

- the use of visual tools to encourage creativity and collaboration (Eppler, Hoffmann, & Bresciani, 2011)

- the implementation of a four-stage initiation, ideation, integration and implementation process (Frankenberger, Weiblen, Csik, & Gassmann, 2013)

- designing the organisational structure and workflow (Osterwalder, 2004)

- focusing on alignment with financial, environmental and societal goals (Carayannis, Sindakis, & Walter, 2014)

- the implementation of a 'virtuous Corporate Social Responsibility cycle' (Oftedal, 2013, p. 272) comprising the articulation of the customer value proposition, analysis of the target market segment, the organisation value chain and the organisation's position in the value network, and the formulation of the competitive strategy.

In summary, discussion of business model innovation in social enterprises has received only limited attention, and this may be on account of the different conceptualisations and theoretical approaches in the literature. In particular, the enterprise factors or capabilities that influence social enterprise business model innovation remain unclear and require further investigation (Certo & Miller, 2008; Yunus et al., 2010).

In this exploratory qualitative research, we seek to investigate firstly why nonprofit social enterprises need to engage in innovating in their revenue-generating activities, and secondly to explore the capabilities that are required by these enterprises in order to innovate their business models. The research questions we addressed in this study, therefore, are:

1. Why do nonprofit social enterprises innovate their business models?

2. What capabilities do social enterprises require to support innovation in their business models?

Research method

In this chapter, we explore the characteristics of business model innovation undertaken by five South Australian social enterprises. We used a qualitative case study approach, as this is appropriate for investigating an under-explored and complex phenomenon within a specific context (Eisenhardt, 1989; Yin, 1996). Prior case study research in the social entrepreneurship domain indicates the value of this approach to investigate and explain phenomena influencing social enterprises (Haugh, 2007; Kistruck & Beamish, 2010; Weerawardena & Mort, 2006). We undertook purposive sampling to capture a range of industries in which social enterprises operate.

Data collection

We used an Australian database of social enterprises as the sampling frame in this exploratory study, namely the 'Finding Australia's Social Enterprise Sector', or FASES (Barraket, Collyer, O'Connor, & Anderson, 2010). This database of 4900 organisations that consider themselves to be social enterprises was developed by Social Traders, an NPO in Victoria that encourages the establishment of commercially viable social enterprises in Australia, in partnership with the Australian Centre for Philanthropy and Non-Profit Studies, Queensland University of Technology.

For this study, we selected five relatively large social enterprises based in South Australia, based on the following criteria, which are consistent with prior research into nonprofit social enterprises (Chalmers & Balan-Vnuk, 2012):

1. the explicit statement of a social objective or mission (di Domenico et al., 2010)

2. not operating as a government department (Haugh, 2005)

3. prohibition of profit distribution to shareholders (Considine, 2003)

4. explicit reference to specific revenue-generating activities that involved the sale of goods and/or services to individual paying customers (Lyon & Sepulveda, 2009), either on the website or in the official organisation reports.

Once we had identified organisations based in South Australia, we reviewed the website and publicly available documentation of each organisation to ascertain suitability for this research. If the organisation met the selection criteria, we contacted the Chief Executive Officer by email and invited them to participate. The sample we present in this research is a sub-set of a larger study of sixty-five social enterprises. For this research, we selected five social enterprises based in South Australia from the larger study to represent different areas of national nonprofit social enterprise activity, as presented in Table 7.1.

Data analysis

We conducted in-depth interviews with the Chief Executive Officer of four organisations (Cases A, B, C and D), and the Chief Financial Officer of Case E (all referred to as CEOs from this point). We selected these executives as the key informants due to their seniority and ability to provide an overall perspective of the activities of the organisation (Snow & Hrebiniak, 1980; Zahra & Covin, 1993). In addition, we examined the website of each nonprofit social enterprise, along with available annual reports, to identify the social mission and trading activities. As the focus of the interview was on the activities undertaken by the organisation, and did not require the CEO's personal experiences and motivations, it is the organisation that is the unit of analysis in this study (Blee & Taylor, 2002).

We asked the CEOs to describe the revenue-generating activities undertaken by their organisation, and explain why these specific activities were selected. We then asked them to give an example of a recent innovation that generated revenue for the organisation, and to describe what was required to implement this innovation. Interviews were audio-recorded and transcribed verbatim for analysis using

Case	FTE(1)	Purpose	Trading activities
A	89	Animal welfare and protection	1) Physical and online retail outlets selling pet accessories 2) Pet cremations 3) Pet adoption and training 4) Lotteries
B	62	Recycling and sustainability	1) Resource Recovery Centres: sales of goods (e.g. in store, on eBay, to recycling centres) 2) Business divisions that employ people with a disability; these included car cleaning services, lawn and garden service, document destruction, firewood sales
C	12	Environmental education	1) Waste audit programs and education 2) Environmental consultancy 3) Retail sales of environmental products
D	110	Disability services	1) Low vision clinics 2) Commercial factory (assembly, packaging) that employs people with a disability 3) Retail sales of products for beneficiaries 4) Property rental income
E	65	Education	1) School fees from domestic students 2) School fees from international students 3) Fees from teaching English to students and adults 4) Study tours for international students 5) Classroom hire outside school hours 6) Fees to allow staff of external firms to use gym facilities outside school hours

(1) Full-time equivalent employees

Table 7.1: Social enterprises participating in this study.
Source: Courtesy of the authors.

NVivo software (QSR International Pty Ltd, 2010). The researchers reviewed the interview transcripts and coded the responses to the open-ended questions into relevant categories (nodes). We then compared the themes that were identified and consolidated the findings. This cross-case analysis was conducted to identify insights not readily available from existing theory and empirical research, and to propose a contextual generalisability (Johns, 2006), applicable to other nonprofit social enterprises in Australia.

Findings

We present the findings in two sections. The first addresses why social enterprises innovate their business models, and the second provides an illustration of the capabilities that social enterprises require in order to innovate their business models. We include verbatim comments from interviews to emphasise the capability requirements identified in this exploratory study.

Research Question 1: Why do nonprofit social enterprises innovate their business models?

We asked CEOs to give details about innovation in their revenue-generating activities, and explain why these were undertaken. Two key reasons emerged. The first was the need to ensure the financial sustainability of the organisation itself so that it could continue to operate, even in the absence of other funding sources. The second was the need to generate surpluses to expand the delivery of services provided to beneficiaries. The distinction between these two reasons is the difference between general survival of the organisation, and the generation of funds for the specific goal of delivering critical services.

1.1 To ensure enterprise sustainability

The CEOs of the five social enterprises in this study emphasised the importance of generating income in order to keep the enterprise operating. Without adequate funds, the organisations would cease to exist, leaving a gap in services important to the community. Four of the CEOs indicated that they were recruited to improve the financial health of their organisations, as the previous CEO and/or senior management team were not equipped or qualified to address these critical issues.

The board here were looking for somebody with a commercial background, rather than a not-for-profit background, because at the time the organisation was struggling financially, so they needed somebody to actually really have a look at the business and sort of bring it into, I guess, the modern era, as such. (A)

I think not-for-profits at some level need to have somebody with commercial acumen, because in the end it's about paying our bills. If we can't pay our bills, we can't deliver the core business. (A)

The CEO of Case A had been in the position for eight years, and spent the first twelve months in the role restructuring the organisation, from the IT system to hiring appropriate personnel throughout the organisation. Investment in infrastructure was made because the CEO perceived that this was critical to support the survival and growth of the organisation.

This comment was echoed by the CEO of Case C, who took on the role of developing new programs and revenue streams to ensure the financial sustainability of the organisation:

When I first came to this organisation twenty years ago or so, I mentioned that they were in a bit of trouble, and it was financial trouble. And it was financial trouble not because of mismanagement per se but maybe it was trying to do things the old way, and not picking up on what had to be done the new way. (C)

The CEOs of Cases D and E also mentioned this:

Many years ago when I first started, the [organisation] was in a fairly precarious financial situation. (D)

Well, going back quite a few years the school was in a little bit of financial trouble … and there needed to be alternate income streams. (E)

Overall, the respondents made it clear that even though they operate nonprofit organisations, it is imperative that they innovate in the ways that they generate revenue in order to survive, as stated by the CEO of Case C:

The organisation has changed how it operates; it's a business, even though we're a not-for-profit, or an NGO, non-government organisation. If we don't apply the business principles we simply don't survive. (C)

1.2 To generate surpluses to fund core services

CEOs also mentioned generating surpluses as a key reason for innovating their business model. Respondents made it clear that if their organisation did not find new ways to earn money, then it would not be able to deliver services or its core business:

> We're very commercial, have no fear about that. I mean, if we don't make money we don't supply services. And for us to make money we have to do it very well. We're not charity-minded in the sense of warm and fuzzies are the important driver; the important driver is to meet the needs of the clients and to do it to the best of our ability, and to do that and to hire the staff we need, and to have the resources we need, we need to make money; we need surpluses. (B)

Case E established a separate entity as a for-profit venture. The sole aim of this venture is to generate funds to support the activities of the organisation, and to minimise the costs borne by beneficiaries of their services.

> It has its own separate board of directors ... [B]ottom line, it's there to make money, okay — it's there to make money so the cash can be released to the [organisation] to build and do certain things. It supplies money so that capital works can be undertaken. (E)

In summary, nonprofit social enterprises seek to capture economic gains by innovating their revenue-generating activities to ensure the continuing operation of the organisation, as well as to provide surplus funds to expand the scope of services provided to beneficiaries. It is evident from the responses from all the CEOs that there was no expectation of ongoing financial support from government contracts or from other philanthropic sources, and they were therefore focused on generating revenue for the organisation.

Research Question 2: What capabilities do social enterprises require to support innovation in their business models?

To address the second research question, we asked the CEOs to give an example of a recent revenue-generating innovation in their organisation, and to respond to the prompt, 'What was required to make this happen?' In the analysis, six themes emerged to describe the capabilities that nonprofit social enterprises require to in order to innovate their business models and ensure that these trading activities are appropriate for their organisation. We discuss the six capabilities separately below, with verbatim quotes to illustrate each.

2.1 Clear understanding of the organisation's social mission

Nonprofit social enterprises in this sample indicated that whatever revenue-generating stream they adopted, these must be consistent with their mission. This suggests that the organisation must be very clear about its purpose, and ensure that it focuses on delivering services that support the core social mission. In effect, a clear understanding of the mission gives guidance and direction for business model innovation by providing a focus which excludes possible directions for innovation that might not support the goals of the enterprise.

> So, I went through a complete review of the whole organisation and the services that we offered. We cut some, what I considered to be non-core services. (A)

> We run a whole lot of businesses, but they all obviously still need to focus back on what our mission and our role is. (D)

> The common denominator — it's got to improve school life — you can't work against school life so if it's going to come with a revenue stream which is going to cause disharmony to school life, you have to balance that … [O]verall it has to contribute. (E)

2.2 Access to specialised knowledge

Specialised knowledge, or intellectual property, held in the organisation or in a partner organisation, was seen to be a requirement for business model innovation. Intellectual property [IP] is defined as codified knowledge, and is a component of innovation capital (Daniels & Noordhuis, 2005). In this sample, Case B highlighted that they actively swapped some of their codified knowledge, or IP, with another organisation undertaking similar activities, so that they could both benefit. Case C explained that it is through their specialised knowledge that they are able to identify new revenue activities. Other organisations collaborated with a partner who had access to technology, but the specialised knowledge for the idea originally came from the social enterprise (Case D).

> We did get a lot of help from other organisations who were doing similar things interstate and in Mount Gambier. For example, [another organisation] was doing something similar but not quite like we were doing. We swapped them some IP on a wood yard, and they gave us some IP on a salvage yard, and the same was done with [a different organisation] in Bendigo; they were very generous with their IP. (B)

We set a little strategy — I mean, we didn't do it by chance, we recognised there was a niche ... We know our business, we know about waste, we know about litter, we know about recycling, we deliver in to schools, we have great friendships with local government. (C)

The idea of this, the concept, is ours, but the technology is actually owned by a company we work in partnership with. (D)

2.3 Access to external expertise

The CEOs surveyed considered that it was important for their organisations to be able to access expertise from external sources in order to develop their business models and revenue streams. This capability differs from '2.2 Access to specialised knowledge', as discussed above, in that this factor [2.3] refers to expertise brought in from external sources that are typically individuals, as distinct from knowledge embedded in the enterprise (or partner organisation). One way these organisations gain expertise is to hire staff or to work with experts who have specialist knowledge that is critical for success. Organisations can also capitalise on their own knowledge by turning it into expertise that they make available to other enterprises (Case C). Organisations also pointed out how vulnerable they were to key staff leaving the organisation, and that it could subsequently take time to find someone else with a comparable level of expertise (Case E).

The skill sets that I had available to me was not going to get me anywhere. So, the whole management team has changed. So, personnel have changed at the senior level. IT, everything that we do, there was no efficiency; there was no nothing. So, I had to effectively rebuild the whole organisation. (A)

Yeah, we hired new staff and transferred some staff from different parts of the organisation to it as well. But mostly, the majority of staff would be new ... But we did hire some staff that had some experience. (B)

One is that we are, I don't like the term 'experts', but we have expertise in education, in community education engagement. (C)

We had a long-standing manager — he left us — he was really good and then we recruited someone who didn't work out and then we recruited someone new, so we had a full staff and it's working out really well now. (E)

2.4 Ability to respond to the needs of clients and/or beneficiaries

Organisations innovate by responding to the needs of their clients and beneficiaries, as well as to new market opportunities. Identifying a specific niche where there is a lack of available services, or expertise, allows nonprofit social enterprises to innovate new revenue-generating activities.

> Because we are able to change quickly and react quickly, we can fill a niche very quickly, and if we're filling a niche that means that we're responding to somebody that's got an issue and they see us as being part of their solution. So sometimes the door opens for us. (C)

> So we identify a niche that the councils were struggling in, that they didn't have the resources, and they didn't have the people on the ground. (C)

Nonprofit social enterprises also innovated by acting on feedback from clients. When clients identified a certain need, organisations responded quickly by providing a solution for a fee (Case A). These organisations also innovated new business activities in response to the needs of clients outside their specific geographical area (Case D).

> Somebody rang us up and said, 'I'd like to have a small service for our animal that's passed away,' and we said, 'Well, that's not a problem, we've got a memorial garden'. But we thought, well if you're going to have a service you're going to need a celebrant, and it occurred to us very quickly that if we had a relationship with a celebrant, have a relationship with a caterer … we could say, well, for $500, 'We'll organise the whole thing, and you just tell us the date that you want, sir'. (A)

> I don't have a charter to go outside of my state, but, demand outside of the state is very high, so, and the board have approved me to basically offer this on a fee-for-service basis to blind people in other states. (D)

2.5 Access to alliances and/or partnerships

Collaborating with partners and forming alliances is one capability that nonprofit social enterprises may draw on to innovate their business models. Partnerships are used to gain knowledge and expertise (Case C), help defray costs (Case E), help distribute services to a wider group of beneficiaries (Case D), and they are viewed as essential to an organisation's long-term success (Case B). Therefore, access to alliances and partners supports the ability of the organisation to develop new and creative revenue-generating activities.

Partnerships are essential to the long-term success of the organisation and the growth of it … I think partnerships are the way of the future. (B)

If there's space there, and it's part of our business, we'll jump in, but we jumped in with partners, we weren't that silly that we're going to jump in and get the cream pie in the face if everything goes wrong. (C)

One of the great things by working with partnerships and stakeholders is that we can double our money. We go to somebody and say, 'We've got a grant of $10 000 or we've got an agreement for $50 000 [and] we could do so much more if you could match it dollar for dollar' — and we're very successful with that. (C)

This partnership acts as a distributor for a service that is valuable for visually impaired people who cannot read a book. (D)

We've got the gym — the new gym now, we've got a corporate relationship with the [fitness company]; they run all our gym equipment and memberships from other organisations which provide us with a little bit of a revenue stream; we wouldn't be able to afford to go and buy that ourselves. (E)

2.6 Ability to experiment with pilot programs

Experimenting with pilot programs provides a way for nonprofit social enterprises to innovate while minimising potential risk. By trying things out on a small scale using existing available resources, the organisation gains knowledge and experience, and can learn from the pilot experience to minimise risk when launching a new revenue-generating program for a larger group of clients or beneficiaries.

We're going to run with it, and benefit from it, learn from it, and then use that as a stepping stone. (C)

We did the first national digital pilot six years ago. (D)

[We] test things out. I mean, I know we've made changes to these structures since we've been here; we're just always looking to make changes every year to do something slightly different. (E)

The findings are summarised in Table 7.2.

Discussion

This exploratory study revealed that the nonprofit social enterprises in this South Australian sample innovate their business models for two key reasons, and identified

Research Question	Findings
1. Why do non-profit social enterprises innovate their business models?	1.1 To achieve enterprise sustainability
	1.2 To generate surpluses to fund core services
2. What capabilities do social enterprises require to support innovation in their business models?	2.1 Clear understanding of the organisation's social mission
	2.2 Access to specialised knowledge
	2.3 Access to external expertise
	2.4 Ability to respond to the needs of clients and/or beneficiaries
	2.5 Access to alliances and/or partnerships
	2.6 Ability to experiment with pilot programs

Table 7.2: Summary of research findings.
Source: Courtesy of the authors.

six capabilities supporting business model innovation. The consistent responses from these social enterprises indicate the critical role the business model plays to ensure the financial sustainability of the organisation and its ability to deliver core services to its beneficiaries. Several of the CEOs had been recruited specifically to innovate existing business models, or create new ones, to ensure the organisation's continued survival.

With regard to Research Question 1, this exploratory study showed that, without adequate funds to operate, a social enterprise cannot create social value and fill the social gap it was established to address (Weerawardena et al., 2010). This supports prior research that emphasises the importance of business models for the survival and effectiveness of social enterprises (Yunus et al., 2010), as well as the importance of business model innovation for sustainability and competitive advantage (Matthyssens et al., 2006).

The findings for Research Question 2 reflect the importance of knowledge acquisition and management, and relationship management, which characterise innovation in general in service organisations (Castro, Montoro-Sanchez, & Ortiz-De-Urbina-Criado, 2011; den Hertog, van der Aa, & de Jong, 2010). In particular, having a very clear understanding of the social mission and overall purpose of the organisation was identified as a requirement for business model innovation for the organisations in this sample. This factor is identified in the business model innovation method proposed by Carayannis et al. (2014), and is also consistent with findings that a social enterprise's revenue activities must 'fit' with the social mission (Foster & Bradach, 2005; Wilson & Post, 2013). McDonald (2007) also identifies that nonprofit organisations with clear, motivating missions tend to be more innovative in general. Although some scholars have perceived the social mission as a constraint on a social enterprise's ability to innovate (Weerawardena et al., 2010; Weerawardena & Mort, 2006), in this research we present it as a capability that assists a nonprofit social enterprise's ability to innovate its business model by providing focus and direction.

Having in-house access to specialised knowledge is identified in the business model innovation method proposed by Frankenberger et al. (2013). This factor is implied in several other business model innovation methods, as knowledge is identified as a key resource that is necessary for sustainability and competitiveness in any organisation (Barney, 1991).

Enterprises in this sample either explicitly or implicitly recognised that they were able to innovate more successfully by increasing the level of knowledge and expertise within specific relevant areas in their organisation. In particular, they recognised that they needed to bring in expertise from external sources in order to innovate their business models. This finding supports the business model innovation process suggested by Frankenberger et al. (2013), which relies on implementing an idea-to-implementation process that relies on transforming knowledge or ideas into value.

We found that having a close understanding of the current and future needs of clients and/or beneficiaries was another capability supporting business model innovation in nonprofit social enterprises. Previous research has identified that social enterprises initiate programs or activities in response to community needs (di Domenico et al., 2010), and also adapt services based on the changing needs of their beneficiaries (Weerawardena et al., 2010). This finding supports the business model innovation process proposed by Oftedal (2013), which relies on the articulation of the customer value proposition.

The importance of relationships, partnerships and alliances for nonprofit social enterprises was identified as a strategy to gain additional resources which would otherwise be unavailable or unattainable (Weerawardena et al., 2010), or as a way to scale operations beyond the current capacity of the organisation (Bloom & Smith, 2010). The organisations in this sample actively sought and valued partners, and used these partnerships as a source of business model innovation.

Finally, as social enterprises are generally resource-constrained, they frequently test an idea through a pilot program as a way to learn what does or does not work, while ensuring that the organisation minimises unnecessary risks (di Domenico et al., 2010; Weerawardena & Mort, 2012). By experimenting or improvising with the resources they have at hand, nonprofit social enterprises are able to gain experience and refine their ideas, using bricolage to further drive innovation in their activities (di Domenico et al., 2010). In particular, McDonald (2007) identifies experimenting and testing ideas as an important aspect of innovation for nonprofit organisations, and this is a key aspect of the business model innovation method involving the use of visual tools to encourage creativity (Eppler et al., 2011).

Overall, the capabilities found to be needed for business model innovation in this sample of social nonprofit enterprises can be seen to be aligned with the dynamic capabilities view of the firm (Teece, Pisano, & Shuen, 1997). In particular, the factors 'Clear understanding of the organisation's mission', and 'Access to alliances and/or partnerships' identified in this study can be regarded as elements of the Teece et al. (1997, p. 521) 'position or strategic posture', and the other four factors ('Access to specialised knowledge', 'Access to external expertise', 'Ability to respond to the needs of clients and/or beneficiaries', and 'Ability to experiment with pilot programs') can be identified as aspects of the Teece et al. (1997, p. 518) 'organisation and managerial processes'.

Future research recommendations

This research highlights the importance of social enterprises having a viable business model in place. However, having insight into what these business models look like — and whether any particular type(s) of business model confer(s) a financial advantage — would be beneficial to social enterprises, and this remains an area for further investigation.

Although a range of approaches have been proposed for business model innovation, this study supports those based on the dynamic capabilities view of the firm (Teece et al., 1997). This finding suggests that dynamic capabilities would provide a useful framework for further qualitative and quantitative research with larger samples to confirm the requirements for business model innovation in nonprofit social enterprises. Undertaking industry sector and international comparisons may also help determine whether industry, geographical or cultural differences exist regarding the requirements for business model innovation for nonprofit social enterprises.

Importantly, in this research we found that the enterprise social mission was not perceived as a constraint on business model innovation, as suggested by previous research (Weerawardena et al., 2010; Weerawardena & Mort, 2006) but was seen in a positive manner, its role being to provide clear and helpful direction for business model innovation. This finding suggests the value of further research into this particular aspect of the social enterprise.

We have also highlighted IP as a business model innovation capability for nonprofit social enterprises. Future research may investigate the extent to which IP contributes to the success of these types of organisations. Further studies may investigate the role of organisational learning in the development of the requirements for business model innovation in nonprofit social enterprises, based on the recognition that organisational learning helps organisations innovate (Bingham & Davis, 2012), and that learning styles may influence the types of innovation undertaken by the organisation (Baker & Sinkula, 2007). Additionally, investigating the types of assets or resources required for social enterprises to innovate may also be valuable, particularly at different stages of growth (Greene & Brown, 1997).

Although social enterprises exist in many varied forms, this paper focuses on social enterprises that operate under the nonprofit legal structure (Considine, 2003). Future research may investigate other forms of social enterprises, including for-profit social enterprises, also known as social ventures or social businesses. Future research may investigate the role of strategic balance theory (Deephouse, 1999) in social enterprises, as they must innovate their business models in order to differentiate themselves while ensuring that these activities complement their primary social mission (Foster & Bradach, 2005; Wilson & Post, 2013).

Conclusion

This research responds to calls from scholars to better understand various aspects of social enterprises, including their business models (Short et al., 2009). We used a small sub-set of South Australian nonprofit social enterprises as the subject of qualitative research to explore why they innovate their business models, and to identify the capabilities required to carry out business model innovation. The findings support those found in other empirical studies of NPOs (McDonald, 2007) and nonprofit social enterprises (Di Domenico et al., 2010; Weerawardena et al., 2010), and contribute to the literature by providing greater understanding of why nonprofit social enterprises seek to innovate their business models, as well as by establishing a preliminary list of capabilities that support this activity.

Nonprofit social enterprise CEOs may use these findings as a framework to examine whether their organisation either implicitly or explicitly uses these six capabilities to support business model innovation. For example, these organisations may review existing alliances and partnerships to identify ways to innovate their business model. Nonprofit social enterprises may also formally catalogue the specialised knowledge they have developed over time and use this, as well as expertise from outside their organisation, as a source of innovative ideas to further innovate their business model. These findings highlight the importance of understanding the needs of clients and/or beneficiaries, as this information can provide useful insights that may lead to future revenue-generating activities. Additionally, in contrast to other studies (Weerawardena & Mort, 2006), the participating CEOs perceived the social mission as a source of business model innovation, rather than as a constraint.

NPOs and nonprofit social enterprises contribute to society by fulfilling unmet needs. These organisations are not just about delivering social services; they also need to be financially sustainable. Continual innovation of their business models is therefore critical to the success of social enterprises, and further exploration and validation of the requirements for business model innovation in nonprofit social enterprises is required.

References

Achtenhagen, L, Melin, L, & Naldi, L. (2013). Dynamics of business models — Strategizing, critical capabilities and activities for sustained value creation. *Long Range Planning, 46*(6), 427-42.

Amit, R, & Zott, C. (2012). Creating value through business model innovation. *MIT Sloan Management Review, 53*(3), 41-9.

Austin, J, Stevenson, H, & Wei-Skillern, J. (2006). Social and commercial entrepreneurship: Same, different, or both? *Entrepreneurship: Theory and Practice, 30*(1), 1-22.

Australian Government. (2010). Contribution of the not-for-profit sector: Productivity Commission research report. Canberra, ACT.

Baden-Fuller, C, Demil, B, Lecocq, Z, & MacMillan, I. (2010). Editorial: Special issue to business models. *Long Range Planning, 43* (2-3), 143-5.

Bagnoli, L, & Megali, C. (2011). Performance measuring in social enterprises. *Nonprofit and Voluntary Sector Quarterly, 40*(1), 149-65.

Baker, WE, & Sinkula, JM. (2007). Does market orientation facilitate balanced innovation programs? An organizational learning perspective. *Journal of Product Innovation Management, 24*(4), 316-34.

Barney, J. (1991). Firm resources and sustained competitive advantage. *Journal of Management, 17*(1), 99-120.

Barraket, J, Collyer, N, O'Connor, M, & Anderson, H. (2010). *Finding Australia's Social Enterprise Sector: Final report.* Brisbane: Australian Centre for Philanthropy and Non-profit Studies, Queensland University of Technology.

Bingham, CB, & Davis, JP. (2012). Learning sequences: Their existence, effect, and evolution. *Academy of Management Journal, 55*(3), 611-41.

Blee, KM, & Taylor, V. (2002). Semi-structured interviewing in social movement research. *Methods of Social Movement Research, 16*, 92-117.

Bloom, PN, & Smith, BR. (2010). Identifying the drivers of social entrepreneurial impact: Theoretical development and an exploratory empirical test of SCALERS. *Journal of Social Entrepreneurship, 1*(1), 126-45.

Bogle, J. (1993). *Caroline Chisholm: The emigrant's friend.* Leominster: Gracewing Publishing.

Carayannis, EG, Sindakis, S, & Walter, C. (2014). Business model innovation as lever of organizational sustainability. *The Journal of Technology Transfer*, 1-20.

Castro, L, Montoro-Sanchez, A, & Ortiz-De-Urbina-Criado, M. (2011). Innovation in services industries: Current and future trends. *The Service Industries Journal, 31*(1), 7-20.

Certo, ST, & Miller, T. (2008). Social entrepreneurship: Key issues and concepts. *Business Horizons, 51*, 267-71.

Chalmers, DM, & Balan-Vnuk, E. (2012). Innovating not-for-profit social ventures: Exploring the microfoundations of internal and external absorptive capacity routines. *International Small Business Journal, 31*(7), 785-810.

Considine, M. (2003). Governance and competition: The role of nonprofit organisations in the delivery of public services. *Australian Journal of Political Science, 38*(1), 63-77.

Daniels, H, & Noordhuis, H. (2005). Project selection based on intellectual capital scorecards. *Intelligent Systems in Accounting, Finance and Management, 13*(1), 27-32.

Darby, L, & Jenkins, H. (2006). Applying sustainability indicators to the social enterprise business model: The development and application of an indicator set for Newport Wastesavers, Wales. *International Journal of Social Economics, 33*(5/6), 411-31.

Deephouse, DL. (1999). To be different, or to be the same? It's a question (and theory) of strategic balance. *Strategic Management Journal, 20*(2), 147-66.

Dees, JG. (1998). Enterprising nonprofits. *Harvard Business Review, 76*, 54-69.

di Domenico, ML, Haugh, H, & Tracey, P. (2010). Social bricolage: Theorizing social value creation in social enterprises. *Entrepreneurship: Theory and Practice, 34*(4), 681-703.

Eisenhardt, KM. (1989). Building theories from case study research. *Academy of Management Review, 14*(4), 532-50.

Eppler, MJ, Hoffmann, F, & Bresciani, S. (2011). New business models through collaborative idea generation. *International Journal of Innovation Management, 15*(6), 1323-41.

Foster, W, & Bradach, J. (2005). Should non-profit seek profits. *Harvard Business Review, 83*(2), 92-100.

Frankenberger, K, Weiblen, T, Csik, M, & Gassmann, O. (2013). The 4I-framework of business model innovation: A structured view on process phases and challenges. *International Journal of Product Development, 18*(3/4), 249-73.

Fritscher, B, & Pigneur, Y. (2010). Supporting business model modelling: A compromise between creativity and constraints. In D England, P Palanque, J Vanderdonckt, & PJ Wild (Eds.), *Task models and diagrams for user interface design* (pp. 28-43). Berlin/Heidelberg: Springer-Verlag.

George, G, & Bock, AJ. (2011). The business model in practice and its implications for entrepreneurship research. *Entrepreneurship: Theory and Practice, 35*(1), 83-111.

Greene, PG, & Brown, TE. (1997). Resource needs and the dynamic capitalism typology. *Journal of Business Venturing, 12*(3), 161-73.

Haugh, H. (2005). A research agenda for social entrepreneurship. *Social Enterprise Journal, 1*(1), 1-12.

Haugh, H. (2007). Community-led social venture creation. *Entrepreneurship: Theory and Practice, 31*(2), 161-82.

den Hertog, P, van der Aa, W, & de Jong, MW. (2010). Capabilities for managing service innovation: towards a conceptual framework. *Journal of Service Management, 21*(4), 490-514.

Johns, G. (2006). The essential impact of context on organizational behavior. *Academy of Management Review, 31*(2), 386-408.

Kistruck, GM, & Beamish, PW. (2010). The interplay of form, structure, and embeddedness in social intrapreneurship. *Entrepreneurship: Theory and Practice, 34*(4), 735-61.

Liu, G, & Ko, W-W. (2012). Organizational learning and marketing capability development: A study of the charity retailing operations of British social enterprise. *Nonprofit and Voluntary Sector Quarterly, 41*(4), 580-608.

Lyon, F, & Sepulveda, L. (2009). Mapping social enterprises: Past approaches, challenges and future directions. *Social Enterprise Journal, 5*(1), 83-94.

Lyons, M. (2001). *Third sector: The contribution of nonprofit and cooperative enterprises in Australia.* St Leonards: Allen & Unwin.

McDonald, RE. (2007). An investigation of innovation in non-profit organizations: The role of organizational mission. *Nonprofit and Voluntary Sector Quarterly, 36*(2), 256-81.

Mair, J, & Marti, I. (2006). Social entrepreneurship research: A source of explanation, prediction, and delight. *Journal of World Business, 41*, 36-44.

Matthyssens, P, Vandenbempt, K, & Berghman, L. (2006). Value innovation in business markets: Breaking the industry recipe. *Industrial Marketing Management, 35*(6), 751-61.

Matzler, K, Bailom, F, von den Eichen, SF, & Kohler, T. (2013). Business model innovation: Coffee triumphs for Nespresso. *Journal of Business Strategy, 34*(2), 30-7.

Miller, D. (1983). The correlates of entrepreneurship in three types of firms. *Management Science, 29*(7), 770-91.

Mitchell, DW, & Coles, CB. (2004). Establishing a continuing business model innovation process. *The Journal of Business Strategy, 25*(3), 39-49.

Morris, M, Schindehutte, M, & Allen, J. (2005). The entrepreneur's business model: Toward a unified perspective. *Journal of Business Research, 58*, 726-35.

Morris, MH, Webb, JW, & Franklin, RJ. (2011). Understanding the manifestation of entrepreneurial orientation in the nonprofit context. *Entrepreneurship: Theory and Practice, 35*(5), 947-71.

Oftedal, EM. (2013). Business model innovation. In SO Idowu, N Capaldi, L Zu, & AD Gupta (Eds.), *Encyclopedia of corporate social responsibility* (pp. 267-72). Berlin: Springer.

Osterwalder, A. (2004). *The business model ontology: A proposition in a design science approach*. (Unpublished PhD Thesis, University of Lausanne, Switzerland).

Peredo, AM, & McLean, M. (2006). Social entrepreneurship: A critical review of the concept. *Journal of World Business, 41*, 56-65.

Pohle, G, & Chapman, M. (2006). IBM's global CEO report 2006: Business model innovation matters. *Strategy & Leadership, 34*(5), 34-40.

QSR International Pty Ltd. (2010). NVivo qualitative data analysis software (Version 9).

Salamon, LM. (1993). The marketization of welfare: Changing nonprofit and for-profit roles in the American welfare state. *The Social Service Review, 67*(1), 16-39.

Schneider, S, & Spieth, P. (2013). Business model innovation: Towards an integrated future research agenda. *International Journal of Innovation Management, 17*(1), 15-35.

Shaw, E, & Carter, S. (2007). Social entrepreneurship: Theoretical antecedents and empirical analysis of entrepreneurial processes and outcomes. *Journal of Small Business and Enterprise Development, 14*(3), 418-34.

Short, JC, Moss, TW, & Lumpkin, GT. (2009). Research in social entrepreneurship: Past contributions and future opportunities. *Strategic Entrepreneurship Journal, 3*(2), 161-94.

Snow, CC, & Hrebiniak, LG. (1980). Strategy, distinctive competence and organisational performance. *Administrative Science Quarterly, 25*(2), 317-36.

Sosna, M, Trevinyo-Rodríguez, RN, & Velamuri, SR. (2010). Business model innovation through trial-and-error learning: The Naturhouse case. *Long Range Planning, 43*(2-3), 383-407.

Stewart, DW, & Zhao, Q. (2000). Internet marketing, business models, and public Policy. *Journal of Public Policy & Marketing, 19*(2), 287-96.

Teece, DJ. (2010). Business models, business strategy and innovation. *Long Range Planning, 43*(2-3), 172-94.

Teece, DJ, Pisano, G, & Shuen, A. (1997). Dynamic capabilities and strategic management. *Strategic Management Journal, 18*(7), 509-33.

Timmers, P. (1998). Business models for electronic markets. *Electronic Markets, 8*(2), 3-8.

Weerawardena, J, McDonald, RE, & Mort, GS. (2010). Sustainability of non-profit organizations: An empirical investigation. *Journal of World Business, 45*(4), 346-56.

Weerawardena, J, & Mort, GS. (2006). Investigating social entrepreneurship: A multidimensional model. *Journal of World Business, 41*(1), 21-35.

Weerawardena, J, & Mort, GS. (2012). Competitive strategy in socially entrepreneurial nonprofit organizations: Innovation and differentiation. *Journal of Public Policy & Marketing, 31*(1), 91-101.

Wilson, F, & Post, JE. (2013). Business models for people, planet (& profits): Exploring the phenomena of social business, a market-based approach to social value creation. *Small Business Economics, 40*(3), 715-37.

Yin, R. (1996). *Case study research — Design and methods.* London: Sage.

Young, DR, Jung, T, & Aranson, R. (2010). Mission-market tensions and non-profit pricing. *The American Review of Public Administration, 40*(2), 153-69.

Yunus, M, Moingeon, B, & Lehmann-Ortega, L. (2010). Building social business models: Lessons from the Grameen experience. *Long Range Planning, 43*(2-3), 308-25.

Zahra, SA, & Covin, JG. (1993, September). Business strategy, technology policy and firm performance. *Strategic Management Journal, 14*, 451-78.

Zahra, SA, Gedajlovic, E, Neubaum, DO, & Shulman, JM. (2009). A typology of social entrepreneurs: Motives, search processes and ethical challenges. *Journal of Business Venturing, 24*(5), 519-32.

Zott, C, Amit, R, & Massa, L. (2011). The business model: Recent developments and future research. *Journal of Management, 37*(4), 1019-42.

Part 3

Innovation management perspectives

Complex systems adjusting stability levels and providing entrepreneurial opportunities

8

Vernon Ireland, The University of Adelaide

Introduction

The purpose of this chapter is to explore concepts of complex systems and how these can be instrumental in generating entrepreneurial opportunities. The focus is on how opportunities are created by changing stability levels within our social systems, of which many have occurred and are continuing to occur. The chapter includes sections on the application of complexity theory to entrepreneurship. It further discusses the resilience of natural systems and the lessons that can be learned in terms of the breakdown of systems.

The world has undergone a number of changes to its complex systems which provide context for individuals and enterprises, and with each change to the level of stability it produces entrepreneurial opportunities. A consideration of complex systems in the operation of the world and society demonstrates these changes of stability levels and highlights the dynamic state of dominant systems in society and business. An example of natural system changes can be drawn from observing the biosphere, starting with 540 million years ago through to the present. In more recent times there have been changes to socio-technical systems which provide entrepreneurial opportunities. This chapter will propose a model of stable and unstable systems; it will model both smooth changes and catastrophic changes and will provide an explanatory model from resilience of the natural world; it will propose tools to model social and business systems; and it will recognise some of the key parameters which affect stability and change.

The analysis in this chapter will assist entrepreneurs as they continually search for opportunities. Social breakdown and changes in business can be studied from the perspectives of a system experiencing changing stability levels. Gunderson and Holling (2002, pp. 93-4) illustrate this. The chapter develops this idea by arguing that entrepreneurial opportunities are generated by addressing emergence as a reconfiguration of complex systems after adaptation due to environmental changes. This section sees entrepreneurial opportunities being released by the process of complex systems adapting, and hence moving from one level of stability to another in their adjustment to environmental pressures. Such pressures can be induced by external systems including financial and economic, technological, political, social and cultural, legal, religious and any other major external forces, or a combination of these forces. This chapter refers to two major publications addressing resilience of natural systems, in that resilience is the 'flip' side of the breaking down of the system (Gunderson & Holling, 2002; Walker & Salt, 2012).

This chapter in the context of entrepreneurial opportunities

This chapter examines previous approaches to the source of entrepreneurship and draws significantly on the work of Schindehutte and Morris (2009). However, such previous approaches only note emergence as providing the entrepreneurial opportunity, and do not link it to complex systems with adapting and adjusting stability levels. The benefits of recognising entrepreneurial opportunities being generated through complex systems adapting and adjusting to different stability levels mean that one can attempt to assess stability and get some indication of when a movement is occurring. In doing this, one can then receive an early indication of a change and thus gain early benefits in competition with fewer others. Schindehutte and Morris's (2009) approach notes that entrepreneurship has been seen as a resource or as a theory of the firm. Entrepreneurship has also been examined through resource-based theories (Alvarez & Busenitz, 2001, p. 772), firm-level entrepreneurship (Sharma & Chrisman, 1999), or entrepreneurial behaviour of the firm (Covin & Slevin, 1991). However, these adaptive approaches contribute to theories of the firm behaviour.

Schindehutte and Morris (2009) acknowledge that entrepreneurial opportunities are generated from complex systems as they seek equilibrium. However, this chapter extends the idea by examining the complex system's adaptation process. This chapter then extends the idea to people making sense of the change in order to identify opportunities, and creating meaning in order to explore the change of direction. Schindehutte and Morris's approach is related to other theories of entrepreneurship in that it 'recognises entrepreneurship is not a competitive strategy, a characteristic of a strategy, or a strategic approach selected from a portfolio of strategies' (2009, p. 267). They recognise that it also differs in important ways from entrepreneurial strategy's competition-on-the-edge (Eisenhardt, Brown, & Neck, 2000) and co-adaptive exploitation of cross-business synergies (Brown & Eisenhardt, 1997), as well as Lavie's (2006) views on the issues that entrepreneurs experience in responding to technological changes. McMullen and Shepherd (2006) comment that entrepreneurship is not about the entrepreneurial actions of individuals or a creation theory of entrepreneurship. In a similar vein, Schindehutte and Morris (2009, p. 267) claim that entrepreneurship is not 'strategy that is entrepreneurial' or 'entrepreneurship that is strategic' or 'entrepreneurship plus strategy' — it is not a 'binary construct'.

In recognising that entrepreneurial opportunities are initiated by a system experiencing changing stability levels, this chapter also recognises that people can benefit from examining the change process. A firm and individuals need to quickly sense the change in a complex system as it adapts, create meaning from the change in order to identify a direction of that change, and respond quickly to initiate a process using the entrepreneurial techniques and processes of the individual or enterprise. Identifying potential changes in complex systems — such as technological, political, financial and economic, cultural, and other kinds of changes — is facilitated by skills in exploring future possibilities, by application of selectionism and by using techniques to create meaning rapidly. '[E]ntrepreneurship, after all, is a science of turbulence and change, not continuity' (Bygrave, 1989, p. 28).

What characterises complex systems?

While there is no generally agreed definition of complex systems, Jackson (2003) comments that they can only be understood in terms of the relationship of the parts with each other and the patterns of the relationships. He recognises that complex systems 'are constantly changing due to the interaction of their parts as they seek to process a continuous flow of matter, energy and information from their environments' (p. 115). Mason and Mitroff (1981) add that such ill-structured problem situations are made up of highly interdependent problems. Developing common meaning as well as understanding the implications for the future and how to leverage change to arrive at the desired position is very useful.

There are a number of bases for complexity, but the fundamental condition is emergence due to inclusions of systems which are autonomous and independent and, as such, systems over which one does not have control. Such circumstances where lack of control can occur may be brought about through the policy of governments and the building of a System of Systems, otherwise known as an SoS (Jamshidi, 2009). An SoS includes existing or legacy systems which were designed and built for other purposes, but which have been retained or added. A simple example is the inclusion of a GPS in a vehicle. The GPS was developed for other purposes than navigating a vehicle, but the system has since been added to a set of systems that comprise the automobile. An extreme example of an SoS is the Air Operations Centre of the US Department of Defence (Norman & Kuras, 2006), which includes eighty autonomous and independent systems, all designed for other purposes (e.g. US airforce, navy and army communications).

Some bases for complexity include:

- integration of separate organisations in a supply chain
- operating in an unfamiliar cultural and business environment (such as operating a business in China or Afghanistan)
- being unclear on the stakeholders for a venture or on the relevant boundaries of key variables
- unclear leadership (such as occurred between the US airforce, navy and army when the US Government invaded Afghanistan, and as similarly occurred when MacArthur attempted to retake the Philippines in the

Second World War and the aircraft carriers were sent to address Japan when MacArthur expected naval support)

- addressing wicked problems that are 'interconnected and complicated further by lack of clarity about purposes, conflict, and uncertainty about the environment and social constraints' (Jackson, 2003, p. 137; see also supporting research by Ireland, Gorod, White, Ghandi, & Sauser, 2012).

Key approach of this chapter: Adaptation of complex systems leading to entrepreneurial opportunities

This chapter argues that a primary basis for entrepreneurial opportunities lies with the recognition of complex systems' changing levels of stability. This is in contrast to addressing a range of reductionist approaches to do with enterprise strategy. It is based on a series of the author's ideas reinforced by other researchers' ideas as noted.

As stated earlier, the chapter argues that entrepreneurial opportunities are generated by addressing emergence as a reconfiguration of stable systems due to contextual and environmental changes. This chapter argues that entrepreneurial opportunities are generated when systems are far from equilibrium; that is, 'the entrepreneurial process begins with the perception of the existence of opportunities, or situations in which resources can be recombined at a potential profit' (Shane, 2003, p. 10). Thus the 'individual-opportunity nexus perspective' (Shane & Venkataraman, 2000) on entrepreneurship depends on, is preceded by, and is in response to, change initiated endogenously, and not through technological innovation as suggested in evolutionary economics (Nelson & Winter, 1982). This is a fundamental change of perspective from many other works on entrepreneurial opportunities.

Reductionist versus complex systems thinking

A fundamental issue for understanding entrepreneurship is the basis of thinking and analysis (Schindehutte & Morris, 2009). Traditionally the world has focused on reductionist thinking initiated by Descartes in 1637. He proposed that breaking up thinking into major separate specialist areas would advance knowledge more rapidly than would occur with scholars addressing a broad set of disciplines. Knowledge has certainly advanced using these techniques; however, a number of problems or issues could not be solved by such specialist approaches.

As a result of this way of thinking, or in parallel with it, reductionist approaches tend to encourage people to think in a hierarchic 'command and control manner', where the person in charge gives a series of orders and the more junior members of the team follow these orders. This methodology has been very successful with some major ventures such as space programs and the development of military equipment — areas which are largely governed by the laws of physics and engineering. There are a large number of defence projects, and many other technological developments, which have been developed using this approach.

Bertalanffy (1968) initiated general systems theory and noted that a system is defined by a boundary between itself and its environment. Within the system there are a series of contributing systems, which could be called sub-systems. Closed systems are those which do not transform — in other words, they have no input or output. An example of a closed system is the structure of the building which supports walls and floors. By comparison, an open system transforms information, energy or materials. Examples are a cell, an engine or an architect's office. The interior of the system is thus a zone of reduced complexity, and many see the interior systems of enterprises — such as marketing, transformation of materials energy, or information — as shielded by managers whose job it is to focus on dealing with the external business environment.

However, Bertalanffy (1968) did not specifically address the issue of complex systems, in which the systems making up the overall system are autonomous and independent. The use of techniques such as operations research to deal with more precise disciplines, such as engineering and physics, proved to be a disappointment in not being able to deal with some of the issues associated with human complex systems, because operations research is underpinned by a reductionist approach. Once systems that are autonomous and independent are included in a larger system, such as a system of systems, techniques which focus on command and control are no longer appropriate and need to be replaced by techniques especially appropriate for complex systems. Hence issues concerning people, politics, culture and human issues generally could not be solved by operations research or similar techniques. This is particularly the case when the objective of a problem, or the goal of an enterprise, is not clear, as demonstrated by Jackson (2003), discussed above. Agreement on common meaning, and the long-term implications of change of policy or action, is crucial to moving forward effectively.

As a result of the development of two alternative ways of thinking — the traditional being reductionist, which is exemplified by a top-down, command and control approach, and the other recognising organisation fit within systems, which are largely autonomous — we find that approaches for contributing knowledge also align with these two alternatives. For example, many of the theories proposed to understand entrepreneurship and research have been set within reductionist frameworks, whereas this chapter is proposing a complex systems framework with extended ideas. People who espouse a reductionist approach tend to focus on the parts and independent interactions, but it is the system of interactions *among* the parts that is critical and that constitutes a complex system.

Table 8.1 summarises some differences between systems that are complex, and others that are intrinsically simplistic because they are theoretically reducible, using entrepreneurial strategy (Brown & Eisenhardt, 1998) and strategic entrepreneurship (Ireland, Hitt, & Sirmon, 2003) as representative examples of the differences. In both instances the firm is the unit of analysis and the focus is on economic (profit) opportunity, routines (simple rules), and incremental, firm-level, continuous innovation in pursuit of competitive advantage.

Stability concepts of complex systems

All systems are challenged by potential lack of stability. The human body is kept in a healthy state by hundreds of homeostatic processes, as shown in Marten (2001, p. 12). Attack by disease threatens the health level of stability; however, people usually fight back and the health stability level is restored. If there is permanent damage a lower level of health stability occurs.

An illustration of such a change in stability levels can be provided by the global financial crisis of 2008 to 2009. In earlier times, wealth creation largely depended on the stock market. However, in the period just before the global financial crisis, US banks initiated change and created derivatives which were largely a product of housing loans that did not depend on the relationship between the value of the housing, or the ability of the loan recipient to repay the loan, and the size of the loan. Loans were driven by bonuses being paid to loan officers purely based on the size of the loan. Banks gave people loans worth 120 per cent or more of the value of the property, and gave loans to people on social security. Furthermore, rating agencies endorsed these derivatives, which were packages of such loans. This became

	Strategic entrepreneurship (e.g. Ireland, Hitt, & Sirmon, 2003)	Entrepreneurial strategy (e.g. Brown & Eisenhardt, 1998)
Main focus	**Behavioural**	**Evolutionary**
System type	**General systems theory cybernetics**	**Complex adaptive systems**
Theoretical foundations	[The Carnegie School] March, 1991; Simon, 1962	[Santa Fe Institute] Kauffman, 1993; Waldrop, 1992
Micro-macro relationship	Social system *and* economic system Firm responds to the environment, i.e. micro-macro interaction	Social system *within* economic system Firm is embedded in and changes its environment
System characteristics	Simple, linear and equilibrium-seeking Whole is sum of parts	Open, dynamic, non-linear Whole is more than sum of parts
Origins	Physics (stability, equilibrium)	Biology (structure pattern, self-organisation)
The nature of evolution	Adaptation and evolution of the firm	Dynamic co-evolution of both the firm and the environment Development of new rules and routines
Focus	Organisational learning Balance (exploration-exploitation)	Variation-retention-selection New opportunities arise from technological innovations
Nature of opportunity	Pre-existing profit-making opportunity to seek out and exploit Technology as a given, or selected on economic criteria	Technology in flux, endogenous to the system
Type of non-linearity	Non-linearity ascribed to negative and positive feedback loops Mostly 'same cause, same effect'	Nonlinear interactivity, i.e. 'small cause, large effect' or 'large cause, small effect'
Type of self-organisation	Primarily self-regulatory processes	Creative, self-generated, adaptability-seeking behaviour conferred by emergent phenomena
Type of equilibrium	System tends toward a final state of equilibrium or homeostasis (e.g. 'equifinality' in General Systems Theory)	System is 'beyond equilibrium' (i.e. multi- or non-equilibrium)
Type of attractors	Only one 'attractor' (i.e. a final state of equilibrium)	Different kinds of attractors (e.g. fixed point, limit cycle, strange)

Table 8.1 Comparison of the theoretical foundations of strategic entrepreneurship and entrepreneurial strategy.

Source: Courtesy of the author, adapted from Table 2 in Schindehutte and Morris, 2009.

a particular crisis, as people became nervous and the value of housing fell. However, the first system change occurred when the traditional system moved to the system described above. Ratings agencies massively traded and endorsed financial products, although they understood them poorly (Solow, 2011).

The second system change came about as the system described above moved to one in which US and other banks were attempting to stabilise the situation and the government was providing substantial loans to the banks and other financial institutions. Both of these system changes should have provided opportunities for entrepreneurs, although the operation of the housing derivatives markets was initially kept very quiet.

A more positive note is provided by the introduction of social networks such as Facebook. New patterns of communication and social engagement were generated and new opportunities created for marketing, information gathering and a range of other products. Stability levels of communication systems rose.

Examples of pressures from the environment exerting forces on a natural system include (but are not limited to) the sun and its relationship with forces reducing global warming, geographic position and the tides. Pressures on business systems include competitive pressures, the capability of the organisation to respond, new technologies being introduced, and new communication structures such as social networking. Examples of pressures on political systems include economic capability and the capability of one's friends and competitors, cultural approaches and society, and the form of the political system, whether democratic or otherwise.

Change in society and communities is driven by a number of factors, including general growth in affluence, population growth through birth and migration, technological development, political change, economic change and attitude change. Such change in society produces entrepreneurial opportunities. This chapter will examine a number of aspects of complex systems to illustrate the benefits and opportunities of these changes in society, which disrupt stable patterns and in doing so create opportunities for innovation and entrepreneurship.

Opportunities released

As systems change from one stability level to another, opportunities emerge and there is increased scope for entrepreneurship and innovation. By comparison, a stable business which is not undergoing any change provides fewer entrepreneurial opportunities. Hence those pursuing entrepreneurial opportunities need to primarily track and detect changes in systems. Schindehutte and Morris (2009) recognise that this changes the way we consider entrepreneurship from a model focusing on strategic possibilities toward a model that addresses shifts between stable states (as cited in van de Ven & Poole, 1995) and toward detectable patterns in continuing cycles of interactions.

The unfolding logics of an enterprise adjusting its stability due to environmental pressures such as business, population, legal and cultural pressures stand in sharp contrast to a strategic management paradigm that prioritises control with a preoccupation on reducing uncertainty (Hitt, Ireland, Camp, & Sexton, 2001). Schindehutte and Morris (2009) caution against trends in scholarly work in which firm growth or superior financial performance is considered the most important yardstick. This trend is partially to blame for the erroneous assertion by scholars that 'we should be very, very worried about the future of entrepreneurship' (Baker & Pollock, 2007, p. 307). The Strategic Entrepreneurship model (Ireland, Hitt, & Sirmon, 2003) is somewhere between a reductionist approach and a systems approach (Schindehutte & Morris, 2009).

Some key points developed from this approach

Emergence takes place *during* the process of interacting and regaining stability, which is not encompassed by the reductionist approach, and as such focuses on the entities within the model rather than the links between entities and the processes. The notion of emergent properties created through interaction and feedback is not part of a reductionist approach.

Changes to complex systems

Examples

Barnosky et al. (2011, p. 51) identified 'the Big Five mass extinction events … exhibiting a loss of over 75 per cent of estimated species'. However, it is not just physical systems that adapt. Gunderson and Holling (2002, pp. 93-4) note changes to social systems which must have produced entrepreneurial opportunities. Findlay and Strauss (2011) describe changes in socio-technical systems from the hunter-gatherer, through the

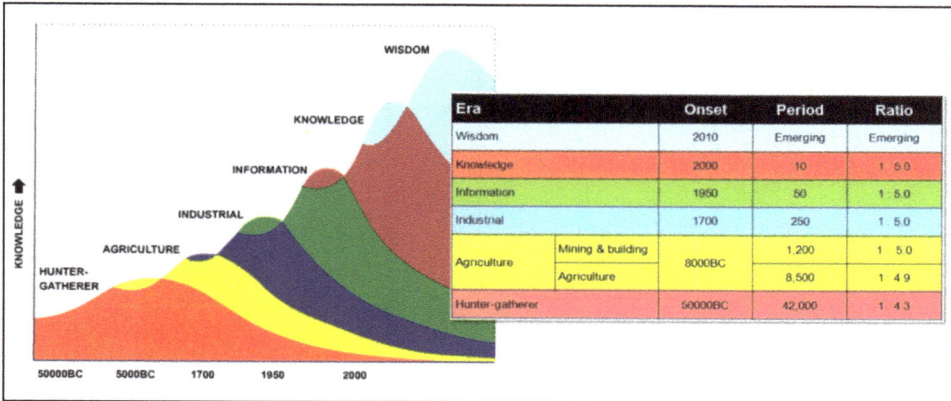

Figure 8.1: Changes in socio-technical systems.
Source: Courtesy of the author, adapted from Findlay and Strauss's model of changes socio-technical systems, 2011.

agricultural and industrial phases, to the current wisdom phase. They also model the approximate periods in which each occurred (see Figure 8.1).

Modelling adaptation and stability

There are a number of examples in the natural world of systems being threatened with change due to the components of the natural system changing. One level of stability is threatened and another takes over. This is illustrated in Figure 8.2, as primarily, but not only, applicable to the adaptation of natural species in three different diagrams. Gunderson and Holling (2002, p. 55) recognise that the model can apply to the entrepreneurial process.

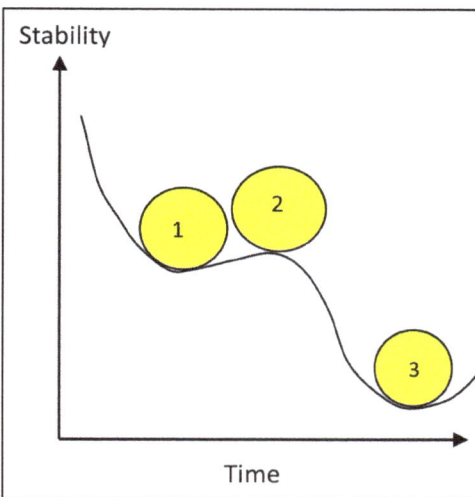

Figure 8.2: Illustration of stability of complex systems.
Source: Courtesy of the author.

Figure 8.3A is a representation of a system which is reasonably balancing the operational forces and is stable. Figure 8.3B represents a system in which the forces are beginning to be out of balance. Figure 8.3C represents a system which is changing stability levels.

In Figure 8.3C, the ecosystem has two alternative stability levels, F_1 and F_2. Figure 8.3C implies that when the ecosystem is on the upper left-hand side branch of the curve, it will not pass to the lower branch smoothly. When the system has changed by passing through F_2, the system changes dramatically to F_1, due to the stress imposed on the system due to the changing environmental conditions. It should be noted that restoring the system to the conditions prevailing before F_2 had been reached is not enough to restore the stability level — one needs to go back much further, to beyond the switch-point F_1. The genie cannot be easily put back in the bottle!

Stability levels can be represented in

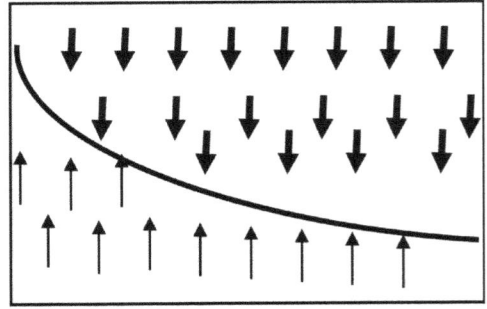

Figure 8.3A: Normal condition.

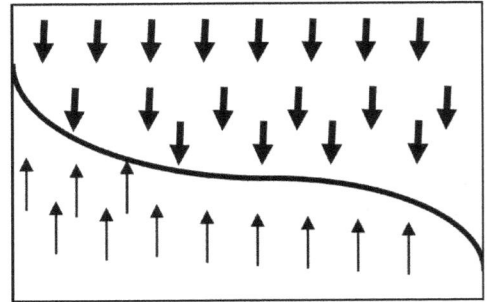

Figure 8.3B: Beginning of stress.

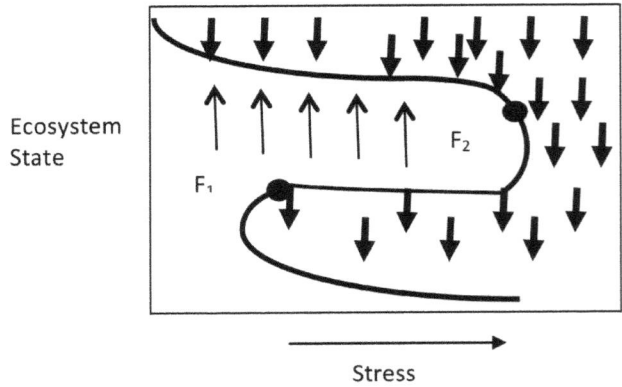

Figure 8.3C: Stress causing a change in stability level.

Figure 8.3: Changes in stability level.
Source: Courtesy of the author.

two dimensions by the troughs in the system between the hills either side in Figure 8.3B (Gunderson, 2002, p. 196). Walker and Salt (2012) describe irreversible threshold changes of systems that will never return to an earlier stability level.

Social systems

Gunderson and Holling (2002, p. 34) provide a generalised adaptive cycle which describes resilient systems but which illustrates changes in stability levels of a range of systems as is shown in Figure 8.5. The model is a 'figure eight' on its side in a two-by-two matrix, with each phase being within a policy area. Note in the alpha quadrant at point 'a', external forces create a reorganisation of the system, which starts occurring. At point 'b' exploitation occurs and at point 'd' conservation occurs. Opportunities are sought by the

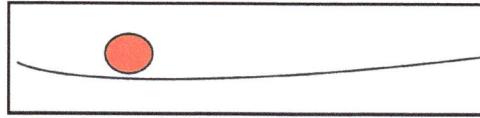

Figure 8.4A: The initial stable state.

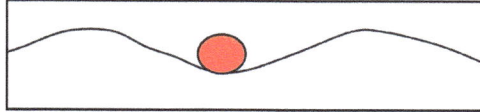

Figure 8.4B: Stress leading to instability.

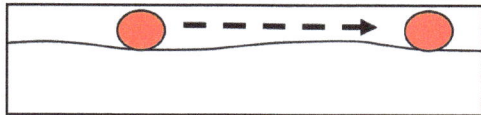

Figure 8.4C: Stress causing a move to a new stable situation.

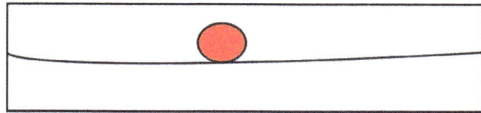

Figure 8.4D: A new stable state F$_1$ in 3C.

Figure 8.4: Movement of stable states.
Source: Courtesy of the author.

system and the cycle moves into exploitation mode, which is represented by the arrows as it moves from quadrant 'r' to quadrant 'K'. Quadrant 'K' is a conservation mode in which the systems are highly connected, which in itself produces instability, and release occurs in quadrant omega [Ω].

A reasonable question to ask is the appropriateness of this model. Gunderson and Holling (2002) illustrate this application through the development of telephony in the USA between the times of its inception to the present. They point out that in the conservation phase the systems are tightly connected, or to use the complex

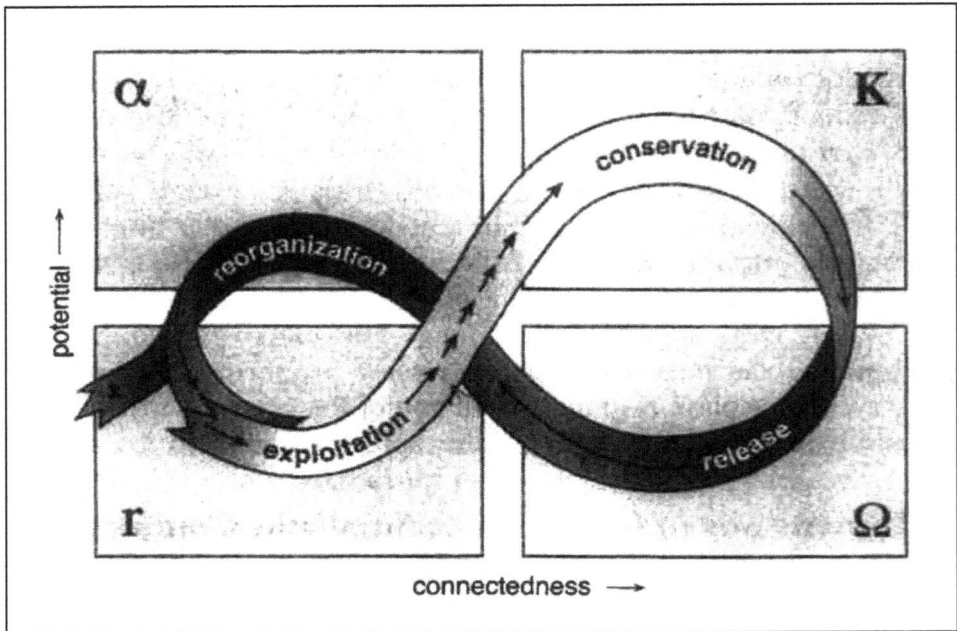

Figure 8.5: The Gunderson & Holling Panarchy model.
Source: Gunderson & Holling, 2002.

system term, they are 'coupled', which in itself produces instability. An example is provided by the major US banks in the global financial crisis in which the inter-lending was correlated at well over 0.9. While such coupling allows no opportunities for entrepreneurship, fortunately it produces its own instability, and another level of stability is sought by the system, which in itself provides many entrepreneurial opportunities.

Modelling key variables

While these models came from natural or biological systems, they have application to social systems. Walker and Salt (2002), while explaining the resilience of systems, provide models which can be applied to social systems as they change and adapt. Gunderson and Holling (2002, p. 34) model systems in terms of a series of crises and dealing with these crises by an adaptive change of rules, response with experience, learning from that experience and creating policy responses.

The efforts of various countries in dealing with the global financial crisis, with large unemployment in the USA and resorting to 'quantitative easing', or printing money, is certainly an example of adaptive change. Europe's attempts to deal with problems in the Euro [€], through conditional loans to various national groups in return for funding to stave off bankruptcy, are further examples of crises and adapting to these. No doubt each crisis brings new and different opportunities amongst the hardships of high unemployment and reducing salaries of government employees.

The adaptation process

The basic adaptation process of the Gunderson and Holling (2002) model, illustrated in Figure 8.5, starts in the alpha quadrant and gathers pace in the 'r' quadrant. At the bottom of the 'r' quadrant there is 'low connectedness which signifies diffuse elements loosely connected to each other, whose behaviour is dominated by outward relations and affected by outward variability' (p. 34). This means that entrepreneurs cannot see how bringing individuals and organisations together will achieve benefits. As the adaptability moves towards quadrant 'K', relationships between people and organisations are developed and cemented in place. This high connectedness is associated with organisations 'whose behaviour is dominated by inward relationships which control or moderate the influence of external variability' (Gunderson & Holling, 2002, p. 34).

Gunderson and Holling (2002) see the importance of low degrees of connectedness in the exploitation of opportunities, which occurs at point 'c' of Figure 8.5. The implication of this is that small groups are more effective in generating opportunities. This means a large number of business and social relations. Furthermore, if large enterprises seek to be entrepreneurial they need to provide a structure which does not constrain employees.

Goldstone (1991) recognises phases in the operation of societies in that Eurasia experienced a wave of revolutions after a period of calm in the seventeenth century. He proposes that state breakdowns occur when there are simultaneous crises occurring at several different organisational levels of societies. Gunderson and Holling (2002, p. 93) point out that simultaneous breakdown of social systems at multiple levels creates the best conditions for change to be reinforced and to feed off itself. Examples of multiple systems breaking down could include the state itself, law and order, currency and social institutions such as religion. The break-up of the Soviet Union provides a good example.

Some processes to manage adaptation

In order for innovation to occur, a range of complex systems concepts, which are relatively natural to human societies, need to be encouraged. These include development of meaning, which Bosch, Nguyen, Maeno, and Yasui (2013) illustrate; they recognise that a range of meanings need to be integrated in, for example, the case of conflict between the benefits of tourism in Vietnam and the potential destruction to the environment. Bosch et al. (2013) find the system dynamics very useful in exploring the potentially unforeseen consequences of current potential actions such that today's solutions do not become tomorrow's problem. Klein, Moon, and Hoffman (2006) have developed processes for creating meaning.

Encouraging self-organisation or bottom-up initiatives is also important, as is allowing citizens scope by not prescribing top-down restrictions. I myself, when investigating the former East German building industry in 1991, found that people had few ideas on how to initiate and manage change (Ireland, 1991). This was because they had only been encouraged to follow the rules and not to take any personal responsibility.

Self-organisation in organisations is encouraged by leaders who do not specify behavioural norms and who provide a very light hand. Leaders who unobtrusively seed ideas for organisational development are appropriate for encouraging bottom-up self-organisation (Uhl-Bien, Marion, & McKelvey, 2007). An example could be unobtrusively putting a question on the notice board for staff to notice and hopefully to consider. Another example is relatively frequent changes in staff roles. Distributed leadership, rather than top-down command and control, is another method of stimulating initiatives. This is related to a modular structure of the enterprise, which includes relatively tight coupling within a module and loose coupling between modules (Baldwin & Clark, 2004).

The ability of humans to self-organise and associate with the meanings they ascribe to social concepts at various levels — from the personal, to the local community, to the enterprise in which they work, to the local, state and federal government, and through to international organisations — provides a rich spectrum of possible initiatives which can play out at various levels. Gunderson and Holling (2002) see this as humans transcending the boundaries of the social systems they have created (p. 110). An example of transcending cultural, legal, local decision-making, language, project and risk management, and other barriers can be drawn from an Australian charity that I have a minor role in, called the Indigo Foundation. The Indigo Foundation has been managing the erection and commissioning of four schools within a three-year period in Afghanistan. Each school is developed for over 1000 pupils and has 40 per cent female admission. The motto of the Indigo Foundation, '[T]he first thing we offer is respect', could be seen as an example of social entrepreneurship through an initiative occurring at multiple levels in various facets. The Indigo Foundation is also taking similar initiatives in other countries.

Emery and Trist (1965) recognise the importance of turbulence in describing social systems. The alternatives are placid and random, placid and clustered, and distributed reactive. The turbulent field is described as dynamic, with dynamic properties arising not simply from the interaction of the component organisations but also from the field itself so that the ground and the figure move simultaneously. This is a beautiful example of complex systems. They point out the importance of values, as values create stability. There are two implications from this: firstly, that entrepreneurs should operate in fields that are turbulent by comparison with those that are placid; and secondly, that values are important in integrating teams and identifying priorities. Gray, Westley, and Brown (1998) recognise that in managing environmental issues one encounters volatile problem domains, which are examples of turbulent environments. The dynamics of the ecological system gets mixed up and interconnected with the social and cultural system. Jackson's description of complex systems as those which are 'interconnected and complicated further by lack of clarity about purposes, conflict, and uncertainty about the environment and social constraints' (2003, p. 138) leads one to use Checkland and Holwell's (1998) soft systems approach in generating entrepreneurial opportunities. Bosch et al. (2013) provide an alternative, which includes the key processes of identifying common meaning amongst the participants, clarifying the implications of this through system dynamics processes and then finally applying a methodology to identify key leverage points. Both of these methods are open to entrepreneurs who seek to generate solutions to complex issues.

The degree of structural rigidity in a system should indicate the possibility of change: the more structurally rigid, the less likely to change in the first instance. Hence structural rigidity and indications of attacks on this, including breakdown of some of the systems, should provide an indicator of possible change and entrepreneurial opportunities. Identifying the boundaries of the system and the range of stakeholders, and significant changes to both, which are key principles of complex systems, is worthwhile.

The Gunderson and Holling (2002) model recognises four distinct phases in the transformation process, each of which requires a different form of decision-making. As the process proceeds from omega [Ω] to alpha, the decision maker has to primarily be a catalyst (p. 250), whereas as the process proceeds from 'r' to 'K' the decision maker is primarily a bureaucrat locking down conservative solutions that work. The catalyst operates largely to change current systems and is required to have strong values to convince others of the need to change and to give them confidence in the leadership of change (p. 353). Furthermore, multiple strategies are required so as not to be too focused on a single approach. The attitudes of the adaptive manager must include that of a collaborator, politician and agency manager, and the adaptive manager must have strong technical skills relevant to the domain. Strong control of emotions, minimum fear of conflict, and humility are required. Adaptive managers need to capitalise on the energy and movement of others. Their role can be seen as catching waves rather than pulling strings.

Describing the system, Walker and Salt (2012, p. 37) point out the importance of simply describing the new concept. They remind the reader of 'requisite simplicity', which relates to Ashby's (1956) requisite complexity, the concept being that in a complex system the control systems have to be as comprehensive as the system which is being controlled. However, Walker and Salt (2012, p. 37) remind us that such entrepreneurial systems need to have a common understanding between participants. They also point out that this is an ongoing process since we are not dealing with a self-organising system. In other words, we need to make the description of the system and the controlling processes simple but as extensive as necessary (including all the critical information) to achieve the objectives (p. 53). Walker and Salt (p. 39) also introduce the concept of focal scale, in the sense that the scale of the new enterprise needs to be clear and the new enterprise must reflect the values practised at that scale. Examples of scale include federal, state and local government. The management processes also need to be appropriate to the scale of the enterprise.

The governance system is crucial in terms of who has power to control, whether they accept this responsibly and the existence of feedback processes to achieve the governance. Governance includes all the aspects and rules and regulations of the organisation that determine how people operate in the system. Resilience literature also reminds us that one needs to look at the dynamic nature of the system by looking at what the system has to deal with in terms of disturbances and their various characteristics. This is somewhat akin to a risk management study but has a slightly different perspective. Disturbances should include the large and infrequent disturbances; an attempt should be made to understand unknown shocks in the systems that might exist but which we cannot anticipate. Loch, De Meyer, and Pich (2006) provide a methodology in their selectionism approach, which this chapter will discuss in a later section.

Walker and Salt (2012, p. 70) introduce the concept of developing a threshold matrix which describes the potential thresholds for a system to fail. These thresholds can be in the form of metrics of scale versus domain. 'Scale' can include an aspect of an enterprise, the enterprise itself or a group of enterprises. 'Domain' may include economic, social and ecological aspects, and disciplines within a business. The benefits of such an approach are to encourage participants to think through further detail, and there are many interactions between thresholds in various domains (p. 71). Walker and Salt point out that as the threshold is being approached the variability of the system increases and fluctuations occur. Monitoring these fluctuations will provide an indication of a likely change and of stability levels.

Walker and Salt (2012) reinforce the benefits of recognising that stakeholders will all have a different mental model of the system that is being conceived. It is important that the differences in these mental models be resolved and all people made aware of what the differences are. It is also important to plot the interaction of variables in the system, as the connections are particularly important. This can be done in a somewhat static way through the use of a systemigram, which is a diagram invented by Boardman and Sauser (2008) to show the relationship between entities and their effects on each other, with the type of effect being shown as a verb on the arrow. An example is provided in Figure 8.6.

A more complex method of describing a system is through system dynamics, which indicates the reinforcing and attracting processes of various variables on each other. There is great benefit in doing this in order to overcome simplistic solutions and particularly to ensure that today's solution does not become tomorrow's problem. Senge (1992) noted this; however, others, such as Bosch et al. (2013), have taken up system dynamics as part of a solution process.

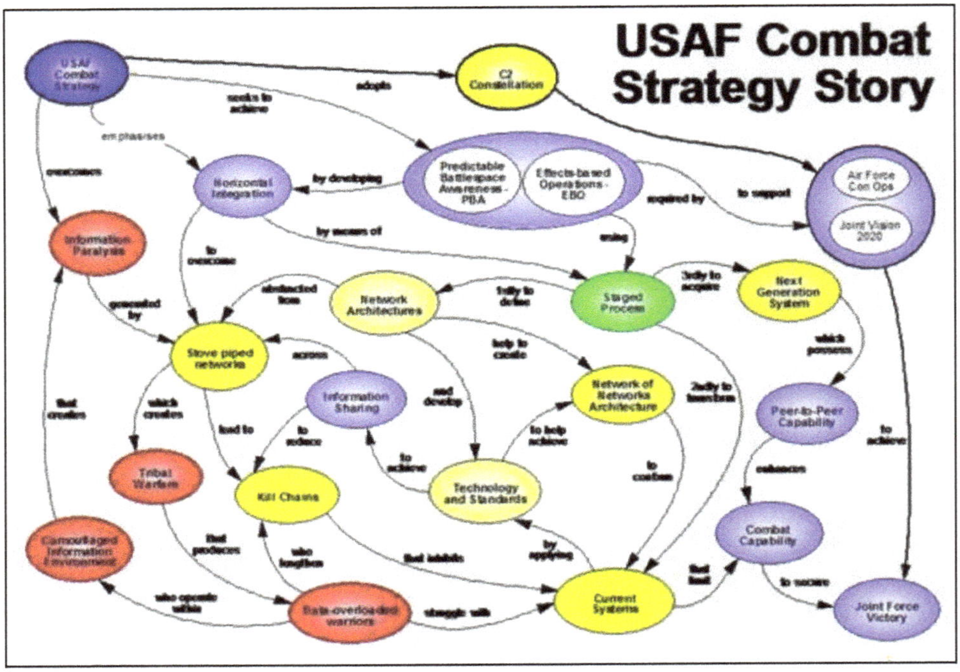

Figure 8.6: An example of a systemigram from Boardman and Sauser.
Source: http://www.boardmansauser.com/thoughts/systemigrams.html.

Senge (1992) comments: '[O]ur mental models determine not only how we make sense of the world, but how we take action' (p. 175). He cites Chris Argyris's (1982) comment: '[A]lthough people do not [always] behave congruently with their espoused theories [i.e. what they say] they do behave congruently with their theories-in-use [i.e. their mental models]' (p. 175). Senge (1992) comments that mental models are simple generalisations but they are also active and they shape how we act. They affect how we see the world. Senge provides the example of the Detroit carmakers who believed that people bought cars on the basis of styling, and not on the cars' quality or reliability (pp. 175-6). While this belief has been overturned since the early 1980s, with the success of the Japanese cars in the USA, the strength of mental models in Detroit is an underlying factor that contributes to the fact that the city of Detroit is currently on the verge of bankruptcy.

Senge was also one of the first authors to popularise system dynamics processes, which he calls reinforcing and balancing processes (1992, p. 70). This recognised that problems have delay between cause and effect, such as adjusting the temperature in a shower with separate hot and cold taps. Finally, Senge also recognises the benefits of finding leveraged points when attempting to achieve the best benefit from action in a group, a methodology taken up by Bosch et al. (2013).

The process of adapting from one stability level to another

Adaptation

As systems adapt from one level of stability to another, the various forces which were balanced at the previous stability level need to change in their configurations in order to be balanced at another level of stability. As this chapter has previously discussed, the various systems within the complex system of systems need to adjust their configurations, and in doing so, entrepreneurial opportunities arise as the businesses which were gaining rent from the stable systems find their stable rents disrupted. The interconnection of the systems means that the behaviour of every part is shaped by feedback loops through the rest of the system. A mixture of positive and negative feedback promotes growth and change in the system as a whole (Marten, 2001).

Emergent properties occur. Genetic evolution and social organisation are examples of emergent properties at the population level. They are not properties of the individuals in a population. They emerge as special properties of populations. Such emergent properties provide the entrepreneurial opportunities. The connections within biological systems are demonstrated by the fact that the food supply for each species is a consequence of what happens in other parts of the complex system. Components at one level of the system interact primarily with other components at the same level and respond to what is occurring at other levels of the system.

Emergent properties shape the ways in which people interact with ecosystems and also with their mental models. For example, an emergent property is the refusal to recognise or accept the truth when it conflicts with existing beliefs. This includes selective filtering of information, which is used to protect existing belief systems of individuals and shared belief systems of society. While governments are encouraging universities to be more entrepreneurial and innovative, they neglect to see that the imposition of more controls on universities is likely to inhibit entrepreneurship and innovation. In this case, the central problem is the assumption in the mental model by government that governments lead and control.

All complex adaptive systems are self-organising, and this explains why they are so well-integrated. Homeostasis creates negative feedback loops which normally keep the body healthy. Negative feedback loops keep social systems within stability domains imposed by particular cultural, political and economic systems, while processes such as cultural evolution gradually change the shape of the domains. However, if the system's environment changes significantly, the social systems will respond and sometimes experience major switches from one stability domain to another. The break-up of the former Soviet Union is a notable example. Glasnost and Perestroika created changes in the external environment of the state which set in motion a multitude of feedback loops that propelled the Soviet Union from the stable form of a single nation to separate nations, a domain which was reinforced by an increasingly failing economy. Rapidly changing economic and communication systems due to boundaries being brought down, and potential opportunities illustrated through handheld communication devices, provide evidence of the likelihood of further change.

Adaptation related to complexity

DeRosa, Grisogono, Ryan, and Norman (2008, p. 4) pick up the issues of a difference between the terms 'complicated' and 'complex', pointing out that the root of the word 'complicated' means 'to fold', whereas the root of the word 'complex' means 'to weave'. Snowden and Boone (2007) echo this distinction. DeRosa et al. (2008) conclude that complex systems require self-organisation, which includes patterns of behaviour that occur in the absence of any external controller. They add that self-organisation is ubiquitous in complex systems, that adaptation covers 'all the various processes that result in complex adaptive systems changing their behaviour, structure and function in ways that improve their success in their environment' (p. 4). Following entrepreneurial actions and change within a system, the effects are evaluated and the changes are accepted or eliminated.

System monitoring tools

The point has been made previously that when systems adapt from one stability level to another, entrepreneurial and innovative opportunities are released. The forces on systems to adapt include a range of aspects relevant to the economic and financial systems, political systems, technological systems and communication systems (including social networking systems). As a consequence, entrepreneurs need to concentrate on developing monitoring tools to indicate when systems are in distress and likely to need a major adaptation to a different level of stability. While monitoring tools exist for mechanical systems, such as the tools devised by Doebling, Farrar, and Prime (1996), reliability needs to be improved for environmental systems, including climate change and tsunamis; computing systems such as Windows 7; financial systems; power systems; pharmaceutical products and systems; and political systems.

Bifurcations, excursions and predictors of change

Bifurcations occur when a complex system changes from one form to another. Excursion occurs when there is temporary movement away from a consistent pattern. Basically, at a bifurcations point, a complex system loses its past stability and moves to another level of stability (Shashkov & Tureav, 1995). Cladis and Palffy-Muhoray (1995) studied bifurcation of chemical systems. They commented that, as part of this process, a host of localised structures are generated. They studied linear stability models and thereby demonstrated that they become unstable due to infinitesimal perturbations. They measured the amplitude and thus illustrated how the structure of the chemical changes dramatically. They also illustrated graphically how one system invades the current dominant system. They recognised that self-organisation plays a critical role in this change of structure. It is possible to plot variables such as the price of gold in order to assess whether the system has undergone an excursion or bifurcation.

It is noted that the change in stability level in the gold price from the early 1970s would lead to significant entrepreneurial opportunities. Developing ideas from Crutchfield (2009) leads one to the following conclusions that systems are more likely to fail if

- they are highly structured (that is, if they have high internal correlation or strong coupling)
- there is exponential amplification of small effects
- fluctuations and noise are amplified.

While Crutchfield (2009, p. 6) notes that fragility cannot be predicted in advance selectionism, which this chapter will discuss in a later section, is a form of model building and makes an attempt to explore the future of systems.

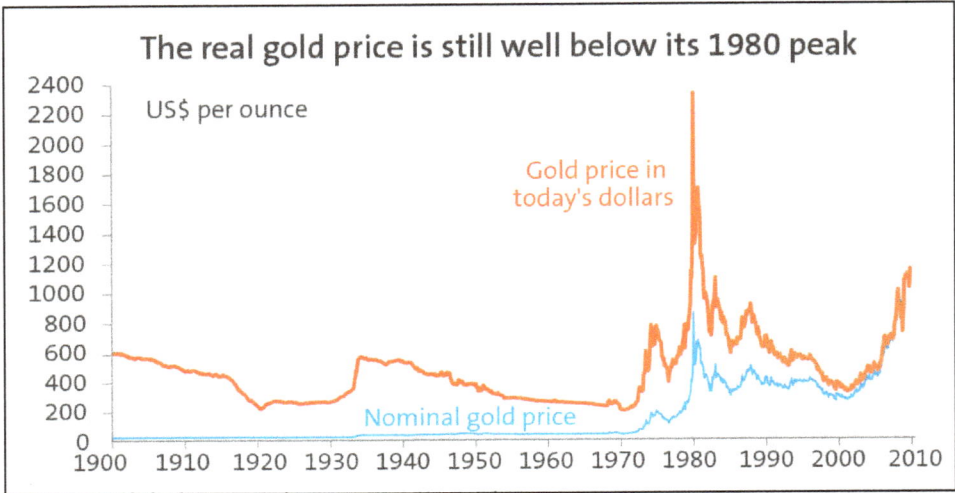

The real gold price is still well below its 1980 peak

Figure 8.7: Variations in the gold price.
Source: AMP Capital Edition 33 17 November 2009, Shane Oliver's insights, http://www.
ccafp.com.au/wp-content/uploads/2009/11/OI-33-2009_Gold.pdf.

A question arises as to whether a high degree of coupling associated with a fragile system increases the likelihood of bifurcation. Crutchfield (2009) reinforces the notion that systems moving to a different level of stability do so 'following the process of functional pattern formation passing through the condition in neutral stability' (p. 5). It is interesting to speculate whether countries which unseat a dictator, to find that another dictator is installed, have not adequately exchanged their basic systems and hence only experience excursions rather than bifurcations.

Some tools to use in managing a complex system

Self-organisation

Self-organisation within an organisation can be described as a group spontaneously coming together to perform a task. The concept of self-organisation echoes emergent properties, and it also echoes the fact that a complex system cannot be understood as the sum of its parts, since it may not be discernible from the properties of the individual agents and how they may behave when interacting in large numbers. For example, studies have shown how highly segregated neighbourhoods can arise from only low levels of racism in individuals (Schelling, 1978, as cited in Ramalingam, Jones, Reba, & Young, 2008). The market is probably the exemplary self-organising system. As the Nobel Laureate Ilya Prigogine has put it (in Waldrop, 1992, as cited in Ramalingam et al., 2008, p. 49): '[T]he economy is a self-organising system, in which market structures are spontaneously organised by such things as the demand for labour and demand for goods and services'.

> Westley, Zimmerman, and Quinn Patton (2006) argue that
>
> > bottom-up behaviour seems illogical to Western minds … [W]e have a hierarchical bias against self-organisation … [which is displayed in] our common understanding of how human change happens, especially in organisations. Our popular management magazines are filled with stories of the omniscient CEO or leader who can see the opportunities or threats in the environment and leads the people into the light. However, self-organisation is critical to achieving change. (As cited in Ramalingam et al., 2008, p. 50, emphasis in the original)

Ramalingam et al. (2008) point out that self-organisation describes how the adaptive strategies of individual agents in particular settings are able to give rise to a whole range of emergent phenomena, including the emergence of resilience (pp. 49-50). They further note that self-organisation need not necessarily be about change, as it can be about resilience in the face of change. They see resilience as being continuous and often simultaneous stages of release, reorganisation, exploitation and conservation, including the possibility of the destruction of some existing organisational structures. This frees up essential resources and enables growth in new areas. Cycles of destruction in economies release innovation and creativity. Reorganisation is where there is competition for available resources which are then exploited by the dominant species or winning proposal.

Recognition of the need for a different leadership style

Leaders of system of systems teams need to recognise the importance of a different leadership style on complex, or systems of systems [SoS], projects. This includes the need for a number of soft skills such as comfort with ambiguity, comfort with being challenged, and even encouraging challenges, emotional intelligence, and other soft skills. These differences are shown in Table 8.2.

Traditional leadership	Leadership for complex issues (Snowden & Boone, 2007) — SoS
Analyse and respond; Create panels of experts; Listen to conflicting ideas.	Probe, sense and respond; Increase levels of interaction and communication; Use methods that can help generate ideas; Open up discussion through large group methods; Create environments and experiments that allow patterns to emerge; Encourage dissent and diversity; and manage starting conditions; Monitor for emergence.

Table 8.2: Leadership styles for reductionist models and complex systems.
Source: Courtesy of the author.

The Helmsman Institute (2009) has found that a better choice of people for working on complex systems is people who are comfortable with ambiguity and have high emotional intelligence.

Entrepreneurship within a process

Bruyat and Julien (2000, p. 173) focus on the issues of new venture creation and recognise entrepreneurial imitation, entrepreneurial venture, entrepreneurial reproduction and entrepreneurial valorisation as part of the process of new value creation. They recognise that innovation is almost always a source of considerable new value creation, at least in a modern liberal democratic economy. They also note that this is consistent to some extent with the work of Baumol (1993, p. 206), who recognises that innovation leading to entrepreneurship adds value as well. They see the entrepreneurial venture as the main example of entrepreneurship, citing examples of creating new value, usually by an innovation, and sometimes creating a new economic sector. They see this as primarily a process of an individual modifying knowledge and relations networks, as well as modifying the speed with which the innovation is taken up by the environment. They also point out that the process timing is extremely important in attempting to understand entrepreneurial ventures. However, while recognising that timing of entrepreneurial activities is of importance, they provide no guidance on what constitutes appropriate timing. Therefore, relating entrepreneurial opportunities to systems that are adjusting stability levels provides a means to anchor a timeframe.

Region of maximum adaptability and entrepreneurial opportunities

It is important to recognise that the region of maximum adaptive change occurs as organisations move out of the control space, which Ashby called 'requisite variety', into the complexity region (Ashby, 1956). Kaufmann (1993) terms this the 'melting zone of maximum adaptive capability'. Bak (1996) argues that, to survive, organisations need to be capable of staying within the melting zone, maintaining themselves in a state of self-organised criticality. The other side of the space is defined by organisations moving out of the complexity area into the chaos space. The space which Ashby called requisite variety is the normal rental space of traditional organisations and performs with normal 'rents'; it is not the space where entrepreneurs make a major killing. Enterprise staff are encouraged to remain in this complexity space by strong adaptive tensions. Jack Welch, the CEO of General Electric, who added more value to an organisation than any other CEO in the twentieth century, an amount of $480 billion, created the adaptive tension by a number of methods. These include his statement, '[B]e number one, or number two, or else' (as cited in McKelvey, 2010, p. 11). He also categorised staff into three groups, essentially as follows: A — you agree with my vision; B — you are undecided and have little time; C — you don't agree and out. 130 000 staff were let go by the operation of these somewhat Draconian measures (as cited in McKelvey, 2010, p. 8).

However, this adaptive tension, aligned with the pressure put on natural systems through environment, will change. This is the pressure that forces natural systems to adjust. In extreme situations it creates change in stability level by the system. However, Bruyat and Julien (2000) recognise that entrepreneurship is enhanced by having a supportive process, and they cite a number of authors supporting this view. They see the individual in terms of someone who is willing to take risks, as someone who is proactive and innovative in the pursuit of the opportunity without regard to the resources he or she currently controls. They recognise the role of the environment but do not address any detail other than noting that researchers in the field of entrepreneurship are concerned with the emerging phase, at a given time in the enterprise life cycle. Some of the supportive processes of complex systems — such as self-organisation, complexity-style leadership, creating meaning and system dynamics — address this need. This chapter will address further approaches in subsequent sections.

Anticipating change

Sensing a change

An important issue to consider is that sensing of a change in a system, in order to maintain stability (such as driving a car and remaining between the lane markers), is facilitated by early detection because one can benefit by early action. The same principle applies in terms of benefiting from detecting the changes due to different levels of stability.

I argued previously that entrepreneurial opportunities are more likely to be available due to a structural change in any one of a number of systems, including (but not limited to) technological, political, economic, social, legal, environmental and cultural systems, or in combination with changes in some of these systems. The current successes of Apple's iPhone and iPad, and some of their competitors, appear to have been supported by the ability of powerful computing division available on a very small disk-space, clever software which allows multi-functions with minimal coupling, touch-screen technology, the development of a clever business model and the software architecture to support it. These allow application makers to develop applications both for the maker's benefit and in recognition of the public's willingness to use tools such as capable Wi-Fi, for which Apple receives a significant percentage. While a number of these systems need to be ready, and in the case of the iPad and the iPhone, were available for a few years before these devices appeared, Apple was the first to couple the possibility with the capability and successfully exploit the timing of systemic change. Steve Jobs was obviously a visionary in seeing these possibilities. However, if tools could be created to balance the vision with the confidence of results from the marketplace, maybe many of us could confidently explore such a venture.

Tools do exist in some applications for sensing a change in a system. For example, Yuan et al. (1993, p. 14936) proposed the use of the global positioning system to monitor and sense changes in the environment. Okoye and Koeln (2003) review remote sensing by satellites and point out that, for remote sensing to be of value, the key variables have to be monitored, and this suggests that an understanding of what the key variables or drivers of entrepreneurial opportunities are is necessary if tools are to be useful.

This chapter suggests that a key variable that can indicate system adaptation could possibly be the recognition of major change in any one of the following systems:

financial, economic, political, social, cultural, technological, environmental, religious and legal.

Indicators of change are likely to be:

- the structure of the system

- the inputs to the system

- the outputs from the system

- the relationship of inputs and outputs to the system

- the relationship between the system and its environment.

A further illustration of systems changing stability level is provided by political change occurring in some Arab countries, such as Egypt and Libya, which has been titled the 'Arab Spring'. This major political change should have provided entrepreneurial opportunities. Further examples (which have been much more obvious publicly) are the change in the role of women (as they become more independent) and the ageing of the population. Both of these changes provided entrepreneurial opportunities. These variables, however, require testing by more rigorous research.

Creating meaning

An issue that is important in recognising a change to a system is the ability to create meaning from a range of inputs. Some useful work has been done on the creation of meaning by sensemaking. Klein, Moon, and Hoffman (2006) propose a model of sensemaking which may assist. It is based on the notion that when people try to make sense of events, they begin with some perspective, viewpoint or framework (p. 88) — however minimal or metaphoric — which Klein et al. call a 'frame' (pp. 88-9). This might be based on a story, a map, organisational diagrams or scripts. Klein et al. further comment that

> [E]ven though frames define what count as data, they themselves actually shape the data (for example, a house fire will be perceived differently by the homeowner, the fire fighters, and the arson investigators) …
>
> [F]rames change as we acquire data. In other words, this is a two-way street: Frames shape and define the relevant data, and data mandate that frames change in nontrivial ways …
>
> [T]he process captures a number of sensemaking activities. Sensemaking can involve elaborating the frame by adding details, and questioning the frame and

doubting the explanations it provides. A frame functions as a hypothesis about
the connections among data. (p. 88)

The approach is to come to a preliminary conclusion in sensemaking and then to attempt to find data to disprove the conclusion and replace it with a better one.

The sensemaking activity here, akin to Piaget's notion of accommodation, is to find some sort of frame that plausibly links the events that are being explained. Each of these aspects of sensemaking has its own dynamics, strategies and requirements. Recognising a frame and recognising data are different processes from elaborating a frame that has already been adopted, and this is different from explaining away inconsistencies. Different still are the reactions to questioning a frame — choosing between alternative frames and constructing a frame where none exists. There is considerable research support for this approach (Klein et al., 2006, p. 88), which suggests that efforts to train decision makers to keep an open mind may be inappropriate. Klein et al. also comment that 'spoon-feeding interpretations to the human (via such methods as data fusion) can be counterproductive' (p. 89). Further:

> [A]nother implication of the Data/Frame Theory concerns using feedback
> to promote learning. Frames are by nature reductive. And yet, frames can
> help overcome the reductive tendency. The commitment to a frame must be
> coupled with a motive to test the frame to discover when it's inaccurate. (Klein
> et al., 2006, p. 89)

Given that the tendency of many people is to provide a response to a situation based on reductionism, which is essentially counter to a complex system explanation, an approach which reduces a reductive response is of significant benefit. Klein et al. further comment that 'the decision research literature suggests that people are inclined to look for and notice information that confirms a view rather than information that disconfirms it' (p. 90).

Kurtz and Snowden (2003) support Klein et al., but question some of their assumptions:

- the assumption of order (i.e. the assumption that cause and effect are related in human interactions and markets)

- the assumption of rational choice (i.e. the assumption that people are rational).

Kurtz and Snowden argue that these assumptions are true within some contexts, but they are not universally true. Kurtz and Snowden endorse tracking patterns, supporting the points above about checking inputs, outputs and the structure of system.

Being ready

Lock, De Meyer, and Pich (2007) address the issue of searching for unknown unknowns; however, their techniques may be applicable in searching for entrepreneurial opportunities. Their methodology is to explore a future situation through a method called selectionism. Their approach is that, in the face of uncertainty, several parallel solution attempts should be launched, or sub-projects, each with a different solution strategy to the problem in hand. The hope is that one of these attempts will succeed and lead to a useful outcome. Success depends on generating enough variations so that, 'ex post, we obtain desirable results' (p. 124).

Loch et al. (2006) refer to a study of fifty-six new business development projects in which the one key difference between firms that are able to adapt to a changing environment and those that fail to do so lies in their ability to apply selectionism — that is, in creating a variety of solution approaches. As the degree of environmental change increases — that is, as the unknown unknowns increase — selectionism increases in importance and produces better solutions than continuous improvement.

What makes selectionism work?

Loch et al. (2006, pp. 133-6) identify the following reasons for selectionism to be successful, which they categorise as questions. These questions are essentially:

- In what space are we going to form alternatives? What is the set space of feasible and practical solutions?

- How many options, sets, or experiments can one afford to carry out simultaneously?

- When do we stop trials?

- How does one ensure that the selection indeed happens, and how does one create a commitment to the selected outcome?

The key to the success of selectionism is the ability to integrate learning across the projects. How does one leverage the learning or other benefits from the non-selected experiment?

Toyota, for example, is very careful to determine the set space. Functional departments within it are required to develop systems simultaneously and to define feasible regions from their perspective. In parallel they put the primary design constraints on the system based on their experience, analysis, experimentation and testing, as well as outside information. These design constraints are translated into engineering checklists, which are used throughout the project to filter possible trials or sets (Loch et al., 2006, p. 132).

How many trials in parallel?

Loch et al. (2006) comment that the answer to the above question depends on four drivers noted above. Clearly the more complex the problem, or sub-problem, the more trials are required. This is strongly backed by research literature. Therefore the organisation needs a manager who can manage multiple projects, which means juggling multiple balls at once. A good system architecture is required.

Leveraging the benefits of non-selected outcomes

Even though a trial may not have led to a result which will be used on the current project there will be benefits which can be used. These benefits are usually embedded in people, and getting these benefits means careful career management of these people.

Selectionism and learning in projects

In order to gain the best combination of selection and learning, Loch et al. (2006, p. 145) outline different approaches: 'The Darwinian approach is pure selectionism with projects running in parallel and allowed to compete, the unknown unknowns are revealed, and the best project is chosen after this'.

The value of Darwinian and sequential learning

For the Darwinian selection process operated by offering multiple models of a manufactured product, the benefit of the information is significant but the cost of developing multiple solutions and projects is quite high. Clearly Darwinian selection is favoured when the cost of running multiple trials is relatively cheap and/or the cost of delays is quite high. A criticism of the methodology is that it can be resource-intensive. However, this resource use is made more economical by preliminary exercises in sensemaking.

Overall comments

The general theme of this chapter has been the application of complexity theory to entrepreneurship and particularly to recognising entrepreneurial opportunities through the breakdown of systems and especially systems changing levels of stability.

This chapter has demonstrated that there are many examples of systems breaking down, from the early introduction of the concept of changing socio-technical systems with six distinct phases. In recent years we have seen possibly the most extreme form of instability in the global financial system. Correcting this instability in the USA, and particularly the European community, has been quite difficult. With such changes occurring in the world, there are a multitude of opportunities for entrepreneurs who recognise a complex systems perspective rather than a reductionist one, and who use the tools of complex systems.

Conclusions

This chapter concludes that there is strong evidence to support the following statements:

- Firms discover and exploit entrepreneurial opportunities to create value and sustain competitive advantage by recognising that entrepreneurial opportunities are released and enhanced as complex systems adjust from one level of stability to another.

- The adjustment of complex systems is due to contextual and environmental pressures on such systems.

- Examples of complex systems include (but are not limited to) political, financial and economic, scientific and technological, legal, environmental, cultural and religious systems.

- Normally, there is interaction between a number of the systems as they adjust.

- Strategic management and entrepreneurship literature examines the nature and character of entrepreneurial opportunities and the entrepreneurial strategies that firms employ to seize and commercialise these opportunities.

- Using the tools of complex systems assists understanding and management of these complex systems issues.

- Such release of entrepreneurial opportunities is recognised to fit within a process in which a firm develops and exploits such opportunities.

- However, in order to benefit from the process of adaptation, a firm and individuals need to quickly sense the change in a complex system and the adaptation process, create meaning from the change in order to identify a direction of that change, and respond promptly to initiate the process using the entrepreneurial techniques and processes of the individual or enterprise.

- Interpreting the potential opportunities is assisted by sensemaking techniques.

- Identifying potential changes in complex systems is assisted by exploring future possibilities in which selectionism assists in exploring meaning more rapidly.

Future research

Important areas to investigate are as follows:

1. **Investigation of system dynamics techniques and whether these suggest complex systems may be under stress:**

   The implications of current initiatives explored through system dynamics techniques may provide a long-term indicator of systems which will become unstable.

2. **Development of the systemigram technique and the relevant power-indicating verbs, which are placed on the arrows:**

   Various alternative approaches can be used to describe the power relationships between organisations; however, focusing on power relationships which support entrepreneurial activity may be possible.

3. **Development of tools to sensitively predict when social and other systems are under stress and moving towards potential changes of stability level:**

   This approach may include Points 1 and 2 above but should go beyond these.

4. **Development of the general techniques of sensemaking in terms of the specialist application to systems changing stability levels:**

   The general approaches to sensemaking have been outlined; however, there are opportunities for a specialist approach for entrepreneurship and innovation.

5. **Investigation of the cost/benefit of selectionism and whether selectionism processes are more costly than the benefits they bring:**

   This requires investigation scenario planning on how this can be brought into the process of exploring the possibility of system changes.

References

Alvarez, S, & Busenitz, LW (2001). The entrepreneurship of resource-based theory. *Journal of Management, 27*(6), 755-75.

Argyris, C. (1982). *Reasoning, learning and action: Individual and organisational.* San Francisco: Jossey Bass.

Ashby, WR. (1956). *An introduction to cybernetics.* London: Chapman and Hall.

Bak, P. (1996). *How nature works.* New York: Copernicus.

Baker, T, & Pollock, TG. (2007). Making the marriage work: The benefits of strategy's takeover of entrepreneurship for strategic organization. *Strategic Organization, 5*(3), 297-312.

Baldwin, C, & Clark, KB. (2004). Modularity in the design of complex engineering systems. Retrieved from www.mendeley.com.

Barnosky, AD, Matzke, N, Tomiya, S, Wogan, GOU, Swartz, B, Quental, TB ... & Ferrer, EA. (2011). Has the Earth's sixth mass extinction already arrived? *Nature, 471*, 51-7.

Baumol, WJ. (1993). Formal entrepreneurship theory in economics: Existence and bounds. *Journal of Business Venturing, 8*, 197-210.

Beinhocker, ED. (2006). *The origin of wealth: Evolution, complexity and the radical remaking of economics*. London: Random House.

Bertalanffy, L. (1968). *General Systems Theory, foundations, development, applications* (Revised ed.). New York: George Braziller.

Boardman, J, & Sauser, B. Worlds of systems. Retrieved from http://www.boardmansauser.com.

Boardman, J, & Sauser, B. (2008). *System thinking — Coping with 21ˢᵗ century problems*. Boca Raton, FL: Taylor and Francis, CRC Press.

Bosch, OJH, Nguyen, NC, Maeno, T, & Yasui, T. (2013). Managing complex issues through evolutionary learning laboratories. *Systems Research and Behavioral Science, 30*(2), 116-35.

Brown, SL, & Eisenhardt, KM. (1997). The art of continuous change: Linking complexity theory and time-paced evolution in relentlessly shifting organizations. *Administrative Science Quarterly, 42*(1), 1-34.

Brown, SL, & Eisenhardt, KM. (1998). *Competing on the edge: Strategy as structured chaos*. Boston: Harvard Business School Press.

Bruyat, C, & Julien, P-A. (2000). Defining the field of research in entrepreneurship. *Journal of Business Venturing, 16*, 165-80.

Bygrave, WD. (1989). The entrepreneurship paradigm II: Chaos and catastrophes among quantum jumps? *Entrepreneurship: Theory and Practice, 14*(2), 7-29.

Checkland, P, & Holwell, S. (1998). *Information, systems and information systems*. Chichester: John Wiley & Sons.

Cladis, PE, & Palffy-Muhoray, P. (Eds.) (1995). *Spatio temporal patterns in non-equilibrium complex systems: Proceedings Volume XXI, Santa Fe Institute studies in the science of complexity*. Reading, MA: Addison-Wesley Publishing Company.

Covin, JG, & Slevin, DP. (1991). A conceptual model of entrepreneurship as firm behaviour. *Entrepreneurship, Theory and Practice, 16*(1), 7-25.

Crutchfield, JP. (2009). The hidden fragility complex systems — Consequences of change, changing consequences. (SFI Working Paper 2009-12-045, Santa Fe Institute, Barcelona).

Davies, R. (2003, November 24-25). Network perspectives on the evaluation of development interventions. *EDAIS Conference, New Directions in Impact Assessment for Development: Methods and Practice*. Retrieved from http://www.mande.co.uk/docs/nape.pdf.

Deleuze, G, & Parnet, C. (2002). *Dialogues II*. New York: Columbia University Press.

DeRosa, JK, Grisogono, A, Ryan, AJ, & Norman, D. (2008, April 7-10). A research agenda for the engineering of complex systems. *SysCon 2008 — IEEE International Systems Conference*, Montreal, Canada.

Doebling, SW, Farrar, CR, & Prime, MB. (1998). *A summary of vibration based damage identification methods*. Los Alamos National Laboratory, Los Alamos: Engineering Analysis Group.

Dopfer, K, Foster, J, & Potts, J. (2004). Micro-meso-macro. *Journal of Evolutionary Economics, 14*, 263-79.

Eisenhardt, KM, Brown, SL, & Neck, H. (2000). Competing on the edge. In GD Meyer & K Heppard (Eds.), *Entrepreneurship as strategy* (pp. 49-62). Thousand Oaks, CA: Sage.

Emery, F, & Trist, F. (1965). The causal texture of organizational environments. *Human Relations, 18*, 21-31.

Findlay, J, & Straus, A. (2011). A shift from systems to complex adaptive systems thinking. In O Bodrova & N Mallory (Eds.), *Complex project management task force report: Compendium of working papers* (pp. 24-6). Canberra: International Centre for Complex Project Management.

Goldstein, J. (1999). Emergence as a construct: History and issues. *Emergence, 1*(1), 49-62.

Goldstone, J. (1991). *Revolution and rebellion in the early modern world*. Berkley: University of California Press.

Gray, B, Westley, F, & Brown, LD. (1998). Where have all the rhinos gone? Working paper, Montréal: McGill University, Faculty of Management.

Gunderson, L, & Holling, C. (2002). *Panarchy: Understanding transformations in human and natural systems*. Washington DC: Island Press.

Helmsman Institute. (2009). *A comparison of project complexity between defence and other sectors*. Sydney, Australia: Helmsman Institute.

Hitt, MA, Ireland, RD, Camp, SM, & Sexton, D. (2001). Guest editors' introduction to the special issue: Strategic entrepreneurship — Entrepreneurial strategies for wealth creation. *Strategic Management Journal, 22*(6/7), 479-91.

Ireland, RD, Hitt, MA, & Sirmon, DG. (2003). A model of strategic entrepreneurship: The construct and its dimensions. *Journal of Management, 29*(6), 963-89.

Ireland, V. (1991). *International comparison of factors affecting productivity*. (Public discussion paper, Royal Commission into productivity in the Building Industry, New South Wales).

Ireland, V, Gorod, A, White, B, Ghandi, S, & Sauser, B. (2012, October). A contribution to developing a complex project management BOK. In *IPMA Project Perspectives* (pp. 16-26). Finland: PMAF.

Jackson, M. (2003). *Systems thinking — Creative holism for managers*. Chichester: John Wiley and Sons, Ltd.

Jamshidi, M. (Ed.) (2009). *System of Systems engineering — Innovations for the 21ˢᵗ Century*. Hoboken: John Wiley.

Kauffman, SA. (1993). *The origins of order: Self-organization and selection in evolution*. New York: Oxford University Press.

Klein, G, Moon, B, Hoffman, R. (2006). Making sense of sensemaking 2: A macrocognitive model. *IEEE Intelligent systems, 21*(5). Retrieved from www.computer.org/intelligent.

Kuhn, T. (1970). *The structure of scientific revolutions*. Chicago: University of Chicago Press.

Kurtz, CF, Snowden, DJ. (2003). The new dynamics of strategy: Sense-making in a complex and complicated world. *IBM Systems Journal, 42*(3), 462-83.

Lavie, D. (2006). Capability reconfiguration: An analysis of incumbent responses to technological change. *Academy of Management Review, 31*(1), 153-74.

Loch, CH, De Meyer, TA, & Pich, MT. (2006). *Managing the Unknown*. Hoboken: Wiley.

McKelvey, B. (2010). Complexity leadership: The secret of Jack Welsh's success. *International Journal of Complexity in Leadership and Management, 1*(1), 4-36.

McMullen, JS, & Shepherd, DA. (2006). Entrepreneurial action and the role of uncertainty in the theory of the entrepreneur. *Academy of Management Review, 31*(1), 132-52.

March, JG. (1991). Exploration and exploitation in organizational learning. *Organization Science, 2*(1), 71-87.

Marten, G. (2001). *Human ecology — The basic concepts for sustainable development.* Oxford: Earthscan.

Mason, RO, & Mitroff, II. (1981). *Challenging strategic planning assumptions.* Chichester, UK: John Wiley and Sons.

Mittleton, KE. (2003). *Ten principles of complexity and enabling infrastructures in complex systems and evolutionary perspectives of organisations: The application of complexity theory to organizations.* London: Elsevier Press.

Mynatt, CR, Doherty, ME, & Tweney, RD. (1978). Consequences of confirmation and disconfirmation in a simulated research environment. *Quarterly Journal of Experimental Psychology, 30*, 395-406.

Nelson, RR, & Winter, SG. (1982). *An evolutionary theory of economic change.* Cambridge, MA: Harvard University Press.

Norman, DO, & Kuras, ML. (2006). Engineering complex systems. In D Braha, AA Minau, & Y Bar-Yam (Eds.), *Complex engineered systems — Science meets technology* (pp. 206-45). Cambridge, MA: Springer.

Okoye, MA, & Koeln, GT. (2003). Remote sending (satellite) system technologies. In HI Inyang, & JL Daniels (Eds.), *Environmental Monitoring I, Encyclopedia of Life Support Systems (EOLSS).* Paris: EOLSS Publishers, UNESCO. Retrieved from http://www.eolss.net.

Prigogine, I, & Stengers, I. (1984). *Order out of chaos: Man's new dialogue with nature.* New York: Bantam Books.

Ramalingam, B, Jones, H, Reba, T, & Young, J. (2008). *Exploring the science of complexity ideas and implications for development and humanitarian efforts* (2nd ed.). (Working paper 285, London: Overseas Development Institute).

Schindehutte, M, & Morris, MH. (2009). Advancing strategic entrepreneurship research: The role of complexity science in shifting the paradigm. *Entrepreneurship: Theory and Practice, 33*(1), 241-76.

Schumpeter, JA. (1911). *Theorie der wirtschaftlichen Entwicklung*. Translated by Redvers Opie: *The theory of economic development: An inquiry into profits, capital, credit, interest and the business cycle*. Cambridge, MA: Harvard University Press (1934).

Schumpeter, JA. (1939). *A theoretical, historical, and statistical analysis of the capitalist process*. New York: McGraw-Hill.

Schumpeter, JA. (1942). *Socialism, capitalism and democracy*. New York: Harper and Brothers.

Senge, PM. (1992). *The fifth discipline — The art & practice of the learning organisation*. Sydney: Random House.

Shane, S. (2003). *A general theory of entrepreneurship: The individual-opportunity nexus*. Cheltenham, UK: Edward Elgar.

Shane, S, & Venkataraman, S. (2000). The promise of entrepreneurship as a field of research. *The Academy of Management Review, 25*(1), 217-26.

Sharma, P, & Chrisman, J. (1999). Toward a reconciliation of the definitional issues in the field of corporate entrepreneurship. *Entrepreneurship: Theory and Practice, 23*(3), 11-27.

Shashkov, M, & Turaev, D. (1995). On the complex bifurcations set for a system with simple dynamics. *International Journal of Bifurcation and Chaos. 6*(5) 949-68.

Simon, HA. (1962). The architecture of complexity. *Proceedings of the American Philosophical Society, 106*(6), 467-82.

Snowden, DJ, & Boone, ME. (2007, November). A leader's framework for decision making. *Harvard Business Review*. 69-76.

Solow, RM. (2011, Spring). The financial crisis and economic policy. *Bulletin of the American Academy*. Retrieved from www.amacad.org/publications/bulletin/spring2011/crisis.pdf.

Uhl-Bien, M, Marion, R, & McKelvey, B. (2007). Complexity leadership theory: Shifting leadership from the industrial age to the knowledge era. *The Leadership Quarterly, 18*(4), 298-318.

van de Ven, AH, & Poole, MS. (1995). Explaining development and change in organizations. *Academy of Management Review, 20*(3), 510-40.

Waldrop, MM. (1992). *Complexity: The emerging science at the edge of order and chaos*. New York: Simon & Schuster.

Walker, B, & Salt, D. (2012). *Resilience practice — Building capacity to absorb disturbance and maintain function*. Washington, DC: Island Press.

Wason, PC. (1960). On the failure to eliminate hypotheses in a conceptual task. *Quarterly Journal of Experimental Psychology, 12*, 129-40.

Westley, F, Zimmerman, B, & Quinn Patton, M. (2006). *Getting to maybe: How the world is changed*. Toronto: Random House.

The world complex. (2011). Retrieved from http://worldcomplex.blogspot.com/2011/09/recognizing-change-in-complex-systems_27.html.

Yuan, LL, Anthes, RA, Ware, RH, Rocken, C, Bonner, WD, Bevis, MD, and Businger, S. (1993). Sensing climate change using the global positioning system. *Journal of Geophysical Research, 98*(8), 14925-37.

Intellectual capital system perspective:

9

A case study of government intervention in digital media industries

Graciela Corral de Zubielqui, The University of Adelaide
Allan O'Connor, The University of Adelaide
Pi-Shen Seet, Flinders University

Introduction

This research examines a case study of government creative industries development interventions in South Australia [SA]. The intervention was focused specifically in improving firms (such as those in advertising, art, crafts, design, fashion, film, music, publishing, video games and TV) which use digital media tools. O'Connor and Greene (2007) suggest that government intervention in entrepreneurship is grounded in two schools of thought. The first addresses information asymmetry and adopts a resource-based view (Barney, 1991), while the second relates to market failures (Parker, 2004) where government intervention substitutes for, or simulates, a market response.

The resource-based view of government intervention follows the argument that governments need to provide resource support to fill knowledge-gaps. These knowledge-gaps may include a lack of awareness of available resources or poor capabilities due to insufficient experience, skills or knowledge to undertake certain tasks or capitalise on opportunities. By contrast a market failure occurs when there is knowledge but insufficient incentive for a market response. O'Gorman and Kautonen (2004) have argued that market failure policy measures, such as those that respond to a financing market failure for early-stage ventures, for instance, are ineffective without the entrepreneurs who perceive or discover market opportunities. This suggests that there may be interdependencies between the knowledge-gaps and the market failure policy drivers. For example, knowledge-gaps or information asymmetry such as poor entrepreneurial capability may underpin the failure of a market response. That is, the market will respond without knowing there is a capability gap. Similarly, failures of market response may exacerbate a knowledge or capability gap or deficiency that remains unfulfilled while there is no market driver. This opens up the need to analyse government interventions by adopting a systems perspective.

We analysed the case study using system perspectives to show how government interventions interlink to support the financial, relational, physical and human resource gaps/market failures. We argue that government plays a critical role in facilitating links between resource sources that would not connect without a structural system and incentive to bring them together. Further, by conducting a systems analysis we highlight the need for strategic engagement between stakeholders which provides focus, intent and competitive direction.

We address our study through two main research questions:

1.   What role does government play in forming regional system interventions?
2.   How would these interventions intersect with an intellectual capital [IC] analysis framework if they were conducted at a regional level?

In this chapter we first introduce the case in focus for this study before briefly reviewing the literature on the two main interventions to exhibit the logic behind these interventions and illustrate the known limitations. Next we discuss an overview of a systems perspective for complexity sciences, and we overlay and present the IC approach as a means of providing specific tools for an industry development system analysis. We then discuss how an IC systems analysis may inform governments that wish to embed interventions in the active market place.

The SA Government intervention

The Government of South Australia promoted an intervention in 2009, the Digital Tomorrow program, to stimulate the growth of the creative industries in South

Australia. According to the Creative Industries Catalyst, the growth rate of the digital media industry across Australia was 138 per cent over the three years prior to the intervention, while in SA that growth rate had been 14 per cent. Further, Parker, Tims, and Wright (2006) highlighted the social inequity encountered by 'creative' individuals moving into the workforce. Essentially they argued that those rich in financial and social capital succeeded ahead of those poor in these areas. Furthermore, the report suggested that the education and training provided by traditional education models left graduates in the field short on commercial, entrepreneurial and networking skills.

The intervention had two main aspects. The first involved addressing the perceived resource gap intervention in terms of education and training. The second focused attention on the Digital Tomorrow Studio (a digital media business incubator), which in effect was a market failure intervention where the government provided small grants, business accommodation and networking support for fledgling digital media businesses. The intervention initiated the development of entrepreneurship education to facilitate regional development and remedy a perceived information asymmetry for intending participants in the higher education sector. This part of the program supported education for both active and potential start-up business founders to increase their skills and capabilities in capturing opportunities and improving their chance of success.

A second part of the intervention was to provide business incubation and funding support through the Digital Tomorrow Studio. Hackett and Dilts (2004) acknowledge business incubation as a means to help minimise the risks while maximising survival and growth of new ventures. In effect, the business incubation intervention was designed to meet a market failure whereby funding and early-stage business development support were unavailable to promising young businesses in the creative industries. Furthermore, the incubator provided companies with the possibility of collaborating with other companies in the same industry, creating synergies in innovation activities. It is well-recognised that innovation results from the interaction of different actors (Corsaro, Cantù, & Tunisini, 2012) and from unique combinations of resources (Cantù, Corsaro, & Snehota, 2012). Westerlund and Rajala (2010) describe the innovation development as a co-creation process.

Rationale for the adopted government interventions

In the following sections, we discuss the rationale and a brief literature review for each of the types of intervention (entrepreneurship education and business incubation) adopted by the government.

Entrepreneurship education

Keogh and Galloway (2004) claim that tertiary education institutions have an obligation to provide appropriate education that prepares students to operate and contribute to an economy. Further, to stimulate industry development, policy makers may turn to entrepreneurship education and training as 'an efficient mechanism for increasing entrepreneurial activity' (Martinez, Levie, Kelley, Sæmundsson, & Schøtt, 2010, p. 43). Adcroft, Willis, and Dhaliwal (2004) argue that education in entrepreneurship, like management, should not be considered alone and without deference to the contributions of other segments of the community that create industry structures, market conditions, labour-cost factors and general resource conditions. These authors promote the idea of the need for entrepreneurship educators to consult broadly with institutional and sectoral stakeholders to identify issues of information asymmetry and strategic resource building when concerns for regional development are priority.

O'Connor (2009) — also one of the authors of this chapter — claims that left to its own devices, the education sector will follow economic rules of supply and demand in response to pressures exerted by potential students and industry. However, as Etzkowitz (2003) points out, ' … the interaction in university-industry-government is the key to improving the conditions for innovation in a knowledge-based society' (p. 295). This implies that if universities are to fulfill broad socio-economic aims, relying on industry demand pressures to prompt development of education will be ineffective. Responses to failures in the dynamics for regional development require instead a proactive engagement between government, industry and tertiary education if regional strategic initiatives are to be conceived and successfully driven.

Carey and Naudin (2006) have examined the need for research to improve the enterprise curriculum for creative industries students. One conclusion they have drawn is that 'more research is required in order to identify how faculties can more effectively share their specific knowledge and work together to make better use of existing internal as well as external resources' (Carey & Naudin 2006, p. 529). Similarly, Laukkanen (2000) has also called for the need to better understand university-based mechanisms that support regional evolution. In essence, entrepreneurship education can be considered as part of a regional innovation system and yet little is understood with respect to questions about how this education links to the innovation system.

Business incubation

Hackett and Dilts (2004) advocate business incubation as a means of overcoming some of the problems of market failure and, to some extent, information asymmetry. They define a business incubator as a shared facility that provides its incubatees with

> a strategic, value-adding intervention system of monitoring and business assistance. This system controls and links resources with the objective of facilitating the successful new venture development of the incubatees while simultaneously containing the cost of their potential failure. (p. 57)

Business incubator programs also serve different purposes. Grimaldi and Grandi (2005) suggest that the incubator concept promotes an effective means for incubator participants to integrate the acquisition of resources and start-up management techniques. The business incubator program is also recognised as a mechanism for uplifting the economy by encouraging development of new practical entrepreneurial ideas, and also increasing the likelihood of a person establishing companies (Aeroudt, 2004; Grimaldi & Grandi, 2005). O'Connor, Burnett, and Hancock (2009) also suggest that a business incubator program can be part of an entrepreneurship education system, and de Foite, Henry, Johnston, and Van Der Sijde (2003) add that they can act as a structured training program. Smilor (1987) summarises the incubation process to illustrate the different inputs and outputs in Figure 9.1.

In the context of new or emerging industries where there are few commercial backers, governments have been stepping in as investors in business incubation, as can be seen in Figure 9.1, which shows government affiliation for some incubators. However, there is paucity in the literature on research that investigates whether the incubation process is actually effective (Hackett & Dilts, 2004), and past studies have highlighted this deficiency. For instance, the OECD (Organisation for Economic Co-operation and Development, 1999, p. 1) found that 'despite the investment of significant public funds, few science parks in Australia are credited with success'. Business incubation plays a part in the regional innovation system but, like

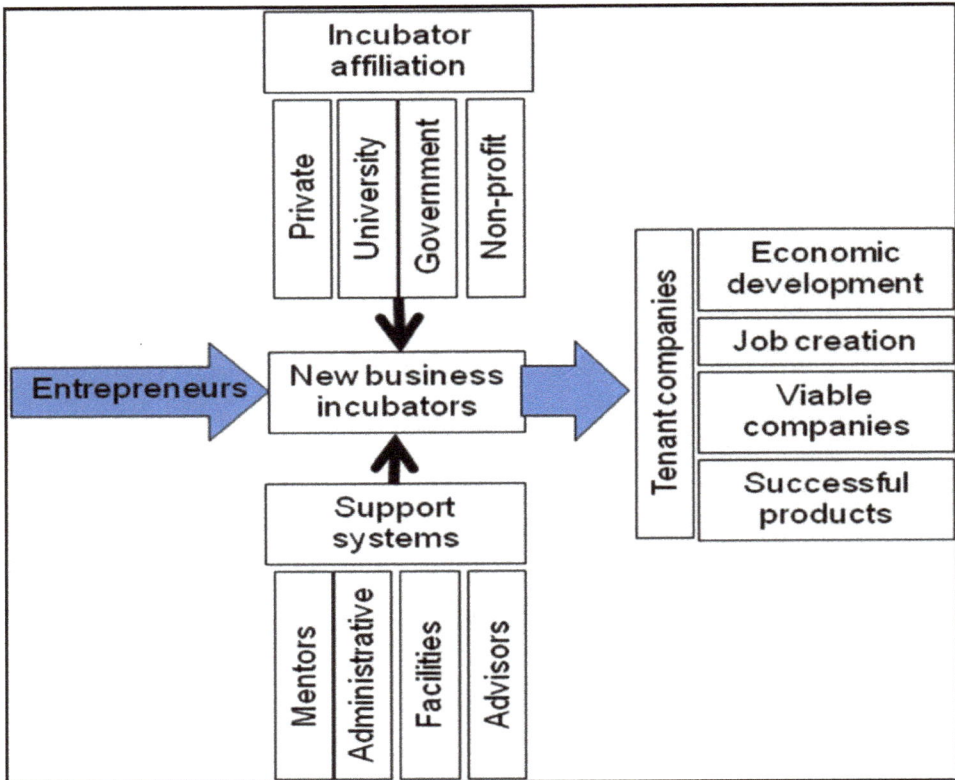

Figure 9.1: A summary of the incubation process.
Source: Courtesy of the authors, adapted from Smilor, 1987.

entrepreneurship education, how it plays a part in the growth of innovation within a region is less understood.

Systems analysis and intellectual capital [IC]

There is a significant amount of literature connected with IC and National Innovation Systems [NIS] which addresses differences between innovative and competitive capacities (Hervas Oliver, Rojas, Martins, & Cervello Royo, 2011). Lin and Edvinsson (2008) recognise that knowledge assets are essential for regional development. Also, regional innovation systems theories can be used as a framework for policy makers where regional resources are used to improve firms and region growth

(Doloreux & Parto, 2005, pp. 1-2). Gertler (1995) also recognises that proximity brings advantages for knowledge dissemination at inter-organisational level, while collaboration is essential in contemporary business (Gulati, Nohria, & Zaheer, 2000; Westerlund & Rajala, 2010).

The IC perspective focuses on country or region differences in outputs from the intangible point of view (Bontis, 2004; Stahle & Bounfour, 2008). This suggests that a systems approach to understanding failures within the market dynamics is important for government if it is to formulate policies that will be effective. However, there is limited beneficial research that assists a systems perspective. For instance, Corsaro, Cantù, and Tunisini (2012) argue that not many studies have focused on actors in innovation networks, and furthermore, given the heterogeneity among these actors, there is a need for more theoretical and empirical research.

In seeking to understand the roles and differing perspectives of government, industry and the education sector, the Triple Helix Model [THM] provides a useful reference that is embedded within the discourse on the NIS. The THM is described as a model useful for analysing innovation activities in a knowledge-based economy. It emphasises the importance of the relationships between firms, government and universities on the transfer of knowledge which is the key factor inherent in innovation systems (Cooke & Leydesdorff, 2006; Etzkowitz, 2003; Etzkowitz & Leydesdorff, 2000; Leydesdorff & Etzkowitz, 1998). The THM recognises the important role that universities play in knowledge-based economies (Etzkowitz & Leydesdorff, 2000). Importantly, though, for our purposes, the THM is an accepted framework that suggests the importance of a system within a region with respect to expanding innovation activity, although we argue that it falls short as a tool for providing deepening understanding of the system elements and behaviours.

Building on systems theory (notably Ashby's [1956] law of requisite variety) and theories of economic demography, Roos (2012) argues that in the context of a small economy, markets are less developed and hence less efficient. While some factors such as job creation and infrastructure investment (or the lack of these) may be obvious indicators of market failure and poor resource endowment or allocation, in certain industries, the intangible and more intellectually focused factors are less obvious and hence harder to track and detect. Scholars such as Lin and Edvinsson (2008) and Stewart (1997) describe non-monetary and non-physical resources as associated with knowledge, intellectual property and experience. Edvinsson & Malone (1997) put it another way, saying that we can view these intangible resource as the basis for future capabilities. They form part of what is known as intellectual capital and we extend Roos, Pike, and Fernström's (2005, p. 19) definition of intellectual capital at the organisational level as 'all nonmonetary and nonphysical resources that are fully or partly controlled by the organisation and that contribute to the organisation's value creation' to apply it at an industry development level.

Because they are non-additive in nature, intellectual capital resources behave differently from monetary and physical resources and should be managed differently. In application, the approach to IC analysis that we adopted for this chapter emphasises clusters of similar marginal utility behaviour[1], which are divided into three categories as follows:

- relational: the social capital associated with individuals and organisations

- organisational: a firm's infrastructure, processes, culture and so on

- human: the skills, knowledge, attitude and intellectual capacities of individuals.

Other grouping approaches have been used to distinguish an organisation's assets and capabilities; however, these have been criticised for lack of clarity in distinction of asset or resource classes, which leads to overlaps (Leliaert, Candries, & Tilmans, 2003; Stewart, 1997) or missing components of value creation (McElroy, 2002).

Past authors such as Peppard and Rylander (2001) have adopted the IC marginal utility for a commercial case, and O'Connor, Roos, and Vickers-Willis (2007) have adopted it for a government case, to illustrate the development and implementation of an organisation's strategy. We argue that industry development takes on similar properties to organisational growth and development strategies, and intellectual capital is critical to addressing the problems that the creative industries sector faces when it comes to market failures and securing resources efficiently and effectively. As such, there can be a role for the government to intervene. The aim of this chapter is to expose the roles of government and to overlay an IC systems perspective on an empirical case to identify the benefits that an IC approach may have for informing government market system interventions.

---

1 Marginal utility behaviour is an economic term that refers to the extra benefit gained from an incremental increase in the asset. It has its roots in consumer behaviour theory; however, here we apply it to the returns that accrue to an organisation through the growth of a particular asset. The economic behaviour may exhibit either diminishing or increasing returns.

System perspectives of government intervention

From the perspective of complexity sciences, in order to understand systems and system interactions, McKelvey (2004) suggests that four types of analysis can be undertaken.

The first type of analysis seeks to identify the actors and boundaries of the system. The second type of analysis is based on efficient economic and other market theories, which provide a causal level of analysis that assumes rational behaviour. This analysis does not so much predict (because the rules of this form of behaviour are influenced by non-rational inputs that are not accounted for by these methods) as suggest the types of input and output relationships that might be expected if all conditions were universally equal. It is upon these sets of conditions that failures are perceived in market response, whereby non-rational economic behaviour can confound the market economic system.

A system(s) examination also needs to take into account a third analysis of the material and localised conditions to comprehend information asymmetries and the ability of the entrepreneur to acquire the skills, knowledge, capabilities and networks necessary to create any certain form of differentiated products/services. For example, if local conditions do not provide access to expertise and knowledge in a particular new technology, then it is unlikely that a local entrepreneur would engage in a new venture creation related to that expertise and knowledge, and the entrepreneur would find opportunities in areas better supported under the local conditions by education, facilities or capabilities. This level of analysis focuses on information asymmetry, which provides the basis for government's reactive intervention.

The fourth type of analysis requires an examination of the structural and institutional drivers that provide the organisational means for actors to interact within and across different system levels. In terms of hierarchy, this analysis, for instance, examines the bottom-up push that may come from industry, which provides a mechanism for actors, legitimises behaviour and creates connectivity between the system levels. Similarly, from a top-down perspective, government may provide structural support by introducing programs and incentives that provide a platform for interconnective behaviours. It is this fourth level of analysis that identifies the infrastructural gaps and the potential policies and programs that are required to fill the market failures and resource gaps not addressed by current infrastructural mechanisms.

IC analysis perspective

While there are various means and methods for innovation system analysis, the tools of analysis are less defined than the models (for instance, the THM; see Etzkowitz & Klofsten, 2005) or the process (see for instance Bergek, Jacobsson, Carlsson, Lindmark, & Rickne, 2008). Intellectual capital, on the other hand, when used as an interpretive lens or research perspective on an organisation, acts as either a measurement tool for establishing intangible value or a strategic management tool for building and deploying knowledge (Pike, Rylander, & Roos, 2002; von Krogh, Nonaka, & Aben, 2001); and it is the latter that is of interest in this research. Peppard and Rylander (2001) suggest that an intellectual capital approach to strategy analysis and development also has four stages.

The first stage is to operationalise the value creation pathway, which entails identifying the stakeholders and the value they seek from the venture. The management team would then seek to prioritise among the stakeholders in order to surface strategic priorities. This is akin to Stage One of a systems perspective of actor identification and defining boundaries. Stage Two of an IC analysis brings into focus the specific strategic intent that the firm needs to follow in order to satisfy the value creation expectations of the dominant or selected stakeholder position. Similar to the second stage systems analysis, this IC analysis stage provides the direction and the coherent and consistent view of the organisation and defines the expected inputs and outputs that would satisfy the value creation system, framing the analysis for the remaining stages.

The third stage of an IC analysis articulates the value creation pathway by describing how the organisation creates value through its use and deployment of resources. Through this process the strengths and weaknesses of the resource base are identified along with the critical priorities for development of particular resources within the context of how they add or create value toward the organisation's strategic intent. This, too, takes on aspects of system analysis in its third stage, which examines the local conditions (or local resource base) as a means to locate areas of information asymmetry, knowledge or resource gaps. Similar to a regional analysis, a firm seeks to maximise its value creation system by identifying and building a functional resource base.

The fourth and last step in an IC analysis framework is to articulate the IC Navigator, which is a diagrammatic tool that visualises and exposes the value creation pathways and resource transformation system. In a similar fashion to the McKelvey system analysis, the concern with this level of analysis is the transformation processes which may be driven from either bottom-up or top-down. The management team of an organisation needs to ensure that the organisational dimensions enable the support of the value creation system in the same way as governments respond to their analysis by formulating programs and policies that provide the structural backdrop to value creation within a region.

The systems view of complexity science and IC analysis techniques therefore have similar stages and are concerned with similar issues, although the IC set of tools is generally applied to a firm level. In the following sections, we seek to overlay the IC tools of firm-level strategy analysis by adapting them to the regional system level. We first review the development of the digital media industry intervention from a THM and systems perspective and then detail how an IC approach would be applied and the outcomes that may follow from such an approach.

Applying the system analysis perspectives to the SA Government intervention case

We first frame the case of the development of the creative industries government intervention within the systems analysis perspective, as suggested by McKelvey (2004), and then adopt an IC analysis approach. Contrasting the two methods helps to understand the system and the type of government response to the failures suggested by each analysis.

A complex systems analysis

The priority of a systems analysis from a government's perspective is to determine the different active stakeholders within the system to understand and frame the inputs and outcomes that are necessary and desired from an intervention. In this analysis from a regional perspective, we aggregate the stakeholders into the three sectors of government, industry and university that comply with the THM (Cooke, 1998; Etzkowitz, 2003; Etzkowitz & Leydesdorff, 2000; Leydesdorff & Etzkowitz, 1998). These three actors are organised in independent institutional spheres (Zhou, 2008).

In the SA context, the state government initiated the discussion in 2009 and set the agenda with respect to purpose and participant inclusion. The state government was looking to provide opportunities for creative industries (more specifically, digital media) participants to improve their social capital and network participation with respect to stimulating further entrepreneurship within the sector. The state government wanted to develop the creative sector through improving the sector's access to different resources. A key objective and motivator for the government was to remediate the slow growth of the sector in SA and position the industry as a key economic contributor to the state. The intervention process was entirely stimulated and driven by the state government's Department of the Premier and Cabinet, which was responding to a broader agenda designed to increase employment opportunities and economic growth within SA. SA's Strategic Plan (Government of South Australia, 2007) outlined several targets which fit together like a mosaic to frame the particular IC intervention. For that purpose the government involved industry members and the university sector, and through them, enhanced collaboration for development of the industry sector.

The industry sector was consulted and played a relatively minor but important role in the development of the intervention. For instance, nineteen industry representatives participated in the education development forum that provided insights into expectations of how education might fill the knowledge-gap in their industry. As the Tomorrow Studio developed, industry became progressively more involved in terms of providing support to the young digital media businesses. The primary aims of the industry as a group were to adequately resource the sector for growth and reach a critical mass that could sustain a skilled and knowledgeable workforce in SA.

The third stakeholder engaged by the initiative was the university sector. There are three substantial universities within SA: the University of Adelaide, the University of South Australia, and Flinders University. There are also a number of smaller outpost campuses from interstate and international universities that offer specialised or niche programs. The SA Government initiation of engagement with the university sector was enacted via agreement with the Entrepreneurship, Commercialisation and Innovation Centre at the University of Adelaide, where two of the authors of this chapter work. The role of the Entrepreneurship Centre became one of facilitator, as a representative from the centre met with stakeholders from each of the main three universities. As a result of this consultation, it was clear that the primary and overarching motivation for the university sector to participate in this initiative was the desire to offer a better student experience and improved student outcomes.

Perceived gaps in the industry prompting government intervention

In sum, the analysis of stakeholders suggested that each had different drivers that motivated a commonly agreed and preferred outcome. The state government subsequently undertook an analysis on the industry issues which it perceived as needing some response, and this resulted in the following list of key issues:

- a lack of global business relationships
- the perception that local business people were not generally risk takers
- entrepreneurial cultural problems within business and government
- the difficulty of attempting to expand out of the local region
- limited creative use or clever use of technologies
- limited creative problem-solving capabilities
- the transition for an individual between being creative and being commercial being thought to be often too difficult.

These points contribute to a lack of industry participation in the creative industries (digital media) — or, to put it another way, there was a low relative proportion of industry in this sector. From a human capital perspective, there are too few appropriately skilled people and there is a lack of entrepreneurial drive among those who enter the sector.

In ideal circumstances the digital media sector would respond to local and global demand, and certainly there were some SA businesses within the sector which had become global players with international reputations. An example is Rising Sun Pictures, which has won industry awards and lucrative international contracts for digital animation in Hollywood blockbuster films; another example is Resin, which specialises in digital effects and animation in the advertising and movie industries. However, this relatively small group of leading-edge industry players was insufficient to fuel high levels of sector growth.

Reviewing local conditions and resource gaps

The local conditions suggested that the industry was poorly supported, and the majority opinion was that the lack of state dynamics in terms of infrastructure and human capital was both a market- and resource-based failure. Despite the presence within the sector of private financial investor networks, government-backed business enterprise support centres and some highly successful businesses, these were insufficient to kickstart growth. From this context the state government could conceive the particular initiatives that formed part of the Digital Tomorrow program.

The first order of business was the need to overcome the market failures in terms of early-stage financing and support for new and emerging businesses within the sector. There was a notable absence of local early-stage financing for ventures in this sector and no dedicated infrastructural support to nurture young businesses. This suggested a need for a place where like-minded young businesses could share ideas, concepts and knowledge with a view to creating a focal point for critical mass. The size of the local market also suggested that private enterprise and local new business-support infrastructure would not substantially support such a narrowly based sector, and therefore government intervention was warranted.

Perhaps more notable was the lack of awareness of opportunities within the sector, specifically the lack of skills in identifying and exploiting entrepreneurial opportunities. The second part of the program would need to involve developing the human capital of the sector, which meant addressing both awareness levels and the entrepreneurial skill shortage problem. It was generally found that there were sufficient technical knowledge and skills-based opportunities through undergraduate courses and programs in digital media offered in the local region, but the missing elements were the entrepreneurial flair and industry readiness of the graduates and anything specifically available at the postgraduate course level.

Government intervention through the education and training systems can improve entrepreneurial skills and motivation (Lundström & Stevenson, 2005). Education and training allows knowledge to be transferred between actors. The government plays an important role in these systems, as sometimes actors are required to exchange information and come together to find innovative solutions through sharing knowledge. In this case, initial discussions between the government and the university stakeholder group centred on the development of a specific postgraduate entrepreneurship study program for creative industries students. Further discussion led to a more refined focus — instead of focusing on creating a *program*, concentration shifted to a tailored and specific postgraduate *course*. From this perspective, the intention was also not that any one tertiary education institution should be dominant, but instead that each university would fit entrepreneurship within their own institutional education objectives and agendas, which were primarily undergraduate offerings.

Creating structural and institutional drivers

In essence, the Digital Tomorrow Studio initiative was designed to fill the gap left by the market failures in terms of early-stage financing and support for new and emerging businesses within the sector. Given the absence of local early-stage financing for ventures in this sector, the program included small competitive grants that aimed to give promising businesses the opportunity to finance the initial stages of business and market establishment. In addition, the Digital Tomorrow Studio provided a place for like-minded young businesses to share ideas, concepts and knowledge. The Studio also ran workshops and invited guest speakers in response to the particular needs that the surveyed participants raised. The overarching aim of this program initiative was to generate new industry entrants and assist in securing the survival of the firms to help the sector achieve critical mass.

Interestingly, as a by-product of the development of the initiative, the industry group itself decided that it could at least attempt to rectify some of the industry barriers. Subsequently, therefore, the industry group involved in consultation with the initiative arranged to meet on a regular and informal basis. The industry participants were sufficiently motivated to continue working collaboratively to address concerns they had that they felt neither government nor universities could satisfactorily address.

The Digital Tomorrow program responded to the perceived resource-based failure by sponsoring the development of a postgraduate Digital Media Entrepreneurship course. In addition, five scholarship places were funded to attract candidates who were not engaged in formal university study to attend the course. The scholarships successfully attracted eighteen high-calibre applicants. In addition the university sector stakeholders agreed to continue working together to make available courses that were both relevant in objective and pedagogy to their particular institutions and would prepare students for further studies in a Digital Media Entrepreneurship postgraduate course if they so desired. From the initiative, a reference group formed with members from different educational settings, who committed to preparing students for the potential of a career in entrepreneurship in the digital media industry sector.

Outcomes and contributions

From the outset it was apparent that the digital media industry faced some difficulties in developing human capital capable of surviving and thriving in the dynamism of the sector. Further, there was the perceived need for the industry to reach critical mass, whereby the networks and opportunities were sufficient to sustain the sector and nurture growth.

From the education sector's perspective, the primary outcome was the recognition that most of the entrepreneurial education and training required by the industry sector already existed. However, it was highlighted that what was missing was a component of entrepreneurship education framed within the context of a rapidly changing and diverse industry such as the digital media sector. This shifted the emphasis of development from that of a program containing a suite of courses to one of a single course developed specifically to fill this knowledge-gap, which became known as the Digital Media Entrepreneurship course embedded in a postgraduate Master of Applied Innovation and Entrepreneurship at the University of Adelaide. The first Digital Media Entrepreneurship course was delivered during Semester One in 2010 (March to May) and today it has evolved into a highly popular dual offering at both undergraduate and postgraduate levels.

The Digital Tomorrow Studio (business incubator), despite creating a small but vibrant start-up business community for the sector, closed at the end of 2011 due to funding restrictions. In total, the Studio supported thirty-one tenant businesses, of which thirty were start-ups (H Park, personal email correspondence, 26 September 2012). Interviews with the tenants revealed that among the incubatees, the value of the incubation experience included the experiential learning and the development of shared experiences and a sense of community (O'Connor, Seet, Ahmad, & Mukhtar, 2011). The businesses found support among their peers in terms of social capital, knowledge and expertise and even sharing of work to generate income. Regrettably, no follow-up work has been conducted but it would be difficult to imagine that none of these relationships would have endured.

Applying an IC system analysis perspective

Applying the above systems perspective to the digital media sector suggests that both the Studio and the education initiatives provided by the SA Government were appropriate responses to the weaknesses in the industry system. However, neither intervention reached full potential with respect to influencing the growth of the industry sector. Ultimately, government funding is limited, and while the programs were achieving good but modest outcomes the investment needed was much more long-term than the government could sustain. This section attempts to provide an IC analysis framework to the problem, with a view to identifying whether a differing perspective may lead to different types of intervention which might be more enduring.

Stakeholder considerations and dominant perspectives

The first stage of an IC analysis operationalises the value perspective. In this case, the three primary stakeholders were aggregate sectors: government, industry and higher education. The value from the government's perspective can be summarised as seeking to increase employment opportunities and economic growth within SA. From the university sector's viewpoint, the value of this initiative was in the creation of better student experiences and improved outcomes, particularly through additional employment opportunities and employment-ready graduates. The industry sector, however, was seeking to gain critical mass to sustain business and a skilled and knowledgeable workforce in SA. From this perspective, it is clear that government was dependent upon industry meeting its aim, while industry relied on the university sector to prepare the human capital of the sector for growth. If the industry sector is vibrant and competitive, world-leading and in high demand, then, by default, government will meet its objectives and the demand placed on universities to fill industry needs will drive the better student outcomes desired. Therefore, rather than industry taking a minor and advisory role, an IC analysis suggests that industry is the dominant stakeholder with a value perspective that drives other stakeholders to achieve their aims.

From this standpoint, the next stage of an IC analysis establishes a strategic intent. The government, as the sector recognising and initiating the drive, has a critical function to provide leadership by assisting both the industry and university sectors to focus on the common goal.

Roos, Pike, and Fernström (2005) suggest that a strategic intent should provide an aspirational statement and should envision a desired future leadership position that provides direction and suggests a means by which the strategic intent could be achieved. A strategic intent is an expression of a principal strategy that focuses attention on the essence of winning, which motivates people by communicating value. It also guides resource allocation, while providing stability under changing circumstances but leaving room for contribution from other stakeholders. Such a strategic intent might be structured as follows: 'Build SA as a leading destination for digital media business, employment and learning, attracting major capital investment and contracts from international private and public sectors'.

This strategic intent immediately focuses on the long term and rules out such interventions that may fill gaps as temporary measures. An IC approach at this point forces stakeholders to examine the resource and capability base it has and examine ways of building the resources and capabilities to achieve the strategic intent. Therefore, as far as government intervention goes, the priority should be on how to build strength within the system, rather than on providing any unsustainable and/or relatively short-term remedy to substitute for market action/reaction.

At the third stage of an IC analysis, attention turns to the value creation pathway — that is, the ways and means that value is created. Clearly, the value sought is the growth and flourishing of the digital media sector for its employment and economic wealth creation potential. The missing elements identified through the earlier analysis were organisational, relational and human capital issues within the sector. A major perception was that, culturally, the state lacked entrepreneurial drive. Relational capital was deficient around global and national business opportunities, and the human capital issues raised were insufficient creative abilities, commercial astuteness and entrepreneurial flair.

Aligning with the strategic intent, these deficiencies suggest a few alternatives that would address these weaknesses and draw upon the strengths of the state digital media sector. Assuming in the first instance that the government could overcome any entrepreneurial inertia (lack of entrepreneurial culture), a priority would be to stimulate the firms in the marketplace to grow their international contacts. As one approach, this may be achieved through financial incentives based on matching funds for firms to seek international business with success bonuses paid to offset some of the risk to international partners or contracts. Addressing the human capital issues would involve working closely with the providers of human capital (the university and tertiary technical education sectors) to strengthen industry links and technical capabilities within the education and training sector. Attracting leading international talent as educators may be an alternative. The commercial and entrepreneurial deficiencies could also be overcome within the tertiary education sector by ensuring that entrepreneurial opportunities are embedded within the system. This implies that digital media incubators and courses would be established and supported within the relevant institutions rather than being outside a government-backed add-on to the system. Industry could be incentivised to contribute to the operations and development of the businesses that could emerge from this sector initiative. Adopting approaches such as these would build the digital media industry system by strengthening the resources and capabilities that were found deficient.

The final stage of an IC analysis constructs the IC Navigator to visualise the system. Although stakeholder input is required in order to construct the system diagram, the above analysis suggests that the intellectual capital in the system will, by far, dominate the Navigator in terms of relative importance. Figure 9.2 is a mock-up to illustrate how an IC Navigator might be interpreted for a region, and in this particular case what the system stocks (or circles) of organisational, relational, human, financial and physical resources and capabilities, and the flows between these stocks (the arrows), may be. A feature of the IC Navigator would be the organisational resources in terms of the tertiary education sector courses and programs and the government programs and incentive schemes that consume financial resources. Of interest is the flow back to financial resources generated by a region's organisational resources, principally the firms and institutions. The objective of the industry development department of the government is not to make money, but the wealth generated by the organisational contributors (firms and institutions) to a system should flow back to the government indirectly through taxes which can again be reinvested in various needs of the region (for example, health, transport and education).

The relational resources that exist within and between the education sector and national and international business sectors will also be critical to value creation within the digital media industry system. Human capital, with its creative, technical and entrepreneurial capabilities, is likely to be the dominant and most highly important resource to the system. Finally, physical resources will be of relatively little importance given the nature of the industry sector. Although clearly some physical resources (computer equipment and offices) will be needed, these are relatively static requirements without the intellectual capital to create and facilitate the software (organisational and human capacity) that drives the system.

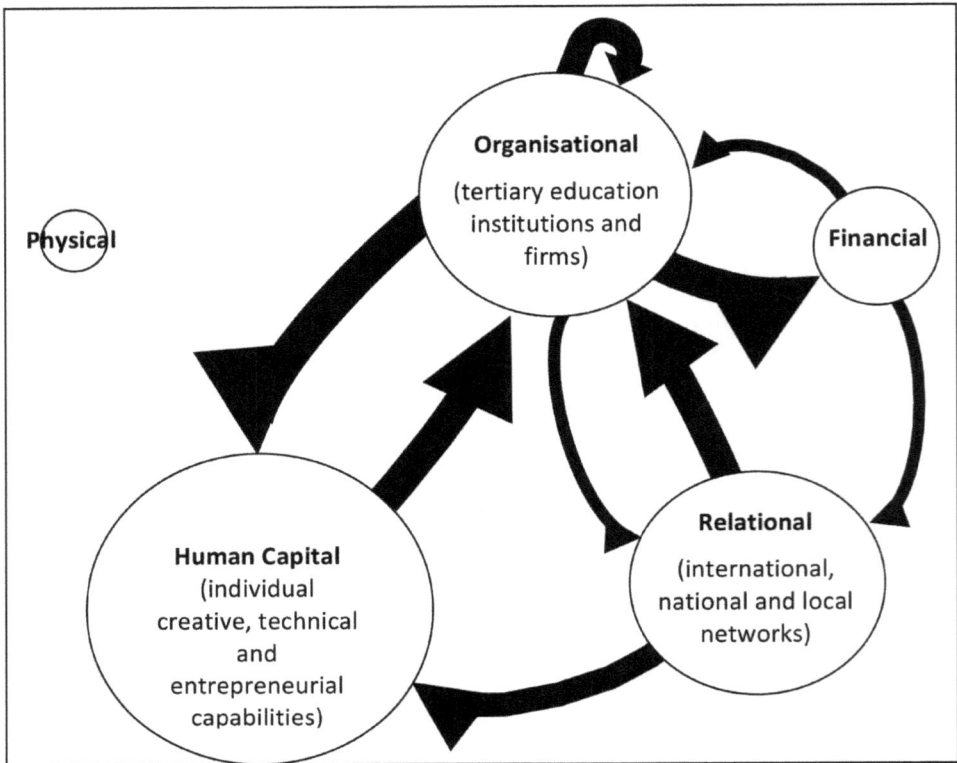

Figure 9.2: An interpreted regional IC Navigator.
Source: Courtesy of the authors.

Discussion and conclusions

By adopting the IC lens, the analysis of the industry system draws attention to the system elements, roles and the interactions among the elements. The alternative system analysis instead highlights the symptoms of the system, which subsequently tend to draw responses that are inadequate for long-term transformation of the system. However, simply adopting the organisational level IC analysis tool to the regional level reveals a number of shortfalls.

First is the issue of definition of the elements involved in the analysis, which, although suitable for the firm level of analysis, does not easily translate to the regional level. For example, what is meant by organisational capital at a region? Is this all soft organisational infrastructure embedded within the region regardless of the level of analysis, or is it, more simply, the organisational infrastructure provided by governments and public institutions? Similarly for human capital: is this the capabilities of the inhabitants of the region or is it the number and type of people who reside in the region? Both have a meaning for regional-level analysis which is less problematic than at an organisational level. Therefore the definition of what is meant by each of these terms when transposed to the regional level is critical.

A second issue is in understanding the operation of the system where there are both flow and transformations that need to be dealt with. For instance, the financial resource element in a firm-level analysis would normally refer to the monetary resources employed by the firm. At the regional level there are two issues that we encounter when considering the financial or monetary resource — that of flow of financial resources and that of transformation of monetary resources. At the firm level, the movement of monetary resources toward other resource forms represents a transformation, as investments of money have a direct influence on the state of the receiving resource (that is to say, money invested in training increases the level of human capital). At a regional level there exists a flow of monetary resource (from a government department to a firm) which results in a subsequent transformation at another level of analysis (in other words, money granted to a firm is subsequently used by the firm to enact a transformation like the purchase of equipment or services). Therefore, while an IC Navigator analysis uses transformations between resources at the regional level, further analysis is required to look at both the flow and the consequential transformations.

A third issue that needs attention is sorting out the different types of investment that might be integrated at one level but might remain distinct at another level. For instance, the intervention of a business incubator is both an investment in soft infrastructure (such as mentors, like-mindedness and training support) and an investment in hard infrastructure (such as a physical space, computer hardware and laboratory equipment). At the regional level an investment in an incubator results in a mixed investment at the (firm-) level of the incubator. Therefore, a regional IC analysis requires a much more careful and articulate distinction between the types of investments than may be crudely observed generally at the regional level.

Further research

As an exploratory study of the role that government plays in forming regional innovation system interventions, this research suggests that the type of analysis of the system alters the perception of the role. Further work could explore the potential variance to an organisation-level representation of an IC Navigator and how the analysis influences the role and intervention design by government.

A system analysis that adopts an approach to understand the system and its failures seems to lead government to design interventions that treat only the symptoms, and the result may fail to leave a lasting change within the system. Adopting a far more structural approach such as the IC Navigator forces the focus onto the behaviour of the system elements, and the role of government shifts from treating the symptoms to embedding deep-seated changes within the system itself and its actors and institutions.

We suggest that further research examining different approaches is required to improve government intervention assessments. We also recommend that researchers work at deeply understanding the element definitions and characteristics of the systems as well as the flows and transformational connections at regional level. Empirical tests will help to assess the use of the IC Navigator at the regional level.

References

Adcroft, A, Willis, R, & Dhaliwal, S. (2004). Missing the point? Management education and entrepreneurship. *Management Decisions, 42*(3/4), 521-30.

Aeroudt, R. (2004). Incubators: Tool for entrepreneurship? *Small Business Economics, 23*, 127-35.

Ashby, WR. (1956). *An introduction to cybernetics*. London: Chapman & Hall.

Barney, J. (1991). Firm resources and sustained competitive advantage. *Journal of Management, 17*(1), 99-120.

Bergek, A, Jacobsson, S, Carlsson, B, Lindmark, S, & Rickne, A. (2008). Analyzing the functional dynamics of technological innovation systems: A scheme of analysis. *Research Policy, 37*, 407-29.

Bontis, N. (2004). National Intellectual Capital Index: A United Nations initiative for the Arab region. *Journal of Intellectual Capital, 5*(1), 13-39.

Cantù, C, Corsaro, D, & Snehota, I. (2012). Roles of actors in combining resources into complex solutions. *Journal of Business Research, 65*(2), 139-50.

Carey, C, & Naudin, A. (2006). Enterprise curriculum for creative industries students: An exploration of current attitudes and issues. *Education + Training, 48*(7), 518-31.

Cooke, P. (1998). *Regional innovation systems*. London: UCL Press.

Cooke, P, & Leydesdorff, L. (2006). Regional development in the knowledge-based economy: The construction of advantage. *The Journal of Technology Transfer, 31*(1), 5-15.

Corsaro, D, Cantù, C, & Tunisini, A. (2012). Actors' heterogeneity in innovation networks. *Industrial Marketing Management, 41*(5), 780-9.

Doloreux, D, & Parto, S. (2005). Regional innovation systems: Current discourse and unresolved issues. *Technology in Society, 27*(2), 133-53.

Edvinsson, L, & Malone, M. (1997). *Intellectual capital*. New York: Harper Business.

Etzkowitz, H. (2003). Innovation in innovation: The Triple Helix of university-industry-government relations. *Social Science Information, 42*(3), 293-337.

Etzkowitz, H, & Klofsten, M. (2005). The innovating region: Toward a theory of knowledge-based regional development. *R&D Management, 35*(3), 243-55.

Etzkowitz, H, & Leydesdorff, L. (2000). The dynamics of innovation: From national systems and 'Mode 2' to a Triple Helix of university-industry-government relations. *Research Policy, 29*(2), 109-330.

de Foite, D, Henry, C, Johnston, K, & Van Der Sijde, P. (2003). Education and training for entrepreneurs: A consideration of initiatives in Ireland and the Netherlands. *Education and Training for Entrepreneurs, 45*, 430-7.

Gertler, MS. (1995). Being there — Proximity, organization, and culture in the development and adoption of advanced manufacturing technologies. *Economic Geography, 71*(1), 1-26.

Government of South Australia. (2007). *South Australia's strategic plan*. South Australia: Government of South Australia. Retrieved from http://saplan/images/pdf/South_Australia_Strategic_Plan_2007.pdf.

Grimaldi, R, & Grandi, A. (2005). Business incubators and new venture creation: An assessment of incubating models. *Technovation, 25*(2), 111-21.

Gulati, R, Nohria, N, & Zaheer, A. (2000). Strategic networks. *Strategic Management Journal, 21*(3), 203-15.

Hackett, SM, & Dilts, DM. (2004). A systematic review of business incubation research. *The Journal of Technology Transfer, 29*(1), 55-82.

Hervas Oliver, JL, Rojas, R, Martins, BM, & Cervello Royo, R. (2011). The overlapping of national IC and innovation systems. *Journal of Intellectual Capital, 12*(1), 111-31.

Keogh, W, & Galloway, L. (2004). Teaching enterprise in vocational disciplines: Reflecting on positive experience. *Management Decisions, 42*(3/4), 531-41.

von Krogh, G, Nonaka, I, & Aben, M. (2001). Making the most of your company's knowledge: A strategic framework. *Long Range Planning, 34*(4), 421-39.

Laukkanen, M. (2000). Exploring alternative approaches in high-level entrepreneurship education: Creating micromechanisms for endogenous regional growth. *Entrepreneurship and Regional Development, 12*(1), 25-47.

Leliaert, PJC, Candries, W, & Tilmans, R. (2003). Identifying and Managing IC: A new classification. *Journal of Intellectual Capital, 4*(2), 202-14.

Leydesdorff, L, & Etzkowitz, H. (1998). The Triple Helix as a model for innovation studies. *Conference Report, Science & Public Policy, 25*(3), 195-203.

Lundström, A, & Stevenson, L. (2005). *Entrepreneurship policy: Theory and practice.* New York: Springer.

McElroy, MW. (2002). Social Innovation capital. *Journal of Intellectual Capital, 3*(1), 30-9.

McKelvey, B. (2004). Toward a complexity science of entrepreneurship. *Journal of Business Venturing, 19*(3), 313-41.

Martinez, AC, Levie, J, Kelley, DJ, Sæmundsson, RJ, & Schøtt, T. (2010). *Global entrepreneurship monitor special report: A global perspective on entrepreneurship education and training.* Retrieved from http://www.gemconsortium.org/docs/cat/2/special-topic-reports.

O'Connor, A. (2009). Enterprise, education and economic development: *An exploration of entrepreneurship's economic function in the Australian government's education policy*. (PhD Thesis, The Australian Graduate School of Entrepreneurship, Swinburne University of Technology, Australia).

O'Connor, A, Burnett, H, & Hancock G. (2009, February 6-9). Converging entrepreneurship education with business incubation: An exploration of the development process for entrepreneurs. *Proceedings of the 6th AGSE Regional Research Exchange*, The University of Adelaide, Australia.

O'Connor, A, & Greene, F. (2007). Does entrepreneurship education support Australian enterprise? *Small Enterprise Conference*, Auckland, New Zealand.

O'Connor, A, Roos, G, & Wickers-Willis, T. (2007). Evaluating the innovation capacity of a public sector organization: An Australian case study. *European Journal of Innovation Management, 10*(4), 532-8.

O'Connor A, Seet, P-S, Ahmad, NH, & Mukhtar, D. (2011, February). Business incubation and entrepreneurial competencies: An exploration of relationships. *Proceedings of the 8th AGSE Regional Research Exchange*, Melbourne, Swinburne University of Technology.

O'Gorman, C, & Kautonen, M. (2004). Policies promoting new knowledge intensive agglomerations. *Entrepreneurship & Regional Development, 16*(6), 459-79.

Organisation for Economic Co-operation and Development (OECD). (1999). *Business incubation: International case studies*. Paris: OECD.

Parker, S. (2004). *The economics of self-employment and entrepreneurship*. Cambridge, UK: Cambridge University Press.

Parker, S, Tims, C, & Wright, S. (2006). *Inclusion, innovation and democracy: Growing talent for the creative and cultural industries*. Retrieved from http://www.demos.co.uk/files/creative_race_finalweb.pdf.

Peppard, J, & Rylander, A. (2001). Using an intellectual capital perspective to design and implement a growth strategy: The case of Apion. *European Management Journal, 19*(5), 510-25.

Pike, S, Rylander, A, & Roos, G. (2002). Intellectual capital management and disclosure. In CW Choo and N Bontis (Eds.), *The strategic management of intellectual capital and organizational knowledge: A selection of readings* (pp. 657-71). New York: Oxford University Press.

Roos, G. (2012). *Manufacturing into the future*. Adelaide: Department of the Premier and Cabinet, Government of South Australia.

Roos, G, Pike, S, & Fernström, L. (2005). *Managing intellectual capital in practice*. Oxford: Butterworth-Heinemann.

Smilor, RW. (1987). Commercializing technology through new business incubators. *Research Management, 30*(5), 36-41.

Stahle, P, & Bounfour, A. (2008). Understanding dynamics of intellectual capital. *Journal of Intellectual Capital, 9*(2), 164-77.

Stewart, TA. (1997). *Intellectual capital: The wealth of organizations*. New York: Nicholas Brealey Publishing.

Westerlund, M, & Rajala, R. (2010). Learning and innovation in inter-organizational network collaboration. *Journal of Business and Industrial Marketing, 25*(6), 435-42.

Yeh-Yun Lin, C, & Edvinsson, L. (2008). National intellectual capital: Comparison of the Nordic countries. *Journal of Intellectual Capital, 9*(4), 525-45.

Zhou, C. (2008). Emergence of the entrepreneurial university in evolution of the Triple Helix. A case of Northeastern University in China. *Journal of Technology Management, 3*(1), 109-26.

A diagnostic tool for assessing innovation readiness

10

Paul Shum, University of Western Sydney

Introduction

Creativity and support for new ideas, their experimentation and development, are key characteristics of innovativeness. Nonetheless, new ideas are not born in 'the full glory of their potentials' (de Bono, 1985). Research has found that for an average of 3000 raw ideas, only one of them reaches the last stage of profitable commercialisation (Kuczmarski, 1996; Stevens & Burley, 1997). It takes both effort and resources to develop and add value to these ideas so that they become marketable. However, even the allocation of additional resources to support further development may not guarantee the desired results. The degree of success of the innovation and commercialisation process is dependent on a wide variety of factors.

According to previous studies, innovation capabilities/practices can be categorised into strategy (Cooper & Kleinschmidt, 1995; Goffin & Pfeiffer, 1999), systems (Christensen, 1997; Leonard-Barton, 1992) and culture (Burgelman, Maidique, & Wheelwright, 2004; Chiesa, Coughlan, & Voss, 1996). However, each research stream looks at innovation capabilities from a narrow perspective. Previous studies have not defined a set of comprehensive innovation capabilities measures that translate innovation inputs into profitable outputs. In contrast, the relationship between innovation capabilities/practices and business performance has been extensively investigated at the industry level (Cooper & Kleinschmidt, 1991; Guan, Tang, & Lau, 2009; Huff, 1990), but not at company level (Adams, Bessant,

& Phelps, 2006). Furthermore, these industry-level studies focus largely on measuring innovation capabilities/practices as monetary inputs in the form of R&D spending or staffing levels, rather than focusing on the capabilities that turn inputs/spending into profitable commercialisation.

The model of this research study captures a common set of innovation- and entrepreneurship-related competences and capabilities that support the innovation and commercialisation process. Using this model may raise the success rate of the conversion of new ideas into marketable products or services. Better still, adopting a balanced approach to this model promises to maximise the financial performance of innovation as well as achieve other strategic objectives such as quality.

Currently, many companies do not adopt a balanced approach. A personal observation, especially among many R&D research centres and laboratories that the author has worked for or visited, is that these entities usually take a biased stance towards the internal view of innovation. These institutions have a high level of innovation input in terms of R&D spending and staff numbers, and a high output of new technologies and knowledge. However, there is no guarantee that their research outcomes will have sufficient market value for profitable commercialisation. These research institutions usually suffer from relying solely on the strategy of technology push. To be more successful, a business must simultaneously adopt an approach to proactively assess its market and technology trends and opportunities. A combined approach taking ideas from both the market ('pull') and technology ('push') usually achieves a higher rate of success, as the model of this research study will demonstrate.

Literature review

Most innovation studies are confined to limited aspects of the innovation process. As a consequence, some published results conflict with others (Wolfe, 1994), either due to different views of the scope of the unit and area of analysis, or because of incomplete specification of the innovation process model. They cannot reach solid conclusions, and their results cannot be generalised to the whole innovation process. Nevertheless, recent attempts to construct an innovation framework or model are paving the way to advance knowledge in this research field.

Based on a small sample of best practice case studies, Chiesa et al. (1996) developed an instrument for auditing technical innovation management. However, they did not test the analytical results with sound statistical techniques. Therefore, the validity and reliability of their instrument is open to discussion. Tang (1998) observed the need for an innovation model to integrate the large amount of research studies on innovation. He developed an integrative innovation framework, and later collected data to test it. Other research studies (APQC, 2001; Belliveau, Griffin, & Somermeyer, 2002; Conceicao, Hamill, & Pinheiro, 2002; Cooper, Edgett, & Kleinschmidt, 2004; Griffin, 1997; Zairi, 1999) have also constructed innovation frameworks that capture a wide range of measurable innovation variables whilst subjecting the data to statistical analysis for validation. They suggest either comparing a company's innovation profile with that of the sample means, maximum and minimum, of another company, or an ideal perfect score position (the highest score on the Likert scale, e.g. 5).

These types of approaches take an initial step to assist practitioners in benchmarking their innovation capabilities against best practice. The innovation framework provides measurement and evaluation methods in comparing a broad range of innovation capabilities and practices. Relevant capabilities and practices can be identified, introduced and developed, with the intention of targeting weak areas for improvement in order to bridge performance gaps (Dence, 1995; Morgan, 1995; Rimmer, MacNeil, Chenhall, Langfield-Smith, & Watts, 1996; Welbourn, Wardrop, & Bryant, 1994). This benchmarking can be extended and generalised to compare similar capabilities and practices in different industries (Karlof, 1993). However, research studies (Porter, 1996; Sheather, 1998) have warned about the pitfalls of simply copying best practice and yet not achieving the desired outcomes. In many situations, Sheather (1998) observed negative effects on performance that might result from benchmarking exercises. One of the reasons is that the company imitates the best practice at the superficial and visible level, but ignores the enterprise-wide interlocking mechanisms and the required cultural change.

In contrast, converting to the same innovation profile as the benchmarked company may not be feasible or economical, in terms of the resources required to achieve the desired outcomes. Due to high demand on the resources for a long intervention period, many firms target isolated areas for improvement. This partial implementation moves the firm closer to the innovation profile of the benchmarked company in the selected areas. However, lack of enterprise-wide alignment prevents realisation of all the improvement potential along the internal value chain. Therefore, the overall benefit of benchmarking is likely to be unsatisfactorily low or uncertain.

The marginal cost would most likely outweigh the marginal return. For companies wanting to improve their innovation capabilities, these innovation frameworks cannot offer a precise and practical intervention program to bridge the performance gap.

This chapter will present a systematically constructed innovation readiness framework that captures enterprise-wide innovation capabilities. However, this research study does not use the sample means, maximum and minimum, another company, or an ideal perfect score position as benchmark. Instead, it uses the data-mining method (neural network) to classify the data set into two classes. One class consists of company innovation profiles that belong to the 'innovation-ready' group. Their scores in innovation capabilities and environment are consistently higher in all dimensions than that of the other 'non-innovation-ready' group. This benchmark is more accurate and objective than the sample means, maximum and minimum, another company, or an ideal perfect score position. It will help practitioners identify important areas for improving innovation capabilities and environment.

Small-to-medium sized enterprises that have resource constraints will especially find this targeted approach more economical by focusing resources in the identified areas for improvement. Since the diagnosis for innovation readiness will be based on an assessment tool constructed from empirical data, it is superior to other methods currently applied. This assessment tool identifies important areas for improvement and guides companies to optimise resources to achieve satisfactory innovation outcomes. Some case studies will validate and illustrate this innovation readiness framework. The field study consists of interviews with twenty senior managers of the three case study companies to validate the data collected previously and test the audit instrument and innovation readiness diagnostic tools.

Methodology and results

The sample consists of eighty-one manufacturing companies in South Australia. This data set contains postal survey questionnaires completed by the managing director, CEO, or senior-level management representative of each sampled company. Morse (1998) has determined these participants as able to best represent the view of their companies. Recording their perception of the company's innovation capabilities reduces the perceptual bias that may not represent the dominant view of the sampled companies. A follow-up study of three case study companies will confirm this assertion and validate the degree of accuracy of the data set.

Data-mining method

After discussion with practising consultants in this field and through a literature review, this research study identified over 150 factors combining to form an important capability set that contributes to superior quality and innovation performance. Using the data-mining method, the research study uses the Kohonen neural network for classifying data into classes. It differs from the feed-forward backpropagation neural network by training in unsupervised mode and recalling a pattern. It does not use any activation function or bias weight, and requires input normalisation as a third layer. The output generates two major classes out of the sample size of eighty-one cases. One class consists of an 'innovation-ready' profile. These companies have a superior environment and innovation capabilities to engage in innovative activities and develop profitable new products. Companies of the second class belong to the 'non-innovation-ready' group. Further field study of several companies of the 'non-innovation-ready' group reveals that even if a window-dressing approach is adopted to provide the public with a corporate image of innovativeness and entrepreneurship, the true level of innovation readiness can easily be detected from the diagnosis. These companies do not score high in the intellectual capital measures due to management's unwillingness to invest in employees in developing their capabilities in entrepreneurship, innovation and quality. Resources commitment is necessary for bridging the innovation performance gap in order to become 'innovation-ready'.

Data validation

This research selected three case study companies for a follow-up field study using the 'innovation-ready' profile for comparison. Two companies were drawn from the 'innovation-ready' group, one of which had higher scores and the other one lower scores relative to the group means. The third company was drawn from the 'non-innovation-ready' group. This follow-up field study required all senior managers of the three case study companies to complete the survey questionnaire. Their survey scores were analysed to detect any pattern that supported the view that using one single survey questionnaire completed by the most senior manager or director sufficiently represented the whole company. The result shows that survey scores of the most senior manager or director have the least deviation from the average of all the senior managers surveyed and achieve the least prediction error. As such, a survey that targets the most senior manager or director can reduce the perceptual bias that may not represent the dominant view of the sampled companies.

Results

The t-Student test examines the statistical uniformity of the means difference between two groups (Hair, Black, Babin, Anderson, & Tatham, 2007). Using t-Student tests with a statistical significance level of 5 per cent, Table 10.2 lists the results of the analysis, showing that fifteen critical factors are statistically significant to distinguish the 'innovation-ready' and 'non-innovation-ready' groups. Such factors might include championship, customer focus, customer interface, diversity, employee involvement, employee training, entrepreneurship, exposure to environment, external knowledge, front-end management, idea management, incubation, management training, market strategy, openness, organisational training, performance, process capability, product development, project management, R&D, scanning, teamwork, and vision. These identified factors have been reported as important characteristics of highly innovative companies by published research studies (APQC, 2001; Belliveau, Griffin, & Somermeyer, 2002; Conceicao, Hamill, & Pinheiro, 2002; Cooper, Edgett, & Kleinschmidt, 2004; Griffin, 1997; Zairi, 1999) that focused on smaller sets of these factors.

This study adopts two popularly used intellectual capital typologies: IC-Index (Roos, Roos, Dragonetti, & Edvinsson, 1997) and Skandia Navigator (Edvinsson & Malone, 1997). The five-dimensional IC-Index framework is composed of a thinking part, the human capital (Human and Intellectual Agility), and a non-thinking part, the structural capital (Relationships, Organisation, and Renewal and Development). The Skandia Navigator consists of four parts, including Human, Customer, Innovation and Process Capital. The Innovation Readiness IC (IRIC) model of this study also has four parts, Leadership and Vision, Renewal and Innovation, Internal Capability and Process, and Customer Orientation. These three IC constructs are closely aligned, as characterised in Table 10.1.

Using these IC typologies, the fifteen factors are categorised into two major IC types, as shown in Tables 10.2 and 10.3. The distances — that is, the difference of the innovation capability scores between these two groups — are wider in the intellectual capital elements Championship, Idea Management, R&D, Vision,

IC-index[1]	Skandia navigator[2]	IRIC[3] model	IRIC components
1. Human	1. Human	1. Leadership and vision	Championship
			Vision
			Entrepreneurship
2. Intellectual	2. Innovation	2. Renewal and innovation	Idea management
			Product development
			Front-end management
3. Renewal			R&D
			Training
4. Organisational	3. Process	3. Internal capability and process	Project management
			Teamwork
			Diversity
			Process capability
4. Relationships	4. Customer	4. Customer orientation	Customer focus
			Market strategy

[1] Originally constructed by Roos et al. (1997)
[2] Originally constructed by Edvinsson and Malone (1997)
[3] Innovation Readiness Intellectual Capital (IRIC) proposed in this study

Table 10.1: The three intellectual capital (IC) constructs.
Source: Courtesy of the author.

Product Development and Training, followed by Project Management, and Teamwork. This research study recommends that the government and industry associations allocate more resources in the manufacturing industry of South Australia to support innovation programs that enhance these innovation capabilities if more profitable innovation outcomes are to be achieved.

The Innovation capability scores of the 'innovation-ready' group are consistently higher than that of the 'non-innovation-ready' group. Furthermore, the distances between these two groups are wider in the Human and the Renewal and Development elements, followed by the Intellectual Agility and Organisational

IRIC Model COMPONENTS	Type of intellectual capital		The difference between 'innovation-ready' and 'non innovation-ready'	
	IC-Index and Skandia Navigator	IRIC Model	Distance	t- statistics
1. Performance	Financial	Financial	0.11	2.18
2. Championship	Human	Leadership and vision	0.41	9.81
3. Vision	Human	Leadership and vision	0.33	8.77
4. Entrepreneurship	Human	Leadership and vision	0.17	3.21
5. Idea management	Intellectual	Renewal and innovation	0.34	9.36
6. Product development	Intellectual	Renewal and innovation	0.33	6.41
7. Front-end management	Intellectual	Renewal and innovation	0.19	4.25
8. Project management	Organisational	Internal process	0.26	6.60
9. Teamwork	Organisational	Internal process	0.21	6.03
10. Diversity	Organisational	Internal process	0.14	3.23
11. Process capability	Organisational	Internal process	0.13	2.96
12. Customer focus	Relationships	Customer orientation	0.15	4.65
13. Market strategy	Relationships	Customer orientation	0.11	2.63
14. R&D	Renewal	Renewal and innovation	0.34	5.27
15. Training	Renewal	Renewal and innovation	0.32	3.51

Table 10.2: 'Innovation-ready' (Class 1) versus 'non-innovation-ready' (Class 2)
— An alignment of the intellectual capital constructs.
Source: Courtesy of the author.

elements, and then the Relationships element, according to the five elements of the IC index.

The purpose of this chapter is to address the research issues overlooked by previous research studies, and to offer a practical solution to guide companies in their innovation journey. Using this framework, companies allocate resources to the five dimensions listed in Table 10.3 to improve their innovation capabilities and performance. To maximise the return on investment in innovation capabilities, a company must be able to identify and operationalise the areas for improvement

IC-Index and Skandia Navigator	IRIC Model	Class 1	Class 2	Class 1 is greater than class 2
		'Innovation-ready'	*'Non-innovation-ready'*	*Distance*
Organisational	Internal capability and process	10.0	7.7	2.3
Relationships	Customer orientation	10.0	7.9	2.1
Human	Leadership and vision	10.0	7.3	2.7
Intellectual agility	Renewal and innovation	10.0	7.6	2.4
Renewal and development	Renewal and innovation	10.0	7.4	2.6

Table 10.3: 'Innovation-ready' (Class 1) versus 'non-innovation-ready' (Class 2) — An aggregate intellectual capital profile.
Source: Courtesy of the author.

in order to select the appropriate tools and techniques to enhance its innovation capabilities. It must also define the performance gap and set a priority to determine the amount of resources and intensity of efforts to realise the performance plan.

As shown in Tables 10.2 and 10.3, the wider the distance between Class 1 and Class 2, the bigger the capability gap, and the higher the improvement potential for enhancing innovation capabilities. Table 10.2 suggests that the 'non-innovation-ready' companies should allocate more resources to promote employee training, championship, R&D, idea management, product development, vision, management training, organisational training, project management, environmental scanning, teamwork, front-end management and entrepreneurship before tackling other less distanced aspects.

When this table was communicated to the senior management of the three case study companies, they immediately agreed on the specified areas for intervention. The next section will investigate the comparative innovation profiles of the three case study companies in depth to validate the data set against the business reality.

Case studies

This research study selects three companies from the sample (manufacturing companies operating in South Australia) for in-depth data collection and analysis. Interviews with members of the senior management team help clarify and validate the previously collected survey data. The interview results prove that their views are consistent with the original survey data. The following sections report the case studies.

Case Study 1 — More innovative company

Table 10.4 shows the innovation profile of Case Study 1 Company, relative to that of the Class 1 (innovation-ready) group. The data-mining method classifies it as relatively more innovative than the innovation-ready group. The scores of this more innovative company are normalised to 0 per cent in all innovation components. For each innovation component, if the relative score of Class 1 (innovation-ready) group is positive, for example, by 16 per cent in external knowledge sourcing, this points to an area of improvement for the Case Study 1 Company. For those innovation components where the relative scores of Class 1 are negative, this more innovative (Case Study 1) company has already developed stronger capabilities, and does not require any improvement in these areas.

The innovation readiness framework indicates that this Case Study 1 Company is scoring higher than the 'innovation-ready' group in management training, R&D, performance measures, product development, entrepreneurship, process capability and teamwork. As a result, this more innovative company has achieved a higher innovation performance when compared to the 'innovation-ready' group. For the areas needing improvement, the diagram identifies two major components. This more innovative company can strengthen further

	Weaknesses[1]	Strengths[2]	Recommendation[3]
Employee training	65%		Area for improvement
External knowledge	16%		Area for improvement
Management training		35%	
R&D		34%	
Performance		25%	
Product development		23%	
Entrepreneurship		21%	
Process capability		17%	
Teamwork		16%	

[1] *(% weaker than the innovation-ready class)*
[2] *(% stronger than the innovation-ready class)*
[3] *for this case study (more innovative) company*

Table 10.4: More innovative company versus 'innovation-ready' group (Class 1).
Source: Courtesy of the author.

through the implementation of a tailored innovation program by addressing employee training and external knowledge sourcing.

The field interviews with all the senior managers of this more innovative company confirm these findings. The interviews indicate that this company

- encourages and sends managers to undertake university management development programs

- has its own R&D establishment and a team of full-time dedicated R&D engineers and facilities

- allocates more resources in product and export market development

- enjoys a higher level of performance in new product development and introduction

- has a senior management with ambitious visions of innovation, higher entrepreneurial propensity and preparedness to take risks

- has employees who are more technically competent, especially in product/process development and technology adoption
- uses project teams widely in new product/process development, quality and productivity improvement initiatives
- has a more sophisticated structure and procedure for managing projects
- has a more sophisticated process for creativity and ideas management
- is highly competitive in pricing and market strategies.

In contrast, further observations are:

- Except for R&D personnel, other employees find themselves under pressure and not provided with sufficient time and opportunities to test or try out more ideas.
- Workers are not familiar with what others are doing, and they do not have the time and opportunities to discuss their ideas with others.
- Senior managers rely more on a small group of people whom they regard as innovative thinkers. Only this group receives training in creativity and problem identification/solving techniques. There is scope for expanding this training to other employees so that all employees can be part of innovation activities and contribute accordingly.
- There is heavy reliance on senior managers as liaising agents to acquire external knowledge sources and circulate the information internally among the upper echelon. There is little direct effort among lower-level employees to access such information or search for external knowledge sources.

These observations agree with the analysis as indicated in Table 10.4.

Case Study 2 — Less innovative company

Table 10.5 shows the innovation profile of Case Study 2 Company, relative to that of the 'innovation-ready' group. The data-mining method identifies it as a relatively less innovative company. The innovation readiness framework indicates that this less innovative (Case Study 2) company scores higher than the 'innovation-ready' group for entrepreneurship and incubation. However, this less innovative company has achieved a lower innovation performance when compared to the 'innovation-ready' group due to a number of weak areas that require improvement, as identified in the diagram. These weak areas include training for management, employee and organisation, championship, idea management, vision, R&D, environmental scanning, market strategy and teamwork. These are areas where this less innovative company can further upgrade through the implementation of a tailored innovation program.

	Weaknesses[1]	Strengths[2]	Recommendation[3]
Management training	69%		Area for improvement
Employee training	65%		Area for improvement
Organisation training	38%		Area for improvement
Championship	33%		Area for improvement
Idea management	33%		Area for improvement
Vision	33%		Area for improvement
R&D	32%		Area for improvement
Environmental scanning	27%		Area for improvement
Market strategy	24%		Area for improvement
Teamwork	19%		Area for improvement
Entrepreneurship		21%	
Incubation		16%	

[1] (% weaker than the innovation-ready class)
[2] (% stronger than the innovation-ready class)
[3] for this case study (less innovative) company

Table 10.5: Less innovative company versus 'innovation-ready' group (Class 1).
Source: Courtesy of the author.

The field interviews with all the senior managers of this less innovative company also confirm these findings. For this company, the owner (managing director) has a strong entrepreneurial orientation. The pace of work is more relaxed. Employees generally have time to pursue their interests or ideas if they want to.

However, a number of other factors need attention:

- There are project teams but the working relationships and communication among team members are fragmented.

- The project engineer takes part in the leadership role, as emphasised by recent studies (Matzler, Bailom, Anschober, & Richardson, 2010; O'Connor, 2008; Tushman, Smith, Chapman, Westerman, & O'Reilly, 2010).

- The project teams need to better manage change and innovation. They are responsible for the completion of the tasks required. However, they have little authority to campaign for resources and priorities. Furthermore, they do not have a strong vision or build coalition across different functions.

- The managing director wants to be informed of all details and is reluctant to delegate any decision-making power. There are some communication problems in vertical and horizontal directions. As a result, this discourages interactions among various functional units and slows down the project execution.

- The pricing and market strategies are not aggressive.

- The managing director is receptive to new technology and is willing to try out new ideas. However, engineers may not have the skills and expertise to integrate them with existing systems. Therefore, reliability is a problem. The marketing manager is sometimes blamed for overselling the product as a result.

- The managing director has undertaken R&D in the past, but this has declined in recent years.

- The managing director has a vague concept of the organisation becoming an innovative company. However, there is no motivating mechanism to attract workers to embark on such an innovation journey.

- Training in creativity and problem identification/solving at organisational as well as individual levels is minimal.

- There is no process for creativity and ideas management.

These observations agree with the analysis as indicated in Table 10.4.

Case Study 3 — Non-innovative company

Table 10.6 shows the innovation profile of Case Study 3 Company, relative to that of the 'innovation-ready' group. The data-mining method identifies it as a relatively non-innovative company. The innovation readiness framework indicates that this non-innovative (Case Study 3) company does not score higher than the 'innovation-ready' group in any innovation dimensions. This explains why this non-innovative company has achieved a much lower innovation performance, as compared with the 'innovation-ready' group. As identified in the diagram, the weak areas that require improvement include vision, training for management/employee/organisation, championship, front-end management, product development, R&D, environmental scanning and market strategy. These are areas where this non-innovative company can further upgrade through the implementation of a tailored innovation program.

	Weaknesses[1]	Strengths[2]	Recommendation[3]
Vision	71%		Area for improvement
Management training	69%		Area for improvement
Organisation training	69%		Area for improvement
Employee training	65%		Area for improvement
Championship	63%		Area for improvement
Front-end management	61%		Area for improvement
Product development	57%		Area for improvement
R&D	54%		Area for improvement
Environmental scanning	51%		Area for improvement
Market strategy	49%		Area for improvement
Entrepreneurship	43%		Area for improvement
Customer focus	43%		Area for improvement
Project management	42%		Area for improvement
Process capability	39%		Area for improvement
Idea management	39%		Area for improvement
Teamwork	38%		Area for improvement
Exposure to environment	35%		Area for improvement
Incubation	30%		Area for improvement
External knowledge	27%		Area for improvement

[1] *(% weaker than the innovation-ready class)*
[2] *(% stronger than the innovation-ready class)*
[3] *for this case study (non-innovative) company*

Table 10.6: Non-innovative company versus 'innovation-ready' group (Class 1).
Source: Courtesy of the author.

The field interviews with all the senior managers of this non-innovative company also confirm these findings. The interviews indicate the following:

- This company is clearly lagging in many innovation capability factors.

- Employees are fully occupied with routine operational activities, with no spare time to test or try out new ideas.

- There is no effort to develop and introduce new products and there are no resources allocated for R&D activities.

- The low risk-taking attitude is clearly demonstrated by an inability to invest in physical and human capital, improvement initiatives, and training/development activities.

- Some managers can sense that there is a need for improvement in people and technology skills from their observation of what other competing companies are doing. However, they do not engage in systematic environmental scanning activities.

After the first survey questionnaire had been collected, a new managing director came on board. Since then, a number of positive changes that are consistent with the framework of this research study have been observed:

- The new managing director has a strong entrepreneurial and marketing orientation, and successfully added a new business that has proven to contribute to company survival and improved financial performance. In fact, these entrepreneurial and marketing-oriented attributes have been identified as areas for improvement in the diagnosis chart. The arrival of this new managing director resulted in turning around this company's performance.

- The new managing director places more emphasis on marketing and business development.

- He has the vision to transform this company into a more innovative company.

- However, his risk-averse attitude is still restraining him from trying out a new innovation program. He prefers to take on proven methods. This pulls back further development of the innovation capabilities and culture.

This research study has committed substantial effort and resources to provide a small-scale innovation training program to the management team of this non-innovative company. Training workshops included a discussion session of what innovation is and how to become an innovative company, strategy and tactics of innovation, creative problem solving, the seven quality tools (that is, cause and effect diagrams, check sheets, control charts, histograms, Pareto charts, scatter diagrams and stratification), fact-based decision-making and setting up an employee suggestions scheme. This innovation training program was supplemented by several 'low-hanging fruit' or 'quick result' projects to improve the factory plant layout and shop floor production schedule and control. The purpose is to create a routine of initiating change and improvement in traditional work culture to pave the way for implementation of radical innovative activities such as new product development. As a result, several innovation capability factors have improved and are reflected in higher innovation performance over the observed period of two years. As a result of collaboration with university research and licensing technology from inventors, the company has developed several new products. These new products have reached the market introduction stage.

Discussion of the barriers and problems

Though the impact of the innovation program has been positive in upgrading the innovation capability and performance, there are resistance and barriers to realising the full effect. Due to the unavailability of some senior managers for training, some managers did not adopt some innovation tools and techniques as part of their daily routine. Senior management found it difficult to understand the innovation process, let alone to commit sufficient resources and expand the training to other lower level employees to make the company-wide intervention a success. Furthermore, employees resisted the extra work required by the innovation program. These observations are consistent with other research findings that resource constraints, lack of competences and skills, lack of commitment to invest in training, competing priorities, and lack of measurement systems have usually caused such implementations to lapse or fail

(Findlay, McKinlay, Marks, & Thompson, 2000; Vossen, 1999). Many organisational analysts blame implementation failure, not innovation failure, as the main cause of not achieving the intended benefits of innovation adoption (Klein & Sorra, 1996).

The other prohibitive barrier is the extensive time-lag from the initiation of an intervention to its effect being noticed. The prime reason is that effective innovation must involve all employees, functions and company-wide activities and processes (Bessant & Francis, 1998; McAdam, 2000). Some research studies (Humphreys, McAdam, & Leckey, 2005) reported a time-lag of five to six years. Many companies could not progress beyond the initial stage of application.

Conclusion

This research uses survey data and the data-mining method to develop an empirically based diagnostic tool for assessing innovation readiness. As such, it has addressed the research problem: can the survey questionnaire serve as a diagnostic tool to validate the survey method and results of the first round of research data, communicate to practitioners their achieved level of innovation capabilities and performance, and provide decision support on improving them? The survey questionnaire is an important communication device for informing and interacting with practitioners about the achieved level of innovation capabilities and performance, and for providing decision support on improving them.

This systematically constructed innovation readiness framework offers more advantageous features than previous research studies. Firstly, the research classified the sample into two classes ('innovation-ready' versus 'non-innovation-ready' companies). Secondly, statistically significant innovation capability factors were selected to identify the areas for improvement which can be operationalised. Thirdly, resources can be allocated based on the identified performance gap in order to optimise return on investment. These features will help practitioners to make sense of the intervention required for enhancing innovation capabilities and environment. This is particularly true for small-to-medium sized enterprises that have inflexible resource constraints, as they will find this targeted approach a more economical way of focusing valuable resources in the identified areas for improvement. The research used case studies to validate the data accuracy and the targeted company representative for survey sampling to reflect the true view of a company. This comparative analysis also illustrates the usefulness of the innovation readiness framework. Using this diagnostic tool, consultants can communicate effectively to management regarding the current state of their company's innovation capability as well as areas for improvement. This helps to bring a company to the state of innovation readiness.

Future research recommendations

In order to increase generalisation of the results of this study to countries other than Australia, as well as to non-manufacturing industries, future research may advance knowledge to sample data from other countries and industries. More accurate and consistent results may be generated by applying an industry-specific framework characterised by cultural setting or orientation, depending on the country in which the framework is used.

In this study, some 'innovation-ready' companies were successfully developing and introducing new products. However, they shared their not-so-successful experience in changing existing business models, especially in relation to the alignment with product and process innovations. The business model literature does not rigorously differentiate between the business model and new product development (Chesbrough, 2010; Gambardella & McGahan, 2010; Sosna, Trevinyo-Rodríguez, & Velamuri, 2010; Teece, 2010; Zott, Amit, & Massa, 2011). It is more difficult and challenging to renew a business model than a product. Therefore, future research in applying the intellectual-capital-based innovation readiness framework of this study to business model innovation will not only advance academic knowledge in this field, but also add value to business model innovation by making it more accessible.

References

Adams, R, Bessant, J, & Phelps, R. (2006). Innovation management measurement: A review. *International Journal of Management Reviews, 8*(1), 21-47.

APQC. (2001). *New product development: Gaining and using market insight.* Houston: American Productivity and Quality Center.

Belliveau, P, Griffin, A, & Somermeyer, S. (Eds.) (2002). *The PDMA toolbox for new product development.* New York: John Wiley & Sons.

Bessant, J, & Francis, D. (1998). Implementing the new product development process. *Technovation, 17*(4), 187-97.

de Bono, E. (Ed.) (1985). *Opportunities: A handbook of business opportunity search.* Hong Kong: WED International.

Burgelman, R, Maidique, M, & Wheelwright, S. (2004). *Strategic management of technology and innovation.* New York: McGraw Hill.

Chesbrough, H. (2010). Business model innovation: Opportunities and barriers. *Long Range Planning, 43*, 354-63.

Chiesa, V, Coughlan, P, & Voss, CA. (1996). Development of a technical innovation audit. *Journal of Product Innovation, 13*(2), 105-36.

Christensen, C. (1997). *The innovator's dilemma: When new technologies cause great firms to fail.* Boston: Harvard Business School Press.

Conceicao, P, Hamill, D, & Pinheiro, P. (2002). Innovative science and technology commercialisation strategies at 3M: A case study. *Journal of Engineering and Technology Management, 19*(1), 25-38.

Cooper, R, Edgett, S, & Kleinschmidt, E. (2004). Benchmarking best NPD practices II. *Research-Technology Management, 47*(3), 50-9.

Cooper, R, & Kleinschmidt, E. (1991). The impact of product innovativeness on performance. *Journal of Product Innovation Management, 8*(4), 240-51.

Cooper, R, & Kleinschmidt, E. (1995). Benchmarking firms' new product performance and practices. *Engineering Management Review, 23*(3), 112-20.

Dence, R. (1995). Best practices benchmarking. In J Holloway, J Lewis, & G Mallory (Eds.), *Performance measurement and evaluation* (pp. 124-51). London: Sage Publications.

Edvinsson, L, & Malone, M. (1997). *Intellectual capital — Realizing your company's true value by finding its hidden roots.* New York: Harper Business.

Findlay, P, McKinlay, A, Marks, A, & Thompson, P. (2000). In search of perfect people: Teamwork and team players in the Scottish spirits industry. *Human Relations, 53*(11), 1549-77.

Gambardella, A, & McGahan, A. (2010). Business model innovation: General purpose technologies and their implications for industry structure. *Long Range Planning, 43*, 262-71.

Goffin, K, & Pfeiffer, R. (1999). *Innovation management in UK and German manufacturing companies*. London: Anglo-German Foundation for the Study of Industrial Society.

Griffin, A. (1997). PDMA research on new product development practices: Updating trends and benchmarking best practices. *The Journal of Product Innovation Management, 14*, 429-58.

Guan, JRY, Tang, E, & Lau, A. (2009). Innovation strategy and performance during economic transition: Evidences in Beijing, China. *Research Policy, 38*(5), 802-12.

Hair, J, Black, W, Babin, B, Anderson, R, & Tatham, R. (2007). *Multivariate data analysis* (6th ed.). New Jersey: Prentice Hall.

Huff, A. (1990). *Mapping strategic thought*. New York: John Wiley & Sons.

Humphreys, P, McAdam, R, & Leckey, J. (2005). Longitudinal evaluation of innovation implementation in SMEs. *European Journal of Innovation Management, 8*(3), 283-304.

Karlof, B. (1993). *Key business concepts*. London: Routledge.

Klein, K, & Sorra, J. (1996). The challenge of innovation implementation. *Academy of Management Review, 21*(4), 1055-80.

Kuczmarski, T. (1996). *Innovation: Leadership strategies for the competitive edge*. Lincolnwood, IL: NTC Business Books.

Leonard-Barton, D. (1992). Core capabilities and core rigidities: A paradox in managing new product development. *Strategic Management Journal, 13*(S1), 111-25.

McAdam, R. (2000). The implementation of reengineering in SMEs: A grounded study. *International Small Business Journal, 18*(72), 29-45.

Matzler, K, Bailom, F. Anschober, M, & Richardson, S. (2010). Sustaining corporate success: What drives the top performers? *Journal of Business Strategy, 31*(5), 4-13.

Morgan, M. (1995). How corporate culture drives strategy. In P Sadler (Ed.), *Strategic change: Building a high performance organization* (pp. 7-32). Oxford: Pergamon.

Morse, JM. (1998). What's wrong with random selection? *Qualitative Health Research, 8*(6), 733-5.

O'Connor, G. (2008). Major innovation as a dynamic capability: A systems approach. *Product Innovation Management, 25*, 313-30.

Porter, M. (1996, November-December). What is strategy? *Harvard Business Review*, 61-78.

Rimmer, M, MacNeil, J, Chenhall, R, Langfield-Smith, K, & Watts, L. (1996). *Reinventing competitiveness: Achieving best practice in Australia.* Melbourne: Pitman Publishing.

Roos, J, Roos, G, Dragonetti, N, & Edvinsson, L. (1997). *Intellectual capital: Navigating the new business landscape.* London: MacMillan Press.

Sheather, G. (1998). Re-engineering Australian manufacturing. In R Genoff & R Green (Eds.), *Manufacturing prosperity: Ideas for industry, technology and employment* (pp. 132-72). Sydney: The Federation Press.

Sosna, M, Trevinyo-Rodríguez, R, & Velamuri, S. (2010). Business models innovation through trial-and-error learning: The Naturhouse case. *Long Range Planning, 43*, 383-407.

Stevens, G, & Burley, J. (1997). 3,000 raw ideas = 1 commercial success! *Research Technology Management, 40*(3), 16-27.

Tang, HK. (1998). An integrative model of innovation in organizations. *Technovation 18*(5), 297-309.

Teece, D. (2010). Business models, business strategy and innovation. *Long Range Planning, 43*, 172-94.

Tushman, M, Smith, W, Chapman, R, Westerman, G, & O'Reilly, C. (2010). Organizational designs and innovation streams. *Industrial and Corporate Change, 19*(5), 1331-66.

Vossen, R. (1999). Relative strengths and weaknesses of small firms in innovation. *International Small Business Journal, 16*(3), 88-94.

Welbourn, M, Wardrop, M, & Bryant, K. (1994). *The pace of change: Technology uptake and enterprise improvement.* Canberra: Australian Government Publishing Service.

Wolfe, R. (1994). Organisational innovation: Review, critique and suggested research directions. *The Journal of Management Studies, 31*(3), 405-31.

Zairi, M. (Ed.) (1999). *Best practice process innovation management.* Oxford: Butterworth-Heinemann.

Zott, C, Amit, R, & Massa, L. (2011). The business model: Recent developments and future research. *Journal of Management, 37*(4), 1019-42.

Developing a framework for the management of Critical Success Factors in organisational innovation projects:

11

A case of Enterprise Resource Planning systems

Jiwat Ram, The University of Adelaide
David Corkindale, University of South Australia

Introduction

Small and Medium Enterprises/Businesses [SMEs/SMBs] constitute an estimated 95.9 per cent of the total businesses/enterprises operating in Australia, employing about 42 per cent (4.1 million) of the employed workforce and contributing about 46 per cent of the Gross Domestic Product in 2006 to the Australian economy (ABS, 2013; ABS, 2010). Apparently due to small organisational size, less business complexity and high flexibility of working with large organisations, SMEs have shown resilience despite the volatility of the global business environment (Gunasekaran, Rai, & Griffin, 2011).

SMEs, however, face a number of challenges to survive. These challenges include, but are not limited to, availability of financial and human capital; expertise and diversity of business management; technological infrastructure and competencies in maintaining and managing such infrastructure; capacity to embrace, integrate and capitalise on innovations; competitive threats from ever-increasing numbers of small businesses; dependence on large organisations; and the ability to attract and retain a skilled workforce (Malhotra & Temponi, 2010). SMEs adopt a variety of strategies to deal with these challenges. The commonly cited strategies include implementing the latest available technologies and systems; aligning to the needs of large organisations so as to be an effective partner/member of the value chain; improving the business processes; enhancing the staff skills; and being ready to adapt to the dynamics of market-based economies (Gunasekaran et al., 2011).

The high dependence of SMEs on larger enterprises for their business survival has led to SMEs adopting innovative technologies and systems which facilitate improved business and relationship management and better communication with their supply chain partners (Gunasekaran et al., 2011; Malhotra & Temponi, 2010). Enterprise Resource Planning [ERP] is one such system that has attracted significant acceptance by SMEs since 2000 (Huin, 2004). ERP is used as a means of automating and standardising business operations, improving information visibility and facilitating supply chain integration. The structural changes brought about by the introduction of ERP lead to innovative practices and ways of operating in today's dynamic business environment. However, the organisational innovation process of ERP is considered a complex endeavour and poses significant challenges to organisations of all sizes, particularly to SMEs (Morabito, Pace, & Previtali, 2005).

Innovation theorists have conceptualised the organisational innovation process as involving multi-stage events that start with the generation of an innovation and then pass through further stages of diffusion, adoption, implementation, use, benefits/impacts and retirement. In addition, scholars have identified factors that could influence, both positively and negatively, the outcome of these stages of the overall innovation process.

Rogers (2003) presented one of the pioneering theories on innovation process, the Diffusion of Innovations [DOI], and described the process from both individual and organisational perspectives, identifying several key attributes that influence the process. From an organisational context, DOI theory describes a five-stage innovation process: agenda-setting, matching (two stages under the 'initiation' sub-process), redefining/restructuring, clarifying and routinising (three stages under the 'implementation' sub-process). The theory also indicates some structural and individual factors which influence the innovation process. DOI theory therefore is a useful lens in this study to identify factors that should be managed carefully along the key stages of the adoption and implementation of the innovation process of applying ERP in SMEs.

Extending Rogers's (2003, p. 392) organisational innovation model, Kwon and Zmud (1987, p. 233) presented a more specific-purpose, multi-stage model in the Information Systems [IS] context called the IS Implementation Model. The model posits that the organisational innovation process is a six-stage process, namely: initiation, adoption, adaptation (development/installation), acceptance, use and incorporation. Kwon and Zmud (1987) also identified a number of categories of factors that could influence these stages: individual, structural, technological, task-related and environmental factors. Analysing the management of Critical Success Factors [CSFs] based on the key stages and factors relevant to stages as posited by this model can help in better management of ERP projects.

The fundamental purpose of innovation, however, has been to achieve performance improvements, and an innovation process is incomplete if it does not contribute to organisational improvements. Delone and McLean (1992), in their well-known IS Success Model, proposed six dimensions of IS success, theorising that the first two dimensions — system quality and information quality — jointly and severally affect the third and fourth dimensions — use and user satisfaction — which, in turn, result in the fifth and sixth dimensions — individual impact and subsequent organisational impact. Further research into the use of this model, however, has led to the addition of two more dimensions: service quality and intention-to-use. Delone and McLean (2004) later combined the individual impact and organisational impact dimensions, replacing it with the net benefits dimension.

The innovation process models seem to embody a common approach consisting of factors related to stages for the management of the innovation process in organisations. The factors described in the innovation process models have been classified under multiple dimensions such as structural/organisational, technological/innovation-related, project-related, environmental and individual (Delone & McLean, 1992; Kwon & Zmud, 1987; Rogers, 2003).

The process and factors approach described above has resulted in the emergence of a large body of research on various stages of the innovation process such as adoption, implementation and use of the innovation process and the factors or antecedents (commonly termed as CSFs) critically relevant to these stages. In particular, due to the complexity of ERP projects, researchers have identified a large number of CSFs in various stages of the ERP innovation process. Conceptually, CSFs are 'for any business, the limited number of areas in which results, if they are satisfactory, will ensure successful competitive performance for the organisation' (Rockart, 1979, p. 85). Knowing or identifying CSFs and understanding synergies among them is assumed to provide a positive, beneficial effect on the outcome of projects and performance of the firms (Karimi, Somers, & Bhattacherjee, 2007).

Despite abundant research on the identification of CSFs, our understanding of how to manage the identified CSFs, or what actions to take in the identified key areas, remains limited (Esteves & Pastor, 2001). The investigation of the management of CSFs is fundamentally important not only to enhance our understanding of why it is necessary to identify CSFs, but also to make use of a large number of identified CSFs to improve the chances of success of the organisational innovation process of ERP (Esteves & Bohorquez, 2007). A number of questions merit further investigations. For instance:

- How do organisations manage the identified CSFs?
- Has identification of CSFs helped in achieving the desired impact on project outcome and post-implementation performance of the firms?
- What processes do the organisations put in place to manage the areas identified as CSFs?
- How do organisations define the actions, and the ownership of the actions, which need to be taken to manage CSFs?
- How do organisations manage and measure the processes in relation to identified CSFs?

Françoise, Bourgault, and Pellerin (2009) have termed the gap between knowledge-ability and operational-ability of CSFs as a missing connection and suggest that the situation accounts for the mediocre results of ERP projects. The key is to manage the underpinning processes and take necessary actions, as 'CSFs are not, in themselves, directly manageable' (Esteves & Pastor, 2001, p. 109).

The above discussion raises the question as to whether identification of CSFs alone can be useful unless it is combined with understanding how the identified CSFs are managed, both by those who thrived on their success and those who failed to achieve it. We argue that the identification of CSFs is not enough: it is essential that understanding the entire process of identification, management and measuring the impacts of CSFs on project success/performance should be undertaken to establish the benefits and purpose of identifying CSFs in the first place. Françoise, Bourgault, and Pellerin (2009) have termed establishing the usefulness of CSFs 'incomplete' without also prescribing the management process of CSFs. The advancement of knowledge on the management of CSFs is important, as it would firstly provide a direction for creating relevant and adequate action plans suitable to the needs of organisations — in particular, SMEs, as they have limited resources and expertise at their disposal. It would secondly improve the chances of successful ERP innovation process. Further, understanding the management process for CSFs would consolidate the research base on CSFs for ERP and provide practical solutions and resultant knowledge transfer from academia to industry. It would also provide new avenues of research in the fuller CSFs context rather than just focusing on the identification of such factors.

Given the above argument, and seeking to fill the gap in our knowledge, this study aims to develop and propose a framework for the management of some CSFs that are important for the adoption and implementation stages of the organisational innovation process of ERP, and to discuss the actions that need to be taken to manage the CSFs. The study seeks to contribute to theory by increasing the body of knowledge on the conceptualisation of CSFs, and to contribute to practice by providing an understanding of what organisations should do to manage the identified CSFs so as to potentially benefit from CSFs.

In this chapter, we first present a review of the literature pertaining to the management of CSFs. We follow with a discussion of the proposed framework for the management of CSFs. Then we present an analysis of the study's findings, followed by the conclusion, implications and limitations of the research. Finally, we discuss the opportunities for further research.

Literature review

Innovation in the Information Systems [IS] literature is regarded as the enabler and vehicle for the introduction of change within an organisation's systems. IS innovations, such as ERP systems, are often expected to spur growth and innovative activities around the system, leading to beneficial economic returns. However, the introduction of these systems carries a certain degree of risk, mainly due to the complexities of adoption, implementation, use and maintenance of them.

Given the high failure rate of ERP projects (for some examples, see Kanaracus, 2011), considerable research has been undertaken to devise solutions to achieve successful outcomes for the ERP innovation process. One such activity is the identification of CSFs as tools for helping to manage ERP projects.

The concept of CSFs has been and is being extensively used in ERP implementation studies to identify the factors considered vital to achieve success in ERP projects. Due to costly failures and to implementation difficulties, many researchers believe that identifying and managing CSFs could reduce or eliminate the problems and assist organisations to adopt and implement ERP systems successfully (Ang, Sum, & Yeo, 2002; Wang, Shih, Jiang, & Klein, 2008). CSFs can be identified in several ways, such as through the analysis of competitor best practices; scanning of the business environment; analysis of industrial structure; analysis of the internal business environment; and analysis of the project post-completion environment to determine what helped or hindered the success of the projects (Leidecker & Bruno, 1984). However, without knowing how to manage the identified CSFs, the usefulness of identifying CSFs remains a matter of debate (Ang et al., 2002).

We define management of CSFs in this chapter as *the planning, organisation and co-ordination of activities in the identified critical areas to achieve project success and performance improvements*. Specifically, management of CSFs involves creating an actionable list of activities structured in a logical flow (Françoise, Bourgault, & Pellerin, 2009). The list of actionable activities should be flexible in character in order to easily adjust it to the particular circumstances of the business or industry. The activities identified to manage CSFs should be clear and explicit in order to establish their effectiveness and to complete them during the management process. The accomplishment of these activities is expected to result in a positive outcome in the areas relevant to CSFs (for example, project management and system integration) and to have a subsequent impact on performance improvement and/or project success.

A review of literature on CSFs for ERP points to a lack of publications investigating the management of CSFs. Highlighting the practical significance of the subject, Françoise, Bourgault, and Pellerin(2009) combined their literature review and results of a Delphi study to propose a set of 151 indispensable actions to manage 13 Critical Success Factors, particularly in the structural, project-related and organisational culture context. They also identified implementation difficulties relevant to each CSF under study. Other researchers (Hawari & Heeks, 2010; Bose, Pal, & Ye, 2008; Koh, Gunasekaran, & Cooper, 2009) have discussed the tasks performed by organisations while managing various elements of an ERP implementation project. For instance, to manage a Project Management CSF, the tasks included the analysis of initial requirements; budgeting, schedule and HR requirements analysis; transition and maintenance planning; business process evaluation; system and software analysis; hardware and software purchasing, installation and testing; and training and transition (Bose, Pal, & Ye, 2008). In addition, a number of studies have offered insights derived from the implementation experience of organisations and have, to some extent, broadly discussed these in relation to key issues in organisations across various CSFs such as top management support, training and education, and project management (Dong, 2008; Muscatello, Small, & Chen, 2003; Subramoniam, Tounsi, & Krishnankutty, 2009).

It is important to note that CSFs are not isolated entities. They interact with other CSFs to influence the outcome (Ang et al., 2002; Grabski & Leech, 2007). Understanding the interactions among CSFs is one of the key requirements for better management of CSFs (Karimi et al., 2007). For instance, the formation of an effective project team is a key element of a Project Management CSF. However, formation of a good project team is affected by another CSF, Top Management Support (Ang et al., 2002). By understanding the linkages among CSFs and activities specific to CSFs, a network of relationships is formed which could then clarify the level of complexities of CSF management, and make it easier to develop adequate plans of actions. Inadequate management of any of the factors in the network, or the absence of a factor from the network altogether, could jeopardise the success of the ERP project (Ang et al., 2002).

CSF management can also be done by linking CSFs to stages of the innovation process or stages of the project life cycle. Ho and Lin (2004) produced an Integrated-Enterprise System Implementation [ISI] framework that classifies CSFs into infrastructure, system design, implementation and organisation types. The framework then provides a description of activities that need to be carried out for each CSF. The individual activities are then mapped into the project life cycle phases. The concept seems to be very useful, interesting and systematic; it could be refined and help to develop a more complete management framework for CSFs to develop ERP projects.

The literature review presented above points to a lack of empirical and theory-driven studies on the management of CSFs. Given the large number of CSFs that have been identified, it is crucial to investigate and propose what managers should do in order for the identified CSFs to achieve the ERP project objectives and targeted performance improvements. The aim should be to make use of CSFs and enhance understanding in a process that goes beyond just identifying them and leads to discussing actual action plans for managerial interventions. This study, therefore, aims to fill this gap in knowledge by proposing a theory-based framework for CSFs management.

A framework for management of CSFs

As discussed in the introduction to this chapter, the three innovation models discussed above allow identification of a number of factors, some of which have been selected for this study to propose a framework for the management of these factors, as shown in Figure 11.1. The factors are organisational readiness; perceived strategic value (structural); environmental assessment (environmental); system quality; information quality (technical); project management; business process re-engineering; system integration; and training and education (project-related). As the unit of analysis of this study is at the organisational level, we have not selected any factor that is related to an individual dimension.

Organisational readiness [OGRD]

Organisational readiness is defined as 'the ability of a firm to successfully adopt, use, and benefit from information technologies' (Fathian, Akhavan, & Hoorali, 2008). Organisational readiness is a multi-context factor and thus has been assessed using a variety of measures including awareness of benefits and risks of innovation; availability of human resources skills and capabilities; availability of technological, business and financial resources; commitment and support by top management; fit between innovation and organisational structure; and goals and values of organisation (Fathian et al., 2008; Molla & Licker, 2005).

To put in place a framework to manage the organisational readiness CSF, we argue that managers need to work on a number of aspects (Fathian, Akhavan, & Hoorali, 2008; Molla & Licker, 2005; Tan, Tyler, & Manica, 2007). We propose a classification of these activities along four major dimensions: strategy and structure,

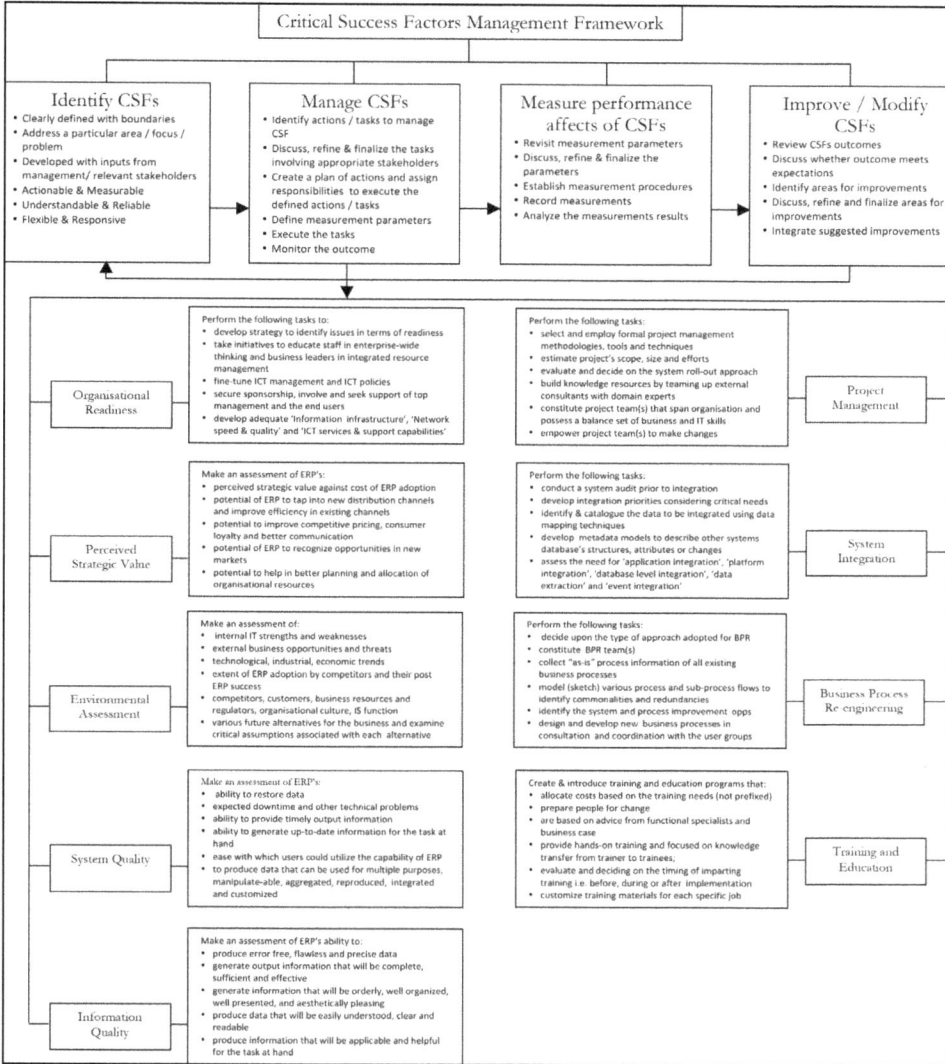

Figure 11.1: Critical Success Factors Management Framework.
Source: Courtesy of the authors.

people, technology and processes. We describe the activities that managers should work on, related to each of the four dimensions, below.

1. **Strategy and structure**: develop and put in place a strategy to assess and identify issues for ERP adoption; form an evaluation committee

to assess organisational readiness; develop an action plan to address the opportunities and constraints in relation to adopting ERP; secure the sponsorship, involvement and support of the top management and end users; assess fit between ERP and organisation; assess general readiness by acquiring knowledge of other organisations' ERP adoption patterns; assess other organisations' ERP characteristics.

2. **People**: take initiatives to educate staff in enterprise-wide thinking; take initiatives to educate business leaders in integrated resource management; assess perception of the benefits and ability of IT/IS staff to support ERP; assess degree of satisfaction of IT/IS staff with organisational systems before adoption of ERP; assess degree of desired and perceived involvement of IT/IS staff in the ERP innovation process; and assess level of commitment of the IT/IS staff to the organisation.

3. **Technology**: fine-tune the ICT management and policies to support ERP adoption; assess 'Information infrastructure', 'Network speed and quality' and 'ICT services and support' capabilities; assess the way ERP would connect the users to an information source relevant to their needs; assess the degree of fit or compatibility between existing data architecture and ERP; and identify potential integration issues associated with the feasibility, cost, deployment and obsolescence of ERP systems.

4. **Processes**: develop and implement procedures that ensure standardisation of information in all business operations; decision-making processes and technology innovation experience; and ERP acquisition and installation processes, particularly in terms of team function, contracts, licensing and vendor reliability assessment.

While several issues need to be tackled, as a minimum we posit here that SME managers should

a. form evaluation committee(s) to assess organisational readiness

b. develop strategy to identify issues in terms of readiness

c. put in place an action plan to address the opportunities and constraints in the adoption of ERP

d. take initiatives to educate staff in enterprise-wide thinking and business leaders in integrated resource management

e.   fine-tune ICT management and ICT policies

f.   secure sponsorship, and involve and seek support of top management and the end users

g.   develop and implement procedures to ensure standardisation of information in all business operations

h.   assess fit between the ERP system to be adopted and the organisation culture

i.   develop adequate 'Information infrastructure', 'Network speed and quality' and 'ICT services and support' capabilities.

Perceived Strategic Value [PSV]

ERP is considered a strategic information system; thus its adoption is usually preceded by a business case and strategic value assessment (Subramanian & Nosek, 1993). Three factors generally measure the PSV construct: operational support, managerial productivity and strategic decision aid.

It is important that organisations understand the cost versus the benefits of adopting ERP. The installation of an ERP system involves monetary, people and organisational commitments. Organisations adopting ERP face short-term as well as long-term affects. Therefore, a number of activities need to be carried out to understand the Perceived Strategic Value of ERP in improving the technological future and technological outlook of the organisation, opening up new business prospects, improving co-ordination and partner relationships, bettering customer relationship management, and improving resource planning and management.

The literature suggests that for a better understanding of strategic value, organisations should assess ERP's possible impacts on productivity; create opportunities to tap into new distribution channels and improve efficiency in existing distribution channels; improve co-ordination and relationships with business partners; improve competitive pricing; improve consumer loyalty; support better communication; support business due to reliance on knowledge workers; help recognise new market potential; generate and evaluate business alternatives; and plan and allocate organisational resources better (Grandon & Pearson, 2004; Saffu, Walker, & Hinson, 2007; Subramanian & Nosek, 1993). Also, organisations need to compare the benefits of ERP against existing technologies within their organisation.

Given the number of recommended actions, we posit that SME managers should at least

a.   weigh the Perceived Strategic Value of ERP against the cost of ERP adoption

b.   assess the potential of ERP to tap into new distribution channels and improve efficiency in existing distribution channels

c.   gather knowledge on ERP's potential to improve competitive pricing, consumer loyalty and better communication

d.   assess the potential of ERP to recognise opportunities in new markets

e.   assess ERP to aid in generation and evaluation of business alternatives

f.   assess the potential of ERP to help in better planning and allocation of organisational resources.

Environmental Assessment [EVA]

'An environmental assessment evaluates external information and identifies business needs, objectives, external opportunities, and threats' (Chi, Jones, Lederer, Li, Newkirk, & Sethi, 2005). Environmental Assessment has been measured using a variety of indicators. The three main indicators are

a.   **hostility**: degree of unpredictability of competitors' market activities; price/product quality competition; labour scarcity (Löfsten & Lindelöf, 2005; Newkirk & Lederer, 2006)

b.   **dynamics**: growth opportunities, change in production/service technologies, rate of innovation, product/technology changes, and so on (Newkirk & Lederer, 2006; Zhu, Dong, Xu, & Kraemer, 2006)

c.   **heterogeneity**: diversity in production and marketing methods; in customer buying behaviours; in the nature of competition; and in product line (Newkirk & Lederer, 2006).

Literature reviews (Newkirk & Lederer, 2006; Löfsten & Lindelöf, 2005; Zhu et al., 2006) suggest that management of the Environmental Assessment CSF can be done through a number of activities, and we have classified those activities into five areas as follows:

1. **Assessment of strengths and weaknesses**: this includes assessment of internal IT strengths and weaknesses; assessment of external business opportunities and threats; examining the technological, environmental, industrial and economic trends; study of external business and IT environment to understand the impact of change and to plan better; and evaluation of possible policy changes.

2. **Assessment of needs**: in-depth evaluation of the needs of all of the functional areas.

3. **Assessment of competitors**: assessment of perceived success of competitors who have adopted ERP; assessment of the extent of adoption by competitors; review of competitors' information technology; and obtaining of appropriate knowledge about competitors, resources, customers and regulators through a careful organisation of teams to obtain and understand that knowledge.

4. **Regulatory assessment**: regulation and government incentives.

5. **Internal assessment**: knowledge of the institutional norms and understanding of enterprise-wide business processes; identification of a number of future alternatives rather than a particular single one; identification of critical assumptions associated with each future alternative; careful study of business, organisation and IS to produce better knowledge about the organisation's requirements; identification and evaluation of opportunities to provide realistic alternatives; identification of IT objectives so as to allow the organisation to align future IT and business objectives; better prioritisation of projects to improve the chances of meeting objectives; change management and a better action plan; better follow-up and control to improve chances of the plan being implemented; better delivery of planning objectives; IS participation in business planning.

Based on the above framework, we propose that SME managers undertake the following activities to assess the environment and identify the opportunities and threats of adopting ERP systems. The organisation should

a. assess internal IT strengths and weaknesses

b. assess external business opportunities and threats

c.   assess technological, environmental, industrial and economic trends

d.   assess possible government policy changes

e.   assess the extent of ERP adoption by competitors and their post-ERP success

f.   obtain appropriate knowledge about competitors, customers, business resources and regulators

g.   assess the company's business, organisation functioning, culture and IS to produce better knowledge about the organisation's requirements

h.   identify various future alternatives for the business and examine critical assumptions associated with each alternative

i.   assess other organisations' ERP characteristics, acquisition and installation processes in terms of team function, contracts, licensing and vendor reliability.

Project Management [PM]

Project Management has been one of the widely cited CSFs for ERP implementation (Ehie & Madsen, 2005; Ngai, Law, & Wat, 2008). An ERP project involves handling IT infrastructure, processes and people issues. The sheer complexity of ERP implementation and enterprise-wide scope necessitates careful planning, co-ordination, budgeting, scheduling and monitoring of the project. As such the use of project management tools and techniques becomes almost indispensible (Ngai, Law, & Wat, 2008). The PM construct has been measured using indicators such as having a formal PM plan and PM team, setting realistic deadlines, defining project scope, and monitoring costs and schedule.

A review of the literature (Al-Mashari, Al-Mudimigh, & Zairi 2003; Ehie & Madsen, 2005; Somers & Nelson, 2004; Ngai, Law, & Wat, 2008) suggests that three issues pertaining to the planning, execution and controlling stages of ERP projects require a systematic and methodological approach. These include:

1.   **Planning issues:** having a formal project management methodology; taking a risk-planning and mitigation approach; adequately scoping the project and the effort required; clearly defining project objectives in terms of business process efficiency, effectiveness and flexibility; evaluating the system roll-out approach for the project; selecting a multi-

skilled and capable project team; achieving a balance of IT and business skills on the project team; empowering the project team to make and execute the changes required; senior management supporting the ERP project *internally* through incentives and bonuses and *externally* through maintaining open and effective communication channels.

2. **Execution issues**: employing experienced consultants and teaming them up with domain experts to facilitate knowledge transfer; removing project constraints (which include financial, legal, ethical, environmental and logic constraints); nurturing and maintaining an environment aimed at enhancing employee motivation and morale.

3. **Control issues**: assessing the earned value management of the project; periodically holding project status meetings and tracking the project's progress; monitoring the cost, time and schedule baseline; establishing proper change management procedures; defining accountabilities clearly.

This study recommends that SME managers undertake the following activities when using project management CSFs:

a. select and employ formal project management methodologies, tools and techniques

b. evaluate, classify and prioritise the implementation risks

c. estimate the project's scope, size and efforts

d. define the project objectives in terms of business process efficiency, effectiveness and flexibility

e. evaluate and decide on the system roll-out approach (gradual versus 'big bang')

f. build knowledge resources by teaming up external consultants with domain experts from within the firm, so as to open up a two-way channel of communication

g. select highly capable and experienced project manager(s) to oversee the project

h. build project team(s) that span the organisation and possess a balanced set of business and IT skills, and empower project team(s) to make and execute the changes required

i. determine the measures for ERP project success

j. nurture and maintain a high level of employee morale and motivation

k. organise periodic project status meetings and track the project's progress.

Business Process Re-engineering [BPR]

BPR involves redesigning or improving the business processes in order to bring them in to alignment with the generic processes defined in an ERP software structure. It is generally argued that BPR should precede implementation of an ERP system. Business Process Re-engineering includes several activities, such as modelling various process and sub-process flows, designing and developing new processes, and process mapping.

To manage the BPR factor, organisations need to pay attention to a number of issues (Bradford & Florin, 2003; Ehie & Madsen, 2005). Deciding on the approach for undertaking the BPR exercise is vital in order to provide direction to people working on the change management. Forming teams that document the existing processes and identify areas for improvements is key to designing new and better processes. Close working of functional and user groups and change management teams should help in the smooth completion of the BPR exercise. It could also feed back into an understanding of the need for training programs for newly installed processes.

We argue that SME managers should undertake the following activities in order to appropriately manage issues for Business Process Re-engineering CSFs:

a. decide upon the type of approach adopted for BPR

b. form BPR team(s)

c. collect 'as-is' process information of all existing business processes

d. model (or sketch) various process and sub-process flows to identify commonalities and redundancies among the processes

e. identify the system, and process improvement opportunities

f. design and develop new business processes in consultation and co-ordination with the user groups

g. provide an understanding to employees on how their actions impact the operations of other functional areas

h. acquire the agreement of representatives of user groups for the revised processes

i. encourage close working of BPR team(s) and 'Change management team(s)'.

System Integration [SI]

Lee, Siau, and Hong (2003) define System Integration as the 'capability to integrate a variety of different system functionalities'. ERP is usually implemented to replace the legacy systems; however, due to regulatory or business requirements, organisations retain some of the existing systems, thus needing them to be integrated with the ERP system.

Given the technical nature of the tasks involved in System Integration, the literature identifies a number of areas that need managerial attention (Ehie & Madsen, 2005; Zhu et al., 2006). These include integration planning activities; developing integration strategies and priorities by considering an Information Systems strategic plan and political consideration; mapping 'as-is' processes; and identifying a need for different types of integration. System Integration can be achieved using a variety of techniques and at different levels. Use of middleware known as Application Programming Interfaces [APIs], data extraction, database-level integration and real-time integration are some of the ways System Integration is done.

We propose that SME managers should undertake the following activities to manage system integration CSFs:

a. conduct a system audit prior to integration

b. develop integration priorities by considering criteria such as critical business needs, cost/resource, system size/complexity, IS Strategic plan

c. identify and catalogue the data to be integrated using data mapping techniques

d. develop metadata models to describe other system database structures, attributes or changes

e. assess the need for 'application integration' by using API for ERP integration

f. assess the need for 'platform integration' (architecture, hardware and software)

g.   assess the need for 'database-level' integration to achieve data management efficiencies

h.   assess the need for 'data extraction' for integration (that is, extract data from one application, and then place the data in a file to translate the data into a format that the other application can understand)

i.   assess the need for 'event integration' as a means of real-time integration.

Training and Education [TED]

User training and education is an important CSF for ERP implementation. It has been found to be responsible for a number of ERP implementation problems and system failures (Somers & Nelson, 2004). Training and education is a continuous process of transfer of both tacit and explicit knowledge of the overall logic, concept and working of the system. A good training program equips users with the understanding of business processes embedded in ERP application. A number of measures have been used to capture the training and education construct, some of which include the length and details of training, the knowledge of trainers, and the transfer of knowledge from trainer to trainee.

Literature has identified and discussed a number of activities for the management of the Training and Education CSF (Al-Mashari, Al-Mudimigh, & Zairi, 2003; Kumar, Maheshwari, & Kumar, 2003). These activities include strategies for allocating training costs; training that is focused on knowledge transfer and on providing an understanding of the implications of System Implementation; preparing people for change; developing need- and consultation-based training policies; ensuring continuous and appropriate training assessments; training project management team(s); developing programs aimed at providing awareness, knowledge and skill in IT, ERP, communication and new working methods; timing training programs appropriately (before, during or after implementation); and taking into account the difference in perception about the adequacy of training programs between user groups and managers.

SME managers could benefit from the appropriate management of the Training and Education CSF. We propose that the SME manager should at least

a.   allocate costs based on the (not predetermined) needs for training and education

b. devise and introduce programs that prepare people for change

c. devise programs which provide managers with knowledge about the implications of the new system

d. put in place a TED policy that is based on advice from functional specialists and the business case documentation

e. introduce training programs that provide hands-on training and focus on knowledge transfer from trainer to trainees

f. devise training programs that take into account the difference in perception (of the adequacy of programs) between user groups and the managers

g. evaluate and decide on the timing of imparting training programs (before, during or after implementation)

h. install training programs with an inbuilt mechanism for continuous and appropriate assessment

i. customise training materials for each specific job, ensuring that the training materials cover the entire business task, not just the ERP screens and reports.

Discussion

The investigation of CSFs is a research issue of ongoing interest, particularly due to its potential practical utility. However, over the years it has been observed that research on CSFs has largely remained uni-dimensional, in that it has focused on just the identification of CSFs. This situation has resulted in a limited understanding of the actual utility of identified CSFs. Going beyond the traditional approach of just identifying CSFs, we have contributed to the body of knowledge on CSFs by proposing in this chapter a Framework for Management that encapsulates the management of CSFs as part of a four-step process to enable the implementation of ERP. In doing so, we propose here a set of actions for each step in the process.

1. **Identify CSFs:** The first step in the use of the CSFs concept is the identification of CSFs. CSFs can be identified in a number of ways, some of which we described above. We posit here that the key characteristics to improve the management and usefulness of CSFs is that each identified CSF should have clear boundaries and a specific underpinning focus

or a problem to solve, should allow strategies and action plans that address the underpinning problem/focus, and should have a process outcome that is measurable as per agreed benchmarks or performance criteria. For instance, identifying 'Top Management Support' [TMS] as a CSF should involve including a definition, having a clear focus for managerial attention, putting up an action plan of how to seek and retain management support, and assessing whether paying attention to the TMS factor has achieved the goals.

2. **Manage CSFs**: The second step in the framework is the actual implementation of actions necessary to achieve the performance goals as set out in the identification process. We posit that some of the key issues that need attention at this step are identifying actions or tasks; discussing, refining and finalising the list of actions/tasks; creating a plan of action with a possible timeline and cost estimates; assigning responsibilities and ownership for accomplishing the tasks; executing the tasks; and monitoring the execution process. Taking a careful and thorough approach at this step is vital to achieving the objectives of identifying CSFs.

3. **Measure performance effects of CSFs**: The first steps, above, set the direction and parameters for measurement of the effects of attending to CSFs. We posit that at this step, it is necessary to revisit and refine the measurement criteria and performance goals; establish appropriate measurement procedures; record measurements against the set parameters; and analyse the results obtained through collected data. The results then feed into an analysis exploring whether the identified CSF is actually a CSF.

4. **Improve/modify CSFs**: The last step in the process is the evaluation of the CSF concept. We posit that not only do CSFs need to be identified, they should also be reviewed, revised, improved and, if necessary, discarded based on their performance against the set goals and parameters. We understand that the identified areas of improvements should feed back into the identification process of CSFs. The continuous cycle of identification, management, performance measurement and improvement of CSFs will result in achieving a set of CSFs that can be utilised for the successful management of projects.

In addition to the basic framework as discussed above, we have described a set of managerial actions for nine CSFs for ERP and we elaborate this in Figure 11.1. We have argued that an advancement of knowledge on the whole process of identification, management and performance assessment of CSFs is essential for providing actionable solutions for industry. This line of thinking is consistent with recent research presented at IS conferences and published in journals, which emphasises the importance of research with the potential for knowledge transfer from academia to practice.

Conclusion and research implications

We have shown that SMEs can potentially benefit greatly from installing appropriate ERP systems, but that the implementation of these is difficult. One proposed aid to achieving this is said to be the identification of Critical Success Factors. We argue that although much research has focused upon this, the mere identification of these is insufficient for the practical implementation of systems like ERP. We make the point again that the key is to manage the underpinning processes and take necessary actions, as 'CSFs are not, in themselves, directly manageable' (Esteves & Pastor, 2001, p. 109). With this purpose in mind we have reviewed the literature on CSFs and combined this with a synthesis of three well-established theories of innovation adoption. From this we have devised a comprehensive framework for managing the many interrelated activities which, if systematically undertaken, can lead to the achievement of identified, relevant CSFs and the operational implementation of a system such as ERP.

The framework proposed in this study systematically sets out the sequence of issues and decisions which the management of SMEs needs to address in order to ensure that an ERP system can be selected and implemented via the appropriate deployment of CSFs. The framework shows how the various key requirements described in the main body of this chapter relate to each other and it also shows the overall requirements for comprehensively managing the implementation of an ERP system. It presents a list of activities and action items that need to be undertaken in relation to each of the nine key factors that will influence the success of the ERP system.

The results of this study can have significant academic implications. Firstly, we have introduced a Framework for Management of CSFs with sets of actionable items at each step in the framework. This is a key contribution to theory building in the concept of CSFs. Secondly, we have proposed a framework for the management of nine CSFs, which provides an understanding of how the identified CSFs can be managed. Thirdly, the study proposes a systematic direction to research on CSFs that may not only help in consolidating the research base on CSFs but may also lead to new avenues of research. Finally, by adopting a structured and integrated approach we show how to overcome the shortcomings of traditional CSF-oriented studies. For instance, the question of how critical the CSFs actually are requires an in-depth examination of the interactive effect of CSFs beyond the particular innovation process.

The framework introduced in this study has significant implications for practice as well. It improves understanding of the management of CSFs related to various stages of the ERP innovation process. This can help SMEs to study their conditions against a set of identified CSFs and devise relevant action plans, which may be expected to improve their chances of eliminating or reducing the risk of failure or improving the chances of success of their ERP projects (Ngai, Law, & Wat, 2008). It is also expected to help ERP vendors understand the needs of potential SME ERP-adopters, and thus formulate their marketing and product development activities more effectively.

Future research recommendations

The next step in this research direction will be the empirical testing and validation of the framework we have proposed in this chapter. It would be helpful for this future research to employ a mixed-method approach to collect the data through a survey and semi-structured interviews. Richness of information obtained through face-to-face interviews and open-ended questions could help in seeking a deeper understanding of the complexities of the processes required for managing CSFs.

The research could be extended further by examining the management of those CSFs that have not been covered by this study. Identifying the possible synergies and interactions between CSFs could help in managing CSFs to gain greater benefits from them, and exploring this presents opportunities for future research work. The empirical validation of the theorised steps in the management framework presented in this chapter will also be another important avenue for further research into CSFs so as to add to the body of knowledge on them.

References

ABS. (2010). Characteristics and performance of small and medium-sized businesses in Australia. *1350.0 — Australian Economic Indicators, Jan 2010*. Retrieved from http://www.abs.gov.au/AUSSTATS/abs@.nsf/ DetailsPage/1350.0Jan%202010?OpenDocument.

ABS. (2013). 8165.0 — Counts of Australian businesses, including entries and exits, Jun 2009 to Jun 2013. Retrieved from http://www.abs.gov.au/ausstats/ abs@.nsf/mf/8165.0.

Al-Mashari, M, Al-Mudimigh, A, & Zairi, M. (2003). Enterprise Resource Planning: A taxonomy of critical factors. *European Journal of Operational Research, 146*(2), 352-64.

Ang, JSK, Sum, CC, & Yeo, LN. (2002). A multiple-case design methodology for studying MRP success and CSFs. *Information & Management, 39*(4), 271-81.

Bose, I, Pal, R, & Ye, A. (2008). ERP and SCM systems integration: The case of a valve manufacturer in China. *Information & Management, 45*(4), 233-41.

Bradford, M, & Florin, J. (2003). Examining the role of innovation diffusion factors on the implementation success of Enterprise Resource Planning systems. *International Journal of Accounting Information Systems, 4*(3), 205-25.

Chi, L, Jones, KG, Lederer, AL, Li, P, Newkirk, HE, & Sethi, V. (2005). Environmental Assessment in strategic information systems planning. *International Journal of Information Management, 25*(3), 253-69.

DeLone, WH, & McLean, ER. (1992). Information systems success: The quest for the dependent variable. *Information Systems Research, 3*(1), 60-95.

DeLone, WH, & McLean, ER. (2004). Measuring e-commerce success: Applying the Delone & Mclean Information Systems success model. *International Journal of Electronic Commerce, 9*(1), 31-47.

Dong, L. (2008). Exploring the impact of top management support of enterprise systems implementations outcomes. *Business Process Management Journal, 14*(2), 204-18.

Ehie, IC, & Madsen, M. (2005). Identifying critical issues in Enterprise Resource Planning (ERP) implementation. *Computers in Industry, 56*(6), 545-57.

Esteves, J, & Bohorquez, VW. (2007). *An updated ERP systems annotated bibliography: 2001-2005.* (IE Working Paper, WP07-04, 1-64).

Esteves, J, & Pastor, J. (2001). Analysis of critical success factors relevance along SAP implementation phases. *Seventh Americas Conference on Information Systems* (pp. 1019-25). Boston: Association for Information Systems.

Fathian, M, Akhavan, P, & Hoorali, M. (2008). E-readiness assessment of non-profit ICT SMEs in a developing country: The case of Iran. *Technovation, 28*(9), 578-90.

Françoise, O, Bourgault, M, & Pellerin, R. (2009). ERP implementation through critical success factors' management. *Business Process Management Journal, 15*(3), 371-94.

Gable, GG, Sedera, D, & Chan, T. (2008). Re-conceptualizing information system success: The IS-impact measurement model. *Journal of Association for Information Systems, 9*(7), 377-408.

Grabski, SV, & Leech, SA. (2007). Complementary controls and ERP implementation success. *International Journal of Accounting Information Systems, 8*(1), 17-39.

Grandon, EE, & Pearson, JM. (2004). Electronic commerce adoption: An empirical study of small and medium US businesses. *Information & Management, 42*(1), 197-216.

Gunasekaran, A, Rai, BK, & Griffin, M. (2011). Resilience and competitiveness of small and medium size enterprises: An empirical research. *International Journal of Production Research, 49*(18), 5489-509.

Hawari, A, & Heeks, R. (2010). Explaining ERP failure in a developing country: A Jordanian case study. *Journal of Enterprise Information Management, 23*(2), 135-60.

Ho, LT, & Lin, GCI. (2004). Critical success factor framework for the implementation of Integrated-Enterprise Systems in the manufacturing environment. *International Journal of Production Research, 42*(17), 3731-42.

Huin, SF. (2004). Managing deployment of ERP systems in SMEs using multi-agents. *International Journal of Project Management, 22*(6), 511-17.

Ifinedo, P. (2007). An empirical study of ERP success evaluations by business and IT managers. *Information Management & Computer Security, 15*(4), 270-82.

Iivari, J. (2005). An empirical test of the Delone-Mclean model of information system success. *ACM SIGMIS Database, 36*(2), 8-27.

Kanaracus, C. (2011). 10 biggest ERP software failures of 2011. Retrieved from http://www.computerworld.com/s/article/9222864/10_biggest_ERP_software_failures_of_2011?taxonomyId=144&pageNumber=1.

Karimi, J, Somers, TM, & Bhattacherjee, A. (2007). The impact of ERP implementation on business process outcomes: A factor-based study. *Journal of Management Information Systems, 24*(1), 101-34.

Koh, SCL, Gunasekaran, A, & Cooper, JR. (2009). The demand for training and consultancy investment in SME-specific ERP systems implementation and operation. *International Journal of Production Economics, 122*(1), 241-54.

Kumar, V, Maheshwari, B, & Kumar, U. (2003). An investigation of critical management issues in ERP implementation: Empirical evidence from Canadian organizations. *Technovation, 23*(10), 793-807.

Kwon, TH, & Zmud, RW. (1987). Unifying the fragmented models of Information Systems implementation. In RJ Boland, & RA Hirschheim (Eds.), *Critical issues in Information Systems research* (pp. 227-51). New York: John Wiley & Sons, Inc.

Lee, J, Siau, K, & Hong, S. (2003). Enterprise integration with ERP and EAI. *Communications of the ACM, 46*(2), 54-60.

Leidecker, JK, & Bruno, AV. (1984). Identifying and using critical success factors. *Long Range Planning, 17*(1), 23-32.

Löfsten, H, & Lindelöf, P. (2005). Environmental hostility, strategic orientation and the importance of management accounting — An empirical analysis of new technology-based firms. *Technovation, 25*(7), 725-38.

Malhotra, R, & Temponi, C. (2010). Critical decisions for ERP integration: Small business issues. *International Journal of Information Management, 30*(1), 28-37.

Molla, A, & Licker, PS. (2005). Perceived e-readiness factors in e-commerce adoption: An empirical investigation in a developing country. *International Journal of Electronic Commerce, 10*(1), 83-110.

Morabito, V, Pace, S, & Previtali, P. (2005). ERP marketing and Italian SMEs. *European Management Journal, 23*(5), 590-8.

Muscatello, JR, Small, MH, & Chen, IJ. (2003). Implementing Enterprise Resource Planning (ERP) systems in small and midsize manufacturing firms. *International Journal of Operations and Production Management, 23*(8), 850-71.

Nelson, RR, Todd, PA, & Wixom, BH. (2005). Antecedents of information and system quality: An empirical examination within the context of data warehousing. *Journal of Management Information Systems, 21*(4), 199-235.

Newkirk, HE, & Lederer, AL. (2006). The effectiveness of strategic Information Systems planning under environmental uncertainty. *Information & Management, 43*(4), 481-501.

Ngai, EWT, Law, CCH, & Wat, FKT. (2008). Examining the critical success factors in the adoption of Enterprise Resource Planning. *Computers in Industry, 59*(6), 548-64.

Rai, A, Lang, SS, & Welker, RB. (2002). Assessing the validity of is success models: An empirical test and theoretical analysis. *Information Systems Research, 13*(1), 50-69.

Rockart, JF. (1979). Chief executives define their own data needs. *Harvard Business Review, 57*(2), 81-93.

Rogers, EM. (2003). *Diffusion of innovation* (5th ed.). New York: The Free Press.

Roldàn, JL, & Leal, A. (2003). A validation test of an adaptation of the Delone and Mclean's model in the Spanish EIS field. In JJ Cano (Ed.), *Critical reflections on Information Systems: A systemic approach* (pp. 66-84). Hershey, PA: Idea Group Publishing.

Saffu, K, Walker, JH, & Hinson, R. (2007). An empirical study of Perceived Strategic Value and adoption constructs: The Ghanaian case. *Management Decision, 45*(7), 1083-101.

Somers, TM, & Nelson, KG. (2004). A taxonomy of players and activities across the ERP project life cycle. *Information & Management, 41*(3), 257-78.

Subramanian, GH, & Nosek, JT. (1993). The development and validation of an instrument to measure Perceived strategic value of Information Systems. *Proceedings of the Twenty-Sixth Hawaii International Conference on System Sciences* (pp. 500-8). Wailea, HI: IEEE.

Subramoniam, S, Tounsi, M, & Krishnankutty, KV. (2009). The role of BPR in the implementation of ERP systems. *Business Process Management Journal, 15*(5), 653-68.

Tan, J, Tyler, K, & Manica, A. (2007). Business-to-business adoption of ecommerce in China. *Information & Management, 44*(3), 332-51.

Wang, ETG, Shih, SP, Jiang, JJ, & Klein, G. (2008). The consistency among facilitating factors and ERP implementation success: A holistic view of fit. *The Journal of Systems and Software, 81*, 1609-21.

Weber, RP. (1990). *Basic content analysis* (2nd ed.) Newbury Park, CA: Sage Publications.

Wu, JH, & Wang, YM. (2006). Measuring KM's success: A re-specification of the Delone and Mclean's model. *Information & Management, 43*(6), 728-39.

Zhu, K, Dong, S, Xu, SX, & Kraemer, KL. (2006). Innovation diffusion in global contexts: Determinants of post-adoption digital transformation of European companies. *European Journal of Information Systems, 15*(6), 601-16.

Conclusion

Innovation and entrepreneurship:

12

Building the systems and strategies for South Australia

Allan O'Connor, The University of Adelaide
Göran Roos, The University of Adelaide

Introduction

This final chapter considers all the chapters in this volume with the following objectives in mind:

- to portray the key issues emerging through a review of the chapter contributions and the interlinkages between the chapters
- to illustrate the integrated nature of innovation systems through an intellectual capital [IC] lens
- to identify strategies to improve the South Australian innovation ecosystem
- to articulate a future research program.

To meet these objectives we first consider the chapters in each of the parts of the book in turn to draw out the common elements and particular issues raised pertaining to the relevant focus. Next, we illustrate how innovation works across the macro to micro issues and identify the key interlinkages that influence the different levels of discussion and the particular focus of the innovation system that each chapter takes. Using this systems perspective we then consider the implications of the work to identify where and how intellectual capital interventions may help to shape and integrate the regional innovation ecosystem. Lastly, we conclude by suggesting a program of ongoing research and development that will increase our understanding not only of how innovation is integrated within South Australia [SA] but also of how the management of the innovation system can be effected, the outcomes improved and entrepreneurship integrated.

Part 1: Regional-level perspectives

The three chapters in this section draw attention to the regional innovation system [RIS]. This is as distinct to the national innovation system [NIS] and brings into focus dependencies on both the local (South Australian) and the national innovation infrastructures, policies and programs. In other words, 'we are not alone' — and for innovation to occur through the RIS in SA, both internal and external contexts need to be carefully considered and monitored.

For instance, Jane Andrew in her chapter makes the case for how both the broad discipline areas of Humanities, Arts and Social Sciences [HASS] and Science, Technology, Engineering and Maths [STEM] are of critical importance for an RIS and yet both of these discipline areas have internal regional influences through the policies, strategies and offerings made by the regional education institutions and the external influences of national government policy on the Higher Education system and national school curriculum. The RIS is sandwiched in between these two dynamic forces.

Kym Teh and Göran Roos, the authors of the next chapter in Part 1 discuss intellectual property [IP] developments, particularly with respect to patents. Their findings clearly articulate both the local dimensions relating to firms, institutions and individuals and the national drivers on IP policy. In this case, the RIS to some extent has little punch with respect to direct impact on the patenting patterns and behaviours, although the authors drive home a key point about the enabling infrastructure of the RIS, which indirectly supports and facilitates patenting activity.

Gavin Artz, in his contribution to the section, uses two local cases — the entrepreneurship education program, MEGA, and *rezon8*, a participant firm. Artz highlights that the RIS can be considered a value network which can host virtual teams. The value of these virtual teams is their capacity to link locally, nationally and internationally, which provides the RIS with outreach and capacity to target expertise, markets and possibly capital from places where it is best sourced. The conception of a virtual team again strengthens the case for the RIS to be the enabling infrastructure mediating between the local and national dynamics.

While the RIS is a sandwiched concept between local and national influences, each of the chapters also points to mechanisms for managing these dynamics. First, we will refer to the chapter by Kym Teh and Göran Roos, who articulate the Triple Helix as the way in which industry, academe and government intertwine within an economy at the macro level as key actors in an innovation system. In considering this view, a point worth noting is that Australia is at odds with the original case study of the Massachusetts Institute of Technology [MIT] in the United States of America, which informed the Triple Helix idea (Gunasekara, 2006). Unlike the MIT case, the historical and cultural roots of the Australian university system are characterised by dependence on government funding, weak private sector funding and, at least until relatively recently, a two-tier Higher Education system. Notwithstanding these historical and cultural anomalies, the Triple Helix is a relevant discussion and starting point for considering the management of an RIS, which brings into focus the role of government policy in facilitating, enabling and catalysing the connections, outreach and knowledge bases that are at the heart of a state RIS.

Jane Andrew, in her chapter, expressly points to the role of design thinking and value network analysis as tools for managing the design of policy as an enabling institutional infrastructure. Andrew argues that design, as a discipline, brings into account holistic approaches and forces strategic thinking for the long term. She points also to the fact that design is an important concept embedded in the state's manufacturing strategy as a critical skill. In order to facilitate good design, Andrew also argues that new ways to measure value are required that will capture the different ways knowledge is captured and contributes to the regional economy. One such means, Andrew suggests, is Verna Allee's (2002, p. 21) value network model, which assists in understanding 'the patterns of value exchange, the value impact of the tangible and intangible inputs … and the dynamics of creating and leveraging value'. For policy makers seeking to develop, grow or establish an RIS, having the right tools to manage the policies and program interventions that add most value would seem to be essential.

The cases provided by Gavin Artz provide some insight into the types of programs that may be beneficial to the RIS in SA, especially around the concept of the virtual team. The critical thought here is that a new venturing team with a well-connected and experienced support network can overcome obstacles and adjust to the innovation pathway in response to new information and opportunities faster than isolated or disconnected teams. Of course the government support and intervention to kick this project off was indeed of utmost importance but probably not more than the team that came together behind the program to make it successful. Together, Artz's cases of the program and the new venture point to the relative importance of human and social capital within and beyond the RIS.

Collectively, the three chapters included in Part 1 make three valuable contributions to understanding how innovation is, or may be, integrated through the RIS in South Australia.

1. The RIS in SA is a dependent system reliant on both local and national/international systems for innovation.

2. Tools and methods to analyse the RIS holistically are required to comprehend and contribute to the RIS in such a way as to bring about growth in the innovation outputs.

3. The approach to policy-making for the RIS in SA will be to create and leverage facilitative and enabling infrastructure that acts as a catalyst for individual, firm and institutional interactions. At the regional level, government needs to identify and use the opportunities presented by both the local and national contexts and be aware of the roadblocks imposed by both local and national constraints to either provide avenues to obvert the obstacles or find the ways and means to remove them from the system. This suggests that the RIS is partly a mediating variable between the NIS and the local infrastructure as it influences the NIS on the local infrastructure, and partly a moderating variable on the local firm innovation system [FIS] as it imposes programs and policies independent of the NIS to influence the local FIS.

Part 2: Firm-level perspectives

The second section of the book comprises three chapters that deal primarily with innovation at the level of the firm. All three contributions highlight the general lack of appreciation of the firm's processes of innovation. As Fiona Kerr states:

> Much has been written on how to facilitate and nurture innovation in organisations, but the concepts are often disaggregated and analysed as individual processes, practices or measures. This fails to take into account the complexity of interconnectedness and interdependence which both creativity and innovation entail ...

In much the same manner as noted in Part 1, this implies that a holistic approach to understanding innovation within a firm is required. Perhaps equally notable and relevant to this discussion is that innovation is a ubiquitous capability (Eisenhardt & Martin, 2000), meaning that all firms need some level of capability to embrace the 'new', whether that be capability in products, markets, processes or any other new approach that accompanies the need to deal with the myriad changing combinations and circumstances that a firm faces throughout its life. It perhaps is also not surprising, then, that the number of responses to innovation, or how innovation is done, can vary in almost as many ways as there are firms who engage in it. This may explain why all three chapters in this section have adopted a case study methodology and have attempted to unpack the principles that support and define innovation behaviour rather than opting to describe specific processes.

Although all three chapters examine the firm and adopt the same methodology, this is where the similarities in addressing the subject-matter end. All three approach the subject from three different vantage points: from the view of clusters, a research and development organisation and nonprofit social enterprise.

Huanmei Li and Allan O'Connor examine a long-standing and successful firm and enquire into the entrepreneurial processes that drive opportunity for such a firm, which is embedded in one of the strongest cluster environments in South Australia, the South Australian wine industry. Interestingly, in Part 1, Teh and Roos expressly pointed out that clusters were not an equivalent to the RIS but rather an associated and related concept that may form part of the RIS. Li and O'Connor break down the cluster concept to expose the different ways in which it can be considered, building from a pure agglomeration (lots of loosely related firms in one place) through to a deeply and intensely networked region of inter-firm, institutional and regionally exposed external networks. However, while clusters have a tighter regional boundary defined by the interdependence between the firms and other agencies, the boundary for an RIS has no such reliance on interdependence, and instead captures all related and unrelated firms and institutions in a geographically defined area. From this context, then, Li and O'Connor's chapter sheds some light into a specific part of firm engagement and embeddedness within the RIS.

The second chapter in the group, by Fiona Kerr, takes a longitudinal view of a research and development organisation that was facing closure, and offers insight into how the firm regrouped and captured value through innovation. A limitation to case study research is the limited breadth of cases that inform the findings, but the principle advantage is gaining a depth of engagement that can potentially surface and crystallise new perspectives. This research achieves the latter and brings together three key principles for creative and innovative firm performances: space, time and diversity. The chapter also raises questions with respect to the relative importance of each of these principles, particularly with respect to the changing dynamics of a firm over time and as the context varies.

Eva Balan-Vnuk and Peter Balan, in the third chapter for this group, particularly probe the business model innovation aspects of nonprofit social enterprises. Focusing on interviews with the Chief Executive Officers of five SA organisations with different nonprofit activities, the study identifies two drivers for business model innovation and six dimensions of innovation capability which fit well with the findings of the other two chapters in this set. The drivers are for sustainability and securing funding to provide core services, and this is consistent with the observations from the other two cases, whereby firm performances and common and/or shared vision and activities play a role in defining the pathway to innovation. Balan-Vnuk and Balan's six capabilities also link to the findings and conclusions of the other two chapters and highlight the critical importance of networks of different types (in other words, the importance of diversity), the need for time and space to experiment, and the value of cohesiveness in mission and customer focus.

In considering the contribution of this section to our task of illustrating the integrated nature of innovation, we find the following:

1. Like individuals, firms are not homogeneous in their behaviours or needs for innovation, and while entrepreneurial behaviours are found to be linked to embedded concepts of the RIS (for example, clusters), the way these links operate, and with what effect, is still not entirely clear.

2. The concept of innovation is not homogeneous across all firms and there are likely to be differences between industry sectors, stage of development of a firm and the management style of individual firms. Nonetheless,

for innovation to occur, general principles apply that create and embed linkages internally and externally for the firm. Hence by seeking to innovate, a firm is consequentially integrated into its regional (and/or other defined boundary) context because networks, by their very nature, are not only organisationally specific or independent.

3.   The types of networks for firm-level innovation need tighter specificity for the firm level. The benefit of networks is derived from the information and/or knowledge flow or access to specialist skills. It is insufficient to assume a general notion of networks when particular types of information, knowledge and skills are needed, as these may be dictated by the sectoral, customer or emerging technology needs peculiar to different firms at various stages of development. For innovation, firms are dependent on the human capital, both as the supply of labour to the firm and the knowledge, information and expertise that is available to it from within its regional (or broader/narrower) context.

Part 3: Innovation management perspectives

The chapters in the third part fall into two categories with respect to the tools and techniques for managing innovation. The first two chapters, one by Graciela Corral de Zubielqui, Pi-Shen Seet and Allan O'Connor, and the other by Vernon Ireland, are more generally dealing with macro or regional-level changes and the tools to manage these changes. The third and fourth chapters, by Paul Shum and by Jiwat Ram and David Corkindale respectively, are directed toward managing innovation at the firm level.

The chapter by Corral de Zubielqui, Seet and O'Connor illustrates the application of an intellectual capital [IC] methodology as a means to examine the types of capital and resources needed in an industry analysis, and how an intervention might flow or transform resources through different elements of the system, impacting the regional firms or businesses and bringing forth consequential behaviour and change. By conducting this analysis the authors reveal the different levels of insight provided by different methodologies, and raise a number of observations and issues that need attention if an IC form of systems analysis is to be conducted.

The primary observation is that an IC analysis trawls deeper into the issues of the system and what is going on beneath the surface of activity. It reveals much more about the transformations between the types of resources and the impact on other resource types. The analysis leads the investigator to cross the boundaries between region and firm and begin to articulate and conceptualise how regional interventions will impact the firm through its resource base and, zooming back out again, what would be the likely consequence back in the region. While a simpler systems analysis exposes the symptoms or conditions at the regional level, following an IC stock and flow approach forces the investigator to ask the critical question: So what happens by changing this or that resource?

The issues that flow from this type of analysis, though, are at best tricky to deal with. For instance, consider the issue of having a common understanding among the stakeholders about what a resource includes and means. This may seem fairly straightforward and not onerous; however, the degree of difficulty becomes greater as the unit of analysis is crossed. For example, defining what we mean by human resource at the firm level is far more nuanced, reflecting the human characteristics of individuals and small groups of people, than what might be considered at the regional level, which is generic and aggregated. But if we are to benefit from the depth of analysis of an IC approach, then it is a prerequisite to come to terms with what effects the interventions and transformations will have. This will take some investment in time and consultation between the regional and firm (industry sector) stakeholders before prescribing interventions.

Vernon Ireland's chapter deals specifically with system complexity and the tools that are used within the systems domain to address the usefulness or otherwise of these tools for entrepreneurs seeking to identify, create or exploit new and emerging opportunities. Ireland finds that there are a range of tools that would assist the entrepreneur and firm managers to comprehend and manage the shifts and changes in the complex social, technical, political and economic systems to unlock potential opportunities. However, the benefits that might flow from these insights rely on the interpretative and sensemaking skills of the management team and the ability to respond and move quickly.

Jointly, these two chapters make apparent an emerging and critical need to find, engage with and master new tools, which echoes a conclusion from Part 1 of this volume. Perhaps more importantly, both chapters identify techniques and practices that are useful and purposeful with respect to developing strategies for understanding and managing complex systems for innovation. Both chapters, though, also point to a critical need for human capital development in the use and application of these methodologies.

The other two chapters in this section surface different types of integration issues. Shum uses a survey and case methodology to examine the difference between the intellectual capital of innovating and non-innovating firms. The chapter articulates a long list of factors that influence innovation in the in-firm context. However, this list is not simply a checklist of independent items that must exist within the firm; rather, the work reveals the necessity to integrate the list within a working FIS. The non-innovating firms tend to not be able to ingrain innovation across the firm, and a common trait is stratification within the firm, which isolates innovation into pockets. More strongly innovating firms appear to have more robust organisational resources to manage projects and share information, knowledge and vision.

Shum also highlights the importance of training and high levels of competence within firms for innovation and the need to sharpen communication between the training providers and the training recipient firms. Research and development relationships with universities and other external providers also factor in strongly. The integration issues, therefore, are both within the firm and across the boundaries of the firm.

Ram and Corkindale have examined a particular application of innovation whereby an Enterprise Resource Planning [ERP] system is implemented within a firm. The focus of the chapter is on the Critical Success Factors [CSFs] and how these CSFs can be managed to achieve successful adoption of an ERP. For our purposes this chapter illustrates two particular types of integration; the first is an integration of different types of resources, and the second is an integration of processes. A key contribution of the work is the provision of a CSF management framework that articulates nine key CSF areas, ranging from organisational readiness through to training and education. Each of the CSF areas is designed with a view to bringing together the different parts of the firm — whether those different parts of the firm refer to sections or divisions, or to types of resources (human, organisational or relational). The authors argue that it is the management of these CSFs which is critical to bringing the ERP project through to successful implementation, and that through this management it is clear that the integration of the new into the firm is the problematic objective.

Ram and Corkindale also illustrate how this type of innovation reaches across the boundaries of the firm and into the value chain within which the firm operates. Management of the innovation — the ERP in this case — is not a straightforward task and the integration challenges, as similarly noted by Shum, are both internal and external to the firm.

Two particular take-outs can be identified through Part 3 which are of relevance to our innovation integration agenda.

1. Managing innovation, whether it is at the regional or firm level, requires new tools and approaches. The key issue is the need to look beyond the surface and the symptoms and to be able to trace the inferences and implications of transformations and change to deeper levels. The tools illustrated in the first two chapters in the section provide some insight into the approaches needed, whereas the second two chapters highlight the depth and breadth of integration issues that management tools need to address.

2. With the introduction of new tools comes the need for new training methods and new capabilities in the application of these tools. The firm-based chapters in this group particularly raise the issue of competence for innovation, but equally, at the regional level, if innovation and entrepreneurship interventions are to be well-designed and implemented, it will be necessary for our public sector and institutions to also raise the bar.

Strategies for RIS integration in SA

South Australia faces the prospect of being a sustained high-cost economy. Smaller and relatively isolated regions, once supported by the value chains of scale-based manufacturing firms, are vulnerable and face a challenging future unless the region transitions to a sustainable industrial base. Detroit, in the USA, is an example of an economy that has not managed this transition well. The prospect of Adelaide facing similar circumstances is looming large in the minds of some in local and state government and community as the automotive manufacturing sector in Australia faces virtually complete shutdown with all of the current Australian motor manufacturing plants closing their doors. Ford announced its closure of car manufacturing in Australia by 2016, which was followed by General Motors Holden announcing closure of its production plant in 2017. In turn Toyota has followed by announcing the closure of its operations in the same timeframe, and all follow on the heels of Mitsubishi, which closed its Australian production operations in 2008, and Nissan, much earlier in 1992. South Australia has been the home of two of these automotive manufacturing plants, and thus with the demise of car production in Australia, the flow-on effect of job losses throughout the Australian automotive value chain raises grave concerns for South Australian manufacturing.

In response, the South Australian state government and Adelaide's local community and local government are turning their attention to entrepreneurship as a means to stimulate new economic activity. But Adelaide is not alone and it can be observed globally that there is an increasing trend for government policy to advocate entrepreneurship. And a number of studies have revealed 'the increasing attention paid to entrepreneurship by governments at all levels all across the world' (Minniti & Lévesque, 2008, p. 605). The value of entrepreneurship, though, is not embedded in the number of new firms that start in any place; instead, it is the new level of industry that flows from the business activities of the entrepreneurs. Seeking new levels of industry places the emphasis on the links between entrepreneurship and innovation.

Through the works presented in this volume, it is possible to see the integrative nature of innovation. Innovation relies not only on the production of new knowledge but also on the carriage of that new knowledge into an application that responds to, or stimulates, customer demand. From this perspective, entrepreneurship is a key contributor to an innovation system, whether that is at the national, regional or firm level.

Innovation is also not simply related to new products but also embraces new markets, materials, processes, business methods, models and practices. Furthermore, innovation may also rely on new insight that reconfigures old systems, processes, practices and methods, or that reapplies old materials and products in new ways or into new markets. Innovation, in all of its many guises, is more complex than a linear model of invention to commercialisation would suggest.

This book started from the perspective that the change and industrial transition that SA needs will be grounded in its ability to stimulate and integrate innovation. Through the analysis of the contributions to this volume, eight key issues emerge for SA (see below). Figure 12.1 illustrates the interconnectedness of innovation when

Key issues for RIS in SA

1. *The RIS in SA is a dependent system reliant on both local and national/ international systems for innovation.*

2. *New tools and methods are needed to analyse the RIS holistically.*

3. *Policy-making for an RIS will create and leverage facilitative and enabling infrastructure to catalyse individual, firm and institutional interactions.*

4. *The RIS is different but linked to embedded concepts — for example, clusters.*

5. *Differences between industry sectors, stage of development of a firm and the management style of individual firms will mean that different treatments are required.*

6. *The benefit of networks is derived from the information and/or knowledge flow or access to specialist skills.*

7. *For innovation, firms are dependent on the quality of human capital, both as the supply of labour to the firm and the knowledge, information and expertise that is available to it from within its regional (and/or broader/narrower) networks and context.*

8. *Managing innovation, whether it is at the regional or firm level, requires new tools and approaches and with this the need for new training methods and new capabilities in the application of these tools is also required.*

considered on a systems level, and how the RIS is a sandwiched concept falling between the NIS (which also links into the international innovation system) and the infrastructure of the local FIS. The RIS will need to account for not only different FISs relating to industry sectors but also for the stage of development of the firm and the sub-systems of different industry sectors that may be characterised by such things as industrial clusters. The idea of New Tools applies not only to the FIS but also to the RIS, where holistic approaches are necessary to fully appreciate and support innovation.

Through an analysis of the chapter contributions to this volume, a layered concept of innovation emerges which reveals the integrated relationships between

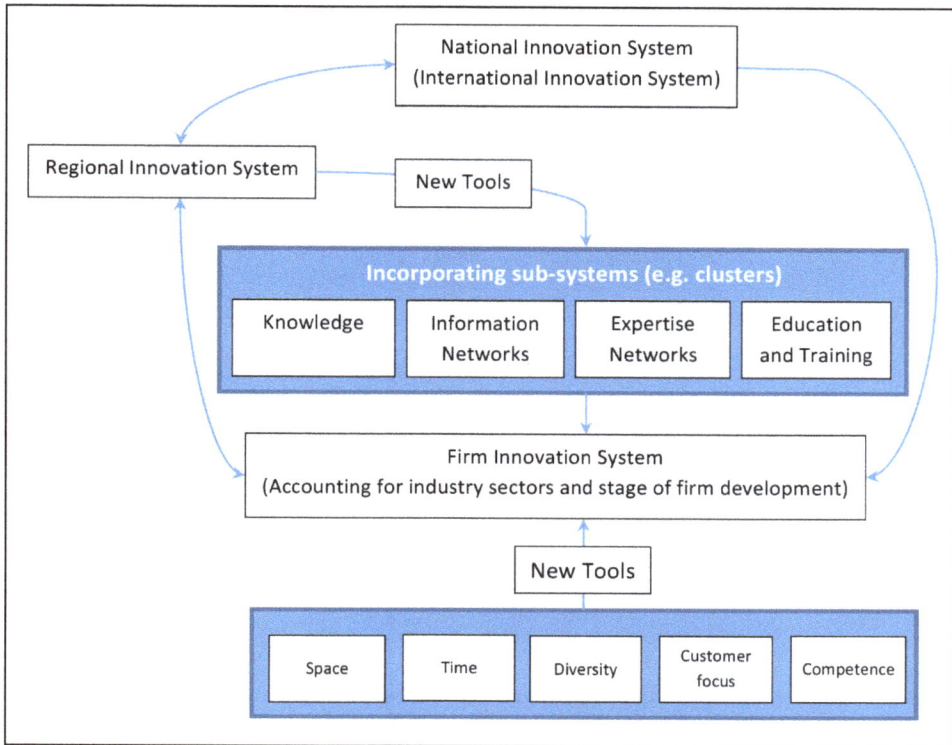

Figure 12.1: Integrated innovation illustrated.
Source: Courtesy of the authors.

the different levels of innovation systems; international, national, regional and firm. Figure 12.2 illustrates the intellectual capital framework for an integrated innovation system.

Successful integrated innovation at the systems level is dependent upon the human capital that supports the system, and this brings into the systems analysis the level of the individual and how each and every one of us plays a part in an integrated system of innovation. Figure 12.2 also highlights other key points. First, it draws attention to the importance of relational capital between the system levels that draws out and makes apparent the needs of the different system levels. Second, it illustrates the critical role of the enabling structural capital, which is responsible for the human capital development (education and training), network development

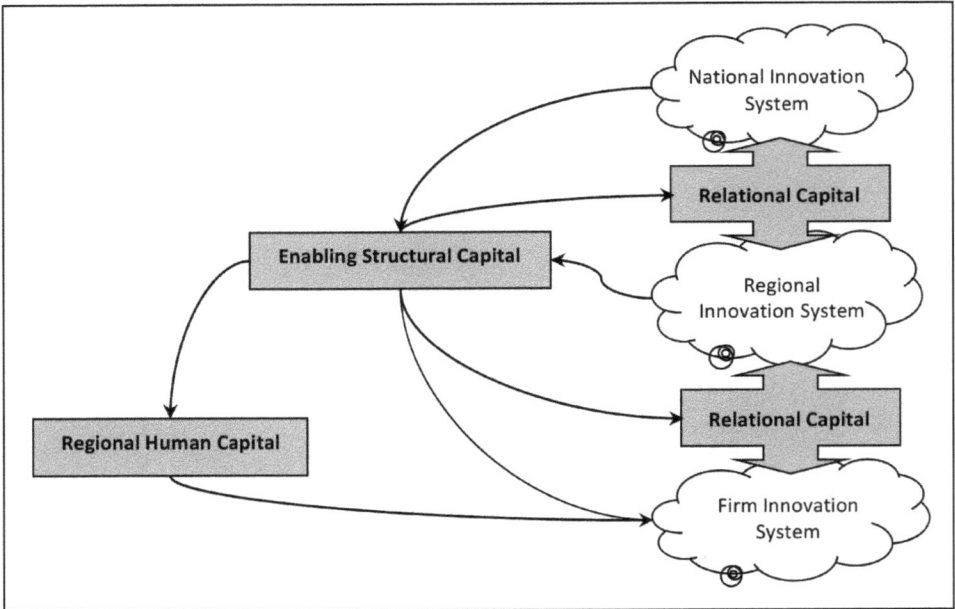

Figure 12.2: Intellectual capital influence on integrated innovation systems.
Source: Courtesy of the authors.

and facilitation of the relationships between the system levels (the organisational structures of committees, boards and councils, for instance).

An analysis of the chapters in this volume suggests four key strategies for SA that will help it enrich its innovation performance and capture value in the state economy. These are:

1. Build strong relationships between the national-, regional- and firm-level systems.

2. Develop new tools and methodologies for data acquisition, management and interpretation which can inform policies and programs at each system level.

3. Identify both the present and absent facilitative and enabling innovation infrastructures including (but not limited to) the knowledge, capabilities and information networks, along with the assistive education and training.

4. Develop a map of the system and sub-system interdependencies and identify weaknesses across variations in sectors and firm stages of development.

The following section discusses each strategy further and elaborates its meaning and intended contribution toward integrating innovation.

Build strong inter-system relationships

Given the sandwiched nature of an RIS and the heavy reliance on systems above and below, it makes sense to strengthen the relationships between the key actors at the different levels, in order to facilitate a pass-through of information and to gain an increased and sensitive understanding of how each system interacts with and supports the other. In practical terms, that means that between the RIS and NIS and the RIS and FIS there should be good and regular correspondence that leverages an appreciation of the diverse industry and policy needs. The policy and program levels should be responsive to variations in regional, sectoral and firm innovation needs. A distinction should be observed between the innovation agenda and other political goals or differences. The flow and transformation of knowledge should be facilitated across the system boundaries. In essence, this strategy signals a shift away from sectoral divisions and toward the means and mechanisms (an Innovation Council, for instance) that have a holistic and integrated focus on innovation (accounting for, managing and facilitating new value creation and appropriation) across the systems.

Develop new tools and methodologies

Going hand-in-hand with the first strategy is the need to develop new tools and methodologies. As discussed in the first chapter and further argued in other chapters, an economy fuelled by innovation and entrepreneurship requires new thinking and approaches. Audretsch and Thurik (2001; 2004) highlight fourteen principle differences between a managed and an entrepreneurial economy. Given the mounting pressures on SA to innovate its economy and move toward an entrepreneurial platform of integrated innovation, the differences are instructive for framing the need for new tools.

The underlying forces in an entrepreneurial economy expose firms and governments to new challenges. Knowledge is a key factor in an entrepreneurial economy (Audretsch & Thurik, 2004) which is less scale-oriented, is relatively

	Entrepreneurial economy ⟷ Managed economy	
Underlying Forces	Localisation	Globalisation
	Change	Continuity
	Jobs <u>and</u> high wages	Jobs <u>or</u> high wages
External Environment	Turbulent	Stable
	Diverse	Specialised
	Heterogeneous	Homogeneous
Firm Behavioural Characteristics	Employee Autonomy	Employee Control
	Market Exchange	Firm transaction
	Competition <u>and</u> Co-operation	Competition <u>or</u> co-operation
	Flexibility	Scale
Government Policy	Stimulation	Regulation
	Targeting inputs	Targeting outputs
	Local focus	National focus
	Entrepreneurial risk capital	Low-risk capital

Table 12.1: Comparison between a managed and entrepreneurial economy.
Source: Courtesy of the authors, adapted from Audretsch & Thurik, 2001; 2004.

high-cost and driven by localised conditions (which is why clusters become more important). Managing within an entrepreneurial framework of conditions places new demands on the tools and techniques which must be designed to deal with the localised conditions, flexibility and diversity. Managing co-operation becomes a dominant logic, and finding ways and means to both compete and collaborate requires a tighter focus on strategic positioning, resources and capabilities.

An entrepreneurial economy is also characterised by less stability and higher uncertainty. This means that firm costs and risks are pushed outward, utilising market exchange between many smaller firms as a hedge mechanism rather than encouraging cost integration into single firm structures where transaction costs are controllable in response to a stable and certain environment. Firms and governments need to recognise the shift in economic fundamentals. This strategy encourages firms and governments to look at and question the utility of their current management and policy tools and ask whether they are appropriate for the task of managing in a brave new entrepreneurial world. The third part of this volume provides some insights into how this economic change influences the tools of management.

Identify and develop facilitative innovation infrastructure

Consistent with the thrust of the works in this volume, this third strategy picks up on a key policy difference flagged by Audretsch and Thurik (2004) between the entrepreneurial and managed economy; that is, an entrepreneurial economy needs a government policy focus on stimulating and enabling infrastructure and the targeting of inputs, while firms need to enable and encourage human capital development, knowledge and innovation. As a starting point, governments and firms should conduct a stocktake to examine their policies, programs and routines to see what exists within their respective structural resource portfolios to enable and facilitate innovation. Keeping in mind the holistic nature of innovation, this stocktake must account for all divisions, sections and sectors. Moving from what is in hand to dealing with the deficits is the next obligation. This task also draws upon the first strategy and emphasises the need for correspondence between the innovation system levels, whereby government enables knowledge and network inputs through the RIS in response to firm and sector input needs at the FIS level. The localised context of the RIS may also force the need for negotiation with the NIS or the employment of policy and program strategies that fill the gaps and voids between the NIS and the FIS.

Education and training will be a key pillar for innovation in an entrepreneurial economy, given the far greater reliance on a skilled and highly competent work force. For firms, this means that support for staff and employee training will become a more critical input, and with this will come a need for encouraging and enabling the culture and practices for innovation. For governments, beyond the firms and NIS, a tight relationship with the education sector will also be needed to ensure that pathways toward advanced knowledge are available, knowledge-gaps identified by firms are plugged, innovation skills are embedded among the RIS human capital, and channels for new knowledge production and industry transference are open. Education and training will be a key input for the FIS, and the importance of the Triple Helix (government, industry and university) sectoral relationships cannot be underestimated.

Map the system and sub-system interdependencies

The final strategy addresses the heterogeneity of the industry, firms and individuals and suggests that while a holistic perspective of innovation systems is vital, it is equally vital to address the differences within the systems to ensure that knowledge capture and transformation is permeating throughout the systems by acknowledging the differences in sectoral needs and stages of development. Some of the interdependencies will be general in nature; for instance, a general level of human capital development will benefit all sectors. However, more specifically the sector needs may differ. For instance, the development of the forestry industry may require higher technical knowledge and skills, while the digital media sector may need stronger relationships to connect firms with lead customers. Further, the innovation resource needs of maturing firms will differ from the needs of new and emerging firms, and again some needs may be generic (access to capital, for example) while others may be specific (key supplier relationships for firms and sectors).

One note of caution to this strategy also harps back to the relational issues across the systems. Mapping the innovation systems and the interrelationships between the systems is a complex, cross-sectoral and multi-level activity and cannot be performed without central co-ordination of sectoral and stakeholder inputs. To achieve well-designed policies and practices that integrate innovation and feed an entrepreneurial economy, a single body with the skills and tools to map, interpret and diagnose the state's innovation needs, to inform policy, and to advise firms must intersect and correspond with the multitude of SA's sectors and stakeholders. This is not a task for an isolated division or a functionally fragmented or under-resourced government department, but it is the domain of a highly skilled, deeply engaged unit that has cross-sectoral representation with sufficient localised resources to help build and leverage a state's entrepreneurial economy.

A future research program

All of the contributing authors have highlighted specific future research opportunities relevant to their research work. In this section we attempt to aggregate the suggestions to articulate the opportunities for a program of research based around the concept of integrating innovation at a systems level. Distilling the core themes leads to five key areas of future research discussed further below:

1. internal holistic innovation system analysis
2. innovation metrics and management tools
3. innovation system policy, program and resource development and implementation
4. the influence of system elements on measures of system success and failure
5. intra- and inter-national comparative and cross-analysis of innovation systems.

Internal-holistic innovation system analysis

The need to investigate the different levels of innovation systems independently in order to understand how they work and how the interactions culminate in outcomes was a common thread. Each system needs its own internal-holistic analysis (that is, holistic within the boundaries defined by the level), which appreciates and accommodates the nuance of the system that may be driven by particular cultures, levels of human capital and specific access (or not) to resources or infrastructure. This research demand responds to the fact that systems, particularly those constructed by and consisting of humans, are not homogeneous in character and will defy any defining rules. Rather, human systems are driven by principles that are adapted to context, and the diversity of contexts requires closer scrutiny if we are to move closer to understanding and refining the general principles. In essence, this research program examines the interplay between general principles of an integrated innovation system and the context that reshapes and redefines the principles originating in theory.

Innovation metrics and management tools

The call for better tools and metrics for innovation was a common cry from the contributing authors. These tools, methods and techniques are needed at all innovation system levels, be it national, international, regional or firm level. The driver for these new tools is primarily the shift in economic logic away from a managed and controlled economy to an entrepreneurial, diverse and flexible economy. This shift has never been more apparent in South Australia than it is at the time of writing in 2014, with the successive closure of the automotive manufacturing plants. Couple this with the interstate plant closures and the entire collapse of the Australian automotive sector value chain, and it is readily apparent that the keystone of Australian scale-based manufacturing is now (virtually) completely gone. To recover from this shock it will take new ways of working, collaborating, communicating, structuring and exchanging, and with this disruptive economic shock comes the urgent need for new approaches to managing our workplaces and political systems.

Innovation system policy, program and resource development and implementation

The development and application of new management tools, techniques and methods is one thing, but the development in response to what these new tools may suggest is another. The focus of this research program is on how the responses to change and the implementation of new approaches — whether these are at the government, industry or education sector levels (the Triple Helix) — are developed and implemented. South Australia is not alone in facing the transition to an entrepreneurial economy, and there is plenty to observe and learn about how policies, programs and resources are developed and how the implementation of new ways and means of doing things is received and integrated into the fabric of innovation systems.

The influence of system elements on measures of system success and failure

While much has been said about the holistic nature of innovation systems, it cannot be denied that systems are made up of component elements. Each of these components has a role and function within the system. Therefore, this research program is concerned with the distinctive elements and how they contribute to the system's performance. Examples of different elements may be the finance sector, social networks and industrial clusters (as a sub-system). The success or failure of a system is determined by the objective design of the system, and objectives such as increasing technology-based start-ups, knowledge transference, employment increases or export sales may be some of the dependent outcomes.

Intra- and inter-national comparative and cross-analysis of innovation systems

This final research program tends to adopt, on the one hand, a system of systems [SoS] approach and zooms out to the level of looking at innovation system interactions and how each system and sub-system is interrelated with, and influenced by, another. But on the other hand, the program seeks to compare and contrast innovation systems across regional and national boundaries to examine how the system elements and the contexts of the systems interrelate. This final program requires a much broader call for input from national and international partners and research collaborators to capture the system dynamics while accounting for variations in innovation system elements and context.

Conclusion

In approaching this volume as editors, we sought to achieve three ambitions. The first was to draw together South Australian research and researchers who are actively engaged in creating and contributing to new knowledge about innovation from a systems perspective. The call for chapters managed to attract fifteen authors (including the editors) whose research has strong links to South Australia. From this position we plan in the future to expand our efforts and reach out further into national and international corners of the globe by inviting other authors to contribute knowledge on other regional and national systems.

The second ambition was to facilitate growth in understanding about the linkages between innovation and entrepreneurship and how these two distinct ideas are necessarily intertwined: how they interact and with what affect. As we reflect on the inputs, it is apparent that there is still much more to be done, as is indicated by the five different future research programs. We have, however, articulated the dramatic shift in the economic base that South Australia is experiencing, which, by its very nature, prods us to move the economy into an entrepreneurial direction and away from the ideas and principles of a managed economy. Underpinning this new form of economy is knowledge, and a prosperous entrepreneurial economy will turn that knowledge into innovation. We aimed high with this ambition, and while we are not there yet we have taken the first step in this journey of discovery by providing the foundations of how and why innovation and entrepreneurship are so closely entwined.

The third ambition was to examine and establish a language that has relevance to the concept of integrated innovation and entrepreneurship. We turned to the field of intellectual capital to provide such a language and consequently we have illustrated the intellectual capital foundations of integrated innovation by showing the interactions between relational, structural and human capital when considering innovation as a system of systems. The work that remains to be done is to gain a much stronger and deeper understanding of the nuances within these interactions. For this purpose we have provided five future research programs which together will assist to illuminate how innovation is integrated through entrepreneurship. The field of intellectual capital facilitates analysis and understanding and should prove useful to scholars willing to plunge into this enticing area of research.

As a small and relatively isolated economy it is imperative for SA to differentiate and build a sustainable base of innovative and entrepreneurial capabilities. The works that make up this volume present a clear case for building the human capital base on innovative and entrepreneurial credentials. As knowledge is key to an entrepreneurial economy, it is also critical that investments are made in developing and growing the knowledge base within SA. That means that we cannot and should not rely on imported knowledge; instead, the state needs to establish the human capital foundations with proficient and competent knowledge and capabilities in areas that will provide the state with an edge in global markets. To achieve this, a strong relationship and structural capital base is also required that can fully mobilise the Triple Helix. This is the practical challenge that is presented through this research-based undertaking.

In closing, please feel free to circulate this volume. We invite your expressions of interest for contributions to future editions of this work and ongoing co-operative research into integrated innovation through the lenses of entrepreneurship and intellectual capital.

References

Allee, V. (2002, November). A value network approach for modelling and measuring intangibles. (White paper, *Transparent Enterprise Conference*, Madrid). Retrieved from http://www.vernaallee.com/images/vaa-a-valuenetworkapproach.pdf.

Audretsch, D, & Thurik, R. (2001). What's new about the new economy? Sources of growth in the managed and entrepreneurial economies. *Industrial and Corporate Change, 10*(1), 267-315.

Audretsch, D, & Thurik, R. (2004). *A model of the entrepreneurial economy.* (Discussion paper series on Entrepreneurship, Growth and Public Policy,

Jena, Germany, Max Planck Institute for Research into Economic Systems).

Eisenhardt, KM, & Martin, JA. (2000). Dynamic capabilities: What are they? *Strategic Management Journal, 21*(10/11), 1105-21.

Gunasekara, C. (2006). Universities and associative regional governance: Australian evidence in non-core metropolitan regions. *Regional Studies, 40*(7), 727-41.

Minniti, M, & Lévesque, M. (2008). Recent developments in the economics of entrepreneurship. *Journal of Business Venturing, 23*, 603-12.

This book is available as a free fully-searchable ebook from
www.adelaide.edu.au/press